T0315000

SHREDDING PAPER

SHREDDING PAPER

The Rise and Fall of Maine's Mighty
Paper Industry

Michael G. Hillard

ILR PRESS

AN IMPRINT OF CORNELL UNIVERSITY PRESS   ITHACA AND LONDON

Copyright © 2020 by Cornell University

All rights reserved. Except for brief quotations in a review, this book, or parts thereof, must not be reproduced in any form without permission in writing from the publisher. For information, address Cornell University Press, Sage House, 512 East State Street, Ithaca, New York 14850. Visit our website at cornellpress.cornell.edu.

First published 2020 by Cornell University Press

Printed in the United States of America

Library of Congress Cataloging-in-Publication Data

Names: Hillard, Michael G., author.
Title: Shredding paper : the rise and fall of Maine's mighty paper industry /
    Michael G. Hillard.
Description: Ithaca [New York] : ILR Press, an imprint of Cornell University
    Press, 2020. | Includes bibliographical references and index.
Identifiers: LCCN 2020012030 (print) | LCCN 2020012031 (ebook) |
    ISBN 9781501753152 (hardcover) | ISBN 9781501753176 (pdf) |
    ISBN 9781501753169 (epub)
Subjects: LCSH: Paper industry—Maine—History—20th century. |
    Paper industry workers—Maine—Economic conditions—20th century. |
    Paper industry workers—Labor unions—Maine. | Strikes and lockouts—Paper
    industry—Maine.
Classification: LCC HD9827.M2 H55 2020 (print) | LCC HD9827.M2 (ebook) |
    DDC 338.4/767609741—dc23
LC record available at https://lccn.loc.gov/2020012030
LC ebook record available at https://lccn.loc.gov/2020012031

To Marcia Goldenberg and the women and men of Maine's mighty paper industry who made their own history

The mill. The rumbling, hard-breathing monster made steam and noise and grit and stench and dreams and livelihoods—and paper. It possessed a scoured, industrial beauty as awesome and ever changing as the leaf-plumped hills that surrounded us. It made a world unto itself, overbearing and irrefutable.

—Monica Wood, *When We Were the Kennedys*

Contents

Preface: "A Cloud of Rocks"   ix

Acknowledgments   xiii

Introduction: The Detroit of Paper   1

Part 1 THE RISE OF MAINE'S MIGHTY PAPER INDUSTRY

1. A Rags to Riches Story   15

2. The Paradoxes of Paper Mill Employment   46

Part 2 TOP-DOWN AND BOTTOM-UP CHANGE
IN MAINE'S MIGHTY PAPER INDUSTRY AND THE RISE
OF A NEW MILITANCY, 1960–80

3. The Fall of Mother Warren   95

4. Madawaska Rebellion   117

5. Cutting Off the Canadians   140

Part 3 FINANCIALIZATION, RESISTANCE, AND FOLK
POLITICAL ECONOMY

6. Fear and Loathing on the Low and High Roads   165

7. The High Road Cometh   180

8. Memory, Enterprise Consciousness, and Historical
Perspective among Maine's Paper Workers   201

Epilogue: Paper Workers' Folk Political Economy
versus Neoliberalism   212

Notes   219

Index   279

Preface

"A Cloud of Rocks"

Between 1965 and 1990, dramatic confrontations punctuated Maine's paper industry. These confrontations included:

- On August 9, 1971, nearly one thousand men, women, and children gathered at dawn to block a train loaded with twenty-seven boxcars full of paper, in a do-or-die last stand to win a month-long strike against Fraser Paper Company. The action was a confrontation between the French-speaking community of Madawaska, Maine, and a Canadian company that had hired English-speaking American managers to rationalize production and raise profits. Despite the presence of children and women on the tracks, a frustrated contingent of Maine state troopers teargassed the crowd, unleashing a riot. With tracks resting on a massive bed of rocks, men, women, and children retaliated with what was at hand. Striker Bob Gogan, a ring leader in local guerrilla actions against Fraser during the strike, remembered that someone in the crowd yelled "rocks!"[1] One of the teenagers present, Phil Dubois, recalls: "I could remember a black cloud of rocks . . ."; a state trooper on the other end described the moment—"Oh, my Jesus, you had a moment there . . . it was almost like an eclipse out there, the sky was so full of rocks."[2] Strikers chased off the police, destroying both police cars and two train engines. The strike ended a month later with a modest but momentous win for strikers. Fraser's owners fired the new company CEO, and workers regained shop floor rights taken away in the previous three years.
- In October, 1975, a ragtag group of independent, mostly conservative men, employed by paper mills as contractors to cut millions of pounds of pulpwood, swarmed paper mills across the state with picket lines for the first time, attempting to shut down the entire industry. Loosely affiliated with a new group called the Maine Woodsmen's Association (MWA), the protest was a spontaneous rebellion of Yankee (local WASP New Englanders) former farmers, whose once lucrative use of new chainsaws and skidders (large tractor-like devices for hauling felled logs out of the woods) had devolved into the economic distress of what woodcutters saw as "pulp peonage."[3] New out-of-state owners of Maine paper mills had squeezed these nominally independent employees, as pulpwood prices

failed to keep up with inflation and as the interest rates they paid on loans to finance their equipment purchases skyrocketed. Holding all the legal cards, the paper companies quickly gained court injunctions against the strikers, while Maine's governor threatened the MWA by declaring he'd "fill the woods with 5,000 Canadians" in order to break the strike if the MWA didn't call off the action.[4] The militant but disorganized MWA action came to a quick end after three weeks. While the MWA effort bore no immediate fruit, it did lead to the unionization of some of its ranks for the first and only time in the industry's history. The paper companies quickly moved to adopt a new regime of mechanization, and within fifteen years put most of those who fought in the strike out of work.

- In 1967, one of the United States' longest standing nonunion companies, S. D. Warren Company of Westbrook, Maine—famed for its founder's paternalism and so beloved by generations of workers that they called it Mother Warren—succumbed to unionization as a major national paper company, Scott Paper, swooped in and bought the 113-year-old company. The mill's largest new union quickly became among the state's most militant and helped stoke a statewide movement against union busting in the 1980s.[5] The same local, seeing their company's flagship mill under threat by new Wall Street forces, attempted to buy the mill a few years later. Scott Paper rejected the workers' offer and was soon taken over by notorious downsizing CEO "Chainsaw" Al Dunlap. Dunlap quickly busted up Scott Paper, rewarding stockholders with a $6 billion windfall. The Westbrook mill would see most of its remaining jobs disappear within five years, and related mills in Winslow, Maine and Mobile, Alabama met a premature end, all closing by the year 2000.

Shredding Paper tells these stories of Maine's workers, but in context. It chronicles the life cycle of one the United States' greatest industrial legacies—Maine's mighty paper industry. It puts these labor stories into the larger story of the ebb and flow of U.S. industrial capitalism. As mass production capitalism took off in the late nineteenth century, wealthy investors discovered Maine's fortunate rural landscape, whose rivers and forests made Maine the heart of this industry's early prosperity. Its mature phase after 1960 saw structural changes in U.S. business that ended the local character of ownership and management prized by its workforce and their communities. New owners "from away" increasingly pressed their workers to accept changes and cuts that violated longstanding norms of reciprocity between owners and workers. Reflecting the boisterous, countercultural tone of the times, workers and their unions fought back.

In the 1980s, a more dramatic structural turn arrived, as Wall Street began to forcefully prioritize a new level of corporate profit making over the needs and stakes of workers. While fighting what became ultimately a losing battle, Maine's paper workers also fashioned a cultural response, using memories of a paternalistic past to build an indictment of the new form of capitalism. Understandably, workers found a new financialized capitalism wanting for its abuse of the very people who form the bedrock of American economic prosperity.

The industrial legacy of Maine's mighty paper industry is of great intrinsic interest. But the voices of these workers, who were on the front lines of a new financial capitalism is itself an urgent legacy. As Americans entering the third decade of the twenty-first century seeking to refashion the current form of capitalism, from one that has come to benefit the few over the many into a kinder system, all can learn from these workers' folk political economy.

Shredding Paper is meant to be both a scholarly and a popular account of the economic and labor history of Maine's mighty paper industry. It is part of a chorus of recent work by academics who find relevance in telling specific stories about American capitalism. These stories help us all to better understand the economic and moral challenges we now face in making choices about the texture of our economic system. For the general reader, I hope that by infusing what is already a gripping story of economic life with this scholarly perspective, she or he will benefit from this new round of insight.

Acknowledgments

At the age of forty (in 1998), I decided that my love of reading and teaching U.S. labor history (I'm nominally an economist) required more—I needed to *do* history, not just appreciate and share it. Maine proved to be a wonderful laboratory. I was lucky to teach at a modest state university whose students were directly connected to its great industrial heritage; to develop relationships with the local labor movement and businesses; and to find a story that needed to be told. From baby steps in the 2000s, to a sustained push in the last six years, finally, I have a book I'm proud to share with the world.

Success has many mothers and fathers. Let me do my best to acknowledge the many who played a big part in the making of *Shredding Paper*. I have benefited from working with a great population of working-class students from all backgrounds and across the globe—some who shared in the research work for this book but many more who brought me stories of their families' mill town lives, interview leads, and who read parts of this work along the way with great interest. Thanks especially to those who directly assisted in my research: Christina Barnes, John Bshara, Molly Dolby, Skyler Gordon, Cliff Gray, Matthew Hopkins, Daniel MacLeod, Rebecca McElrath, P. Kim Ouellette, Janet Peterson, and Kim Sanders. Lifelong friend Ira Peppercorn won the informal contest to help name the book. Thanks to these scholars who helped shape the research and writing of this book in significant ways, all of whom were generous with their time: Jonathan Goldstein, Lloyd Irland, Sandy Jacoby, Nicole Lang, Pauleena MacDougal, Jason Newton, and Lise Pelletier. Also helpful along the way were: Gregory Field, Julius Getman, and Lydia Savage. Thanks also to two anonymous referees. I am grateful for my opportunity to work closely with Gabriel Grabin, Claire Holman, and Jessica Lockhart, who taught me proper recording techniques, helped digitize my oral history interviews, and collaborated with me to produce two audio documentaries associated with this book—*Remembering Mother Warren* and *Madawaska Rebellion*—before podcasting was a thing. Three librarians at the University of Southern Maine were always available to help me with problem solving on finding sources: Cassandra Fitzherbert, Zip Kellogg, and Pat Prieto; Cassandra also was a great partner in making my oral histories live on the web. Thanks to these mentors and colleagues whose good cheer, insight and inspiration, and support over the years mattered very much. These include mostly colleagues at the University of Southern Maine and also a few whom I've met along the national academic trail: Rachel Bouvier, David Carey, Lorrayne Carroll, Susan Feiner, Julius Getman, Margaret Gray, Lynn Kuzma, Penny Lewis, Vaishali Mamgain, Joseph Medley, Rebecca Nisetich, Bruce Roberts, Howard Stanger, Adam Tuchinsky, and Jeannine Uzzi. Thanks to ILR Press editorial director Fran Benson, who offered great encouragement, insight, and patience over a long period of time, and whose faith in this project meant a great deal to a first–time book author. Her staff and the editing assistance of Westchester Publishing Services, especially production editor Michelle Witkowski, ensured a professional manuscript and solid marketing plan. Special thanks to my graduate school mentors Jim Crotty, David Kotz, Stephen Resnick, and Richard Wolff, who taught me how to think rigorously about capitalism and economic history.

I always describe the work that went into this book as ethnography in the finest sense. I spent eighteen years crisscrossing the state of Maine, cold-calling leads, settling into rural communities for a week at a time, and mostly sitting with folks in their living rooms and community buildings, hearing their stories about work in paper and logging. I got to know much about their communities, families, and the way of life, past and present, in the mostly rural stretches that define most of Maine's geography. The some 150 or so folks I've met along the way both made this book possible and changed me indelibly. A few in particular became true guides and gate openers, many of whom I've stayed connected with over time (except for those who've passed away). An incomplete list, with apologies to those I've left out: Claire Bolduc, Paul Cyr, Bob Dorr, Arthur Gordon, Barry Kenney, Tom Lestage, Howard Reiche Jr, and Jan Usher. Special thanks to renowned Maine writer Monica Wood, who shared her special insights about Maine paper communities both in writing and in person.

Let me especially thank a group of four colleagues/friends/mentors who truly made this work possible. My University of Southern Maine colleague and accomplished historian, Ardis Cameron, led me to the literature and practice of oral history with an appreciation for community memory, and strongly encouraged my early endeavor to transform myself from a political economist interested in history into a full-fledged historian. Peter Kellman, perhaps Maine's most important labor activist of the last forty years and whose remarkable life story deserves a full biography, has been a constant source of friendship, insight, encouragement, connections to labor folks throughout Maine, has provided me crucial leads on some of this book's most important stories, and was a careful reader of my work from start to finish. Richard McIntyre, my bestie from the earliest days of graduate school at University of Massachusetts-Amherst, has formed the better half of a two-person think tank with me over our career on the connections between political economy, U.S. labor history, and U.S. labor and employment relations. His good cheer, close friendship, generous help with any and all thinking and writing, and encouragement to believe in my scholarly talents, can't be fully put into words; I would not be the thinker or writer I am had it not been for our long friendship and collaboration. Foremost inspiring me to do this work, mentoring my scholarship, and reading this work critically at every step is Bruce Laurie of the University of Massachusetts. More than forty years ago, I somehow lucked into what would become a lifelong personal and professional friendship with of one of the most important U.S. labor and social historians of the late twentieth and early twenty-first century. He has been a remarkable role model and teacher, and a truly generous mentor who helped me first to become a decent undergraduate labor history instructor and now a published labor historian. To these four, words can't fully express my gratitude and good fortune to know and be inspired by them.

My biggest thanks go to my wife Marcia Goldenberg. Our marriage inducted me into a rich Jewish extended family and the world of Yiddish and Jewish humor, which I can't get enough of; who makes every day fun, and life worth living; and who would accept nothing less than a completed and published manuscript. Apologies to her: she had to find out the hard way it can take an academic forever to write a book. I am so glad we're both alive to enjoy the final result together, and even more so to have her at the center of my life.

SHREDDING PAPER

THE DETROIT OF PAPER

Introduction

Maine is well-known as a place of natural beauty, a notable Republican tradition ("As Maine goes, so goes . . ."), and as a summer home to generations of middle- and upper-class residents of the eastern seaboard. Less well-known is its long tenure as the leading producer of the nation's finest papers. From the late nineteenth century until the 1960s, Maine was to paper as Detroit was to American automobile industry. But unlike Detroit, with its aura of Henry Ford, the Flint sit-down strike of 1936–37, and the rise of the United Autoworkers (UAW), the U.S. public knows little about Maine's paper industry's history.[1] To locals, paper was king, with a pervasive economic and political presence that led local critics to dub Maine "the paper plantation."[2] Built deep in the Maine frontier, companies like Great Northern Paper (GNP) and Oxford Paper came to own more than half of the state's considerable land mass, an area equal to New England's five other states combined. GNP, Oxford Paper Company, and S. D. Warren Company set the rules in their company towns and exercised complete sovereignty over their commercially owned forests in what are still known as Maine's unorganized territories.[3] Their political dominance over state and local governments ensured control over economic, workplace, land use, and water use policies, securing company rule and profitability. The owners of these mills also spawned a new industrial culture infused with paternalism and craft pride. For a century and a half, behind the nation's most widely read glossy magazine covers, gorgeous corporate annual reports, S&H Green Stamps, Chinette fine paper plates, IBM card stock, and Sears

1

catalogs—ubiquitous commodities in modern life, taken for granted by most as part of modern American prosperity—was a rich and evolving story of the capitalist history of an industry and the relations among the owners and managers of these companies, their workers, and their communities.

At the time of this writing, Maine paper and logging industry employment had in the space of one generation shrunk by roughly 80 percent to just over six thousand.[4] The twenty or so mills still operating in 1990 have been purchased, sold, temporarily shut down, reopened (often by hedge fund investors), and, as of late, routinely closed for good. Once prosperous rural towns have depopulated, and the connection that much of the state had to the industry has now been severed by time and loss. In 2014, 2015, and 2016, four of the remaining mills shut down for good, sparking sustained public interest in the industry's dénouement. Print and media journalists, community leaders, experts, and ordinary citizens lament the serial closings and wonder aloud about just what forces caused the industry's decline. Was it globalization? High energy, unionized labor, and regulatory costs? Or a vague corporate malfeasance? Besides making sense of paper's legacy, locals ask: How best to mourn its impending extinction? Finally, the events of 2016 in the U.S. election, Brexit, and cross-national political currents have put the politically loaded issues of global trade and income inequality on the front burner. As we'll see, the story Maine's mighty paper industry's fall has much to offer to this discussion.

Shredding Paper recounts the colorful origins of this industry and economic culture, with an eye toward addressing these questions. The rise and fall of Maine's mighty paper industry is an example of the most familiar story of the arc of modern industries: a dynamic industry bursts onto the scene by virtue of well-placed entrepreneurial innovation, grows to maturity and literally transforms a landscape, along the way builds a prosperous but complicated way of life, and then ultimately faces stagnation and decline. At the level of broad strokes, there is nothing unique about the fact of the Maine paper industry's decline, nor the late twentieth century timing of its demise. Indeed, Karl Marx was already writing in the mid-nineteenth century about capitalism's tendency to kill off industries and regions as innovation and even globalization undermined mature industries.[5] Joseph Schumpeter coined the term "creative destruction"—the widely used name for this pattern—in 1942.[6] But the details of decline in a particular time and place can bring to light new insights about the process and reinforce a gathering critique of a system that routinely punishes huge segments of its participants.

Shredding Paper joins a number of recent histories of companies such as Walmart, Campbell's Soup, or branches of U.S. capitalism such as finance or merchants—in performing what might usefully be described as an autopsy of twentieth-century capitalism.[7] Such autopsies allow historians, economists, and an interested public to better understand how and why American workers have increasingly wound up on the wrong end of the economic stick while providing a balanced account of the benefits and undersides of a more prosperous era, now bygone. Since the late 1970s, well-paying and economically secure employment has quickly waned, the political power of American business has reshaped the U.S.'s economic policy to primarily serve business interests, and both the power and validity of unions and labor movements have been crushed on our way to a new Gilded Age. Learning about the forces underlying industrial decline—and especially the way that workers understood and challenged it—is essential to re-thinking an economic system whose ability to provide a good economic life for all has dramatically eroded.

While *Shredding Paper* tells a big story about the history of a regional industry, the core thread is the experience, thinking, and actions of its workers, managers, and owners. Written primary sources—newspapers, company records and histories, and other archival materials, along with many valuable studies over the years by Maine-based graduate students and authors—help to tell this story. But foremost, this account features the voices of the more than 160 workers, managers, and community members interviewed by the author.

One important example is my ethnography of the iconic strike at the International Paper Company (IP) in Jay, Maine 1987–88. Brilliant activism by Jay strikers enlisted workers across Maine in a statewide movement.[8] The strike and local solidarity efforts generated intense, plant-by-plant discussions of the threats that new outside managers were making; included statewide protests against IP; and featured paper workers joining civil rights leader Jesse Jackson's 1988 presidential campaign (Jackson placed a surprising second place in the primary to regional favorite and eventual nominee, Michael Dukakis—notable in one of the nation's whitest states). As the struggle evolved, strikers and supports alike fixed on a simple slogan: "stop corporate greed."

Digging beneath this slogan, I discovered paper mill workers and many of their managers had a cogent and original analysis of the history of Maine paper capitalism. Interestingly, they did not see globalization as a prime cause of recent industry and labor-management troubles. Instead, they understood what had been clearly true: prior to the mid-1980s, stable, regional owners and long-term mill managers operated their mills fundamentally as community-based enterprises. Workers had always been central to their mills' success, and the most senior workers not only held essential skills but also had a deep say in day-to-day production decisions. Management clearly was at the top of a workplace hierarchy, and owner and/or shareholder profit was ostensibly the leading purpose for their mills. In practice, a significant share of company earnings was turned back to the community. A virtually feudal—not capitalist—reciprocity bound management in a web of obligations to workers and by extension workers' families and ultimately entire local communities. Thus, profit making was but one of the mills' objectives.

Foremost, ensuring the long-run stability of employment and local prosperity was, or at least seemed to be, just as important as the company making a buck. Thus, paper mill workers were shocked when new, unfamiliar managers "from away" (in Maine lexicon, clueless outsiders) arrived, demanding that workers accept deep cuts in wages, benefits, and, most ominously, jobs, while unilaterally ending the generosity and respect implicit in both formal union contracts and less formal timeworn obligations. It was clear that distant corporate leaders at IP and Boise Cascade had intentionally provoked strikes so that the company could permanently replace their unionized workers with nonunion scabs. For Maine paper workers, this drastic shift in the companies' creed and actions constituted a hostile takeover, ending the community nature of their mills and bringing an end to a morale and legitimate capitalism that had reigned for a century. The new capitalism had a twin character—not only was it morally bankrupt, but it also introduced a panoply of incompetence. Bad investment and management decisions compounded disenfranchisement of the skilled and dedicated workers—a, if not *the*, major source of much of their companies' profits. This understanding of history and critique of a new corporate greed amounted to a folk political economy, every bit as valid as academic theorizing and possessed of unique insights.

I first came across this folk political economy at the historic S. D. Warren mill, founded in Westbrook, Maine in 1854 and thus Maine's oldest mill still in business at the dawn of the twenty-first century. The mill was first owned and maintained by three generations in the Warren family, followed by a small group of professional managers who took charge of the company in the 1920s and then passed control of the operation to their sons and sons-in-law, who held sway until 1967. Warren began as a technology leader, and it maintained this lead in the twentieth century by building a powerful onsite research and development center, making endless new capital investments, and staffing a sophisticated national sales force. By the 1880s, the Warren works had become the world's largest paper mill, with over eight hundred workers—eventually employing over three thousand at its mid-twentieth-century peak. The bond between the mill and its workers was so strong that the company came to be known as Mother Warren.[9] While workers at all of Maine's other paper mills had joined unions at various points between 1900 and the 1940s, Warren workers routinely rejected organizing efforts.[10]

In 1967, Warren's longtime owners sold the mill (and three others acquired or built by Warren in the previous decade). Its workers then unionized. Over the subsequent twenty years, the mill's unions, particularly Warren's largest—United Paperworkers International Union (UPIU) Local 1069—built a strong, combative leadership that led two strikes. Warren workers readily joined the statewide paper workers' movement against IP during the 1987–88 Jay strike. Local 1069 also spearheaded growing opposition by Maine paper workers to company initiatives to remold union contracts and collaborate with unions on high-performance work redesigns. When IP managers commingled work redesign with its assault on unions, Local 1069 helped spread the word to other mills across the state that these ostensibly progressive initiatives were a Trojan horse, a tool in the effort to break paper worker unions.

About this time, a turnstile of new managers with little expertise in paper making began to lead—mismanage, really—the mill. Losses of markets led to layoffs. When I began to interview Warren workers a few years later, I found a readymade critique of the new hostile capitalism. Chris Murray, a thirty-year-old electrician, born after the sale of Warren to Scott, invoked founder S. D. Warren's memory to decry the brutal downsizing and delinquent management that arrived in the prior decade.[11] To Warren's workers, these new governors were not only attacking their unions but were responsible for hastening the local industry's decline through growing strategic and managerial missteps and incompetence.

Paper workers at S. D. Warren and other Maine mills clearly developed an understanding of the history of their industry and their place in it. They built their folk political economy from community memory, applying it to make sense of the wrenching change they suffered and had to come to terms with. A major thesis of the book is that this morally infused historical analysis has something to teach us all.[12]

This class war and advent of managerial incompetence formed a key moment, but it can be best appreciated in the context of the industry's long history.

The Rise and Fall of Maine's Mighty Paper Industry in Brief

Before 1870, U.S. paper production was concentrated in southern New England and the mid-Atlantic states. After 1870, Maine's unique·geography made it the place to be for late nineteenth- and twentieth-century paper mass production.[13] It is the nation's most heavily forested state, and its seven major rivers cut a deep path through its rich woodlands. In all, the Maine frontier offered a resource bounty unavailable elsewhere on the East Coast.

Thanks to exploding demand for newsprint, book papers, and other products, stoked by rapid population growth and the full force of America's industrial revolution, national paper production tripled between 1869 and 1889, and it increased tenfold by 1919 when output exceeded six million tons.[14] Following

FIGURE 0.1   S. D. Warren Company, Westbrook, Maine, circa 1970. Maine's oldest integrated paper mill; note massive woodpile in upper right and location over the Presumpscot River (Westbrook Historical Society).

Samuel Dennis Warren's example, captains of industry backed by well-funded investment consortiums began to build massive works deep in the Maine woods, creating new industrial towns such as Rumford and Millinocket, founding the Oxford Paper Company, GNP, and IP in short order.

Thus, around a river bend or over the next ridge of Maine's mountains, one is likely to encounter a factory complex with one or more soaring smokestacks and a complex of medium-sized, nondescript metal factory buildings, along with a wood yard with mountainous piles of logs (see figure 0.1).

Maine became attractive for one simple reason: by the mid-1800s, paper mills could no longer rely on a dwindling supply of used cloth rags—paper's traditional raw material since the era of Gutenberg—and hope to mass produce paper.[15] By then, frantic fights over access to rags played out across the globe and hampered what was otherwise a huge business opportunity. A massive, cross-national race to find a way to make paper from wood pulp carried on for several decades. Successful experimentation finally allowed companies to switch from rags to wood by the 1870s. Replacing rags with tree fibers freed paper manufacturers of this supply constraint, but dictated moving away from southern New England where forestry resources had been depleted by land cleared for farming. Maine's eighteen million acres of spruce and fir forests, and its experienced woodcutter workforce, made it possible to rapidly grow a new mass production industry. Investors found this huge woods' workforce at the ready, comprised of farmers from Maine or nearby Canadian provinces who were happy to make additional cash income cutting trees in the winter, while larger logging camps attracted urban proletarians from major seaports on the East Coast. Water provided a cheap source of power, and it was paper production's second most important input after trees. To power their mills, companies built a system of hydroelectric dams starting in the 1880s. River systems also served as the prime means of delivering a massive supply of pulp logs to the mill by a distinct workforce that had mastered the tricky and dangerous practice of log drives. Maine had been a northern outpost in New England's early to mid-nineteenth-century industrial revolution, offering a workforce skilled in both paper production and machine production in textile factories. Maine's new major paper companies emphasized high-end publication papers, cornering niche markets with high profit margins. With ingenious technology labs and capable, skilled workers, its flexible mills also produced an astonishingly wide array of other items. The state's biggest company, GNP, found a profitable niche making newsprint for decades after Canadian mills put most other U.S. newsprint concerns out of business by dumping cheap paper into the U.S. market.

This bounty was turned back on itself, as companies needed to maintain and reward a stable team of workers who could master the finicky and quite difficult challenge of making paper profitably. Paper manufacturing was and is a high-tech, capital-intensive pursuit, but it was also heavily dependent on the skill and myriad unsupervised judgments of workers who kept the huge paper machines thrumming out tons of paper every hour, day and night, running all but a few days out of the year. (For perspective, one machine could make enough paper in one eight-hour shift in 1920 to stretch over one hundred miles; by the 1970s, one machine's output in a shift could stretch from Boston to Virginia.) Some jobs, like cutting, packaging, and inspecting finished paper became routinized, and the woodlot and pulp mill included many brute jobs, but the shop-floor ethos of a twentieth-century paper mill would remain quite different from the technical control that emerged in assembly line industries. Maine's paper workers recognized the critical role their special skills played in their companies' success, priding themselves as world's best paper makers, able to point to the most elite periodicals in the country and know those glossy pages came from their hands.

The tens of thousands of paper makers needed once the industry was in full swing enjoyed relatively high wages and lifetime jobs. Mills virtually guaranteed that paper workers' daughters and sons would almost certainly follow their parents into the mill for generation after generation. In exchange, workers endured a punishing work routine, toxic environment, and their employer's local and state political dominance. Manglings, severed limbs, and deaths were a constant, especially in the industry's earliest years but not unknown in recent times. Harshest were the pulp mills—the chemical works that pulverized logs into wood chips and cooked these chips into the pulp that became paper when dried on paper machines. Pulp works thus churned noxious odors apparent throughout nearby communities. Workers and their families awoke—sometimes at dawn, sometimes midday, sometimes late evening, due to the rhythms of shift work—to what locals called in a profound if understandable act of rationalization "the smell of money."[16]

Despite these challenges, mill workers, specialist engineers, and managers known as paper makers had deep pride in their companies' leadership in high-quality products such as glossy magazine paper, and recognized their central role in the making of this industrial success. Imaginative names such as Mother Warren and Magic City, and the legends of great founders like Hugh Chisholm and Samuel Dennis Warren, together conjured a particular mystique of these companies as exceptional bastions of craft skill and a superior economic life.

Logging was another story. While paper mill work had its own challenges, woodcutting was done under the harshest imaginable conditions. The prime cutting season was in the dead of the frigid Maine winter, when logs could be dragged across hard, frozen surfaces to water bodies that served to convey the wood to mills in the spring thaw. From the start, it employed a somewhat different segment of the population than the industrial immigrants attracted to mill jobs. Drawn from farmer stock, and employed both directly and through a complex and constantly evolving system of subcontracting, woodsmen worked for a piece rate, consuming up to eight thousand calories a day to avoid weight loss and maintain sufficient energy. They braved death by widowmakers—hidden dead tree limbs or tree tops that can suddenly let loose and crush a logger to death—and a host of other lethal hazards. Rivaling northern Minnesota, if not Alaska, midwinter temperatures in the north Maine woods were as low as fifty degrees below zero Fahrenheit. For most of its history, woodsmen found compensating solace in the independence, skill, and the famous manliness of these Bunyanesque proletarians.[17] For the entirety of its history, woodcutting remained a parallel economy to paper making, with a largely separate workforce and lower standard of living.

We will learn a great deal more about the years of dominance and overall prosperity, and especially about the complex community and institutional life that sprung up in its wake in part 1 of the book. Parts 2 and 3 describe the disruption of community and institutional life that issued from changes in the larger capitalist world.

Maine's paper industry reached a crest in 1960, when Maine lost its place as the nation's leading paper producer that it held since 1920.[18] The Maine industry's fall would await the 1980s and 1990s, but its antecedents came in the form of a merger wave that began around 1960. For business purposes—access to capital, diversification, and a general fad for mergers and the supposed advantages of what economists called bigness—already national companies were buying up local mills, while regional companies joined in by matching up with partners from other regions.[19] Corporate headquarters were increasingly located away, making it harder for local mills to secure capital and introducing an element of instability in local labor relations. These developments provoked bouts of squeezing that, with greater frequency, set off strikes, protests, and resentment.[20] Maine's conservative paper workers and woodsmen acted in sometimes shocking and daring ways, seeking to turn back new chinks in the armor of traditional reciprocity. Workers also insisted on large increases in compensation as the peak of postwar prosperity became evident to Mainers who routinely traveled to Connecticut for work in the nation's highest paid union shops, spent stints in the military, or availed themselves of new consumption standards revealed by television. By the 1980s, the hostile takeover of these firms by new investors and the open season on unions brought the fall into full swing.[21]

Historians of U.S. capitalism and labor relations offer a useful frame for understanding about the fall of Maine's mighty paper industry. If this volume has a voice, it comes from pairing scholarly thinking with the practical political economy of Maine workers.

The History of Capitalism and Labor in the Paper Plantation

History from the bottom up—all the way to the top.

—Cornell History of Capitalism Project

Schredding Paper is a work of U.S. labor history and the history of American capitalism. It brings bottom-up stories of workers' lives, and especially how these workers at times accommodated and other times rebelled against their employers, together with a top-down analysis that shows how the broader forces of capitalism were at work in changing the character of Maine's companies. It presents a rich and particular story, and it also has several worthwhile lessons for understanding the nature and ultimate fate of one of U.S. capitalism's lesser-chronicled industries.

Capitalism is not just a market system; it is a complex economic structure comprised of businesses and other institutions that change over time and across national boundaries. The most common way of thinking about the United States' economic history sees the years from 1900 through the 1970s as a halcyon period, where manufacturers enjoyed the fruits of a large, closed, domestic market. Workers shared in unparalleled prosperity, especially after the 1930s, when mass unionization spread higher wages and benefits across much of the American landscape.[22] In popular and academic thinking, this era of American industrial capitalism has been crushed by globalization, where low-wage bastions like Mexico or China put an end to the privileged position of America's blue-collar workers.[23] While globalization certainly impacted the U.S. paper industry, it was not as much as most might assume. To really understand what happened to Maine's paper companies, and why, we'll look a little deeper.

A good place to start is by examining profound changes in what economists call corporate governance—the institutional forms of ownership and management. For most of its history, and with only a couple of exceptions, Maine paper mills were the central production sites for their owners. They were supported by long-term investors, allowing senior managers to concentrate on building their businesses through research and development, marketing, and brand loyalty. Maine companies were exemplars of this managerial era of corporate governance, where company leaders shared profits with stakeholder constituencies— shareholders, of course, but also their workforces and mill communities. Managers could direct resources into capital and technology investments that sustained the competitive strength of their companies over the longer term.[24] Any such expenditures other than shareholder profits would later become targets for Wall Street investors, who after 1985 can and did oust CEOs who rewarded multiple stakeholders or focused on the long term.[25]

This managerial corporation came under increasing strain after 1960. Beginning in the late 1950s, Maine paper company executives found it advantageous or necessary to merge with companies located elsewhere in the United States. As numbers-driven, short-term profit demands from Wall Street crept in, long-time local managers fought rearguard actions where they saw their access to investment capital reduced. Increasingly, new outside managers took actions that undermined local stability while ripping at the sinews of past mill–worker relationships. By the 1980s, new international competition and greater demands from Wall Street investors (generally known as the shareholder value movement) drove new corporate owners to pursue transformative strategies to increase the Maine mills' profitability. Together, these changes replaced one form of corporate governance with another. That is, the financialized corporation replaced the managerial corporation. This change in corporate governance was perhaps the most distinctive force accounting for the decline of Maine paper mills. Illustrative of this shift was the hostile takeover of Mother Warren by the notorious corporate hatchet man, "Chainsaw" Al Dunlap mentioned in the preface.[26]

As a work of labor history, *Shredding Paper* is an account of how workers at the time accommodated the labor practices imposed by their employers, and also of resistance to their employers when times turned tough. Most Americans share a common understanding of the rise and fall of unions. It begins with a dark era of child labor and sweatshops that ended when Franklin Delano Roosevelt's New Deal helped usher in big and powerful unions like the UAW, followed by the end of union power with the advent of 1980s' globalization. Maine's paper industry in some ways tracks this story, but it also departs from it. Pioneers like S. D. Warren Company, GNP, and Oxford Paper Company built a generous and informal paternalism prior to the 1930s. In the late 1930s and during World War II, a conservative, craft-oriented unionism formalized and modified the substance of reciprocity that defined the paternalism of Maine's paper companies. The national unions that came to Maine's paper industry were not powerful national industrial unions like the UAW or United Steel Workers; rather, they were a relatively weak and divided set of accommodative unions that thwarted grassroots union activism, much to the liking of midcentury paper industry managers.[27]

After 1960, Maine's paper employers, often under new ownership, first stressed and then abandoned the industry's hallmark reciprocity, prompting workers to resist, often dramatically. In the process, Maine paper workers reformed and vitalized once staid and top-heavy unions. Rather than a story of labor's decline in the face of powerful new economic currents is a compelling story of resistance. When confronted by new changes from the top, Maine's paper and woods workers mobilized within existing structures (for example, conservative, divided unions and paternalistic managements) and ideology (a general acceptance of capitalism, at least of the sort they long knew) to contest new management forms and reform efforts that they saw as undermining not just their own prosperity but also that of their companies.

The context for *Shredding Paper* is what journalists and scholars describe as the neoliberal era.[28] Neoliberalism uses an older connation of the word "liberal"—for instance, the small government, free market era that precedes the New Deal state that arrived in the 1930s and 1940s. From a labor perspective, virulent suppression of strikes and unions was the core of worker experience prior to the New Deal. The New Deal era, especially in the postwar decades from 1950 through 1980, saw a degree of stability and continuity in unionized labor relations in certain industries, including paper.[29] Then, a new antiunion liberalism entered with a bang in the Reagan era, as the United States deregulated banking, transportation, and financial industries, rapidly opened global trade, and U.S. industry accelerated capital flight to low-wage regions in the United States and in other countries. Ronald Reagan's forceful union-busting drive sewed together these new policies and helped to decimate the industrial, unionized workforce; President Bill Clinton's embrace of free trade accelerated employment loss to globalization. The Clinton years also saw a complete capitulation to Wall Street forces as his administration aggressively deregulated the U.S. financial system. Together, these developments initiated the relentless trend of income and wealth inequality that has marred U.S. capitalism ever since. This reversal of fortune for American workers has pushed scholars of U.S. labor toward a new emphasis on political economy, what the historian Leon Fink usefully refers to as the "forces acting upon workers."[30] The overarching question in this new work is the "why" of the devolution or declension of working-class power, and the declining employment standards that have been its fallout.

The early years of neoliberalism—the 1980s and 1990s—was a time of transition when the survival or decline of major U.S. manufacturing enterprises was still a contingent matter, as employers and unionized workers grappled with these new challenges.[31] Many experiments and new strategies came to the fore.[32] Maine's paper industry was a hothouse of labor relations' initiatives, as the interaction of new economic forces, employer proposals and actions, and proximity provoked a geographically focused and highly intense worker resistance. Work reorganization based on Japanese principles were widely seen in the United States as a way out of the competitiveness dilemmas faced by workers and companies. This gambit proved to be a dead-end in Maine, almost on arrival; chapters 7 and 8 offer a ground-level view of why this strong reform movement floundered, questioning and revising what experts and corporate progenitors once thought about its power and promise. Not surprisingly, financialization is key to explaining why these initiatives were ultimately destined to fail. Moreover, poor corporate strategy issuing from this so-called shareholder value movement gratuitously accelerated decline by undermining production and marketing competencies.[33] Maine's paper workers and their union leaders—and many local managers as well—were particularly astute in grasping this reality, which appropriately informed much of their resistance and disgust.

Ultimately, *Shredding Paper* tells a story of how ordinary folk, with extraordinary industrial talents and a rich, recalled heritage, confronted the new forces of neoliberalism and financialization. Their folk political economy, grounded in deep experience with the old and the new, fueled both resistance and a constructive search for alternatives. Underlying this perspective was a moral code that offers us all a valuable way to think about the benefits of a now bygone (but perhaps worth reviving) view of economic life: that industrial enterprises are community institutions with many stakeholders; that enterprises properly supported by patient sources of finance can and still do thrive in our current global economy; and that skills and resources built up over a hundred years need not be destroyed. I argue that despite the long-term defeat of worker resistance to corporate change and economic decline in Maine's paper plantation, the culturally rich vision workers developed as to what made for good industry, how best to resist corporate assaults, and what a future for American industry under new conditions might look like contain valuable lessons that cry out to be heard in current debates about future of U.S. capitalism.

Part 1

THE RISE OF MAINE'S MIGHTY PAPER INDUSTRY

1

A RAGS TO RICHES STORY

Why did Maine come to be the Detroit of paper? Certainly, no observer in 1850 would have expected that Maine would become a paper industry hub. Most American paper mills were located close to cities in southern New England and the Atlantic states; Maine was still a remote outpost. By 1900, however, Maine's preeminence in paper production was obvious. It retained this prominence into the last third of the twentieth century, when new economic tectonics would erode its special place in making of paper. This chapter answers: Why Maine? That is, just what forces accounted for the rise of Maine as a leading paper making state? The story has four dramatis personae: raw materials, technology, geography, and markets. Together, they called forth a massive increase in paper production over the nineteenth and twentieth centuries and steered much of this increase to new mills in Maine.

In the nineteenth century, both native and immigrant white Americans were a highly literate and highly political lot; books, pamphlets, newspapers, and eventually magazines were in high demand.[1] Population growth alone dictated a breathtaking rise in demand for paper. The U.S. population was just under four million in 1790, the year after the United States approved the Constitution. Population roughly doubled each ensuing generation—to 7.2 million in 1810, 12.9 million in 1830, 31.4 million in 1860, 63 million in 1890, and 105.7 million in 1920.[2] As the number and kinds of paper products grew, per capita annual consumption also grew rapidly, rising from 58 pounds at the end of the Civil War to 120 pounds in just after World War I, and more than doubling again to 254 pounds in 1940.[3] Altogether, between 1869 and 1920, total U.S. production grew more than fifteenfold, from 386,000 tons to 6 million tons.[4]

In the United States as a whole, rapid economic and population growth spurred mass production across a host of new and old industries. A massive network of canals and railroads made production for regional markets economical by the mid nineteenth century and created a truly national market in the ensuing decades. As Adam Smith astutely observed: "The division of labor is limited by the extent of the market";[5] by 1900, the U.S. economy was twice the size of Britain's, and four times that of France or Germany.[6] The uniquely powerful U.S. Industrial Revolution achieved astonishing scale, harnessing mass-production methods uniquely perfected by American enterprises. By the 1880s, steel and iron works grew to employ three thousand. After 1900, Ford, Kodak, General Electric, and Goodyear Tire, among other companies, built works with tens of thousands of employees. Advances in steel-making technology, the U.S.'s unique machine-building technology culture, and innovations in large-scale corporate enterprises fostered mass-production enterprise. Rapid technological change, the continuous invention of new commodities, and capital accumulation together brought production and consumption to a staggering scale.[7]

Paper was no exception. Nineteenth-century paper consumption was mainly for publications, especially books and newspapers. Production methods before 1820 were crude and little changed from the previous half millennium. But paper quickly became a high-technology enterprise, as companies ceaselessly improved chemistry-based production methods while inventing a steadily growing number of new products.[8] We think of the early twentieth century as the time when electric products, the Model T, radio, and movies created a new consumer culture. Paper was a major player, too. By 1920, Americans could read bright picture magazines like *National Geographic* and enjoy the civilizing personal convenience and hygiene of newly invented Kleenex, Kotex, and toilet paper. For the first time, the mass of goods shipped to national markets were packaged in cardboard boxes. By the late 1930s, paper ranked as the tenth largest industry in the United States by total sales.[9]

The raw materials and technology that prevailed into the 1850s were in no way up to the task of serving this rapidly growing market. The first American paper mill was the Rittenhouse mill, founded in 1690 in Pennsylvania. Using a technology little changed since the Guttenberg era, historian A. J. Valente notes: "The Rittenhouse mill employed time-honored techniques brought from the old country [Germany]. The making of pulp was backbreaking work, as old linen rags were ground by hand using mortar and pestle, a process that took a good worker an entire day to make sufficient pulp for just one-half ream of paper (a ream is 520 sheets of paper)."[10] Paper was molded by hand-stampers and laboriously dried. By 1800, most paper was still made by hand in this craft process in small works employing fewer than twenty workers. A large and efficient hand operation might produce five reams of paper a day, a scant fraction of the millions of reams per day made by a contemporary machine.[11]

Paper production made the leap to modern factory methods over the next half century. New beaters shifted pulp production from a hand to machine process. The key invention was the fourdrinier machine, invented in stages by French and British manufacturers around 1800 (see figure 1.1).[12] The fourdrinier is a long and wide machine that makes paper in a four-step continuous process. Pulp is sprayed onto a wire, where two moving screens at ninety degrees agitate, forming a crosshatch of fibers that gives paper its strength. From this wet end, paper then runs through a series of cylinders: a first set that presses out water and forms the paper, followed by a lengthy set of drying cylinders, and then a final squeezing of nearly dry paper into a fixed width by running it through a two-sided blade, or nip, in a process known as calendaring.

Southern New England and Philadelphia-area companies began purchasing English-made machines in the 1820s, and a cottage industry of American machine

FIGURE 1.1   Early twentieth-century fourdrinier, Eastern Manufacturing Company, Brewer, Maine, circa 1920. Note the two carts filled with paper scraps from paper machine tears, known as broke (collections of Northeast Archives of Folklife and Oral History at Fogler Library Special Collections, University of Maine). Maine Folklife Center Photo # 10088.

makers set to work making improved American versions. Starting with early textile American manufacturers, budding U.S. industrialists closely studied English and other European machine technologies, recruited British millwrights to design prototype machines, and then expanded their machinist workforces by further training local farmer-artisans, bringing their machines to market when their designs proved successful.[13] A powerful technological culture emerged as mechanics and later engineers constantly improved methods and materials, especially metallurgy, powering America's rise to mass production prominence by expanding the application of machine-building and problem-solving skills to a growing list of new commodities. First with textiles and gun making, and then in a broad range of industries like paper, American industrialists leapfrogged British and Continental factory methods.[14] In paper, after several decades of experimentation, refinement, and fights over patents, fully modern fourdriniers became widely available in the United States by 1860.[15] While leading paper mill operations built proprietary technology and could get ahead of competitors for short periods of time, the emergence of paper machine-making companies meant entry into the industry was limited only by the large scale of investment required to build a major paper operation.

Book, pamphlet, and newspaper markets were already growing rapidly after the War of 1812. Dozens of small mills cropped up near population centers—especially the Delaware River north of Philadelphia; the Connecticut River Valley in western Massachusetts and Connecticut; and later the Berkshire Mountains west of the Connecticut River.[16] Flammable materials and the use of heat at various stages of papermaking meant fires were common. Dozens of mills had fires during this era, often resulting in their being razed. Spring freshets wiped away entire works. Small paper mills were located near cities—the best source of rags. Railroad expansion and a mass mobilization of rural merchants located along rail lines helped support the growing hunger for rags. Nevertheless, continued growth of paper markets soon outstripped domestic rag supplies. It was thus common by midcentury for paper merchants like Boston's Samuel Dennis Warren to make regular trips to Europe to procure even more rags. This increasingly desperate effort set off rag wars on both sides of the Atlantic. At a time of great chemical, metallurgical, and machine evolution, numerous inventors and mill owners engaged in a furious effort to find ways of using more plentiful raw materials to make paper. The chief candidate was wood—especially poplar and spruce.

Rag and paper shortages became acute during the Civil War, and rapid postwar growth in paper markets made clear to all that rag supplies could no longer match burgeoning demand.[17] For several decades, inventors and manufacturers on both sides of the Atlantic experimented with wood fibers, along with a wide array of other cellulose-based natural materials, a list that included corn husks, straw, hemp, manila, bamboo, wasp's nests, silkweed, tobacco, hay, cattails, cottonseed hulls, and horse manure. In the end, none could match wood for sheer quantity of raw material or final paper quality.

Inventors created three techniques for making wood pulp. The first was groundwood pulp. Larger mechanical grinders pulverized logs into fibers that were washed by copious amounts of water. Groundwood pulp was workable, but the quality was poor; it could be used to make newsprint cheaply—indeed, newsprint prices dropped by more than half in a couple of decades. This method dominated that market for a short time, but it made relatively brittle paper that would quickly yellow when exposed to sunlight. Paper makers thus looked to other methods.

Two other methods applied chemical treatment to wood fibers. Wood chips were cooked in heated cauldrons—double boilers with removable linings called digesters—with caustic chemicals. Initially, however, pulverized trees retained too much lignin, a wood polymer that makes for good fuel but results in a course paper. The first innovation was using a new soda process that helped remove lignin. Soda pulp, adopted in the 1870s by Maine's S. D. Warren Company, made excellent book and stationary papers. Both soda and groundwood processes relied on mixing in rag-based cloth fibers to achieve better quality, which added cost and continued the supply constraint. Thus, the most important innovation was the sulfite method. Using sulfurous acid and calcium sulfite to cook wood pulp resulted in better quality paper, all the while lowering costs. The sulfite process became available in the 1880s and soon became the industry standard.

Pulp makers tested a wide range of trees, resting on poplar and spruce as the highest quality sources. A growing focus on the sulfite method opened production to locales near greater supplies of spruce. Together, these three methods ended reliance on rags and superseded most experimentation with other sources. As historian David Smith noted, it was game on: "With this discovery, the three major methods of making wood pulp were available—groundwood, soda and sulfite pulps. And with these discoveries, a revolution was born. A cheap, readily available paper was now in the hands of everyone."[18]

The established paper manufacturing centers in southern New England and Pennsylvania were no longer the ideal locations. Extensive farm settlement (meaning fewer trees) and existing tree mixes put a limit on how much useful wood could be brought to mills. As wood pulp methods gained favor, traditional paper making regions moved to more rural areas, where larger poplar stands were available. As early as the 1860s, American Wood Paper Company built two larger pulp and paper works, one each on the Shuylkill River west of Philadelphia, Pennsylvania, and one in Providence, Rhode Island, using the soda method and mixing wood and straw in its pulp, with an output of fifteen tons of pulp per day.

However, the company quickly ran out of local tree sources. Thus, "the mills found themselves searching as far as Maine for their supply."[19] Maine's eighteen million acres of trees, heavily spruce and fir, were a resource bounty unmatched on the east coast.[20]

Paper manufacturers first took advantage of Maine's forests by driving wood down the Penobscot and other Maine rivers to lumber mill centers such as Bangor, Maine, and then shipping them to Pennsylvania, Rhode Island, and Connecticut. This alleviated supply shortages, but it was costly. Yet, the industry was hesitant to move north. Managers of American Wood "believed that to locate further north was of no great use."[21] The firm's wood-buying agent was dumbfounded, confronted by his bosses' fears that it would be impossible to operate there because of Maine's deep winters. But such resistance did not last, and by the late 1870s and 1880s the state attracted more investors and began to build larger mills.

Even before then, the state was home to a number of small paper mills serving local markets. By 1846 these operations employed roughly one thousand workers, and double that a decade later.[22] Manufacturing per se already had a presence in Maine. Lowell and Company and other early textile companies built large mills on the Saco and Kennebec rivers by the 1830s. Railroad building after 1850 proceeded steadily, supplementing ships as a means to gain cheaper access to East Coast markets. And new manufacturers could draw on a ready-made skill base. In addition to paper and textile workers, Maine was thick with the kind of New England farmer-mechanics who used the anvil on the farm to fix tools and farm implements, engaging in a variety of home-based manufacture—especially, but not only, wood products and textiles—and who easily made the transition to the skilled factory work of building, repairing, and operating complex machines.[23]

Some Maine mills had already installed groundwood pulp operations in the 1850s. Soon after, paper entrepreneurs were snapping up rag mills across the state, converting them to soda-based pulping. A number of businessmen built larger companies with production in varying locales. Besides S. D. Warren, there was Adna C. Denison, who built five new Maine mills using the new methods and machines to manufacture book and magazine papers, producing 175 tons per month by 1878.[24]

Benjamin Tilghman was the chief American inventor of the sulfite method. He traveled back and forth between his Philadelphia home and German locales where chemists were already working on the process during the late 1860s and 1870s. Crucially, sulfite pulp production could use a much larger and diverse source of spruce trees rather than just poplar. By the early 1880s, he had solved a series of engineering problems to make the technology viable. Tilghman's success started Maine's paper gold rush, and he was hired to build or convert Maine pulp mills to the sulfite process. He helped Penobscot Chemical Fiber Company adopt the method in 1882, which was quickly copied at mills throughout the state. By 1889, the state had thirteen groundwood mills producing fifty-seven tons of pulp per day, and twelve sulfite mills cranked out 182 tons per day. By 1890 Maine had twenty-five pulp mills, almost all using the new methods, ranking it as the top pulp producer in the nation. As new companies were founded and major works built, the price of wood pulp dropped dramatically. By 1900, Maine had the third largest share of U.S. paper production, gaining lead status in the nation twenty years later.[25]

Founding Fathers and the Rise of Maine's Mighty Paper Industry

Maine's modern paper industry was founded by a short list of men who built industrial empires across the Northeast and Midwest. Among many, three stand out: Samuel Dennis Warren, Hugh Chisholm, and Garret Schenck.

Warren was a mid-nineteenth-century captain of industry. Born in 1817, he moved up from middling circumstances to found a small factory that grew gradually over several decades into a large manufacturing operation. Chisholm and Schenck were of a later generation—paper makers—men who pulled together investment consortiums made up of money men from Portland, Boston, or New York and who financed the building of huge operations from scratch. Their efforts also played a role in jumpstarting a new era of oligopoly, where just a few companies dominated major product lines—in this case book and magazine papers, and newsprint.

With the advent of the soda and sulfite processes, rapid advancement in machine-making capabilities, and an exploding market, the 1880s represented a takeoff point for the large-scale U.S. paper industry. S. D. Warren Company led the way.[26] Founded by Boston paper merchant Samuel Dennis Warren, the company grew steadily from a small three-room mill in 1854 to a large, three-mill operation centered in a village that later became the city of Westbrook. By the time of Warren's death in 1888, his original works employed nearly a thousand and was briefly the largest mill in the world, while two other Warren-owned mills nearby employed several hundred more. S. D. Warren Company targeted the growing book paper market, steadily built expertise, and made continuous investments in the Saccarappa Falls site, located just outside of Portland, Maine on the Presumpscot River (see figure 1.2). The company moved quickly into soda pulp production, riding strong sales growth to become one of the nation's first mass production paper operations.

FIGURE 1.2   S. D. Warren Company works on the Presumpscot River, 1884 (Walker Memorial Library, Westbrook, Maine).

While S. D. Warren Company's inception spanned several decades, three behemoths signified the takeoff of the Maine industry: Great Northern Paper Company (GNP), International Paper Company (IP) and Oxford Paper Company. These three companies moved to scale virtually from scratch in a big bang between 1898 and 1901.

Between the late 1880s and 1901, paper merchant Hugh Chisholm gathered investors and built a series of large mills on a twenty-five-mile stretch of the Androscoggin River, from Rumford to Livermore Falls (see figure 1.3). Chisholm focused on newsprint, the biggest segment of the national paper market. In 1898, he further pulled together a large New York-based investor consortium that bought out his Androscoggin holdings, along with mills owned by others and located in four other states, to form IP.[27] IP was the industry's first effort to form major trust—a model like that of U.S. Steel, which formed in 1901, consolidating 70 percent of U.S. steel-making capacity—in a naked bid to create a near monopoly of the U.S. newsprint market. IP, comprised of over twenty mills, for a time did garner a prodigious 60 percent share of the domestic newsprint market. But this was a high point, quickly eroded by competitor efforts.[28] While national in scope, its origins and core operations made it a Maine-based enterprise, at least in its earliest years.

In 1900, encouraged by major newspaper publishers, GNP began construction of a huge operation deep in Maine's interior, entering the newsprint industry in order to compete with IP. Finally, while president of IP, Chisholm organized

FIGURE 1.3   Rumford, Maine—Multiple paper works, circa 1900. By 1900, Hugh Chisholm and his investors built several paper mills in Rumford, shown here. These mills mass produced pulp and paper products including newsprint, bags, and envelopes (collections of Greater Rumford Area Historical Society, courtesy of www.VintageMaineImages.com).

Oxford Paper, a new company, seeking to join S. D. Warren Company as a major player in coated magazine and book papers; the two companies would share a dominant role in these markets into the mid-twentieth century.

These three companies required prodigious amounts of capital. The first of Chisholm's mills, Rumford Falls Paper Company, was completed in 1892; it was initially capitalized at $500,000 at a time when its four paper machines would have cost about $50,000. Hollingsworth and Whitney, an early paper maker that started in Massachusetts, also capitalized itself in 1882 at the same amount in financing construction of two new Maine mills. These companies started with a few fourdriniers and enough pulp-making machines sufficient to run them. By the 1920s, most had at least ten fourdriniers each, coupling fast new machines with older machines that were completely rebuilt to double or triple their capacity. Beaters, boilers, extensive piping, pulpwood grinding machines, steam turbines, and other plants and equipment were also essential. Initial works were housed in buildings well over 100,000 square feet. While much of the capital raised when IP was formed went to acquiring existing mills, the $45 million figure was still an enormous undertaking.[29]

These new companies undertook prodigious construction projects. Paper mills depended on water for production: as a route to bring massive quantities of wood to mills; as a power source for hydroelectric dams and steam-driven turbines; and directly for use in the processes for making both pulp and paper. To these ends, companies built canals, dams, hydroelectric stations, and sluiceways that allowed logs to be driven past dams—all huge endeavors. To ensure wood supply, huge tracts of forestland had to be purchased. GNP's original investors spent over $1 million in 1899–1900 purchasing 252,000 acres of timberland.[30] Towns had to be built, and paper makers like Chisholm and Warren inaugurated a generous paternalism, contracting with famous architects to build high-quality housing for workers, community institutions like churches and gymnasiums, while providing residential electricity. Rumsford and Westbrook were among the first communities in the nation to enjoy electrification. For construction, logging, and mill work, companies needed to recruit large numbers of workers, mostly to frontier locations where hundreds might live in tents for up to a year before housing could be built.

Hugh Chisholm was a looming presence over the formation of these companies. If Warren was a captain of industry, Chisholm was a general. In a two-decade span, he would directly develop eight mills or electric generation companies, assemble the twenty-mill IP merger, and then immediately built the mighty Oxford Paper Company. While Chisholm was not a party to GNP's creation, GNP's formation was a direct response to IP's bid to monopolize newsprint, and it was spearheaded by Chisholm's former right-hand man.

Monica Wood, a noted contemporary Maine author who grew up in Mexico, Maine, was among the throngs of children who grew up learning the tale of Hugh Chisholm.[31] Chisholm began as a newspaper seller in Canada, and a childhood friend of Thomas Edison—with Hugh Chisholm the smarter of the two children in the local telling. At age twenty-five, Chisholm was already a Portland, Maine-based owner of a national publication distribution company when, in the 1870s, he sought to get into paper manufacturing. Chisholm, like Warren, was among the many paper merchants and lumber barons who saw vast wealth potential in building paper mills. After the first mill he owned burned to the ground, Chisholm travelled by horse and sleigh in the winter of 1882 to a pristine locale in the western Maine mountains, a near wilderness area where he would begin carve out his new manufacturing empire. Beholding a breathtaking, 180 foot drop in the Androscoggin River—three sets of falls, any one of which would be sufficient to power a large mill—he envisioned a massive industrial enterprise that would be able to dominate national paper markets. Chisholm later recalled:

I appreciated the possibilities of that stretch of river, and I pictured to myself the industrial community which might grow up there. Here was a water power greater than any other in New England—greater in fact than the combined strength of those water powers which have made Lewiston, Lowell, Lawrence, and Holyoke thriving and populous cities— and the idea of developing and making productive the great unchained power before me . . . came to me.[32]

To locals in later generations, the intrepid Chisholm was likened to a modern Columbus, going into the Maine wilderness to found a new civilization.[33]

Chisholm and a series of partners acquired land at the falls and first built a hydroelectric facility called the Rumford Falls Power Company.[34] The Chisholm interests also built a modern industrial town with tasteful, well-designed housing, bridges, and churches, transforming Rumford and adjacent Mexico from a tiny, declining farm village into a bustling urban-ish community of nearly ten thousand by 1900. Residents enjoyed electric city streetlights and electrified homes from the early 1890s. Chisholm contracted with architect Cass Gilbert, who later designed the U.S. Supreme Court Building, to design Straithglass Park's beautiful homes and duplexes that were rented to workers for a modest sum. Chisholm and his partners also founded a railroad company that built two railroads connecting Rumford to major rail lines in both the east and west. Large-scale paper production commenced in 1893, and over the next several years, the Chisholm group built the Umbagog Pulp Company, the Rumford Falls Paper Company, Continental Bag Company, and the nearby huge Otis Falls Pulp and Paper Company, the third largest in the United States when completed in 1889 in Jay, Maine. The initial Rumford paper mill churned out sixty tons of paper per day at the start, and Otis Falls pumped out 150 tons of newsprint daily.[35]

IP came together as a response to the doldrums in paper prices 1890s. It was just one of dozens of first-of-their-kind horizontal mergers that swept American manufacturing in the years between 1897 and 1903. ("Horizontal" means two or more companies in the same market join together to increase market share). From the onset of the 1873 depression, into the 1890s, price wars were the bane of new mass production manufacturers, as dramatic productivity gains and overcapacity drove down prices and often bankrupted companies. Leading companies in steel, petroleum, tobacco, and virtually all major mass-production manufacturing organized trade associations to fix markets and prices, and some of the largest formed trust companies to further stabilize price fixing.[36] These trusts and trade associations were unwieldy and were outlawed by the Sherman Antitrust Act of 1890. In the late 1890s, a new class of New York financiers led by J. P. Morgan took advantage of a modernized stock market to create oligopolies or monopolies as a means of ensuring stable prices and rising profits. IP was one of the first such amalgamations, formed in January 1898. Its board of directors came from the owners of leading companies that joined the newly formed mega-company, and a group of New York City financiers, but leadership came from Chisholm and his top Maine associates.

At its inception, IP controlled 60 percent of national newsprint production. It was immediately highly profitable, but by arresting a decades-long fall in newsprint prices, IP spurred reaction by newspaper interests. Newspaper moguls successfully lobbied for an end to a large Canadian tariff in 1911 and then gathered New York investors to build competitor mills in Maine and Canada. IP itself would eventually move much of its new investment in newsprint to Canada. It quickly lost its Maine-centric identity, as its increasingly far-flung empire was coordinated from the company's Stamford, Connecticut headquarters. Over time, it had a less pervasive influence in Maine than other large upstarts like GNP and Oxford.[37]

It is hard to imagine a bigger side project than Chisolm's Oxford Paper Company. Rounding up yet another group of investors in 1899, he envisioned moving into the fine publication paper market, diversifying from IP's focus on newsprint. He recognized that book and publication papers offered great potential as a growth market and a higher margin venture than newsprint. In 1901, Oxford's enormous operation commenced production with four paper machines and a sulfite pulp mill. It secured a massive contract with the U.S. Postal Service for three million postcards a day, even before it opened in 1901. Over the coming decade, Oxford steadily added fourdriniers and coaters, and it absorbed Continental Bag's facilities while adding new physical plant. Its works quickly grew to more than 500,000 square feet and achieved annual production of sixty-six thousand tons of pulp and forty-four thousand tons of paper annually. Together with the one remaining IP mill, Rumford paper mill employment exceeded three thousand by 1906.[38]

GNP would carve a paper empire out of the deep, sparsely populated West Branch of the Penobscot River in the North Maine Woods, becoming the very rural tree and paper plantation that later inspired the industry's critics. To locals, GNP earned the friendlier title of Magic City. Garret Schenck, Chisholm's chief hands-on paper manager in the years leading up to IP's formation, had built mills around the country in the 1870s and 1880s. He first came to Maine in 1886 to run the new Penobscot Chemical Fibre Mill before Chisholm hired him to run Rumford Falls Paper Company. He was briefly vice president of IP, but he then headed up a closely held consortium of Maine and New York money men to build GNP. As a matter of geography, the Penobscot River's West Branch was the state's greatest woods and water bounty, reaching deeply into the North Maine Woods and uniting a remarkable complex of lakes and tributaries. It had long been a main thoroughfare for lumber river drives to Bangor, supplying Maine's lumber barons with tens of millions of board feet of lumber a year for much of the nineteenth century. No other location promised as much clean water, potential for dams and hydroelectric facilities, or massive forest resources. As investors looked to Maine's frontier to cash in on the opportunity in the 1890s to mass produce paper and profits, the West Branch would inevitably be attractive.[39]

GNP grew out of several halting efforts during the 1890s, including the building of a newsprint mill in Madison, Maine that struggled with red ink from its 1892 inception. The Northern Development Company preceded formation of GNP; it included a number of leading Bangor lumber mill owners who saw a repeat of Chisholm's development of Rumford as a way out of their long-run decline. This entity did succeed in acquiring lots of land, but it lacked the capital or wherewithal to launch a full mill-building project.

New York City financiers associated with J. P. Morgan swooped in, led by Oliver Payne (a director of Standard Oil), who bought out the Bangor sawmill interests.[40] Payne had already acquired the struggling Madison mill and was able to have the new investment consortium buy out his interests—a nifty coup not unlike the slick wizardry of modern private equity companies.[41] With Schenck joining the group as the operational leader, GNP began construction at the outpost of Millinocket, seventy miles north of Bangor in early 1900, and like Oxford, commenced production in 1901.

The rise of these mills sparked a new era of industrial logging. The biggest Maine lumber mills that exported wood to U.S. and international markets were located far down river from wood sources, where ships could traverse to the sea without hindrance. The practice of high-grading enormous trees in areas adjacent to lumber mills over time forced woodcutting to move ever deeper into the North Maine Woods. To make this work, woodcutters and lumber mill owners relied on an elaborate system to support cutting in remote woods. Trees were felled in remote camps during the winter, logs were then yarded—dragged by oxen or horses to nearby water bodies—and brought to mills in the spring and summer river drives of tens of millions of board feet (the standard measurement for lumber).[42] While these drives happened on most of Maine's rivers, none matched the Penobscot River drive to Bangor, which landed one-fourth of the total annual cut that reached mills; the mill owners earned the moniker "lumber barons" due to their large scale, prosperity, and political influence throughout the nineteenth century.[43]

Maine's lumber industry peaked shortly after the Civil War and then declined dramatically over the ensuing twenty years. By the 1900, new giant paper enterprises were the dynamic factor in the Maine woods. In 1900, lumber production peaked at two million cords per year, while pulpwood cuts were a mere one-fourth that. By the advent of the Great Depression thirty years later, paper mills consumed an annual cut of one million cords, more than twice lumber production.[44]

Crucially, Chisholm and Schenck built mills far upriver from the lumber mills, locating closer to the wood and then shipping paper out by rail rather than over the water. River drives required dams, and woods crews spent summers into early fall building them on small and large bodies of water; water was then released in the spring when needed to maintain water flows sufficient to keep the river drives at full speed. As soon as paper mills were located upriver, the timing and the amount of such water regulation sparked direct conflict with lumber mill owners; there was no clear legal doctrine as to how to resolve these disputes.[45] After a major battle between the two industry interests broke out in the courts and legislature, specifically over use of the Penobscot River, GNP emerged victorious.[46]

When GNP began production in the late fall in 1901 in Millinocket, its first mill soon produced 240 tons of newsprint and 360 tons of pulp per day—a massive scale for its time and at the time the world's largest. GNP aggressively added capacity, building the world's largest private dam and a second newsprint mill in East Millinocket, all by 1915. The Bangor and Aroostook railroad invested to connect Millinocket to main rail lines and conceded rates that ensured GNP's freight costs were modest. Land purchases continued, and GNP would eventually own 2.3 million acres, giving it effective control over three million acres of remote woodlands and waterways—an area more than three times the size of Rhode Island. By 1909, GNP's three mills produced five hundred tons per day—equaling one-third of IP's production with its twenty mills. In its first thirty years, it often strained to meet its customer demand, supporting steady growth in production, sales, and profits.[47] GNP's success was remarkable, given that it moved into newsprint shortly before the end of Canadian tariffs. Its ability to achieve low costs allowed it to retain a solid footing in the U.S. market into the 1970s and remain highly profitable.[48]

Having grown more slowly, the smaller and older S. D. Warren Company was able to rely on hiring from local Yankee farmer stock, and it later drew on the steady flow of French Canadian immigrants into New England to augment its workforce. For the new huge mill complexes in Rumford, Livermore Falls, and Millinocket, the sudden need for more than one thousand workers to first build and then staff the mill, and to also develop the prodigious river infrastructure associated with it, meant turning to labor recruiters in New York, Boston, and in Europe to bring in a workforce. These workers represented typical new immigrants of the era. These included Italian stone masons who literally laid the mill works' foundations and then stayed to work in the mill; they were joined by Polish, Finns, Latvians, Estonians, Germans, Russians and Hungarians and larger numbers of migrants from French Canada and the ethnically Scots-Irish-English

Maritime Provinces.[49] The vast and rapid expansion of pulpwood logging drew on the same immigrant flow, to a lesser extent; unlike the new paper mills, logging had long been the domain of local Yankee farmer loggers and seasonal migrants by nearby French Canada and would be almost solely so from the 1930s on.[50]

The Factory in the Forest

The millions of chords of spruce and fir cut annually as pulpwood was the raison d'etre of Maine's paper industry. Wood production was the very premise of paper production, and for mill managers, ensuring pulpwood supply was a dictum. Foresters and woodlands managers strove to "feed the mills" without interruption, and warned: "woe to the woodlands manager who let the wood run out."[51] Paper companies steadily acquired woodlands, eventually owning a prime ten million acres, half of Maine's landmass. Like GNP, each company asserted control over the water systems needed to bring wood to the mill and supply production operations as well. If the industry was a plantation of sorts, this was clearest in its elaborate system of wood procurement.

Woodcutting, in stark contrast to work in the mills, remained labor-intensive. The technologies used in woodcutting and delivery remained largely unchanged from the 1850s into the 1950s, with little physical capital but axe or saw and horses.[52] Rather than the well-defined mill workplace, logging was a massive battle with nature: with the great variety of terrain that affected the ease of accessing tree stands and twitching cut logs to yards or water bodies; the tree stands themselves that were of uneven quality and were thus aptly named chances, whose bounty could promise either riches or disappointment and poverty; pestilence like the spruce budworm that periodically devastated millions of acres of trees; woodcutters who faced the elements in the deepest winter, the essential season for woodcutting because of the benefits of hardened ground to twitch logs and also for the availability of a farm-based workforce free for labor after the farm growing season; winters that were not only harsh but could slow production when snows deepened to as much as ten feet and temperatures dropped as low as forty below zero Fahrenheit; and the vagaries of the spring melt on water systems through which millions of logs were driven to the mills on colossal river drives, making wood deliveries and quality unpredictable.

In order to feed the mills, companies relied on a fluid set of economic arrangements to procure wood that looked nothing like factory employment. One of the most interesting industrial economics questions is known as make or buy. Does a company vertically integrate backwards into the production of its raw materials, or does it purchase them at arms' length? If a company does not vertically integrate, or make, then what kind of enterprises sell them raw materials? In the past generation, large U.S. companies and new businesses like Uber have chosen to fissure—contracting out noncore operations (think food, security, or janitorial service for a large office or factory), shifting even more activities from make to buy.[53] While companies formally lose direct control over a bought operation, fissuring can cut costs dramatically by eroding labor standards. Generally, the story of the rise of mass production around 1900 in industries like paper is one of vertical integration, preferring make over buy to assure uninterrupted supply of essential inputs. Or, where companies bought rather than made raw materials, rapid technological development and capital intensity were typical. Indeed, in most of the U.S. woods product industry after 1900, companies made—for instance, owned their woodcutting operation and employed loggers directly. However, in Maine, buying rather than making would long persist, with the small-scale independent woodcutter at the center of its wood purchasing arrangements.[54]

From the mid-nineteenth century on, Maine's paper companies would find a readymade workforce, and the informal buy relationships were well established when large-scale paper production began. Paper and other wood product companies did build company camps with waged workers, an economic form that would grow at times to account for roughly half of pulpwood production.[55] But companies relied as much and at times more on two overlapping groups drawn from farmer-loggers from Maine or nearby Canada: independent contractors, who worked in crews of one to perhaps four, and the distinctive category of jobbers, who acted as general contractors with their own networks of contractors and subcontractors. As historian Jason Newton has shown, the nineteenth-century Maine or Canadian farmer developed an intimate knowledge of the forest, matched to their versatile woodworking skills that ranged from tree cutting to the making myriad wood products for home and market.[56] Compared to farming, woods work offered both a supplement to home production and a ready means for securing precious cash income, and for many it was a greater source of both play and remuneration than actual farming.[57] Moreover, as a largely winter pursuit, woodcutting was an excellent opportunity to augment farm income in the offseason. Thus, when industry began to boom, first in lumbering and later in paper, these homegrown woodcutters in northern New England and from nearby Canada numbered in the tens of thousands.[58] Their skill, resourcefulness, hardiness, availability in fall and winter, desire for independence, and satisficing mentality of the farmer-logger—who aimed for a certain level of annual income rather than a specific hourly pay rate—made him an altogether especially useful workforce.[59] After 1850, Maine and nearby states sold off woodlands with an eye toward development—a modern enclosure movement that pushed more farmer-loggers into a dependent relationship with lumber and paper companies, and making them more likely to be either in a company camp or acting as a subcontractor to a jobber.[60] Even as lumber and then paper companies grew larger and built more camps, local jobbers generally retained a better knowledge of who were the best woodcutters. Thus, the jobber who hired a host of small independent crews became the most distinctive way in which Maine's paper companies procured wood, a form that would persist in Maine after 1900, while logging in the rest of the country became proletarian wage work. Indeed, at the very end of the twentieth century paper companies moved back almost entirely to contractors and jobbers.

In manufacturing, where work could be standardized, worker productivity could be monitored, and capital and technology could revolutionize production, having workers under the roof of the capitalist was essential. But Maine's paper companies could and would, where possible, remain free of the risk and capital costs associated with the uncertain enterprise of securing pulpwood. Indeed, the reality for woodcutters was a precarious existence that teetered between a moderately paid independence and a feudal-like peonage. Yet for the companies, it was a system that brought wood to the mill with great certainty and at reasonable cost. But the mills were always at some risk in not fully controlling wood production, and at times the system would go into crisis, creating great suspense and providing impetus for major restructuring. One story of this will feature importantly later in the book.[61]

In areas close to paper mills, or in the southern part of the state, companies could simply use local farmers and later small woodcutting contractors. For instance, in the 1880s, S. D. Warren Company's wood procurer relied on sending out hundreds of postcards to nearby farmers soliciting wood.[62] During the paper industry's takeoff period from the 1890s to the 1920s, the need for labor outstripped these traditional sources of woods workers, and led to the recruiting of the same new immigrants—eastern and southern Europeans—making up the new paper mill workforces. Again, fluidity was the order of the day; the Great Depression ended the need for recruiting immigrants from afar, and throughout the rest of the twentieth century Maine pulpwood logging would be done mainly by French Canadian guest workers and local Yankee stock.[63]

Chandlerian Companies

In *The Visible Hand* and other writings, business historian Alfred Chandler discovered a new form of industrial enterprise driving the U.S. mass production revolution—the "second industrial revolution" in historians' parlance—after 1880.[64] These companies built three distinct, interrelated capacities, investing heavily in capital-intensive mass production facilities; sales and distribution operations (or sales effort); and a large middle management that coordinated production, sales effort, new product invention and innovation, and other important functions ranging from purchasing to accounting.[65] To Chandler, this visible hand of management created markets for new products, drove down costs, standardized quality, and, where relevant, built brand reputation. In quick order, makers of steel; machines; new consumer products such as toasters, cigarettes, radios, breakfast cereal, and other ready-to-eat foods; and Ford's Model T fed a national system of production and mass consumption that vaulted the U.S. economy far ahead of Great Britain, Germany, and France.

The product life cycle was mass production companies' greatest challenge. Markets for particular products would eventually be saturated, growth would slow, and then decline.[66] The only way for business enterprises to avoid the slow euthanasia that resulted from stagnant sales was to continuously invent new uses for existing products or invent new products entirely, to have a sales effort that ensured new products had markets, and to deliver products efficiently by means of economies of scale that drove down costs. The technological and business capacity to design and create new products using existing capabilities, under the most favorable cases, provide ample opportunities for economies of scope, where existing expertise is used to make and market a new product without having to build expert capabilities from scratch. A company newly entering the same market would face huge startup costs that would put it at an inherent disadvantage. Mass production enterprises thus needed to continuously plow profits, new stock issues, and bonds into exploiting economies of scope. In short, product invention was the best route to warding off stagnation. Maine's major paper companies were major practitioners of an early Chandlerian form that implemented these strategies, and their heavy reliance on research and development (R&D) and new product innovation embodied key elements of the highest Chandlerian form, the multidivisional company exemplified by General Motors and DuPont.[67]

A specific form of corporate governance underpinned the Chandlerian corporation. Economists define "corporate governance" as the varying forms of ownership and control—the latter signifying the locus of effective management power—and how ownership and top management together determine who has de facto control of company strategy. Corporate governance structures vary widely over time and across different economies.[68] In the United States, early industrial companies were typically proprietary or partnership-based, like S. D. Warren Company in its earliest days. Early founders ran their companies directly, in concert with a small group of initial investors that often included relatives. With the rise of the stock market, ownership was at least in principle dispersed among a large group of shareholders. Stock or public companies, however, vary quite a bit in terms of practice. In the first half of the twentieth century, many companies in and beyond the paper industry started out as closely held, with a group of founders and their offspring that was often synonymous with top management. This leadership group steadily diluted their ownership share as more and more stocks were issued.[69] The S. D. Warren Company had been wholly owned by the Warren family in the nineteenth century. Common and preferred stock was then held by a small group of Warren family members and top managers until the 1920s. S. D. Warren Company first issued common stock to the public only in 1929; by the early 1950s it had 4,200 shareholders, nearly identical to the four thousand stockholders in Winslow, Maine-based Hollingsworth and Whitney at that time.[70] Thus control—embodied in this small group selecting the board of directors and top management—persisted even as the core ownership group owned a dwindling share of a company's wealth. Eventually, control required a relatively small ownership share by the corporation's leaders. At this point emerges the full-blown managerial corporation, where, as economists Adolph Berle and Gardiner Means first professed in 1932, control was actually divorced from ownership.[71] The separation of ownership from control, as in the case of U.S. Steel when formed in 1901, sometimes commenced with a bang.[72] The other path was a case like Maine-based paper firms that when first incorporated were closely held, adding thousands of small passive stockholders over time until they merged with larger managerial corporations like Scott Paper or IP in the 1950s and 1960s.[73]

Prior to the 1890s, most factories were run by a captain of industry like Samuel Dennis Warren, who assembled partners to arrange funding and who personally oversaw management of the company. The demands for capital and the growing power and importance of upper management proficient in Chandler's three prongs meant Maine's paper companies soon outstripped this model. Building large paper mills required much larger, incorporated, investment consortiums that initially were closely held by lead investors, who in turn recruited professional managers who joined founding families. Over time, Maine paper companies would sell stock to thousands of small investors, diluting the control of founding investors but further empowering top managers. Each of the companies described here thus underwent a gradual evolution from closely held to truly managerial enterprises.[74] In the case of powerful founders like Samuel Dennis Warren and Hugh Chisholm, second and third generations of Warrens and Chisholms would remain in effective control, embodying the tradition of founding fathers who saw through a direct paternalism where mills remained like a family. At both Oxford and S. D. Warren Company, however, third-generation leaders could not match the power or acumen of the earlier founders, opening the door to leadership by professional managers.

The stability of mill leadership cemented the fundamentally local, paternalistic character of the mills. Workers and community members attached great importance to the palpable presence of mill and company leaders in the mills and their remote communities. Beginning with the likes of Samuel Dennis Warren and Hugh Chisholm, company presidents might live in Portland or Boston but could be seen regularly at the mill site. Crucially, the figure of the mill manager, invariably a key member of the controlling management group, was the onsite embodiment of what to workers and their communities were company patriarchs. These were men who lived in the mill towns; they were ubiquitous in both mill and town; enjoyed the same pursuits like hunting and fishing as their male employees; and typically retired locally. From Oxford Paper Company's founding until its purchase by Ethyl Corporation in 1965, the mill managers' average tenure was twelve years; for S. D. Warren Company, mill manager tenure over the 113 years before merging with Scott Paper was eighteen years.[75]

Whether closely held or fully managerial, this corporate governance structure had enormous implications. Berle and Means, and later John Kenneth Galbraith, depicted how separation of control from ownership gave the controlling management group in modern corporations an independence from shareholder demands. With the growing dominance of the American economy by a few hundred large corporations, corporate leaders exercised a great deal of power over their own operations, and by extension to the economy and polity. Berle and Means emphasized the abuse of power and challenge to American democracy posed by a small and powerful group of corporate leaders, an emphasis Galbraith would continue and update. However, Berle and Means also crystallized a broader understanding that this type of corporate governance fit with the large, domestic market created by managerial capitalism in which top managers built a stable, and under the right circumstances, equitable economic life that could benefit themselves, passive owners, but especially workers as well. The shareholder value movement that later emerged narrowed the choices available to top managers and put the generous employment system in crosshairs.[76]

Thus, if there is a tradeoff between short-run profit maximization and long-run growth with solid if not maximum profits, Chandlerian corporations pursued the latter. With shareholders dispersed and without influence over corporate strategy, the controlling management group could satisfice—ensure solid dividends for its shareholders, while taking a long view. Indeed, corporate stocks like those of paper companies became a tool for the well-to-do to save for retirement—purchases of GM, AT&T, and perhaps S. D. Warren Company stock offered ample dividends that offered a source of income in retirement. There was little chance these passive investors would carefully scrutinize the fine details of corporate performance other than regular delivery of dividends.[77] Thus, whether it was research or the cost of a highly-paid workforce, more of a company's surplus revenues could be devoted toward long-run growth and vitality, to a certain degree at the expense of short-run profits. Corporate leaders could plow back profits into the business and favor stability and growth over *maximizing* shareholder profits (thus satisficing).

With a satisficing strategy, an enterprise could also afford slack—a kind of inefficiency that served certain purposes.[78] Paper companies were avid practitioners. Companies could afford to put money into basic research that would take years to pan out or equally benefit competitors. They could acquiesce to unions and pay high benefits and wages—less of a burden than in apparel or retail industries because of the relatively small share of total costs labor represented in paper production and the market power over prices these companies were able to wield as lead producers in narrow product segments; but higher labor costs also meant sacrificing short-term profits. Rewarding labor well was also critical to company performance because of the centrality of skilled labor in the paper production process.

Paper makers cultivated gemeinschaft—the spirit of shared industrial community built on company generosity to its workers.[79] Slack and gemeinschaft were intertwined in practices that built cultures of trust and familiarity. For example, Maine paper mills maintained large forces of skilled maintenance workers, including carpenters, machinists, pipefitters and the like. The workforce was essential to respond when machines broke down, as even minutes of downtime could be enormously costly. The nature of work was episodic, with bouts of intense effort and extensive summer rebuilds; at other times, these workers might go days with little to do. It was common to have some of these workers be sent to a nearby lake and set to work building their supervisor a new summer cabin (which Mainers refer to as camps). In turn, workers were able to pilfer with impunity such materials as they might need to build their own camp, an indulgence that at least part of management would be in on.[80]

In the 1970s and 1980s, Jim Shaffer was in charge of paper purchasing for major newspapers, including the *Los Angeles Times*. Paper mill executives engaged in a courtship with its major customers. Price competition was limited by oligopolistic cooperation among paper companies. The two variables in sales were thus the firm's reputation for quality and timely delivery, and the other was sales effort. What did this effort look like? Dwarfing the classic three-martini lunch, one company invited Shaffer for an all-expenses-paid trip by plane to a lodge in the Canadian wilderness for two weeks of big game hunting. He recounted a similar sales pitch involving a trip to Block Island (a resort off of Rhode Island) where prostitutes were provided (Shaffer demurred the latter offer). Later theorists would target this sort of thing as management gold-plating, but at the time it reflected norms about using company resources to maintain sales growth and security.[81]

A revolution in U.S. corporate governance would question this entire set of practices. Reaching maturity in the 1980s, the shareholder value movement or simply financialization, attacked Chandlerian managerialism.[82] Powerful new institutional investors who controlled the investment of hundreds of billions in pension fund savings recognized that slack and satisficing came at the expense of shareholder returns. These Wall Street powerhouses were quick to punish firms that appeared guilty of either slack or too much emphasis on long-term capacity, in part because the metrics supporting R&D, work reorganization, or similar efforts were perceived as nebulous.[83] Major investors no longer held stocks for a long time: the average length of time an investor held a stock fell dramatically from seven years in 1960 down to one year by the 1990s.[84] This made dividends less important and pushed companies to meet demands to raise short-term profitability and thus stock prices. Whether it was wasteful gold-plating, or overstaffing, or economically sensible long-term investments of the very type that defined the Chandlerian corporation, the late twentieth-century revolution in corporate governance would attack every feature of the structures and strategies that had defined Maine's paper companies for nearly a century. After 1985, CEOs and their top management teams, in the paper industry and elsewhere, could and would be fired and replaced if they didn't abandon traditional Chandlerian strategies.[85] This development is a central part of our story that we'll return to later in the book.

In just what ways were paper companies like GNP, IP, and Oxford Paper Chandlerian? After 1880, paper quickly became one of the most capital-intensive of U.S. industries.[86] The sales effort was modest but significant. But it became a high-tech industry; paper companies constantly applied their capacities to new products and improved processes. Like the chemical industry, the paper industry is more a genus than species; for instance, it is constituted by a wide range of categories of goods, and companies could use their tech prowess to add new types or versions of products well into the twenty-first century. This is the very definition of economies of scope. Besides new personal hygiene products, and every imaginable form of boxing or wrapping of the myriad consumer products of the modern age, new avenues for printing opened markets for those Maine mills best practiced at innovation. By the 1920s, most major integrated mills—the dozen or so major Maine mills that produced pulp and paper together—built formal R&D operations and forged an array of formal and informal relationships with chemistry and chemical engineering programs at schools that included MIT, Syracuse University, and University of Maine. In the 1990s and 2000s, Maine paper labs were creating new products including stick-and-peel labels, release papers for molding car interiors and synthetic leather products, and new ways of making pet food bags.

For the big Maine companies, many of who recognized the loss of competitive advantage when newsprint tariffs ended in 1912, rapid improvements in the machinery used to make coated paper and the simultaneous advent of new printing methods meant that companies like Oxford and S. D. Warren Company had no problem proliferating new products and matching or even creating new growing markets.

None was more important for Maine than twentieth-century magazines. Oxford's and S. D. Warren Company's focus on publication papers was opportune. In the 1910s new coater machines capable of adding glossy sheen to high-quality printing papers became widely available; Maine companies invested heavily in them. Recognizing coaters' potential, publishers quickly developed specific demands for new specifications.[87] For instance, colored ink for photos work only if paper can absorb a great deal of additional ink, and paper had to be stronger and maintain a precise tension needed for accurate printing at higher speeds. Each new demand required a major research effort, which Maine companies were well positioned to conduct.[88] Prior to the Civil War, Americans read newspapers and books, but magazines had yet to capture a large readership. The numbers and circulations of magazines grew in the late nineteenth century; the modern magazine with a national readership and a new kind of ad copy emerged at the turn of the century. Printing and paper innovations began to drastically improve a magazine's looks and possibilities of design, especially color prints. Four-color printing was a crucial advance.[89] Older periodicals like *National Geographic* and the *Saturday Evening Post* were using four-color pictures by the early 1910s, remaking their look and increasing readership dramatically. By the 1920s, new popular magazines like *Time* and *Readers' Digest* created a new type of reader, as millions joined a national news media audience, with specific periodicals appealing to particular ideological sensibilities. By the 1930s, publishers were able to create magazines with full-color photographs. *Vogue*, using Maine-produced paper, created a sensation in 1931 with its vivid fashion photography, followed in the later 1930s with the new era of photojournalism led by *Life* and *Look* that achieved circulations in the millions within months of first publication.[90]

Thus, at the very time that Maine began building a large industry concentrated on publication papers, the magazine entered its golden age. The number of magazine reading households grew from 750,000 in 1899 to 32,300,000 just after World War II. In 1900, the United States had 3,500 magazines with a per issue circulation of 65 million; by 1947 Americans consumed 384,628,000 per issue—a 591 percent increase.[91]

TABLE 1.1   Tonnage and value of coated publication papers, U.S. 1947–63

YEAR	$(000S) VALUE	TONS
1947	100,609	623,724
1954	252,617	1,222,873
1958	362,505	1,547,408
1963	498,637	2,171,778

Source: Hannes Toivanan, "Waves of Technological Innovation: The
Evolution of the US Pulp and Paper Industry, 1860–2000," in *The
Evolution of Global Paper Industry, 1800–2050, A Comparative Analysis*,
ed. J. A. Lamberg et.al, (New York: Springer Dordrecht Heidelberg,
2012), 49–80, 64.

The amount of paper this segment came to produce was massive. A ton of paper translates to 500,000 sheets of paper; 1924's annual publication paper consumption tonnage—354,000 tons—would translate to an astonishing 177 billion
sheets of paper. Production in this segment grew sixfold from 1924 to 1963.[92]
Post-World War II was the industry's biggest boom period (see table 1.1).
Crucially, prices not only held firm as productivity grew but in fact increased,
leading to an impressive growth of sales revenue and profitability.

Besides glossy coated papers, Maine mills continuously churned out a great
variety of other products. Some, including GNP's three mills, Eastern Seaboard
of Bucksport (built in 1929), and the Pejepscot mill in Topsham were able to op-
erate profitably for decades as newsprint mills, though all diversified into also
producing publication and specialty papers over time. Oxford secured the U.S.
Postal Services' entire national contract for postcards. Hollingsworth and Whitney was a powerhouse of product innovation, cornering a number of markets,
including the cardstock for tabulating machines and later computers (notable for
the ubiquitous warning "do not fold, bend, or mutilate" familiar to baby boom-
ers); paper for paper cups including the Dixie cup; mimeograph and later photo-
copy paper; and as a major producer of wrapping papers, especially those used
in butcher shops.[93]

S. D. Warren: Becoming a Chandlerian Company

S. D. Warren Company is a signal case of a company that evolved from a highly
informal firm into a Chandlerian company that secured its long-run growth po-

tential. It had grown prodigiously since its founding through engineering acumen, craft skill, and a knack for identifying growing product lines large and small. By 1900, it had hired a couple of full-time chemists and had recruited a regional sales force. In other ways, it remained backward and absurdly informal in its paternalistic management structure and treatment of its workforce.[94]

From its earliest years, one feature of the mill's history stood out: the astonishing degree and density of nepotism in both management and the workforce. From its inception in the 1850s and 1860s, the mill had been run by the "poor Warrens"—nephews, cousins, or in-laws of founder Samuel D. Warren, who was one of eleven children.[95] Contemporaries and later historical chroniclers of S. D. Warren Company's history noted the extraordinary "rank nepotism" that the founder consecrated, with the "poor Warrens" still in charge of the mill into the 1920s.[96] Meanwhile, founder Samuel Dennis Warren's five children—the rich Warrens who lived on tony Beacon Hill in Boston—remained the company's principal owners after Samuel Dennis died, in 1888 through the 1920s. For the twenty-three years after the founder's death, S. D. Warren II remained company president, commanding the enterprise like his father from its Boston headquarters while also building a prestigious national law practice with soon-to-be Supreme Court Justice Louis Brandeis. S. D. Warren II ran the company ably enough but also cheated his siblings out of their full share of the mill's profits. His siblings sued, prompting his suicide in 1911, just the day before he faced an inevitable loss in court.[97] This event was the first of several that left a leadership vacuum that would finally be resolved in the 1920s.

Its labor relations policy was a crude though effective paternalism, modeled by the founder and perfected by John E. Warren, Samuel's nephew and mill manager from 1885 until his death in 1915.[98] The death of the company and mill leaders left the mill in the hands of John E.'s son Joseph, and an evolving group of the rich and poor Warrens took the helm. Joseph apparently lacked his father's touch both in management and labor relations, provoking a strike in 1916 that the company barely defeated.[99]

In 2001, retired S. D. Warren Company mill manager Howard Reiche Jr., provided a rich account of S. D. Warren Company's managerial and organizational history, including the story of the managerial coup in the 1920s that ended the reign of the poor Warrens.[100] Reiche had grown up in Portland, Maine, the son of a beloved school principal and a 1954 graduate of nearby Bowdoin College. While born and raised less than five miles from the Westbrook mill he would one day manage, he could have easily lived in another state, because insular Westbrook and S. D. Warren Company had little to do with its urban neighbor. He and his college friend Karl Dornish joined S. D. Warren Company and were assigned to its production management apprenticeship program, a notable development because they were the first liberal arts graduates in the program. S. D. Warren Company, like most paper mills, favored engineers, normally recruiting men like Reiche and Dornish into its sales force. Reiche quickly worked his way up the steps of management and was elevated to mill manager in 1970, a post he held until he retired in 1988.

The cumulative problems facing the company from growing mismanagement and poor investment strategy under the poor Warrens reached a crisis point in the early 1920s when a group of recently hired professional managers grabbed the company's helm. The core complaint: the company's increasingly modest scale and ad hoc approach to new technology would not sustain the long run.

According to Reiche, and the official company history, this group was led by John Hyde, George Olmstead Sr., and Oscar Fick Sr. They went to the rich Warrens in Boston and insisted that they be given control over the company. This group argued that the company would fail without a major spate of investment in new capital equipment, the creation of a well-funded technology center, and improvements in the company's sales approach. The rich Warrens heeded their demands, and a truly Chandlerian company was born. By 1925 the company had reorganized under the new leadership, effected a new sales and production strategy, and created one of the industry's most robust research outfits.[101]

First was to shore up a new production and sales approach that began just before the deaths of S. D. Warren II and John E.[102] The company had traditionally contracted with various publishers. Orders had a happenstance character. With no set standards for features like color and constant tinkering needed to meet customer demands, many orders lost money and profitability was unpredictable. Roger Day, a senior salesman who would join the 1920s' leadership group, crafted the idea that the company develop standardized papers, brand them, and advertise the brands nationally. Beginning with Warren Cameo, the company developed a range of specific coated papers targeting various aspects of the growing magazine and book market, especially those featuring glossy color printing. It then refined standardized production to lower costs and raise quality.

After Cameo came a series of new brands including Lustro, Cumberland Coated, and Printone. These brands came online just when glossy magazines were taking off. S. D. Warren Company advertised the new brands with what became a famous slogan, "Better Paper—Better Printing," with the first advertisement being placed in the high-circulation *Saturday Evening Post*. When first introduced in 1908, S. D. Warren Company produced fifteen hundred tons of these standardized grades; five years later, standardized grades production had risen to thirteen thousand tons. While only 25 percent of the year's tonnage, the new grades accounted for 72 percent of profits that year.[103]

S. D. Warren Company also reorganized its sales effort around its brands. It had long worked with—and against—paper merchants. Merchants had no particular allegiance to the company, and they could overcharge or otherwise act in ways that hurt the company's reputation; and the company could go around merchants and deal directly with customers, often at merchant's expense. The new S. D. Warren Company standard grades afforded an opportunity to move beyond these limitations. In 1917, it organized the new Warren Merchants' Association (WMA). These were authorized sellers, not legally associated with the company but bound by a set of agreements as to prices and practices. From an original dozen or so, there were over one hundred members of the WMA by 1954. The company did all it could to help the merchants, paying for marketing materials, routinely bringing them to Westbrook where they were put up in luxury—the mill built a fancy inn across the street, with professional chefs on staff—ensuring they had a close relationship with the company's researchers and engineers and a first-hand knowledge of product characteristics. The dynamic relationship between merchants and engineers became a source of product innovation. Within a few years, the company had built this successful merchant network; streamlined their own national sales force with offices in New York City, Chicago, and other major printing centers across the United States; and established a brand identity that created robust and growing sales, especially as S. D. Warren Company added new products.

The core of the company's identity was its growing capacity to innovate. For most of its first fifty years, mill leaders led by the first two agents (mill managers), George Hammond and John E. Warren, made constant improvements in machine capacities while solving of production problems large and small on an ad hoc basis. Two areas were a constant focus of improvement: the quality of pulp and the challenge of improving the coating sheen that made publishers prize S. D. Warren Company's papers. Toward these ends, S. D. Warren Company began hiring college-trained chemists. The first was Professor Carmichael, hired away from Harvard University in 1893, and then Edwin "Sutie" Suitemester in 1899; Sutie was still working in the lab in the early 1950s. Carmichael perfected a new technique for making chlorine, the chemical used to bleach pulp for whiteness, and also improved production of caustic soda. Sutie invented a variety of improved coating adhesives and pigments as well as a test for purchased pulp, and he redesigned the mill's pulp bleaching process in 1913. Two more chemists were brought on in 1900, one of whom, George Oneslager, later became chief chemist for Goodrich Corporation. Together, these chemists were central to the elaboration and refinement of the new S. D. Warren grades. Besides process improvements and product innovations, S. D. Warren Company pioneered what would become a standard feature of modern paper mills—a testing lab where sheets of paper were regularly brought to an enclosed room on the shop floor. This created an endless, hour-by-hour feedback loop for adjusting pulp and paper processes on the fly, typical of statistical control practices that define modern total quality management. The effectiveness of testing-induced adjustments integrated the roles of paper machine and pulp mill operators and technicians, whose unsupervised judgments would spell the difference between tens of thousands of dollars of profit or loss on each shift.

The company built a new technology center in 1926, separating the daily paper testing function and using the new center to accelerate process improvements and the creation of new lines of paper.[104] By 1929 it had a full-time staff of twelve chemists and engineers housed in a separate building. New paper products could thus be tested and refined entirely within its operation: the center grew to include a small fourdrinier, a machine shop, and laboratory rooms as well as offices. By the end of the 1920s, GNP, Oxford Paper Company, and others had also built their own formal R&D departments. Over the years, chemists and engineers in S. D. Warren Company's technology center invented new materials and chemical processes, improved the quality of coating and pigments on papers, developed entirely new grades, and made improvements to pulping processes that enhanced paper quality while cheapening production costs. It made machine improvements as well, such as the air knife coating principle, a technique that it patented and licensed to other companies. It worked with a consortium of paper and chemical companies to improve the quality of starches used to make the adhesives in paper coatings. During World War II, it created papers that remained strong when wet, which was then used to make millions of maps for the U.S. military.

By creating a strong research operation, S. D. Warren Company could find new markets during the halcyon era of magazines, riding the wave of new color and glossy journals and building a reputation for both making the finest and competitively priced papers while responding to new needs by publishers. It came to be one of the country's most prominent suppliers of papers used in company annual reports of the Fortune 500. Its WMA grew rapidly and standardized relations with the national market for its goods. While no new paper machines were purchased between 1920 and 1950, its fourteen paper machines were rebuilt from end to end many times, increasing speed, reliability, and thus the productivity of these machines tripled.[105] Over that period, sales also tripled, and before the headwinds of the 1970s and 1980s, the mill regularly turned in strong profits. As Karl Dornish, who had become the mill's production manager in the late 1960s, recalled, most grades ran at a gross profit margin of around 30 percent during its most prosperous years.[106]

Post–World War II Peak

Postwar United States experienced unsurpassed economic growth; it too was the peak of the Maine paper industry's prosperity and growth. State annual paper production grew from roughly one million metric tons in 1947 to 2.5 million metric tons by 1970. Employment and productivity both grew steadily during peak growth years: the number of paper and logging jobs grew from about eighteen thousand at the end of the Great Depression to roughly thirty-two thousand at the industry's all-time peak in 1967.[107] Oxford Paper's and S. D. Warren Company's Maine mill complexes saw employment grow from roughly fifteen hundred to over three thousand, and GNP grew even more to eventually employ forty-five hundred in its Millinocket, East Millinocket, and Madison mills. These figures don't account for the huge and growing numbers of woodcutters, who numbered greater than ten thousand. New capital equipment was crucial. At the time, machine makers built fourdriniers with on-machine coaters; these new machines were much wider, so the economies of scale were immense. For instance, GNP installed a massive new machine in 1954, then the biggest in the world and capable of producing up to 250 tons of newsprint per day—equal to GNP's entire operation around 1910.[108] New off-machine coaters permitted flexible production of a greater variety of products, including plastic wrap, paper cups, and paper plates. Keyes Fiber, founded in 1907 and located in Waterville, grabbed a dominant share of this market. By the 1920s it was mastering the making of paper plates; and by using new technologies during and after World War II, it eventually made the famous Chinet brand of fine paper plates and bowls.[109]

Maine held its geographic advantage and leading production status into the middle of the twentieth century, enjoying its place in overall postwar prosperity. This would not last. Trees in Southern pine forests grew more rapidly than in the North, but its trees were far too resinous to make good pulp via the sulfite method. In the 1920s, a Southern chemist created a new process based on sulphate that allowed good pulp to be made despite the resin problem; by the mid 1930s the process was refined enough to make large-scale production work.[110] In the ensuing twenty years, process improvements made it possible for Southern mills to diversify beyond cruder products like paper bags into printing papers; by 1970 high-grade publication papers and printing grades were in production throughout the South.[111] Thus, the 1950s and 1960s saw a massive growth in the South's share of national production. Most new Southern mills were built by Northern-based paper companies rather than new enterprises, with S. D. Warren Company, Scott Paper, and IP among them. Advances in transportation technology and infrastructure—notably the new interstate highway system—reduced regional location advantages; mills could produce anywhere and ship to a national market, eroding the benefits of regional proximity. At the same time, the great advantages to R&D that had long spurred growth began to be exhausted, allowing for further incremental changes in products but not the kind of dynamism seen from the late nineteenth century into the 1960s. The industry was becoming mature, with slower growth ahead. Consolidation into larger national enterprises through horizontal mergers became the order of the day.[112]

The Multidivisional Consolidations of the 1960s, 1970s, and 1980s

From their inception, with their hometown mill managers and highly visible company presidents, the great Maine paper workers were truly local—notwithstanding the location of central corporate offices in Boston, Stamford, or New York. For workers and local communities, wages and employment grew rapidly in the postwar years, typifying the great period of overall U.S. middle-class prosperity that stretched from the end of World War II into the 1970s. By that time, the family ethos was understandably entrenched. But the emergence of national markets, shifting of population centers and thus markets away from the Northeast, and new norms and practices in corporate business ushered in a change in organization and corporate governance. At first, Maine-based companies joined the rush to become national enterprises. In the 1950s, S. D. Warren Company purchased an existing mill in Muskeegon, Michigan, and built another in Mobile, Alabama. Hollingsworth and Whitney of Winslow also built a new plant in Mobile that went into production at the start of World War II. By 1967, both had been purchased by Scott Paper Company.[113]

The nationalization of paper production and markets and the prodigious capital requirements needed to match both dramatically growing markets and greater competition together provided impetus for Hollingsworth and Whitney to sell out to Scott Paper. In Howard Reiche's telling, a similar calculus drove S. D. Warren Company president George Olmstead Jr. to sell out to Scott in 1967. According to Karl Dornish, Olmstead had "bet the farm" on the Muskeegon mill purchase, which proved costly to operate and drained capital more than it added to the company's bottom line, constricting the capital needed to grow and maintain profitability. Oxford Paper Company joined the movement, selling out to Ethyl Corporation, a chemical company based in Louisiana, in 1967.[114] GNP first merged with a Southern company in 1965 and then Wisconsin-based Nekoosa Company, forming the new Great Northern Nekoosa in 1970.[115] As we will see in chapter 5, Fraser Paper Company's Canadian owners successfully fought off several hostile takeover attempts in the late 1960s but then was absorbed by an international mining company in 1974.

For the leadership of S. D. Warren Company and Hollingsworth and Whitney, there is little doubt the major owners walked away with a windfall, but at least in their own telling, they trusted the quality of Scott's corporate leadership and especially the much greater ability of the new parent corporation to further support research and marketing capacity and invest in new capital.[116] The Hollingsworth and Whitney mill did in fact thrive under Scott for another four decades, and its skilled workforce formed the core of workers at a new Maine S. D. Warren Company Division of Scott Paper Company built in the 1970s.[117]

All leading companies adopted the organization of large-scale, vertically integrated, multidivisional, and multiproduct forest product enterprises, thus achieving a version of the most advanced Chandlerian type, the M-form (multidivisional). Given truly national scale, the era of regional specialization and stable company and mill leadership for Maine's mills was now waning. As branch plants of these national mega-entities, this diminished status would change local management practices and put increasing pressure on mills and their workers. This would change relations between workers and their employers in ways that sparked protest.

THE PARADOXES OF PAPER MILL EMPLOYMENT

In Maine's integrated pulp and paper mills, on each and every of the year's 365 days, up to and sometimes more than a thousand workers would enter the mill three or four times a day for the shift change.[1] Paper mill workers spent their adult life-times in the mill, starting out of high school and retiring in their sixties or seventies, or earlier if they suffered permanent injury.[2] To those who have never seen or entered a pulp and paper mill complex, a paper mill is an astonishingly intense environment, with extremes of heat and cold, intense chemical smells, and the pervasive presence of large and deadly machinery. In a word, paper mills, to use S. D. Warren Company millwright Barry Kenney's favored word, are "harsh."[3] Every mill accumulated a legacy of horrific accidents and grisly deaths. Perhaps just as astonishing was that paper workers embraced this life. One might surmise that it was because paper mill work delivered high wages and benefits, and it of-fered remarkable job and economic security with few parallels in Maine's gener-ally lower-wage, blue-collar sectors. But a deeper look at the lives of these workers revealed the crucial place of skills, craft pride, and, foremost, member-ship in a high-status industrial community. In this chapter, we'll depict and un-pack the nature of production and work, the special skill profile that made paper mills distinct if not unique, and look especially at how over time owners and work-ers forged a mutually acceptable paternalism. This paternalism was the glue that made Maine's paper mills both successful businesses and durable communities during the industry's halcyon years from the late nineteenth century through the 1970s. To understand the critical role of skill, and the paradox of suffering and success, that marked these workers' lives, we will look closely at life in S. D. Warren Company.

"They Stood Behind You"

I interviewed Mae Bachelor in 2003 when she was in her early eighties.[4] Mae worked at S. D. Warren from 1940 through the mid-1970s. She toiled, as did hundreds of other women, in the finishing department, inspecting paper and counting out reams by hand. As a highly productive worker, she got plum assignments and earned ample bonus money. She married a fellow Warren worker and began a family in the late 1940s. She remained a loyal worker until "they retired her" in the 1970s because of a lung condition caused by her exposure to chemicals in the mill. Looking back on her time with Warren, she celebrates it.

> It's all family-connected. I mean, my cousins worked there, my brothers and sister worked there, and when you went in, it was just a nice atmosphere, and people were really happy in them days. They were lucky they even had a job! They *wanted* to get into S. D Warren: where could you go and get a better job, better-*paying* job, better health insurance, everything? *You had security down there, and they stood behind you.* Like I said, if your children went to college, they'd even help you if you wanted to buy a house, they'd help you. That's what I liked about it. It was a good company.

Her shop was a site of conviviality and solidarity. They worked under a beloved supervisor named "Poppa" Roy Gory, took up collections when someone was ill, and spent their shifts working at tables and socializing with coworkers who became best friends. Togetherness at work spilled over into the neighborhood, where mothers would keep an eye out on fellow workers' children when their parents were at work—necessitated by the complex timing of shiftwork. Security and stability were the keys to the exchange between Mae, her family, and the mill. She believed that in exchange for her hard work, the mill took care of her and her family and provided the essential stability and security needed to make a good life. Injuries and maladies were unfortunate but normal.

Mae also described many notable sacrifices and hardships that came with the job, but to her they seemed commonplace and barely worthy of comment. She had four children; during the years that her kids were growing up, she would work a six-hour shift from midnight until six a.m. After her shift, she went home and got her kids off to school and husband off to work, making both breakfast and lunches, cleaned the house during the day, then greeted her children and husband with dinner, followed by putting the kids to bed, and finally getting her only daily sleep from about 8:30 to 11:30 p.m. Her children, one of who was present during our interview, were unaware that she continued to work until their teenage years. When she was pregnant, she was required to take off several months from work late in the pregnancy and right after childbirth; each time, she lost all of her accumulated seniority (this was during the nonunion era): "If you had a child, you had to leave, and come back. This is before the union come in. And when the union came in, of course, they reinstated everybody so they got their equal time [seniority], but back in our time, it didn't. We lost all of our seniority, everything."

In the 1960s, her husband was injured in a horrible chemical accident/explosion that killed two men. The explosion draped his body in caustic liquor, and he was fortunate to survive. After a stay in the hospital for many months, he was picked up daily and brought to the mill's medical clinic to change his extensive bandages. Once he recovered, roughly half of his body's skin was permanently disfigured. In recalling this horror, she finishes with the optimistic spin that, "He never lost a day's pay."

Mae's coda about her husband never losing pay is crucial, because it was more important to her understanding of the incident than the fact that her husband had horrible scarring over 40 percent of his body. In the 1970s, a lung condition typical of those who suffer with cystic fibrosis forced her to stop working. She eventually returned and moved into a job that was away from areas that had high chemical intensity in the air, but her breathing problems were too much and she was forced to retire. She recalled with acceptance that this was also part of the normal course of events: "I went in and had one lung operation. . . . I was out . . . for a year and a half, and I went back to work, and it happened again. So, when I went back to work a second time, they [the mill] said no, they had to retire me."

What lay beneath Mae Bachelor's frame for interpreting her past? As we'll see, workers and managers together forged a belief system that elicited needed commitment and loyalty from workers, including an accommodation to a lifetime of difficult circumstances—the paradox of suffering and success—and made sure that each side of the employment bargain served each's material and mythical understanding of success.

S. D. Warren's Employment Bargain in Historical Perspective

Economists consider labor a factor of production; employees exchange their time for a compensation package defined by wages and benefits.[5] In the standard undergraduate textbook, a worker receives a paycheck and then literally enters a black box on a diagram, and there ends the discussion. Interdisciplinary scholars of work and capitalism see a much more complex picture. Employers construct a social system in which workers are directed, compelled, inspired, or otherwise impelled to get a certain quantity and quality of work done. Workers bring or develop an identity and a set of attitudes about work, indelibly shaped by their daily experiences as part of an organization in which friendship, fear, hostility, loyalty, organization, danger, the inability or opportunity to develop and exercise skill, and a host of other factors help to determine the quantity and quality of work that is done. And history plays a huge role. Economists speak of path dependence, in which legacy shapes current economic reality, creating some possibilities and foreclosing others.[6] At the end of the day, a company produces commodities that are sold and that do or do not turn a profit, and workers go home happy, exhausted, injured, or otherwise affected by that particular working day, to hopefully return tomorrow. As Mae's story illustrates, work at S. D. Warren Company and other Maine paper mills was a rich and complicated matter, typical of big mass production companies in some ways and deeply atypical in others.

These complexities inhere in the incomplete wage bargain. Once an employee is hired for a set time (9 to 5), managements face a human and organizational challenge: how to exact the maximum quantity and quality of effort from the worker, something not specified in the wage bargain.[7] America's transition to mass production in the late nineteenth century sparked an array of managerial and technological practices that grew up to address this challenge. Henry Ford and Frederick Winslow Taylor emerged as iconic innovators.[8] Taylor created the method of scientific management, using engineering study to break down industrial work into discrete, repetitive tasks. Appropriating the specific manual skills used by frontline workers meant engineers could collaborate with supervisors to redesign and speed up work, making it ever simpler—and punishing. Engineers and managers could take advantage of the huge armies of southern and eastern European, Chinese, and Mexican immigrants to insist on rapid, repetitive work, selecting only the most physically able and psychologically susceptible, and offering modest wage gains in return for extraordinary returns of increased productivity. Ford raised the profile of this new mode of factory work to an even higher level with the advent of the assembly line, which featured a worker assigned to a singular, repetitive task at a speed dictated by the advance of work along a line. Isolation of individual motions on an assembly line had many implications. It brought about a superworker whose repetition bred speed, expedited the setting of ever-increasing production standards, and gave impetus to mechanization where a new machine could replace the continuously studied and monitored

motions of a human being. Mostly, it produced mind-numbing work, and the relation of the worker to their work was in equal amounts alienating and punishing.
The heart of the employment bargain became *acquiescence* to shop floor tyranny
executed by powerful foremen out of fear of being fired and replaced; this dour
bargain was leavened only by the hollow rewards of a new consumerism, as Model
T cars, radios, movies, and new home conveniences for women holding down the
second shift became available from these very mass production companies who
needed to sell to the working class in order to grow profitably. This so-called Fordism posited a story of deskilling and of a defeated and compliant workforce.[9]

Labor scholars for a time (the 1970s and 1980s) came to assume this narrative
of deskilling, tyranny, and alienation was a universal tendency that could be
tracked across every and any occupation work researchers could turn their attention to.[10] Another perspective questioned this blanket characterization of the
history of work in mass production industry.[11] This work cast doubt on the image of a beaten down and submissive worker. In fact, massive informal workplace
resistance to Taylorite methods emerged and continued for much of the twentieth century. In the 1910s, 1930s–1940s, and late 1960s–1970s, shop floor rebellion erupted into mass labor movements that challenged, modified, and, in some
instances, beat back Taylorism, if not always deskilling.[12] Moreover, in exemplary
cases like Kodak Inc., the character of production was itself less amenable to the
kinds of standardization and control implied by the deskilling narrative.[13] Overall, workers often found myriad ways to resist the most onerous aspects of Taylorized work and found ways to make meaning through daily modes of solidarity.

In 1984, Michael J. Piore and Charles F. Sabel's *Second Industrial Divide* claimed
that the Fordist labor process was on its way out with the arrival of a new era of
"flexible specialization," as globalization and information technology gave impetus to new forms of competition and methods for profitable growth.[14] Piore
and Sabel projected a third industrial revolution, where the pursuit of global niche
markets called for a new labor process, one where workers used higher-order skills
and information technology to crank out a greater variety of products that also
had to meet higher quality standards. They cited historic examples of European
industrial districts in Italian textiles and German machine production, and they
joined many in celebrating contemporary Japanese automakers' ability to change
production models frequently on the same assembly lines. Notably, their description of work under the new flexible specialization regime closely matches what
arose a century earlier at Warren and other integrated paper mills.

Indeed, mass production pulp and paper mills over the century from 1880 to
1980 defies this epochal view of work Taylorism dominating American capitalism. For the typical Maine paper mill, with its focus on high-quality publication
and a plethora of specialty papers, mass production included standardized prod-

ucts for which achieving high and consistent quality was a daily challenge. Also, most mills still made a wide variety of smaller batch runs of specialty products. As we'll see, some paper mill tasks were of the repetitive type subject to standardization and Taylorist control, but movement toward a deskilling regime was mitigated by the presence of difficult elements and unpredictable conditions; authoritarian supervision was thwarted by the communal dynamics of workplaces, where one might have dozens of relatives and close neighbors in other parts of the mill. Thus, the combination of fear-driven shop floor tyranny and the instrumental rewards of a high wage that typified Fordist mass production would not only fail if applied but was largely irrelevant.

Even in the most conventional mass production company, management of the wage bargain dilemma during the mass production era was anything but static. Workplace resistance and constant threat of labor rebellion inspired new managerial techniques that sought to reach the human element of the worker and supplement or replace the brutish incentives of Taylorism and Fordism.[15] Variants of paternalism meant to inspire loyalty, acquiescence, and effort dominated many nineteenth-century factories, and persisted to a degree in smaller firms through the course of the twentieth century. Paternalisms operated through either personally or institutionally delivered "protection, provision, and control" that created an informal authority that could elicit worker commitment.[16] With the advent of large, mass production manufacturing companies after 1890, paternalism was hard to maintain at this larger scale and for long periods of time. A self-named corporate welfare movement began in the late nineteenth century, promising better and safer work settings and the beginnings of fringe benefits such as death benefits and public facilities like gymnasiums and ball parks, while favoring more formal and bureaucratic structures in place of the highly personal style of paternalistic owners. From its start, corporate welfare efforts were motivated by a combination of a desire to produce a better motivated workforce and a persistent managerial commitment to thwart unionism in any form.[17] Labor rebellion and war-induced labor shortages inspired the first efforts to build personnel management practices in the 1910s. A more enduring set of innovations came in the 1920s, constituting what historian Sanford Jacoby dubbed "vanguard welfarism." Jacoby depicted the efforts of firms like Kodak and Thompson Products, which revolutionized shop floor supervision by selecting and training a more humane foreman, stripped of the most powerful tool of tyranny—the power to fire.[18] These employers also gave workers the semblance of a say over their work and more generous benefits and job security than previously conceived. Such firms, and academic advocates like Harvard's Elton Mayo, joined in pioneering the sophisticated field of human resource management that became the standard for post-World War II corporate employment.[19]

Using S. D. Warren Company as our chief example, we will see how a highly idiosyncratic system of company-worker relations grew out of paper's distinct production processes, a system that did not fit any of these widely-used categories. The mill maintained an extraordinary paternalistic legacy that persisted for over a century, adopted some elements of welfare capitalism, but did not create anything resembling modern personnel management.[20] S. D. Warren was in this sense a labor relations oddity: it maintained paternalism long after scale and new personnel techniques typically made paternalism obsolete. Another idiosyncrasy was that, in the absence of sophisticated human resource practices, S. D. Warren still succeeded in remaining union free for more than a century. Despite being out of step with twentieth-century standard labor relations practices, S. D. Warren's approach in fact worked incredibly well at ensuring the company's production prowess that made it a strong, profitable, and growing company. What is most remarkable is just how well this managerial alchemy ultimately worked—workers were inspired by the myth and substance of life at Mother Warren and made the contributions at work needed for the company's success. At the same time, the system did have its problems that accumulated over time.

How does paper production specifically stand out from conventional mass production? Paper mills were highly capital intensive and produced paper on a mass scale. But the nature of the critical pulp and paper mill work obviated deskilling and placed the quest for commitment beyond the reach of standardization and tyranny. Less skilled jobs in materials handling, finishing (cutting, processing, and wrapping completed paper), and testing—and lower-level, highly physical jobs on digesters, paper machines, or in the woodlot—were nonetheless integrated into a team setting; family and personal connections among skilled and nonskilled workers precluded compartmentalized shop floor management strategies. In Maine's major integrated pulp and paper mills, such as Westbrook, Maine's S. D. Warren Company, motivating work and the work itself operated on a basis alien to the methods of Taylorism and the deskilling found in assembly type work. Rather, every shift was an act of individual and collective innovation.

Paper workers had to be trusted to make endless, unsupervised judgments; to apply skills, not rules; and to constantly draw on long-won experience to ensure that the collective resources represented by massive machines and physical plant, the huge quantities of processed raw materials, a large and expensive workforce, and the final product in its multiple stages of production and finishing, were not wasted and the chance for making profits ruined.[21] Each shift was an act of great contingency, a baking of the proverbial touchy soufflé. No rationalization of work or supervision could replace the artistry of teams of workers who were led by first hands in pulp and paper operations—first hands being the lead workers on these operations, promoted on the basis of decades of skill and experience on a particular operation—along with a handful of foremen and managers with deep production and quality expertise. While still capitalism, based on an exchange of a wage for a worker's time so that the employer could produce commodities and garner profits, workers and company owners and managers went beyond this exchange, bestowing collective gifts to each other.[22] For those involved, the market nexus of hired employment could not be separated from a deeper relationship of community.

It is important to remember that two agents come to the table in any employment relationship. The lesson of several generations of research on work is that people do not just submit or agree to the terms of both the wage bargain and shop floor expectations; they go further by building either an entire identity or a place where work fits into one's identity. Work can be just a paycheck, or it can be all-consuming and all-defining, in the way of a career, a vocation.[23]

Maine paper mill work for most was firmly in the latter category, despite its blue-collar character. A paper worker spent much of her or his life mainly in the mill (with its seven-day work weeks and irregular short breaks each month), but she or he also lived in towns in which the mill extended itself into every aspect of people's physical and social existence. Moreover, identity in company towns was a collective project of making meaning—actively producing one's sense of place in the world and the import of being subjugated to an innately harsh daily life defined by heat, stress, injuries, and the toilsome burden of shift work.[24] In S. D. Warren Company's Westbrook, denizens stressed the very uncapitalist, all-encompassing security of being taken care of cradle to grave—and beyond the grave by none other than Mother Warren. While they credited the company's founder and his heirs for creating a special worldly and material status, they also clearly identified their own immense contributions of collective skill and effort. This included the ability to withstand the extraordinary challenges of their work, and also the embrace of psychic income earned from the very success and high-profile status of their products—as makers of the world's best paper.

At S. D. Warren, the final sinew in this great and mutual bargain was an indulgency pattern.[25] The mill, starting with the mill manager but down to front-line supervisors, acted as an informal but ubiquitous social work agency, both seen and truly used as a source of advice and material assistance that workers asked to reach down into every facet of their lives and help them with daily issues and struggles. Foremost, the company took care of all workers as members of a collective family. A worker who might be a self-destructive and unreliable alcoholic, suffered mental illness, or who was permanently injured was seldom if ever let go; in each case, the worker and his/her family would be aided, but never fired.[26]

The company fostered and the workers embraced a system with far more resem-
blance to a private Scandinavian social democracy than the U.S.'s social Darwinian capitalism. It was S. D. Warren Company's superior commitment to its
workers' and their families' security and prosperity—though one with many cave-
ats including the injuries and mistreatment typical of Mae Bachelor's and her husband's experiences—and a recognition and deep pride in their role in their
company's success, profitability, and reputation that secured, *where most needed*, an
extraordinary commitment of workers' energies and skills. Finally, this was a system that reflected the prosperity and the freedom of management in the Chandlerian era to generously share the company's resources, a freedom that would erode
and ultimately evaporate over the final third of the twentieth century. We turn now
to a historical account of production and employment at S. D. Warren Company,
beginning with a depiction of the mill's operations in the mid-twentieth century.

Production and Skill at S. D. Warren:
Supervision, the Skill Hierarchy,
and 287 Factors

> Because of the many variables both in the raw materials and in the operation of
> the individual machines . . . it had been considered impossible to establish a stan-
> dard specification that could produce a given quality of paper every time. The
> men used to say that there were 287 different factors that varied in the produc-
> tion of any single paper.
>
> —S.D. Warren manager, Glower and Hower, *The Administrator* (1950s)

The nature of work and supervision varied dramatically across the mill. In 1948,
at a time when the mill employed about three thousand, senior and middle management on site consisted of only about twenty positions, including fewer than
ten full and assistant department superintendents overseeing production. Below
them were foremen who often oversaw multiple machines or an area of the mill,
working mostly on the day shift. The woodlot, wood room, and pulp mill all included a great deal of brute labor, as small groups of workers were given discreet,
often highly nasty tasks to conduct;[27] this was the part of the complex with the
greatest concentration of chemical vapors that caused illness and "would gag you"
and cause you to "throw your guts up."[28] Supervisors were present—though minimally so on night shifts—but men were typically left on their own to move materials, clean machines, and pour and process chemicals, often troubleshooting
situations where machines clogged up.

The paper mill was the heart of the operation. Here, the first hand—historically known as the machine tender—and his underlings often spent stretches of time doing apparently very little, even taking catnaps in the middle of the third shift, and only swinging into dramatic action when there was a paper break.[29] In fact, we'll see that a great deal of skilled monitoring work was essential to prevent costly breakdowns or poor paper quality. Only the finishing department most closely resembled a traditional Taylorized factory setting. One group of male workers cut paper to size, another female group then counted and inspected reams by hand, a third wrapped paper for shipping, and then a fourth loaded paper on to trucks and railroad cars. Many of these jobs were timed and closely supervised, and a bonus system was at the heart of an effort to maximize production speed.

At the pinnacle of integrated pulp and paper mills were the first hands on pulp and paper machines, and the maintenance crew—machinists, pipefitters, electricians, and others who repaired machines throughout the mill. The greatest prestige, remuneration, and responsibility for making the company's profits rested in the first hands on the digesters and especially the paper machines. These workers were men whose skill and responsibilities were like that of a chef in an elite restaurant, artists whose decades of machine-specific knowledge was crucial to making high-quality paper that, when done correctly, could bring the company great profits.

In the pulp mill, a large number of semiskilled workers processed and delivered materials and chemicals to digesters and beaters. The first hand on a digester was responsible for the cook—literally the cooking of pulp, which had to have a requisite set of physical and chemical characteristics; the brown stock from the digester then moved through the mixing of additional ingredients in order to create the furnish that was the prerequisite to making paper that could meet their customers' standards. Pulp was then piped to paper machines.

Thus, some work was relatively simple and could be learned by newcomers, but most jobs required skills learned through experience. The higher-skill jobs invariably required the longest periods for gaining experience, and many workers advanced through mill employment to jobs of greater responsibility only as they acquired the necessary experience and skills, with some notable exceptions like the "women's work" in the finishing department (see figure 2.1). While supervisors wielded authority, their role was often to set the terms of the work and then either worked in tandem with senior hands or left their charges to their tasks, intervening only if problems arose.

An unusually precise look at the challenges in running these complex processes profitably emerges from the observations of four Harvard researchers who spent lengthy stints in the Westbrook mill in a span during the late 1940s and early 1950s. (Hereafter referred to as the *Harvard study*.)[30]

FIGURE 2.1 It was common for women to staff finishing departments where paper was processed, inspected, and packaged. Here are women workers at Oxford Paper Company in 1903, processing some of the 3 million postcards for the U.S. Postal Service for Oxford's exclusive contract on these cards (collections of Greater Rumford Area Historical Society, courtesy of www.VintageMaineImages .com).

In depicting how and why paper production was so difficult, the study points out:

> The work of producing paper that was satisfactory to the customer was highly complex. The characteristics of the ingredients—water, pulp, filler, sizing, color, and other materials—were never exactly predictable or controllable. . . . From the pulp mill through the paper mill, *an infinite number of combinations of mechanical adjustments were possible in order to get a limited range of desired results.* . . . On the paper machines . . . more than 100 of these adjustments were possible and less than half a dozen automatic devices had been found useful in controlling them.[31]

Daily production encompassed a range of products. They included Warren Standard grades of printing paper sold to book and magazine publishers; high-end coated paper for products such as corporate annual reports; and specialty papers, such as coating and wrapping papers for retail products, which were produced on its older and smaller, less efficient paper machines. The mill's chief production manager observed: "It is no small trick to make all these different kinds of papers so that there will be a profit from the total operation at the end of the year."[32] So, managers and first hands juggled allocating many runs of different products across the mill's fourteen paper machines, constantly mobilizing where needed to solve difficult production problems that arose on almost every shift.

Achieving requisite quality was a constant battle. Their customers' quality requirements were steep—the printing presses their customers ran typically required paper thickness of a specific width, often to one-thousands of an inch.

What was at stake? Even minutes of defective paper or a paper break meant thousands of dollars of lost revenues. Fraser Paper machine tender Jerry Cyr recalled that in the late twentieth century at Fraser, one minute of paper machine downtime was a loss of $3,000—or $180,000 an hour; the many hours it sometimes took to get a machine up and running meant losses on just one paper machine over a shift could approach $1 million.[33]

Making a good run of paper in the face of so many problems meant coordination among the leaders of the pulp and paper making processes, along with key managers that may include the very top leadership at the mill. On the machines, the first hand took the lead in examining the results of the constant tests of samples, as "tests were run to measure and control such characteristics as basic weight, bulk, bursting strength, tearing strength, opacity, ash content, acidity, and porosity . . . [while assessing] surface characteristics, fiber formation, dirt, color and similar matters."[34] Upon identifying errant watermarks and other blemishes, paper whose color or tolerances (width) were off, or dealing with a run with serial breaks, the first hand could make on-machine adjustments. However, major or persistent problems often required the cooperation of workers and department supervisors in other parts of the mill, and scientists and technicians from the technology center.

The result was a form of work organization anathema to Fordism and Taylorism: production based on the skills of the employees rather than on prescribed rules of action. The willingness to apply these skills, without supervision, was the key to the company's success.

On the paper machines, decisions that involved both the volume and quality of production might be made by one of the hands. Even in rolling paper on the reels, which was usually done by the least skilled worker on a paper machine, many things could be done that spoiled the paper and lowered the salable production. The skills necessary to make adequate decisions at all operating levels were usually of a type that could not be carefully formulated and must be learned by experience over a number of years. The men had to know what to do with many of the innumerable problems that arose in the ordinary operations. They often had to act quickly and effectively.[35]

The nexus of the mill's paternalism undergirded a production culture focused on workers' skill acquisition and their freedom *and willingness* to make decisions without direction or monitoring by supervisors. Workers understood that their actions were crucial to making the company highly profitable, and they generally applied their skill with dedication and élan.

Harvard Business School researcher Shoshana Zuboff, in her 1980s study of several Southern paper and pulp mills, depicted the way in which years on a paper mill machine or processes yielded a deep, internalized set of knowledge and skills. Workers, calling on their senses, tapped into a massive well of experience when confronted with new problems in a way that could be quickly translated into effective, corrective action. Notably, much of this knowledge was implicit and second nature, and even ineffable. This made it nigh impossible for managers to appropriate or even study the skill of workers, a prerequisite for classic Taylorist management. She notes: "There are operators who can run the paper machine with tremendous efficiency, but they cannot describe to you how they do it. They have built-in actions and sense that they are not aware of. . . . There are operators who know exactly what to do, but they cannot tell you how they do it."[36] DesCartes's dictum is revised thusly: "I see, I touch, I smell, I hear; therefore, I know."

Notably, the potentially powerful leverage emanating from these workers' critical skills was not used to restrict work. In Taylorized, assembly-line type work, study after study across the twentieth century documents the endlessly clever efforts of workers to restrict the pace of work;[37] here, mill workers sought to solve production problems, giving their all when needed, all with an eye to helping the company earn profit.[38] Close supervision and control by managers was simply not necessary nor would work as an incentive.

Many contemporary paper workers across a number of mills in Maine described their work in precisely this way. Long-time Fraser Paper machine tender Jerry Cyr, whose career working on paper machines spanned the 1960s through the early 2000s, recalls listening closely to sounds from motors and pumps, as well as visual clues, and "if you *feel* that something's going bad, you call for somebody to check it out."[39] Cyr also knew intimately the connection between problems on the machine and the demands of the ultimate customers: "If you are having problems on the machine, whoever is buying it will have problems with that paper."[40]

Production Management at the S. D. Warren Company

In addition to workers' considerable skills and deep commitment to the work, a lean management structure was also crucial. This structure linked production to the mill's onsite research department and its sales force, the latter managed out of the company's Boston headquarters. As the mill slowly evolved from a small operation to a major mill with fourteen paper machines, its management structure that had emerged incrementally, punctuated by the shift from the poor Warrens to control by a senior management group in the 1920s.[41] These new managers forged a nimble organization focused on the constant endeavor to match machines and processes to myriad orders, and to build, encourage, and reward the continual development of worker and managerial skills needed to keep the mill profitable and competitive. As we will see, the production and marketing acumen of the managers meshed with the skill and commitment of the hands met the company's objective to deliver quality paper that met the customers' demanding requirements.

What did this management look like? The informality of this management's lines of authority was notable; the *Harvard study* research group had to create an organization chart to make sense of what it learned about the mill's operation; the lack of such a chart was an odd absence from a midsized manufacturing company of four thousand employees in the post-World War II era.[42] Warren management's signal character was to devolve as much responsibility down to workers, trusting in their skills and devotion to success. A small group of managers with exceptional troubleshooting expertise backed up the shop floor.

Each section the mill—the pulp mill, paper machines, coating, supercalender, and finishing—was headed by a superintendent. Below were a couple of layers of production leaders, each with critical knowledge on how the production processes worked, and especially how to make effective adjustments on the machines and in the processes in order to achieve quality and cost-effective runs of paper. Mill management had grown organically from the mill's earliest days—expanding and specializing according to the emergence of the necessary talent to ensure successful production. Early on, production managers often grew out of the ranks on the machines. After 1920, the mill increasingly recruited college graduates, especially from engineering schools at University of Maine and Syracuse University.[43] New hires began with a management apprentice program that put the men in the various departments of the mill to learn production processes. Many company leaders, including George Olmstead Jr., Rudy Greep, Howard Reiche, and Karl Dornish, were first trained in this program. This training lasted six months, with apprentices rotating through various parts of the mill, spending weeks or months in each operation, gaining familiarity through both observation and participation.[44]

As we'll see, production leaders, whatever their title, maintained a constant communication with the sales staff, the customers themselves, inspection, and the research department—identifying problems when they arose and trying to find solutions to them.

On any given day, two or more dozen different products would be made on the mill's paper machines; they came to each machine as a production order. Each machine ran a minimum of two or three product runs a week, but orders could change more than once on a given shift. The company's sales force put in orders to the mill, with responsibility for getting the order made falling to the mill's scheduling office. The scheduling office would create a production order, making some twenty-two copies that went to each part of the mill with specifications for making the pulp and mixing the furnish, adjustments and settings on paper machines, and for cutting and wrapping in the finishing department; the order also went to the control room where samples of the order were constantly scrutinized. The chief scheduler had sole responsibility for scheduling product runs. He had worked in various parts of the mill for many decades, and he knew the characteristics and vagaries of the mill's many processes and machines. Each order specified the machine to be used for a run of paper, and it detailed the precise characteristics the customer required. There could be innumerable variations from run to run—in width (bulk), color, strength, sheen, and so on. Variations arose even on the mill's standard printing grades—customers were guaranteed tweaks to paper specifications. Deciding which order went on which machine, the scheduler had to take into account a range of characteristics in determining how to optimize the use of machines among competing applications.

The journey of a product order began with the pulp mill and the beaters. The beaters were the nexus of the pulp mill and the paper machines. There were two sets of beaters adjacent to the two groups of paper machines, with one or more beaters dedicated to each machine. It was here that the furnish was created—the combination of purchased pulp, pulp made in the mill, and waste paper mixed with a variety of materials, dyes, and water based on the specific character of each product run.[45]

The relevant supervisor and first hand on a paper machine would make the necessary machine adjustments to produce the specified product, with the assistance of the testing department. Once a run was under way, constant testing of samples at the machine and in the central control room allowed continuous monitoring of the paper quality. While paper breaks constituted one type of routine problem that could often be dealt directly with by the machine hands, a host of other defects could only be identified by testing. At the time of the *Harvard study*, the mill's chief quality inspector oversaw a staff of three inspectors and a larger number of "test girls" (who were young adult women), who worked on hourly tests from all of the machines, with young men who acted as runners bringing samples from the machines and instructions back from the control room to the machines, all supplementing on-machine testing by the first hand. The "girls" checked to see that physical and chemical features of the paper met routine specifications, including weight, thickness, opacity, and various measures of strength, as well as chemical features of the paper such as acidity or ash content. Inspectors looked closely at the presence of dirt, whether or not the paper met color specifications, and the features defining strength. As flaws were identified, the runners returned to the paper machines, conveying to the first hands needed adjustments.

Just as often, a more complex set of possible adjustments was needed. In one case, one of the mill's standard Warren printing grades continually exceeded the specified width.[46] The senior production manager and the chief inspector identified a number of possible fixes. One was to make the fibers in the pulp smaller, which would require increasing the water content of the furnish; this in turn would require slowing the machine speed down by 100 feet per minute (fpm) to allow the paper sheet a longer time to go through the dryer rolls. Another was to change the chemical content of the furnish, adding cellate to the pulp which would result in smaller fibers. They contemplated running the order on another paper machine. And the head of the specialty department actually went to the customer—a Buffalo, New York book printer—to see if adjustments could be made on the printer's printing presses. In each case, there were important disadvantages at the time to any of these solutions, rendering the judgment as to which was the preferred approach a delicate call. These kinds of decisions had to be made on a daily basis.

The mill created similar control rooms in the coating and supercalendering departments. Feedback from these tests added a layer of both quantity control and critical information about possible adjustments at earlier stages of production.

The sales department, headquartered in Boston, supplied a critical link in the feedback loop between the customer and the men on the machines. Sales staff communicated with the chief inspector and direct supervisors on specific machines. The salesmen were mainly recruited out of Williams College, a member of the "little" Ivy League colleges, located in western Massachusetts. Like production managers, they began their careers with a lengthy training program in the Westbrook mill, which ensured they were intimately familiar with the substance and vagaries of the production processes that resulted in the paper they sold and especially the sources and solutions for quality issues.[47] Constant communication between sales and production concerning customer needs and problems with defective paper—via telephone from around the country and through constant visits of sales staff to the mill's shop floor—acted as a stimulus to endless tweaking and problem solving. Similarly, production managers also did field visits to learn about technical challenges publishers experienced and would return to the mill to seek to implement fixes for problems their customers faced.

The *Harvard study* illustrated how these relationships played out in the specialty papers group, focusing on the role played by the group's hands-on manager,

Ned Kenyon.[48] His boss, the assistant mill superintendent, credited Kenyon for being deeply interested in the technical details of production of coated specialty papers, "thinking like a research man":

> As far as specialty papers are concerned, Ned Kenyon does practically all of the detailed work. He talks directly with the salesmen and with the customers when it is necessary. Many of these papers involve the research department, and Kenyon works closely with them. He works out all the details that he can handle, and when he gets stuck, he comes to me. In dealing with the sales office I usually take only the situations where there is some policy decision involved. Once a month, Dunn, the salesman for these specialty papers, comes to the mill. We get together with Kenyon and Pete Fraser of the research department for one or two evening sessions. I keep a record of our general conclusions in this little black book. In meetings of this sort we can keep the manufacturing problems and the customer requirements clearly in front of us.[49]

Karl Dornish, who joined Warren management in 1954 and was a senior production manager by the late 1960s, learned that "it pretty much had been a sales-driven company" whose success was the ability of this complex to ensure higher quality than its competitors: "Your quality had to be better than anybody else's. Particularly the attributes of your product. Everybody struggled for consistency back then. But we always had attributes that were better than anybody else's."[50]

Last and certainly not least were the women who inspected paper and counted reams in the finishing department. At S. D. Warren's employment peak in the post-World War II era, nearly five hundred women, working in four six hour shifts, formed the lynchpin in the mill's quest to meet customer requirements.[51] Paper came to finishing in large rolls and first was cut to size for packing by men on guillotine presses. Then, enormous stacks of sheets, several feet high and typically three to five feet wide and long, were brought to female inspectors in two rooms: the big room and the count and fan room. The big room got the more expensive coated publication papers; plain and specialty papers went to count and fan. Staffed by dozens of women on shift work, here the paper was inspected twice and counted into reams. In the count and fan room, the types of paper being inspected tended to have easily identifiable blemishes. Some twenty-four women worked on pallets of paper, fanning each corner of the stack of papers, making a tear on defective sheets, until they had done so for an estimated ream of paper. This was done on each of the four sides of paper. Two-man teams of pilers removed defective sheets set aside by the women, then removed them two reams at a time and transported them to an adjacent room for one last inspection. The count and fan girl would eventually return to each pallet with a fresh, uncounted stack of paper exposed after the counted paper was removed. In this procedure, if a worker identified a large number of defects in a stack, the paper would then be moved to one of eight tables where another group of women inspectors table sorted the paper, placing good sheets to one side of the table, and defective paper into a bin on the other side of the table, and then repeating the counting exercise on the good paper.

The *Harvard study* noted the importance of this work:

> Inspection in this department constituted the final stage in the efforts of the mill to make high-grade paper. The girls who worked here were aware that as the last people to handle the paper, they were responsible to the customer for quality. They soon learned what grades of paper had to be sorted with particular care and what minor defects each customer would accept or would not accept in his orders.[52]

The many different types and quality levels of paper made specific paper grades distinct in the amount of attention and the speed with which they could be inspected and counted. Smaller-sized paper was easier, and paper with fewer defects meant quicker work and less stress. Crucially, supervisors constantly reminded the women of just how fundamental their role was in making sure customers did not wind up with defective paper. A female inspector in an adjacent room did a final quick inspection, making each woman in either room accountable for being effective in identifying defects. When bad paper accidentally got through and shipped, it would often come back from the customers. The male supervisors would take time at the end of a shift to gather all of the women in the room and examine the defects, and the specific inspector responsible for letting through bad paper would be publicly accountable. For the most part, this was done not to shame a worker but to collectively figure out how best not to allow a certain kind of defective paper to get through.

The mill's management generated a constant stream of daily reports with key data that allowed management to identify problems in need of correcting and distinguish between its most and least profitable lines. Foremost was the tracking of waste throughout the mill. Paper was often ruined on the machines and coaters, while defective paper was separated out in the finishing department. Most of this defective paper was recycled, so it wasn't *completely* wasted, but rather was "expensive pulp."[53] As noted, some defective paper identified and separated out by the women inspectors in the finishing department was of sufficient quality to be sold to jobbers at positive but low profit margins. Each day, a record of waste in each department would be forwarded to the central production office, compiled, and shared with production managers across the mill.

The finishing department had a special form to track waste on coated papers counted in the big room; their inspections were so precise that they were able to track thirty different types of defects. This data was used to develop an ongoing chart made in the production office that could be used to make machine adjustments. Similar charts were generated to track the defects found in the pulp mill and other stages of the production process.

The assistant production manager examined the gross profit by each paper grade; the sales department calculated this profit rate by examining cost, waste, and production data along with actual sales revenue from each run. Except when there were major problems, the typical profit rate per run ranged between 10 and 30 percent, with the former typically being the big-volume Warren standard grades and the latter the specialty grades run on smaller, older machines.[54] Notably, they kept these records on seventy separate grades. This data helped the company's sales force to drive a sales strategy that privileged the highest profit lines. When a particular grade deviated from its past norm, gross profit data was a stimulus to diagnose why something went wrong and how to correct it.

Finally, the mill production manager looked primarily at reported tonnage and waste by machine. "If production was up to schedule and waste was not abnormal, he knew low costs would result."[55] Mill manager John Hyde received concise reports on production, waste, and costs throughout the mill, as well as updates from the research department, monthly first-aid reports, and employee earnings and how they compared to other Maine mills. This data gave Hyde a precise running account of costs and profitability, problems and high points. Once a month, Hyde would travel to Boston to brief the company's board of directors and senior sales staff, where long-run company strategy was ratified or altered to improve company profitability.[56]

Work across the Departments

Roughly 10 percent of the mill's workers were on the paper machines.[57] Machines typically had five-man crews. On each shift for an individual paper machine, the first hand and second hand exercised full control of the operation. A given shift was both a team effort to maintain production and function as a learning system. A shift team that worked effectively required little supervision or managerial intervention, while another might struggle because of the poor skills and leadership of first and second hands and would elicit intervention by managers.

Third, fourth, and fifth hands did most of the physical labor, tending to the winders at the ends of the machines and changing rolls, performing routine maintenance, and jumping in to action when a routine break occurred at the dry end in the dryer stacks or at the calendar, and doing routine maintenance. When they were not actually working, they wandered around the machine watching the others and asking questions. The second hand usually directed the remaining hands, and the first and second hand conferred regularly over the course of the shift. "The second hand actually directed the others, trained them, answered their questions, and worked directly with them on many occasions such as changing the core on the drum reel or handling a break at the dry end."[58] Typically, the first hand had a table near the wet end of the machine, where he spent much time reviewing samples, receiving instructions from the inspection department, and taking time to confer with the second hand and others over a cigarette.

Effort on the machines varied by position and circumstance. A famous feature of paper machine work is the inverse relationship between effort and productivity on paper machines: "Well, also, in the paper machine department if [the] machine is running the operators are sitting around. They're just sitting there watchin' it run."[59] "When things ran fine, you were just monitoring some gauges."[60] In contrast, Tom Lestage describes the intense efforts of the lower hands, under the first hand's supervision, when paper broke:

> You worked the hardest when you didn't make any money—i.e., when paper would break. . . . That was physically demanding . . . from say June to September, the average temperature on a machine runs between 110 and 115. . . . . Your major job was pulling paper out of the machines and off the dryer cans and getting the machine as quick as you could back online. . . . It was endurance and just brute strength that you had to induce.[61]

During the interstices when paper ran flawlessly, machine hands balanced routine tasks and monitoring with teaching underlings. The *Harvard study* explained: "Each man was technically responsible for training the man under him. . . . The first hand trained the second to be a first hand; the second hand trained all the men under him . . . You really just learn by doing. You master your own job and then you watch the next fellow working and do as much as you can."[62]

With its massive amount of physical capital, hundreds of millwrights, pipefitters, electricians, instrument technicians, carpenters, and other trades workers had to be onsite at all times to keep every and all machines and processes working. Pipes, boilers, digesters, steam turbines, paper machines and other equipment were constantly repaired and rebuilt. After several decades, each paper machine was substantially a new entity rebuilt with replacement parts or new features added to increase speed. On any given shift, one or more paper machines, rewinders, digesters, and cutting and wrapping machines could malfunction. A team of maintenance workers would show up, ask first hands and other workers what they had seen, smelled, heard, and knew, and then set to work troubleshooting, followed by fixing or replacing parts, wiring, or other features in order to machines up and running.[63] And these workers loved the challenge. Barry Kenney recalled with pride: "I liked the sense of accomplishment that I got, from being able to fix something that nobody could fix. . . . That was always my big thing. [A first hand might say] 'Oh, we can't fix it, we can't fix it. It won't work. What're we going to do?'" And then I'd go fix it."[64]

Maintenance workers could have lots of down time. Some I interviewed recalled underutilized carpenters and masons being sent to nearby Sebago Lake for a week to construct a vacation house—colloquially known as a camp—for one of the senior managers at a time when their mill-based work was at a low point.[65] Phil Lestage, after years as a first hand, switched to a paper machine maintenance crew that was assigned to several machines, a version of maintenance work that differed from skilled workers who had mill wide duties; Lestage took the job because he only had to work days, which synced with his wife who worked at S. D. Warren Company on days. The crew did routine maintenance, such as changing wires and felts, oiling and greasing the machines. Lestage noted that they could be extremely busy, or have nothing to do:

> A lot of times, stuff would go wrong with the machines—you'd have to go down there and guide a wire, change a dryer felt roll. There were days when we didn't do too much, we'd sit around, do some shop work, stuff we'd be fixing. We had a nice little shop—we had power rolls in the machine shop [to] get the bearings changed and stuff like that, put them away, haul them back, file them—[we] kept busy. A lot of times we didn't have that much to do. We'd sit around, read the paper, do what we wanted to do.[66]

For the hundreds of women who inspected and counted reams by hand for many generations, their work exemplified detail work—work that was highly repetitive, and largely never changing, that required and engendered a super but narrow skill. At S. D. Warren Company, a legacy of work sharing in the Great Depression left in place four standard six-hour shifts after World War II, and women returned day after day to sit and count out reams of paper, all the while inspecting and pulling sheets with blemishes or other defects. Most became very quick at it, fanning paper over and over to count rapidly and see the paper's quality. Some women like Mae Bachelor became super counters, uniquely able to work many times faster than most of her colleagues, allowing her to earn substantial bonus pay.[67] Repetitive stress was tolerated; Shirley Lally noted the standard treatment that kept them going was "old Ben-Gay."[68] Estelle Maelot, daughter of two S. D. Warren workers, worked there in the early 1960s during summers while attending college. She recalled the work and its indignities, including one hundred-degree heat that was "comfortable" after a visit to hotter environs of the paper machine department, and endless paper cuts: "My hands really hurt me during that time, that short time. . . . The thing that bothered me the most is that my back hurt me at the end of the summer, and . . . you would get a lot of cuts. . . . If you bled on [the paper], you'd have to throw it out. And you did, bleed on it."[69]

Every stage of the mill required a great deal of low skill and often brutish work. In the finishing department, scores of men had pallets of paper placed under guillotine cutters; the men would reach up and pull on a broad bar that brought down an enormous, razor-sharp blade to slice paper into smaller sizes. Especially because the work was on bonus (essentially piecework), this classic-type factory job was legendary for producing advanced carpel tunnel in men long before their fortieth birthdays.[70]

Howard Parkhurst and Tom Lestage began their careers in 1960 and 1980 respectively, both assigned to handle wood, coal, or chemicals. Parkhurst's first job was the coal hopper—he had to climb on to the top of railroad cars and maneuver the coal from the top so that it would move from the bottom of the car into an external chute that would deliver the coal to belts that conveyed the coal to the mill's steam boilers. The work was intensely physical, and particularly harsh in the winter. Parkhurst recalls his shift was seven days a week, for seven and a half hours, including allowance for a shower at the end of his shift. Summertime work was relatively easy—they could finish their work in a mere three to four hours: "We'd work our ass off and go home by noon—and still get our seven hours." But in the winter, when there were three or four coal cars to unload, and he and his one fellow coal hopper worker—an alcoholic who downed a six of beer on the job to be able to work—would have to use sledge hammers to break up frozen coal. His shift officially was 7 a.m. to 2 p.m., and 6 a.m. to 1 p.m. on Saturday and Sunday, for a scheduled total of forty-nine hours, but he and his one fellow coal worker would often have to stay until "eight, nine, ten o'clock at night" to get finished. In the winter, he brought and ate seven sandwiches a day, and still lost twenty-five pounds.[71]

Tom Lestage, like some of his uncles and his grandfather, started in the woodlot. It is notable that Lestage and his Uncle Phil perceived this as a function of being "French" (French-Canadian heritage) and of being "the brawny type";[72] historian Timothy Minchin's *The Color of Work* depicts how Southern US paper mills built after 1940 segregated woodlot and other "brawn" type jobs so that African American hires were assigned to these same jobs on the "bull gang," and never allowed to progress on to paper machines.[73] Lestage began by pruning and poling logs on the conveyer belt that brought pulpwood to wood chippers, work so strenuous that he and fellow workers would pole wood for one hour, and then shift to cleaning screens and sweeping the general area for another hour, before returning to loading logs. He then moved in the pulp mill, where in one job he was required to gather samples of pulp to bring to a testing room; in a manner similar to siphoning gasoline from a car, he had to suck on a tube and periodically would get a mouth full of caustic chemicals, requiring a mouthwash of vinegar and then weeks of discomfort as his mouth's lining of skin was assaulted by the chemicals. At other times, he worked on cleaning Jordan machines (a massive conical cylinder that further cleaned pulp) and moving materials, requiring crawling into large, dangerous pieces of machinery and using shovels and even a shotgun to remove undesired materials from the machines.[74] Others describe a shift consisting of two workers periodically grabbing huge bags of dry chemicals, climbing up a ladder and dumping the chemicals into a vat, and repeating this procedure again and again. Again, the work here was irregular at times, and lightly supervised. Crews would be pressed into action when needed, but still might spend hours in a shift killing time, or simply leaving early without loss of pay because they weren't needed, and the mill wanted to ensure workers got paid a full shift (more on this below).

"It's Harsh"—Discomfort, Danger, and Death in the Mill

It is harsh—the language you use is harsh, the way people deal with one another is harsh—very short with one another . . . And the work environment is harsh— it's hot, stinks, it's humid—you name it—it's dirty, just as dirty as can be, greasy, you name it—it's loud, all bad things. So, it is harsh.

—Barry Kenney, interview

Working in a paper mill isn't the easiest job in the world. It's hot—boiling hot in the summer, to the other extremes of cold in the wintertime. It's loud—most of the old-timers, if they have their back to you, they can't hear a thing you are saying. It can be extremely dangerous. For example, from time to time, working on number 9 paper machine, we have to crawl into the machine on our bellies in order to clean the coating rolls, while the machine turns at 1200 feet a minute, and one false move would mean you're a hurting unit or you never go home again.

—Tom Lestage, interview

Paper mill work is defined by a relentless combination of heat, humidity, noise, danger from chemicals, steam, heavy machinery, shift work and long hours, and rough treatment by coworkers and supervisors. While physically difficult and psychologically intense, paper workers invariably adapted to their environs, embracing the challenge as the price of admission to a unique industrial community.

Long hours and shift work were the norm. Paper mills are among the most capital-intensive industries; owners from the start put a premium on keeping expensive machinery working twenty-four hours a day and as close to 365 days a year they could compel workers to work. In its earliest days, S. D. Warren Company was typical in having two shifts—one thirteen hours, the other eleven hours—six days a week. Night shift work was facilitated by S. D. Warren and other mills' adoption of electric power beginning in the late 1880s. In the early twentieth century, Warren led the way for large integrated mills in adopting three eight-hour shifts, both a tip toward being a generous employer but also recognizing that shorter shifts translated into greater care and productivity.[75] Between 1900 and 1960, most Maine mills ended the practice of Sunday shutdowns, which were costly and required intricate measures to power down the mill Saturday evenings and back up on Monday mornings. S. D. Warren Company was an early adopter in 1915. Over the course of the twentieth century, Sunday work was a labor relations sore spot across all of Maine's paper mills, as workers fought, mostly through their unions and often through strikes, to first stop the move toward Sunday work. Unionized International Paper workers once got the right in a union contract to dictate whether the mill operated on Sundays, a prerogative that didn't last.[76] Once imposed, workers then successfully fought and earned double pay for Sundays. Premium pay for Sunday work was a bitter topic in 1980s labor struggles when employers successfully ended the practice in most Maine mills.

The mill's white-collar workforce of engineers, chemists, and higher level managers escaped shift work, as did skilled maintenance workers, though for the latter the reality differed as they were on call to ensure the mill's machines and equipment ran continuously. Despite a typically normal 7 a.m.–3 p.m. shift, maintenance workers routinely worked ten to twelve hours per day and fifty plus hours per week. When machines broke down, or during machine startups, they worked longer hours, sometimes twenty-four hours straight. Many maintenance workers, especially those assigned to specific parts of the mill, could also find themselves whiling away the day, chatting with coworkers or perhaps playing cards.

Production workers were mostly on the Southern swing shift, or tour (in Maine, pronounced "tower") work, a difficult rotating shift. When asked, Warren workers like Shirley Lally frequently and precisely recall: "I worked seven days, then had one day off, I worked the 'set-up' shift seven days, had two days off, then the 'get-up' shift, and then four days off." The four p.m. to midnight set-up and midnight to eight a.m. get-up shifts were a local vernacular invariably explained thusly: "The reason they call it 'get-up' is because the wife had to get up in the morning when he came home from work to get him breakfast. And they call it 'set-up' because she sat up at night waiting for him to come home at midnight."[77] Arthur Gordon recalled that the stress of shift work, and of required extra shifts: "as we get older, it's more, more difficult. . . . During the midnight shift, I generally speaking was a zombie."[78] Being on shift work meant working most Sundays—typically thirty-nine—and holidays throughout the year, a sacrifice that meant not just missing church but many if not most of their kids' notable events.

Summer temperatures throughout the mill but especially in the paper making areas range between 100 and 130 degrees Fahrenheit, and even in the finishing department temperatures approached this range in the summer. Bob Dorr recalled carrying an electronic thermometer when fixing machines and one reading of 157 degrees Fahrenheit; second-degree burns from hot pipes or steam from pipe breaks were routine.[79] The cacophony of machines, trucks, and steam made for very loud atmosphere at 100 decibels or more. When I toured the Westbrook mill in 2001, one was required to wear earplugs, but that was a recent practice. Massive hearing loss was typical.

Paper mills are extremely dangerous. Every mill has a legacy of grisly deaths and maiming. Serious and fatal injuries were a commonplace right up until contemporary times (post 1990), but they were truly egregious in the industry's formative years.[80] Exposure to dangerous machinery is routine. Burns, lost digits and limbs, crushed bodies, and widespread soft tissue injuries are still commonplace. For instance, paper machine workers routinely walk on catwalks under machines next to drums rotating at thousands of fpm to adjust machinery or deal with paper tears; a worker needs to duck to a height of under five feet to avoid the drum—standing up straight would mean a swift and ghastly death. The narrow catwalk with no railings drops directly to the basement floor approximately 25 feet below. At least six Warren workers were killed on the job between 1950 and 2000, including two who died in the solvent coater explosion in 1966; two deaths in the 1950s: a man caught in a debarking machine and died alone being literally ground to death, another burned to death by a sudden burst of steam; a man pulled into a coater machine in the 1970s; and, finally, a worker whose forklift fell through a hole left when a steel plate wasn't in place, falling many stories to his death in 1996.[81]

Finally, a paper mill is a chemical factory, with little safeguards to exposure, a constant arduousness that is hard to imagine people sustaining for years and decades. Dave Martin recalled working around coating machines: "The chemicals they had in the coating, the smells they had, the aroma, just would gag you. And the engineer would come by with the wand and test the air and say it was fine, and then he'd go outside and throw his guts up. But we had to work in it eight hours a day."[82] It was also common to insulate pipes with asbestos—making this toxin ubiquitous in mills. When I interviewed Lucien Mazzerolle and Ron Chasse in Madawaska about their role in the 1971 Fraser strike in 2012, I learned they were leaders of a large lung disease support group of Fraser retirees.

So, if the work and social environment was so fundamentally harsh—why was paper mill work so prized and welcomed? High pay and good benefits were part of the answer, but ultimately it was the extraordinary bond forged by all of those who worked at Mother Warren.

Paternalism, Welfarism, and the Mill's Commitment to its Workers in Context

From the mill's start in 1854, the harshness of paper mill life was balanced by a paternalism in which the mill would care for its workers, who were both proud and independent individual workers but also participants in the extraordinary system of gift exchange: the worker committed her or his life to the company, did all they could to build and exercise skills that made the company profitable, and endured hardships but counted on being taken care of in a way unlike any other employment available in the region. In a tradition that began with the company's founder, S. D. Warren Company gave its workers status and security; progressively layered on new benefits; invested extensively in community public works; guaranteed a worker and his/her family's economic security, taking care of even those whose personal challenges or failures of character made even showing up to work regularly unlikely—all cemented by the practice of mill managers knowing and caring about virtually every individual in the mill. And when this system eroded after Warren's sale to Scott Paper Company in 1967, it would be this past that the people of Westbrook and nearby communities would recall as a remarkable economic system to be remembered, celebrated, and sought after under new circumstances.

However, it would be naïve to depict the Warren traditions of paternalism, high wages, and generous welfare capitalism without acknowledging the centrality of union avoidance, a deep commitment that goes back to the founder. U.S. labor historians have identified the uniquely antiunion tradition in American manufacturing, where being unionized was generally perceived by owners as an existential threat and even a challenge to the manhood of senior managers and company owners.[83] The New Deal era between the 1930s and 1970s, when northern, Midwestern, and West Coast manufacturers were forced to accept unionization that came to cover the vast majority of American manufacturing workers, is in fact an anomaly in the longer view of American labor history—obvious now that private-sector union density has declined to single digits from a high of 35 percent in the early 1950s.[84] We'll see that other Maine-based companies acquiesced to unionization in the New Deal era, or earlier in the case of Great Northern Paper; they did so in part because the principal unions in the paper industry were among the nation's most deferent to employers, and the companies successfully maintained a modified paternalism even after unionization.[85]

Warren differed from other Maine companies in the exceptional character of its paternalism, which was also intertwined with a deep commitment to keep unions out of the mill. Founder Samuel D. Warren noted in his 1883 Senate testimony his clear desire to provide for his workers so they would not join unions or strike.[86] The *Harvard study* noted that in the 1940s, mill manager John Hyde was careful not to promote lower-level supervisors if they showed any union sympathies.[87]

Dana Babb worked in the mill's small accounting operation from the 1930s into the 1970s. He recalled how the mill's leaders carefully followed the wage and benefit packages granted Maine's unionized mills in the 1940s and 1950s, taking care to match or exceed these packages for its own employees, constituting an excellent example of what labor economists call the spillover effect on the wages and benefits of nonunion workers in predominantly unionized industries.[88] The mill thus continually went far beyond relatively high pay and benefits to ensure that its workers would remain unsympathetic to union organizing campaigns.

Mother Warren: Familiar Paternalism and Warren's Gift Exchange

My father and grandfather, and six of my uncles all worked at S. D. Warren.[89] When Samuel Warren ran this facility, it was a family-orientated business. My grandfather would tell you that if he couldn't work this week and he needed oil in his tank, Samuel Warren would send an oil truck to his house and fill his tank. He needed his crews to be at 100 percent, not preoccupied, worrying about whether their families had food on the table or heat in their pipes. That was a prerequisite at the plant when S. D. Warren ran it.

—Tom Lestage, interview

In interviews in the early 2000s, Westbrook workers' and community members' accounts of work at Warren, and life in the mill's shadow, were saturated with this narrative. As noted, these recollections of the mill's paternalistic past—the uniform reference to Mother Warren and various stories, real or embellished, about mill loyalty and kindly mill managers who knew workers as individuals and who were prepared to listen to workers' complaints and to always meet their occasional needs for extraordinary help—were mobilized to make sense of the destructive forces and people that were destroying their institution in the 1990s and 2000s. These were memories. What actually happened in the Warren era before the mill was taken over by an out-of-state company—Scott Paper Company—in 1967?

One of my first interviewees, Chris Murray, offered a clear place to dig in, in September 2000 when he came for his interview with a stack of manuscripts and newspaper clippings. They comprised the file he had compiled around the time he recently had left the mill in anticipation of soon losing his job. They included the company's self-published *One Hundred Years at S.D. Warren*. Murray had heard from parents and fellow coworkers about the great founder, and he dedicated himself to learning everything he could about him. He shared his copy of the company history with me, and I retraced Murray's research, finding documents that included a memorial book of eulogies for the founder Samuel Dennis Warren upon his death in 1888.[90] Tom Lestage, Arthur Gordon, Shirley Lally, Mae Bachelor, Karl Dornish, Curtis Pease, Ron Usher, Frank Jewitt, Phil Lestage, Harry Foote, Karl Dornish, and Howard Reiche, among others, served up a steady diet of anecdotes and confirming evidence of both the myth and the reality of the Warrens' extraordinary paternalism.[91]

During his thirty-four years as principal owner of the mill, S. D. Warren hired less well-off relatives and in-laws to manage the mill on a daily basis. His deep well of siblings, in-laws, and nephews—he was one of eleven children who lived to adulthood—provided an ample pool to draw from to staff the leadership of his growing works. He participated actively in the mill's management via frequent train trips to Maine from his posh Boston home on Beacon Hill.[92] Much recorded and remembered was S. D. Warren's willingness to get to know his workers and to seem to care about them. "Mr. Warren made frequent trips from Boston to visit his beloved paper mill, and he was remembered for his kind personal interest in those who worked for him."[93] At the time of his death, he was extolled for regarding "each one of his employees as a personal friend, and not as so much bone and brawn to be minted into wealth for his personal aggrandizement."[94] John E. (Johnny) Warren, S. D. Warren's nephew and agent (*the* mill manager) from 1884 until his death in 1915, cemented this legacy and practice, and was similarly praised:

> Anyone having a grievance, either real or fancied, would be certain of a sympathetic listener in Mr. Warren [Johnny], and after an interview with him would generally leave with the satisfaction of having received a square deal. It was this generous yet just manner of dealing that endeared him to the hearts of everyone.[95]

It is evident that the Warrens both declared their commitment to and were credited, indeed celebrated, for their fatherly relationships with employees. Johnny Warren even built a home on a hill overlooking the mill in 1880s, alongside of the one that S. D. had built to stay when in Westbrook on business, evoking the classic physical arrangement of a Southern slave plantation. Mill managers continued to live in the house built by Johnny Warren into the 1960s, and importantly upheld S. D.'s and Johnny's familiarity and accessibility.

John Hyde helped lead the 1920s' managerial coup, and he was mill manager from 1931 to 1949. Despite gaining leadership more than a generation after Johnny Warren passed away, he kept the practices and symbolism of the early Warrens' paternalism fully intact: getting to know the workers, management by walking around, continuing the practice of employment security for the worker and the worker's extended family, and an open-door policy that kept him busy day in and day out with great numbers of workers and managers seeking help—all the more remarkable given that mill employment grew to twice the size of what it was during Johnny Warren's reign. Frank Jewitt, who later became a top paper executive at a series of Midwestern mills recalled his impressions of Hyde from his ten-year stint as a research chemist in the 1940s and 1950s.

> John Hyde was an exceptional man. He knew everybody. . . . For example, whenever a guy had hard luck—if somebody was awful sick and he needed money for surgery or some other damn [thing]—he'd go down to see John Hyde. John Hyde would tell him he'd help him. He'd pick up the phone and call the person—whoever has charge of payroll there, that he was lending, the company was lending this man so much money, and he was paying it back at the rate of a dollar, or a dollar and a half a week, to be deducted from his paycheck. . . . And he'd shake the guy's hand, and the guy would be happy. He seemed to care about the personnel, and they knew it. And he was for the city's interest, and he was quite a guy.[96]

Finishing department worker Shirley Lally couldn't wait in September 2000 to tell me about a grandfather who both worked at the mill and ran a neighborhood store, and had a customer early in the Great Depression who got $200 behind on bills. According to Lally, the mill stepped in and paid off the debt for that $1-a-week deduction arrangement described by Jewitt. In case one assumes that this was just mythology, the *Harvard study* vividly describes what for Hyde sounds like an all-encompassing, and likely exhausting, paternal responsibility:

> Workers often sought Mr. [Hyde's] advice on personal problems. The problems which the "help" brought to him were frequently financial; an employee might come, for instance, to get Mr. [Hyde's] advice on

whether the house in which he was interested was a good "buy"; employees might come because they needed a loan to pay for a new home, for a new baby, or a divorce. Often, an employee raised questions relating to his position, his desire for a transfer or promotion, or dissatisfaction with the way a supervisor handled him. One of the employees remarked about Mr. [Hyde]: "He's a great guy. He ain't no different from us."

S. D. Warren solidified what historians call a durable founder's culture that persisted into the 1980s.[97] His management vision clearly derived from classic New England religious sensibilities, trust in his talented relatives who led the mill early on, and likely a recognition of the need for extra commitment from skilled workers in the tricky business of mixing pulp and running fourdriniers at a time when modern paper making technology was a fresh affair.

S. D. Warren was born into a modest Congregationalist family in Massachusetts in 1817, joining a Boston paper merchant company at the age of fifteen and was made a partner at age twenty-one.[98] He was a New England religious leader, a pious Congregationalist who married the daughter of a leading Puritan minister, and he was one of a group of eighteen people who supported the Anglo-American revision of the bible finished in 1881. While he delegated day-to-day mill management to the poor Warrens, continuing his Boston residence and primary work in the merchant business, he was an innovator in the paper business— for example, creating and dominating, for a time, the new practice of importing large quantities of rags from Europe. His relatives made innumerable technological innovations in the mill while he was alive and in the generation following his passing; business and technical wherewithal was a prerequisite to credible paternalism, as workers recognized their employment was dependent on the unique talents of their superiors. His business success and especially his distinctive labor practices attracted national recognition, particularly in his widely reported and acclaimed testimony to the 1883 Congressional commission on capital-labor strife in describing how his beneficence toward his workers had inspired loyalty and efficiency. As a biographer of the Warren family summarizes:

> It was not just as a pile of dollars, of purchasing power, that the Warren fortune stirred up such strong excitement, but as an achievement, as a manifestation of the father's energy, imagination, self-application, and virtue. S.D. Warren's life was an American success story and a moral exemplum. He had started with nothing and ended up with a fortune, and it seemed that he had made it without cheating, indeed by being good, on the way up. He was seen as a hero of the business ethic, a man who showed that Christianity was good for business. . . . Thus, a large audience surrounded and applauded his later years.[99]

Grounded in his Biblical perspective, S. D. Warren practiced what is now called the dual bottom-line of matching profits with social responsibility to stakeholders. Warren was explicit in his testimony that his beneficence was meant to ward off the labor militancy that was becoming widespread in 1870s and 1880s manufacturing. Take, for example, this exchange during his famous 1883 testimony to the U.S. Congress.

> Q: How does it happen that you have got on this way with your help without strikes or disagreements? You must have had some principle on which you conducted business in dealing with your help.
>
> A: Well, I have always felt my interest consisted in taking good care of the help, and giving them good homes and the best sanitary conditions, and to show an interest in them.
>
> Q: Do you think it makes a difference to operatives or working people whether their employer manifests that disposition or not?
>
> A: I do, most emphatically. I think it pays to take the best care of the help.
>
> Q: Why?
>
> A: They are more loyal and do more labor, and more careful to see that the labor they do is good labor. They will be more interested in the success of the employer.[100]

An exemplar of Weberian Protestant rationality, Warren's Puritan-rooted perspective looked for, and found often enough, a double coincidence of motives in his business actions. It is possible to read Warren's motives several ways. A cynical reading is that he opportunistically offered benevolent purposes where the ulterior motives of profit and union avoidance was clearly the prime purpose. Martin Green provides an example:

> It is said that Mr. Warren was sociable and jocular with both other businessmen and his workers. But, says his nephew John E. Warren, "What might to a stranger seem like thoughtless banter was to him a screen from which he looked out to take the measure of the man before him, and in this estimate he was rarely mistaken." At the same time, when a competitor had to sell his machinery at a loss, Mr. Warren put himself out to get him the best price. And when, in 1858, he bought a spring a mile or more from the mills, although his prime object was to supply his customers with "uniform clean white paper at all season of the year," he also wanted his employees to have pure drinking water. He managed to make the two motives coincide.[101]

Thus, Warren's benevolence reflected of a Biblical sensibility that saw business and community purpose as inextricably bound together. S. D. Warren's son Fiske wrote a letter to S. D. Warren's grandchildren "describing him as a man whose religion it was to benefit his fellowmen, a purpose to which he subordinated his church creed, his business interests, and even his work hours."[102]

Secondly, company and town histories offer ample confirmation that Dennis Warren offered his employees *provision, protection, and control*—the three prongs of classic paternalism.[103] Historian Phil Scranton notes that these features made working for the paternalistic owner better than other available options—typically rural poverty—while legitimizing an encompassing authority.[104]

Provision was certainly in evidence. The mill was reputed to have paid good wages from the start. The company's self-published history, *A Hundred Years of S. D. Warren Company*, observed that in 1869, "men on the paper machines received $2 to $2.50 per day; the second hands received $1.55; the engineers on the washer and beaters received $2.10 to $2.25; and the women and girls received 83 cents per day."[105] If true, the better paid hands and "engineers" were substantially higher than $1 to $1.50 per day average wage for the Gilded Age.[106] In the post-World War II era, workers recalled Warren's starting wages being 60 to 100 percent higher than in the comparable local blue-collar jobs they left when finally hired by Warren.[107] While S. D. Warren and Company cut wages during recessions, the company history claims that the mill avoided layoffs, even during the 1870s' depression.[108] The company also began a long-standing practice of offering broad credit to its workers, including making loans for home purchases, bill payments, and children's education. Employees founded the Cumberland Mills Mutual Relief Association around 1880.[109] In its earliest years, the company contributed 10 percent of the fund. The death benefit was $200 at its inception and benefit levels for injured workers were rather meager but by contemporary standards generous. Seriously sick or injured workers and their family members could stay at one of the hospital beds the mill leased from Maine General Hospital.[110] According to an 1899 letter from Johnny Warren to its workers, when this contract was ended, the company offered to pay the $1.50 per day cost of the hospital stay for workers and would then collect repayment, according to the worker's means, arranged through the mill's main office.[111] Johnny Warren had clearly already inaugurated the practice of paying for a worker's overwhelming expenses with the long-term expectation of getting back that "dollar per week."

Like most nonunion companies in decades before the Great Depression, the declared existence of pensions for some didn't necessarily mean real security for most older workers. Some Civil War vets got pensions under Johnny Warren, and they were widespread enough in 1916 for mill manager Joseph Warren to make a point to cancel the potential for pensions for those who participated in a strike that year. Most notable was simply that it was common for mill workers to simply stay on in their elderly years.[112] Notes Phil LaViolette, recalling the 1940s:

FIGURE 2.2   As early as the 1860s, Samuel Dennis Warren built housing and public works for S. D. Warren Company workers. Here, the Warren Block, completed in the 1880s, included a gymnasium and other facilities for use by workers and their families (collections of Maine Historical Society).

"Back then, they worked until they dropped dead—there was no pension. When I went there, there were some people 75 or over still working." In the typical paternalistic twist of making lemonade out of lemons, the mill created a fifty-year club that celebrated these very long-term employees.[113]

The mill, of necessity, had to and did embark on a substantial home-building program, beginning first with boarding houses and then later, over the period from the 1860s through the 1880s, constructing approximately two hundred single-family homes. Also, as a somewhat denser rural area, workers from the start also came from local farms or boarded with them. But rather than build minimally acceptable tenements, Warren commissioned John Calvin Stephens and other leading architects to design modest but tasteful new homes. By 1883, the company had built and either leased or sold to its workers some 150 homes. Leases on homes ranged from $75–$200 per year. Warren claimed that they were provided roughly at cost. The homes were considered by contemporary observers to be of superior quality for company-built housing. By the 1880s, the village and mill grew to the point where private contractors began building housing, particularly for the growing number of Franco-American immigrants who came to work at S. D. Warren.[114]

Protection and control were also clear features of employment at the Westbrook mill. Strict rules about conduct were enforced for those living in the boarding house and also applied to workers renting houses from the mill. S. D. Warren sought to "keep his employees away from saloons, or rather keep saloons away from any part of the town."[115] S. D. Warren himself contributed half the funds for a Congregationalist church to be built in 1869, and later all of the funds for the construction of a school and a number of community buildings, so as to keep his workers from drink and to provide proper educational and spiritual uplift (see figure 2.2). He disliked recruiting immigrants, even though he had begun to hire significant numbers of French-Canadian immigrants after 1870. In his 1883 Congressional testimony, he was comfortable in stating that he still had control of his main mill, in contrast to two other smaller mills he purchased or built during the latter part of his reign. Company documents from shortly after Warren's death show that the mill compelled its employees to follow a strict nonsmoking policy—even while working offsite, and threatened dismissal for employees whose children trespassed on mill property.[116]

Thus, S. D. Warren's relationships to his workers contained many elements of what historian Phillip Scranton describes as familiar paternalism.[117] However, historians of nineteenth-century familiar paternalism was typically limited to a certain maximum scale, perhaps two hundred employees at most.[118] The Cumberland mill's plant grew well past that scale during the 1870s and 1880s, when employment surged from 250 to 800.[119] This meant that the Westbrook mill's scale quickly stretched the foundation for familiar paternalism and brought about the dilemma of how to maintain a personal connection between ownership and its workforce.

The founder and his heirs dealt with this dilemma by steadily adding welfare practices to paternalism.[120] These programs came to be associated with the most progressive of the newly large corporations at the dawn the mass production era, notably the Pullman Corporation and National Cash Register, among others. These large companies, worried about strikes and union organizing, sought to build loyalty through bureaucratic personnel management and by offering workers measures of comfort, safety, and security—the latter through pensions and death and injury benefits, and moving away from the heavy if generous hand of the individual owner. As we've seen, S. D. and Johnny Warren and later mill leaders clearly kept their informal paternalism intact while steadily expanding piecemeal characteristic welfare practices. Already, quality housing, mill relief, hospital assistance, good wages, employment security, a mill reading room, a school and church, pensions for at least a few,[121] and a profit-sharing plan introduced in 1890 meant that S. D. Warren Company was a leader in early welfare benefits characteristic of turn of the century innovators.

From the 1890s through the 1950s, the company offered an expanding roster of benefits or improvements. One was the eight-hour day, first implemented in 1901.[122] Of course, the year 1901 was a time of rising labor militancy in both the United States and in Maine. Paper workers in a number of other Maine mills had, or were in the process of, organizing union locals and seeking recognition.[123] By the 1920s, trusts endowed by Susan Warren, wife of the founder, and Cornelia Warren, the founder's daughter, had established a library, a swimming pool, ball fields and athletic facilities, and a resting room in the mill for female employees.[124] The pervasive presence of these public works, and ongoing funding from the mills to support local sports and other community activities, figured large in the thinking of locals long after the Warren era was over.[125] These trusts later funded an S. D. Warren band and the men's singing and women's glee clubs. A mill medical department—a characteristic welfare practice of the 1910s—was added in 1918. The Warren Company's emphasis on free hospital care and onsite medical assistance obviously grew from the daily list of small injuries and frequent grave injuries characteristic of paper production.[126] Much later, around 1950, a more extensive medical facility was built at the edge of the mill's grounds, replacing the earlier operation that had been located in the heart of the rambling mill; notable was its substance abuse treatment ward, a "drunk tank" in contemporary parlance. Health insurance was introduced around 1950, as the company recognized that newly unionized mills around the state were granting these benefits.[127] Indeed, by the 1950s, S. D. Warren Company remained as the only major nonunion mill in the state.[128]

The mill also went to great lengths to subsidize workers' consumption, using credit and discounting at its company store, stretching workers' wages at a time when credit for working class Americans was still somewhat limited. In accounts of workers who came of age in the mid-twentieth century, the company store helped workers to buy a wide range of products, including all manner of furniture and housing appliances that could be purchased on installment credit provided by the mill and repaid through deductions from weekly paychecks.[129] Employees could even turn to the company to secure a mortgage, which took on added significance to Franco Warren workers whose relatives toiled in lower-paid work in nearby shoe and textile towns:

> Like all the houses that were built, if you wanted to build a house you went up—you didn't go up to the bank—you went up to the S. D. Warren main office, and tell them you wanted to build a house, and they'd arrange a loan through the bank, take so much out of your pay every

week. That's how come people in Westbrook were able to prosper better than people in Biddeford and Lewiston.[130]

Employment security was the most profound link in S. D. Warren's relationship with its workers, and both recollections and records indicate that Warren from the start made efforts to ensure workers kept their jobs during recessions, a notable benefit that set the company apart. The company history notes: "During the Depression years of 1873–75, there were no layoffs at S. D. Warren's mills, even though other mills were shut down or on half time. Construction was continued where possible."[131] Later, during the Great Depression, the company history states that workers accepted a work-spreading scheme: "The men and women of Cumberland Mills voluntarily went on a six-hour tour in order to spread the available work among employees."[132] Phil LaViolette recalled that this immediately created nearly one thousand new jobs. The move was such a success that the mill maintained the four-shift tour for females for over twenty years, where most U.S. manufacturers used the tactic only in the heart of the Depression for a few years.[133] Howard Reiche recalled that employment maintenance during the Great Depression and other forms of assistance by the mill left a lasting impression on workers.

> The Warrens made a great effort to run the mill if they possibly could. . . . And that carried up into the forties and fifties, because it was so much a part of the culture. And if you were a child, and your father had been home and his paycheck continued, or your brother had gotten a job when he really needed it, that registered.[134]

Former workers also say that loyalty from workers who started before or during the Great Depression contributed to the failure of several union elections at the mill in the 1950s and 1960s.[135]

Perhaps most signature was the mill's family hiring system, one that privileged the hiring of family members over generations and that created a mill landscape dominated by extended families and serial generations; it was common in interviews for workers to describe themselves a third-generation paper worker, like David Martin when he said: "I'm a third-generation paper worker. My grandfather worked on the paper machines, my father worked on paper machines, as did I." The reader will recall Mae Bachelor's characterization that "it's all family-connected. I mean, my cousins worked there, my brothers and sister worked there." Harley Lord, who began at the mill in 1924, recalled: "It was a growing family affair. As your father got in, your mother got in, all of your children, and grandchildren." And Estelle Maelot, who worked summers while in college around 1960 described an entire extended family: "My mother and father, sister, husband, brother in law, aunts and uncles, and grandparents—all worked at the mill."[136]

From its inception, Warren's wage scale was significantly higher than other blue-collar employment in southern Maine, and its overall generosity kept it in a labor surplus situation for most of its history.[137] It's self-described male entry level wage in 1953 was 200 percent of the minimum wage at the time. In the post-World War II era, the mill maintained an employment office across the street from the mill.[138] Many I interviewed—Phil Lestage, Howard Parkhurst, Dan Parks, Curtis Pease and others—described going to that office weekly for many years, knowing that this persistence was crucial in signaling to the company a potential worker's commitment; regardless, the favored were typically from extended mill families. Phil LaViolette recalled that French Canadian locals actually went through their priest: "Between Father Desjardins and Reverend Townsend they ran the city. If you wanted a job down at S. D. Warren, you didn't go down to S. D. Warren, you'd go see him, or Reverend Townsend, and they'd call up S. D. Warren. I have a man who wants a job; you have an opening, they'd give it to him."[139]

A gruesome feature of this system was a heightened commitment to the families of workers who were permanently injured or who lost their lives. LaViolette tells this story:

> My father's uncle Theopile . . . worked over there, he worked in the color room. And in those days, they didn't have all the monitors and machines that they have today. They had to *walk the plank*—a catwalk over the tanks. And from experience they were able to tell the consistency, the right color, and so forth. Well he fell in! All they found was his buttons.
>
> But S. D. Warren had a policy that anybody killed working S. D. Warren, the next generation would have a job. So my father got a job there. I got a job there. My sons got a job there. And if it was still S. D. Warren, well my grandchildren would have a job there.[140]

The mill prioritized male employment during downturns. In an era where the mill literally kept separate pay scales for men and women, it was straightforward to reinforce the patriarchical family wage, in which women's earnings were strictly seen as a supplement, and thus making female employees the buffer during frequent slowdown in sales during recessions. Phil LaViolette recalled: "If there was any firing or laying off to be done, it was not the men that were laid off, it was the women. I remember the one time, there was about five hundred women were laid off. Why did they not lay off the men? Because the men were supposedly the breadwinners."[141] Like most U.S. industry during World War II, dozens of women at Warren were pressed into "men's" jobs during the war, including running guillotine presses, but were shoved back into their narrow slot of finishing department work in the mill's occupational structure when the war ended.

Mill domination of town politics was another notable feature of this post-founder paternalism. While Cumberland Mills remained a company town only through the life of its founder—or really a two company town, as Dana Warp Mill a mile up the Presumpscott also dominated its own end of the town—it began an ostensibly independent political existence when the city of Westbrook was incorporated in 1891. But from incorporation into the 1960s, mill managers dominated city, and to some extent Maine, politics. Joseph A. Warren, great-nephew of the founder and active in mill management into the 1950s, was elected the city's youngest mayor in 1901. The city council, school board, and other bodies, along with the city's delegation to the Maine legislature, were filled primarily by middle and top executives from the mill until unionization came in the late 1960s.[142] Managers who began at the mill in the 1950s describe the expectation upon hiring that as a manager one would have to live in Westbrook (rather than nearby affluent communities) and get involved in the town's political administration.[143] Employees at all levels were allowed to leave the mill for critical community activities, such as volunteer firefighting, without loss of pay for time not spent at work. The official company history claims that: "All of these public activities by employees have been encouraged by the company, which nevertheless has maintained a strict policy of never trying to influence the city government through its employees."[144]

Protests of innocence aside, it is, however, conspicuous that shortly after unionization in 1967, a number of union leaders—including one who had been previously active as a Republican in city politics—ran successfully as Democrats for posts in the city and state government.[145] Westbrook has remained a Democratic city since that time. Finally, until it was abolished in the early 1970s, Maine state government had a nonelected executive council of seven nonelected appointees selected by the state's governor that represented the state's leading business interests and dominated by paper executives. S. D. Warren Company always had one of these seats. The council had the unusual power to veto any legislation that the governor was considering signing.[146] "Slim" Travis was the mill's purchasing manager in the 1960s and Warren's representative in the council. Former mill manager Howard Reiche described how Travis was able to insist on legislation containing only those measures favorable to Warren on water, power, and timber issues of great import to the company's bottom line. "If it doesn't have *this* in it, we'll veto that."[147] Obviously, this gave the council the power to influence or even dictate legislation and appointments.[148]

A signal part of the mill's paternalism was the mill as social work agency, collaborating with local priests and ministers, and with managers high and low, in assisting workers with personal or familial problems, and the oft-mentioned need for hospital bills to be paid for via loans before the advent of health insurance around 1950. Reiche recalls what he found when he arrived in the mill in 1954:

> This was a time, when if someone is in trouble, he got some help. This was a time, if somebody had a drinking problem, the priest, or the minister, might call up the mill manager and say "so and so is having some problems," and [so] arrangements were made, things were done. This astounded me when I came. Say there was a four-man crew, the person has had an automobile accident, is going to be out for three weeks, the other members of the crew would say "we'll do his job . . . for three weeks, and we'll put his time card in," and the guy's time card would be put in. And no one questioned it—it was okay to do that.

Reiche continued, "I remember one guy, wasn't all there, we handled his money, we practically fathered him. . . . The company tended to make all the decisions for you." The *Harvard study* noted a story of a worker using John Hyde's open-door policy to address physical problems on the job because "his job was giving him severe headaches and [he] couldn't work continuously." The worker turned out to both have a college education and a talent at the work, and was subsequently recruited into management. The worker went first to his church: "Rathbun finally went to see the Baptist deacon about it. . . . The deacon spoke to Mr. [Hyde] and Mr. [Hyde] said he would like to see Rathbun—you know his door is always open to the men. When Rathbun went in, he took his wife and child along with him. Mr. [Hyde] got quite a chuckle out of that."[149]

Even lower-level supervisors were thrust into this role. Finishing department foreman Robert Burton, recalling his first years in the 1940s and 1950s, discovered that once he earned his female charges' trust, they brought their marital problems to him: "I always felt that they would come to me because they knew I wouldn't say nothing. . . . . And it was good. Because they would come to you when they had a problem, and you could help them work it out."[150] Oscar Fick Jr., the son of one of small group of managers who took the company's reigns in the 1920s, moved up quickly in the 1930 and 1940s to take over his father's leadership of the utility operations—primarily the production of electricity from the mill's hydroelectric dams and the mill's electrical system. As he assumed managerial duties, he was shocked by what his employees would discuss with him: "I would never go to my supervisor for something like that. But they did. They came to us, and they wanted help. Advice, mainly advice. I think that's [what gave rise to] the term "Mother Warren" . . . I was listening to people's problems more than I was trying to solve the mill's problems."[151]

Production manager Karl Dornish frequently arranged to send his employees up to Westbrook Hospital "to be dried out."[152] The mill's accounting office would manage the finances of spendthrift employees, and at tax time prepared returns for hundreds of workers for free.[153]

Both managers and workers present in the mill in the 1950s and 1960s note that the mill rarely fired people. Karl Dornish went through the management apprentice system with Howard Reiche in 1954 and 1955, spent ten years in the technical department interfacing between the technology center and the men on paper and coating machines, and later rose to be the mill's number 2 as head of production: "the plusses [of getting hired by Warren] were that if you got a job there, you pretty much had to murder, rape, or pillage to lose your job." Once hired, you were there to stay; Dornish followed "there was supposed to be a probationary period . . . [but] once you were in, you stayed."

The mill also kept on dozens of injured workers, assigning them to light-duty jobs such as monitoring gauges. The *Harvard study* highlights this tolerance of underperformers and nonperformers with numerous examples. One case, described here by the paper mill superintendent in the 1940s, illustrates:

> I never drive men—or at least I don't any longer. I try to find ways of making them better workers. If I can't do anything with them, I don't fire. I send them to [John Hyde], and he usually finds some way of giving them another chance. He has been able to straighten out a lot of men we haven't been able to do anything with. There is one we have been having a lot of trouble with lately. He'll stay out three or four months at a time, and we are all trying to keep him on the payroll until he gets his pension. He'll get his pension in a few months now. **He lost his wife a while back and has been no good ever since**. [Hyde] has been a lot of help with him.[154]

Karl Dornish's recalled that after World War II, the mill had a large number of men returning from war with what would likely now be recognized as posttraumatic stress disorder, and others just likely victims of alcoholism. Finally, Shirley Lally lauded what she saw as the mill's willingness to hire and retain underprivileged workers:

> I don't like to say that, but [Warren employed] a lot of uneducated ladies, housewives—Some of them didn't know how to read or write. The mill was good like that. They took in some deaf-mutes, who were excellent workers, and they took in people who were not educated and gave them a good job, and gave them a good week's pay, and these people really worked hard, they were very dedicated.

These stories—about managers keeping workers on the payroll after personal crises such as losing one's spouse, an inability to cope with what we now know to be posttraumatic stress disorder, addiction problems, or the company's willingness to hire handicapped and illiterate workers, speak to the logic of this indulgency pattern. The city of Westbrook was under the shadow of S. D. Warren Company, and of course, the mill itself was a dense, closely knit community anchored by extended and multigenerational families who worked at the mill. Knowing the mill's loyalty and kindness extended to a family member, friend, or community member—no matter what—stoked and maintained workers' unselfish contributions to the company's success.

Conclusion

Founder S. D. Warren was among the first large nineteenth-century U.S. industrial employers to address the conundrum of effective paternalism and rapid growth by means of welfare activities. While maintaining the founder's personal approach and upholding its family myth, its managers continued to add the new benefits and welfare practices characteristic of their later contemporaries. As we've seen, this created an overarching belief in the loyalty and generosity of Mother Warren, and it elicited the needed commitment from its workers and long papered over the flaws in its underdeveloped personnel system.

Warren's extraordinary paternalism was thus crucial to the company's success and was paralleled by Oxford Paper, Great Northern Paper, Hollingsworth and Whitney, and the other large Maine-based companies. Maine's major mills were ruled by paper makers who came to their rural locations, settled in for long durations, and maintained their companies' lineage of early founders or previous generations of professional managers. True of all of these companies—whether production managers, chemists, or engineers—the managerial hierarchy held and wielded their own extraordinary command of a high-technology production culture. Legitimacy thus grew from production competence and from the kind of commitment and familiarity that came from sharing both mill and community life, enhanced by managerial generosity to its workers and towns. Family hiring systems were the norm, and whether or not the mills unionized in the early twentieth century, paper mill workers across the state enjoyed the same high wages, cutting-edge benefits, employment security, and craft pride, along with other signal benefits such as the much-noted Great Northern Paper Company policy of giving its workers virtually free plots on the company's most beautiful lakes, where workers built their summer camps, and over time, year round homes.[155] At Fraser Paper, the ability of the company to pay a family wage where families had anywhere from five or six to up to twenty-four children made it prized employment.[156] There, an ethnic and class divide absent the extensive paternalistic generosity of other Maine mills mattered little as the prized family wage and an inherent work ethic made for a different bargain. This exception aside, the all-encompassing security, provided by leaders who were perceived as local, loyal, and generous, cemented a material existence and industrial culture that kept paper mill employment at the top of Maine's blue-collar pyramid for a century.

As for S. D. Warren, the company built and sustained a sophisticated, high-technology production operation that after World War II grew to employ nearly four thousand salesmen, managers, chemists, engineers, and workers. It was prosperous enough to maintain an immense amount of workforce slack. The mill's all-encompassing security permitted some workers to do little, but it created an atmosphere where men and women would knock themselves out if physically called upon. Crucially the key, most skilled, workers were inspired to keep expensive equipment up and running, applying skills gained through many years of experience on specific machines in an endless problem-solving loop that was the difference between profit and failure for the enterprise as a whole. At its extreme, Warren had what sociologist Alvin Gouldner has described as an indulgency pattern—a combination of leniency and nonrequisite generosity—that formed a gift exchange between worker and company.[157] For many in the mill, one knew of a troubled relative or friend was taken care of, rehabilitated where possible, or otherwise treated compassionately in a way consistent with company culture and lore. And the mill's legitimacy was synched by the mill manager—with his sincere appreciation of most if not all workers in the mill, and remarkable, perhaps even excessive, open-door policy. This loyalty to one's friends, neighbors, and especially extended family meant that workers in the most critical jobs would be sure to do what it took to not cost the company the loss of thousands of dollars an hour on a machine.

In the twenty-five years after World War II, the company's relationship with its workers drifted into crisis. While the managerial system it built worked to deliver on production, it contained inherent weaknesses because of the mill's informal personnel and human resource practices. A lack of modernized and professional personnel practices allowed a variety of local problems in the various parts of the mill that accumulated over time, eventually leading to a crisis that produced unionization. After unionization, the unique leadership of one mill manager, Howard Reiche Jr., who began as a management apprentice at S. D. Warren Company in 1954 and rose rapidly to become mill manager in 1970, allowed for the Mother Warren culture to persist into the 1980s. Reiche reestablished the informal bargains and ethos of company paternalism while working with new unions to bring a new measure of standardized equity missing from the chaotic local cultures within the mill that flourished prior to unionization. Under Reiche, Warren's halcyon production culture strengths were continued for an additional two decades after the mill unionized and was sold to Scott Paper Company in 1967.

Appendix: The Layout of Production in a Mid-Twentieth-Century Maine Paper Mill

The types and areas of work track the progress of materials through the mill. Raw materials were delivered to the mill via truck and railroad car: coal, and later oil, to run up to a dozen large steam-producing boilers; a host of chemicals and raw materials, some highly toxic, such as chlorine; inert materials like clay and ash that were essential to making varieties of pulp needed for different paper types; and, foremost, pulpwood. As paper's prime raw material, a typical large Maine mill might have received one thousand or more chords of wood daily—some four million pounds of wood; Great Northern Paper by the 1970s received more than that, amounting to twelve million pounds daily.[158] Pulpwood was originally transported via spring river drive and, in S. D. Warren's case, horse and wagon deliveries. For some mills, railroad spurs were another mode of conveyance. After 1950, truck delivery became the favored means. Until the 1970s, pulpwood was cut at the source into four-foot lengths, especially auspicious for river drives; with the advance of mechanical tree harvesting and delivery technologies, delivering tree-length logs became possible, economizing on intermediate labor.[159]

Once at the mill's woodlot, a combination of cranes, pulleys, and inescapable and dangerous brute labor conveyed logs onto belts delivered to a large wood room. After logs entered the wood room, they were fed into debarking and chipping machines; wood chips were then moved on belts aloft to the pulp mill.

The pulp mill is a chemical plant. Closed off completely from outside light, pulp mills are a maze of pipes, intermediate vats, and digesters. A digester is a tall chamber, with even early versions four or more stories tall; much later they would grow to 150 feet in height, including those in S. D. Warren Company's most modern pulp mill completed in 1990. A mix of chemicals known as cooking liquor, wood chips, and water are poured into the digester; the mixture is sealed, pressurized, and heated, and after four to eight hours, a cook is complete. The result is a suspension of separated and chemically treated wood cellulose fibers, with the wood's lignin and resin removed. At the end of a cook, the residual mix of chemicals and lignin is extracted from the bottom of the digester, forming a black liquor that is piped to recovery boilers where it is burnt as fuel. With a variety of dials indicating heat, pressure, and other factors, a successful cook is the responsibility of the first hand who listens, smells, touches, and feels to see if the pulp is up to standard. Pulp is then piped into vats where dyes, inert materials, clay, alum, and resin are mixed with the wood fibers, depending on the specific paper's specifications for strength, color, and other features; the resulting mix is known as the furnish. Fibers are further brushed and cut in a cylindrical device known as a Jordan, which resembles a large, conical space capsule. Fibers are then further cut and brushed in large round, open tubs known as beaters; beaters are enormous vats with rotating blades not unlike a professional kitchen mixer. The resulting processed pulp is kept in large beater chests that continually agitate the pulp so it is ready for the paper making process.

With a basic design unchanged for two centuries, we return again to the fourdrinier. The battleship-sized contraption—modern paper machines can be 100 yards long or longer and are many stories high—is bookended by the wet and dry ends, the former where pulp with up to 99.5 percent water concentration is first sprayed onto the wire, and the latter where fully formed, sized, and dried paper is wound on to multiton rolls.

The first step is a head box, where pulp is pumped in through a screen to remove last-minute impurities, creating a closed, upright, rectangular well full of a pulp made up of uniform, brushed, and chemically treated fibers ready to be conveyed onto the paper machine. Pulp is then directed downward from the head box through a slice with top and bottom blades that deliver an even flow of pulp onto the all-important wire. The wire is a fine metal screen that loops several dozen feet like a conveyer belt. It is in a constant state of agitation, in order to shake the pulp and produce a crosshatch of fibers, a structure crucial for ensuring the strength and overall quality of paper. Water drains below the machine, and as agitated pulp is moved toward the paper machine, additional water is removed by suction boxes under the wire. Uniform width is ensured by high-pressure squirting jets on each side of the wire (and the watery quasi paper is removed and returned to beater chests); a roller presses from the top near the end of the wire to impart an even width. The formed paper, perhaps down to 80 percent water, is wound on to a felt belt that begins the paper's journey through the heart of machine. The first set of cylinders is the press roll and squeezes water out while smoothing the paper. The second set of rolls are drying cylinders, heated by pipe from the mill's boilers. Here, the variables are temperature, the number of cylinders (typically in the dozens), and their speed, which together reduce water content from around 65 percent to roughly 10 percent and further smooth the paper. The final stage is a series of rollers known as the calender that imparts a final smoothing and produces finished paper that winds up on a large reel at the dry ends of the machines. In the case of coated publication papers, the paper may have gone through another section of press rolls where a coating is applied.

A final step for many printing grades is supercalendering. A supercalendar is a separate machine that looks like a smaller, vertical fourdinier—still several stories high—through which paper is buffed into a higher gloss or sheen. After 1950, paper machine makers could deliver a continuous machine that integrated the fourdrinier and supercalender processes.

Fourdriniers ran just a few feet wide in the mid-nineteenth century and grew to 10, 20, or more feet wide by the second half of the twentieth century. Wider machines presented more opportunities for paper to break but also created dramatic economies of scale. The speed of the machine, the other major productivity variable besides width, began in the nineteenth century at perhaps 200–300 feet per minute, and reached 3,000 feet per minute after 1900. Together, these two scale variables increased productivity by thousands of percent.[160] By the mid to late twentieth century, one paper machine could produce upwards 600 miles or more of paper in a shift.

Paper mills in the coated publication paper business were advantaged in the latter half of the twentieth century by integration of coaters and paper machines. S. D. Warren's Westbrook works was unable to take advantage of this innovation because of the dense and happenstance arrangement of machines in the mill. The Westbrook mill thus retained, in later years, a large materials handling army with forklifts and other machines used to move product from one stage to another, a staff not needed in new mills. Indeed, in the 1970s, S. D. Warren, by then a division of Scott Paper Company, decided to build an entirely separate and thus more efficiently laid out mill 75 miles north in Hinckley, Maine to install these most modern machines.

Finished paper rolls are typically routed to rewinder machines, which even rolls and cut them to various sizes. In mills like Oxford and S. D. Warren, some rolls were sent to the finishing department directly to be packaged as-is to be shipped to customers; many went to the supercalender machine for further buffing. Once ready, paper rolls were moved via forklift to an entirely different building. Looking back at S. D. Warren's antiquated layout in the mid-twentieth century, one would find labor-intensive processes that compensated for the sprawling mill's inefficient design. There, paper was cut, counted, and inspected. Here were large banks of paper cutting machines; men ran guillotine cutters that use human power to bring down sharp blades that cut paper to various sizes, typically about three to five feet to a side. The now cut paper was brought to hundreds of female workers who inspected the paper and counted reams by hand. Paper was then ready to be wrapped and brought to shipping to be delivered by truck or rail.

This mass of machinery required a very large workforce of expert craft workers who staffed the mill's maintenance section. Maintenance workers made up about 15 percent of the mill's workforce. At S. D. Warren's peak, this division numbered more than five hundred workers. Of these, the usual array of machine fixers—millwrights, electricians, and boilermakers—supplemented by builders, including carpenters, and the many machinists who fabricated replacement parts for the mill's complex of machines. Indeed, during the post-World War II era, the mill's final growth spurt involved so much construction that old timers recalled as many as two hundred brick masons on staff in the peak postwar era.[161]

Part 2

TOP-DOWN AND BOTTOM-UP CHANGE IN MAINE'S MIGHTY PAPER INDUSTRY AND THE RISE OF A NEW MILITANCY, 1960–80

THE FALL OF MOTHER WARREN

In 1967, Mother Warren's profligate paternalism and century-long bond between local owners and its loyal workforce came to an end—of sorts—with the mill's surprising unionization that coincided with the company's sale to Scott Paper. To some, Scott Paper's purchase of S. D. Warren was a shocking end to the mill's local identity and also the key event sparking unionization. But prior to Scott's purchase, abusive treatment by foremen, discrimination against female employees, and rank unfairness in job assignments and pay bred widespread resentment. As Warren's paternalism broke down, the mill and its workers were also swept by top-down and bottom-up national currents that changed the economic and labor landscape throughout the United States. New levels of blue-collar prosperity could not suppress growing conflict.

In a dialectical irony, the biggest of Warren's new union locals became the state's most militant. Facing this new militancy was Howard Reiche Jr., who took the helm as mill manager in 1970. Reiche worked cooperatively with the new unions, even embracing their constructive role in rectifying the mill's plainly outdated pay and supervisory practices. But Reiche's steady hand alone did not ameliorate the growing tension that new forces stoked across all of Maine's mills—and in the factory in the forest as well. Conflict in Westbrook that led to two strikes, was alive throughout the state, as more socially and geographically distant corporate leaders narrowed the space for any continued paternalism.

Part II explores these new circumstances as the industry matured. Postwar prosperity was impressive: state paper production grew from one million metric tons in 1947 to 2.5 million metric tons by 1970; woods and paper mill employment grew from eighteen thousand in 1940 to thirty-two thousand in 1967; real wages doubled in the postwar upswing, and mill workers enjoyed a vast expansion of benefits. True decline was still decades away—employment declined only slightly to twenty-seven thousand in 1989, and production actually grew by 40 percent over that period as automation dramatically boosted productivity.[1]

The 1960s and 1970s was more than just a watershed between the industry's rise and the painful and caustic developments of the 1980s and 1990s. The great Maine mills already were losing their status as the central stars of their companies' solar systems; their local character was stripped away as they become mere branch plants of national corporations. New corporate combinations were enamored with newer Southern plants that offered higher profits and (for the most part) more pliant workers. Local Maine mill leaders now had to fight for investment resources that previously were guaranteed.

These new forces acting upon workers precipitated tension and conflict. Also, World War II and later wars brought many young Mainers into contact with a wider world at a time when unionism was in a great upswing. The anti-Vietnam War and other 1960s movements not only had a Maine component, but brought new political radicals and union activists to Maine. World War II also sparked a long-term back-and-forth migration between central and northern Maine and unionized Connecticut military factories, movement that imported new sensibilities and activism. As the industry underwent significant changes, a new combative ethos would emerge in the mills and the woods.[2]

Paper Unionism in the United States and Maine

With the exception of S. D. Warren Company, Maine's paper workers gained union recognition in the late 1930s and World War II.[3] A national labor uprising between 1908 and 1912 saw a first wave of successful labor organizing and strikes in Jay, Rumford, and Millinocket. This early movement was led by the International Brotherhood of Paper Makers Union (hereafter Papermakers) and the International Brotherhood of Pulp, Sulfite, and Paper Mills Workers (hereafter Pulp and Sulphite union), laced with socialist and anarchist radicals.[4] After a decade, International Paper (IP), led major paper companies in a campaign to defeat these unions, with the national IP strike ending in 1926. Few U.S. paper mills had union representation over the ensuing decade.[5]

A renewed national wave of striking and union organizing swept the United States beginning in 1933; national union membership grew fivefold, from three million to fifteen million in 1945.[6] By 1954, 39 percent of nonagricultural private sector workers were covered by union contracts, up from 12 percent in 1932.[7] In the late 1930s, the new Congress of Industrial Unions (CIO), comprised of new unions such as the United Autoworkers and the United Electrical Workers, represented the labor movement's insurgent wing. The CIO's rise spurred older craft unions of the American Federation of Labor (AFL) that had long eschewed organizing mass production workers to begin to organize on an industrial basis (an inclusive model that sought to bring all workers in an industry into one union versus the earlier model of organizing only highly skilled craft workers by occupation, leaving most workers unrepresented). Previously antiunion employers threatened by militant CIO unions prompted a new embrace of the older, more conservative AFL unions. The Pulp and Sulfite union, already an industrial union though associated with the AFL, skillfully exploited this to organize previously unrepresented workers in Maine and elsewhere.[8]

According to Robert Zeiger, paper employers frequently reached out to the Pulp and Sulfite workers, offering "friendly cooperation" in signing their workers up.[9] Historian and activist Peter Kellman offers the intriguing anecdote of Mickey Poulin, a worker at Jay, Maine's IP plant, being told by a foreman that:

> "If [Poulin] wanted to continue in the employ of International Paper Company he would have to join the union that night and bring a union card to work the next day." A 1937 contract between IP and four new locals boldly stated: ". . . its local management will cooperate with the local unions in every way the management of the Company considers proper and lawful to assist in obtaining and retaining members."[10]

Zeiger notes just how forcefully the CIO's arrival in 1937 proved a boon to the Pulp and Sulfite union:

> Everywhere, any hint of CIO activity drove employers into the arms of the paper unions. . . . Everywhere, employers dropped their opposition to the Brotherhood, collaborated with its representatives to direct workers into the AFL organization, cooperated in isolating CIO activists, and zealously enforced union security provisions against workers agitating on behalf of the CIO.[11]

The Pulp and Sulfite and the Papermaker unions were quintessential business unions. They focused on bread-and-butter issues—wages, benefits, hours, and working conditions. They also represented a highly bureaucratic version of business unionism, emphasizing cooperation between professional union officials and company executives, avoiding strikes, and limiting local workers' voices in making key decisions. By the 1960s, "the Brotherhood . . . gained the unenviable reputation . . . for its cozy bargaining relationships with paper companies, timid grievance handling, and for having apathetic and somnolent local unions."[12]

Companies benefited from divided workforces. A typical postwar paper mill had one to as many as four union locals representing the Papermakers and the Pulp and Sulfite union (these two unions would merge to become the United Paperworkers International Union [UPIU] in 1972), and a collection of craft locals representing skilled maintenance trades.[13] Bargaining in the industry was highly decentralized, with separate contracts often negotiated for each mill, with the exception of IP. Within each mill, contract negotiations would take place at separate dates across the mill's locals.[14] Union business agents and regional executives dominated negotiations; professional union negotiators often formed closer relationships with corporate officials than with local union members. This hierarchical and bureaucratic style brewed in the paper unions' dark days in the 1920s and early 1930s. Over time, the unions' bureaucratic style became a source of growing tension between local leadership and the national union. These tensions emerged in the 1960s, and crystallized during the 1987–88 Jay strike.[15]

Paper worker unions were at their best in creating income security and fairness for workers through the practice of job control unionism. Job control union contracts specified every job in the mill, with standards for the amount and types of work to be done in a job. Especially important was the seniority-based system of promotion up lines of progression. Moving from being a sixth hand upwards to a first or second hand meant moving into more skilled and less physically taxing jobs.[16]

Job control unionism had a special importance to paper workers. As we've seen with Warren's pre-union bonus system, it was common for management to set great differences in pay for similar jobs, and even larger differentials in the pay for different job assignments. In S. D. Warren's finishing department, for example, some jobs offered up to three times the pay of similar jobs nearby because of productivity-based bonuses.[17] Rampant inequity along with nepotistic awards of better-paid work made careful specification of wage levels for job definitions, and strict rules about progression from lesser to high paid jobs, central to shop-floor justice.

By the 1960s, Maine's paper workers had become more involved in conducting the work of their locals—particularly shop stewards' defense of the contract through the grievance process. With as many as eight or nine union locals at single mill, it was common for dozens of workers to take a turn at one point as union leaders, as shop stewards (the shop steward is a fellow worker who acts as the union representative in charge of grievances and contract enforcement in specific work areas), as an elected leader, or on a governing executive committee that ran the local. Participation in governance was thus widespread, and thus so was a daily discussion of the exact rules for fair treatment. Contracts stipulated due process seniority in allocating jobs with a strong bonus, or, in the case of a double shift, whether one has to do it without choice, or who has the priority in getting a huge (earned) windfall in a weekly paycheck the so-called extra offered. Another commonplace was the worker who was sent home without pay for several days because of some mistake or infraction, a particularly onerous penalty long built into contracts by national union officials. In all, stewards and higher-level union officials litigated these issues on a daily basis. Shop stewards and union leaders were quick to defend job definitions, seniority and seniority-related job security, and general due process in matters such as seniority-based allocation of overtime shifts.[18]

Historian David Brody aptly named this activism "workplace contractualism."[19] Vigorous contract enforcement gave workers a significant say over the conditions of their work. While not quite a full-blown industrial democracy, these practices were a meaningful form of worker power. For managers, especially front-line supervisors, this system was an impingement and a burden—an unfortunate opportunity for workers to be litigious, avoid work, or get free money. To workers, it was the premise of fairness and dignity on the job. The ability to insist on fair treatment through the contract and its daily enforcement became a widely held ethos for the thousands of workers across Maine's sixteen major postwar paper mills.[20]

For union officials, the manly practice of standing up to and even intimidating managers in union matters provided both psychic as well as pecuniary benefits. Frank Poulin was president of UPIU Local 9 at S. D. Warren's new Somerset mill from the mill's opening in 1976 until 1985. Poulin spent many years in senior union leadership at the former Hollingsworth and Whitney mill in nearby Winslow, and he brought to Somerset a fighting sensibility about defending contract provisions. He recounted once pounding his fist so hard on a table during a negotiation that he broke his hand. He proudly recalls getting disability payments as prescribed in the union contract for the month of work he lost while recuperating.[21] UPIU Local 1069 president Tom Lestage put it this way: "We question authority at all times. We don't have a problem filing fifty grievances on an issue. . . . If there's a practice that they're trying to establish, we'll grieve it and we'll—our term has been 'we'll bury them in paper work.'"[22]

It was this specific legacy that shaped the ways in which militancy would emerge in Maine paper mills in the years after 1964.[23] Defending workplace contractualism was central to ensuing struggles. On the one hand, it marked a growing split between local militancy and the national unions' cautious culture. Long before the hyper-charged rift erupted in the 1987–88 Jay strike, distrust in "the international" was a broad if not ubiquitous sentiment among rank-and-file union officials.[24] On the other hand, union contracts had codified ways of working that predated unionization, and, as we've seen, made the independence and centrality of the unsupervised lead hand the core of company identity and success. In the name of efficiency, companies led by Boise Cascade and IP would aim to squash this form of worker control.[25]

One last feature of note: prior to 1985, the new conflicts had a local flavor and are best understood through mill-specific case studies. This would later change in the 1980s, when struggles across companies fused in a statewide movement culture.[26]

Maine workers' militancy was part of a national wave of labor activism. Worker rebellion was a constant throughout the post-World War II era, with two notable peaks: during the Korean War, and then between 1965 and 1975. For comparison, the average annual number of major work stoppages—strikes and lockouts involving more than one thousand workers—in the United States between 2002 and 2011 was a mere 16.3. The annual average for 1967, 1971, and 1975—the moments when workers at Fraser Paper, and Maine Woodsmen struck, and S. D. Warren unionized—was 220 major strikes, roughly fourteen times as many in the decade after 9/11.[27] In 1966, over two million workers struck; at a similar point in the most recent business cycle—2006—a mere seventy thousand did. Also, in contrast to the 1980s or later, unions actually won strikes. One happy outcome for unionized mill workers of pre-1980 militancy was a sharp rise in living standards made possible by wage and benefit improvements, with the biggest growth of wages at the peak of this militancy in the 1970s.[28]

How did militancy arise? From the top—Northern mills faced growing competition from the Southern U.S., Canada, and Scandinavia. Maine paper mills lost, or were in the process of losing, what might be termed their independence, as they merged with or were bought out by larger national paper companies, thus joining multiplant operations that in most cases included locations in the lower-cost U.S. South. Independence in what sense? Investment and management decisions were previously overseen by a small group of principal owners who overlapped with top management. With few likely uses of retained earnings and depreciation before 1960, S. D. Warren, Oxford, Great Northern Paper, Fraser, and other Maine giants pursued a truly Chandlerian strategy of retaining and reinvesting profits. The principal use of profits besides investment was shareholder dividends. Companies could satisfice by rewarding stockholders with a steady income.[29] But unlike the financialized era to come, shareholders other than the main owners were passive—that is, they did not place short-term profit demands on companies that would undermine the plowing of most profits back into research and development, marketing, upgrading, and expanding machinery and other physical capital. Long-term managers with appropriate financial backing could maintain long-term norms of reciprocity with a mill's workers.

Workers reacted to the changing character of ownership and management. One factor was the growing flow into Maine mills of middle and upper managers who had not come up through the company's ranks. Over time, the tendency grew for these newer managers to disregard or be simply ignorant of existing workplace norms or even the very skill of the workers.[30] At first, it was a lack of knowledge of or respect for local norms, but eventually it was gaps in their practical knowledge of production that were a particular sore spot. Also, facing intensified competition, managers new or old sought to speed up work in ways that violated either the spirit or letter of union contracts.[31] A similar and parallel dynamic took place in the Maine woods, as companies progressively squeezed logging contractors after 1965.[32] As we'll see, conflict was also intramanagement. For instance, local management leaders of the S. D. Warren Division of Scott after 1967 distrusted and even mocked the sensibilities of Scott Paper executives.[33] This combination of factors, in local variations, gave impetus to S. D. Warren's 1967 unionization and two strikes at Warren in 1977 and 1983, major strikes at Maine's largest mills such as Boise Cascade (the original Oxford mill), GNP, and Fraser, and stoppages at smaller mills such as the Pepjepscot in 1976.[34] In each case, new ownership, or the threat of hostile takeovers, combined with competitive pressures, translated into shop-floor practices that ignited conflict.

Worker combativeness thus issued from quite distinct local sources, though influenced by some of the common developments shaping national labor relations—including veterans' rebelliousness, participation by New Left activists in labor struggles, and the migration of militant unionists from other regions.[35] With new leadership from below and new pressures from above, workers utilized the framework of traditional union contracts to practice a militant workplace contractualism. This daily resistance, combined with strikes large and small, defined a new era of labor relations. A growing penchant for militancy blossomed into even sharper acts of resistance when paper companies fully turned on workers and their unions in 1986 and 1987.

The Fall of Mother Warren

And then, all of a sudden, there was talk in the late sixties that they were going to sell the mill. . . . And I think people got a little panicky, they didn't know anything about this *out-of-town, out-of-state organization* going to come in, and buy the mill. So, they didn't know how they was [*sic*] going to be treated, how it was going to affect them. And I think there was a lot of concern about the sudden change from that closeness that was originally there in the mill for years. Now it was going to change. And I think people was [*sic*] a little concerned about that—maybe we ought to have a union here looking over things to make sure we're treated all right.

—Dan Parks, production worker and later president of United Paperworkers
International Union (UPIU) Local 1069-Westbrook, interview

When asked about the fall of Mother Warren, former workers like Dan Parks pointed to Scott's purchase of S. D. Warren Company from its long-term inves-

FIGURE 3.1   S. D. Warren workers and representatives of the United Papermakers and Paperworkers Union and International Brotherhood of Pulp, Sulfite, and Paper Mills Union who worked together to secure victory in an October 1967 National Labor Relations Board election, taken the day after the election victory. Joseph Jensen (standing, third from left), Omer Charest (kneeling, far left), and Clyde Harriman (kneeling, far right with his son) were S. D. Warren workers who convinced union representatives to speak respectfully of the Mother Warren legacy and focus on women workers and wives in building support for the union campaign (photo in author's possession, given as a gift by Joseph Jensen to the author in 2002).

tors and company leaders. They feared the loss of family ownership that symbolized Mother Warren's exceptional treatment of its workers. In turn, they faced an uncertain future at the hands of an out-of-state, corporate entity whose governance and management approach was unknown; workers did not know what to expect but feared the worst. As Ron Usher—a mill worker who would soon successfully run for the state legislature at the union's urging—recalls: "Scott Paper—what was it? Scott purchased us and that scared the people. . . . And after we [had] had a homey atmosphere. Warren, Mother Warren, participated in everything. If anybody needed anything, they was [sic] always there. And when another company comes in, it scares people."[36]

Workers from the postwar era can recall minor skirmishes with management in the past but nothing that fundamentally challenged the company's nonunion standing in the years before the 1960s.[37] When paper worker unions attempted to organize the mill prior to 1960, they were defeated in three postwar National Labor Relations Board votes, as only a minority of Warren workers saw any value in union representation.[38] There was even a serious organizing drive and strike for union recognition that ended in defeat for workers in 1916, though few workers who started after 1960 recalled it.[39] Despite these skirmishes, Mother Warren's outstanding reputation for providing economic security and it is like-a-family culture remained intact well into its second century of being (see figure 3.1).

The substance of Warren's indulgency pattern evolved over time.[40] The generation who lived through the Depression and World War II recall Warren's extraordinary efforts to sacrifice profits on behalf of its workers' well-being during hard times. After the war, the mill took special care of its veterans. Production manager Karl Dornish portrays the workforce of the 1950s and 1960s as populated by a large number of World War II veterans, who undoubtedly suffered varying degrees of posttraumatic stress, drank heavily, and showed up for work irregularly.[41] Supervisors and the mill manager routinely indulged this part of its workforce by sponsoring rehabilitation and by maintaining employment and paying wages, even when these workers disappeared for weeks at a time.[42]

For the early postwar generation at Warren, the guarantee of economic security and financial generosity toward its workers was thus both real and often extraordinary. Therefore, a deep loyalty made unionization unnecessary to a majority of Warren's workers, even when virtually every other mill in the state unionized, making appeals by professional organizers of little interest. Clyde Harriman, a key member of the 1960s' organizing committee, described professional union organizers from United Papermakers and Paperworkers, and International Brotherhood of Pulp, Sulfite and Paper Mill Workers international unions attempting to derogate Warren as an exploitative "overbearing robber baron";

Harriman found this language to be "garbage."[43] This cluelessness about Warren's deep and unique bond with its workforce sent unionization efforts in the late 1940s and 1950s to defeat.[44]

But underneath the apparent strength and durability of the company's legend as a superior employer was a fundamental contradiction that explained new support for unionization. The company as a whole had made an explicit compact of deep economic security for its workers in exchange for their robust commitment to making Warren's finicky products and for their willingness to tolerate the onerous character of the work. But below the kindly concern from the mill manager—a concern which atrophied in the hands of mill managers after John Hyde—were serious shop-floor problems. An archipelago of kind treatment by easygoing, warm, and approachable managers could be found in the mill's geography. However, in other sections of the mill, workers found that when as they walked through the factory gates, the most immediate reality was of a foreman or more senior manager's abusive behavior. Widespread favoritism was a huge problem. Warren had so many extended families that nepotism more than any other factor guided access to higher earnings. It is a sign of the failure of the post-1920s' top management group that the problem of nepotism, in this instance practiced not at the company's higher levels as described in chapter 1, but in its lower ranks, persisted. Thus, as the postwar years wore on, Mother Warren's mystique eroded, giving a new and different momentum to organizing efforts in the 1960s.[45]

This problem had long been papered over by senior managers, and especially the mill managers who maintained an informal grievance system—a substantive open-door policy. Behind the indulgency pattern, and the great pride Warren workers had in being an essential part of a first-tier paper producer, the last line of defense against worker unhappiness and interest in unionization was the mill manager who spent much of his time meeting individual workers about their complaints. As the mill grew from one thousand to over three thousand employees in the fifty years prior to unionization, the effort to maintain loyalty was a monumental task. A Harvard researcher, who had spent a good part of his four months in the mill in the late 1940s shadowing John Hyde, witnessed the bizarrely large scope of the mill manager's grievance efforts. The researcher notes "he had never been in Mr. [Hyde's] office without being preceded or followed by men and women from every working level in the mill."[46] At the end of one such meeting, a more than sixty year old Hyde is described as looking pensively out the window of his office, wondering if the handful of men he had trained to replace him were adequate to the task.[47]

So the story of Warren's shop floor after 1950 is one of growing abuse in what may best be described as the department supervisors' empire and a simultaneous failure to replace the last of the great Warren leaders who workers could turn to for redress. Karl Dornish recalled Hyde's replacements, Everett Ingalls in the 1950s, and later Rudy Greep (1958–70), as both absent from the shop floor and willing to leave personnel matters to department superintendents and their underlings.[48] In short, they ignored growing problems and lacked the special touch for salving frustrations wielded previously by Hyde. While the sale of the company to Scott was the coup-de-grace in creating majority support for unionization, these shop-floor problems were at the heart of the company's labor relations problems.

Favoritism and the Shop-Floor Experience

> And I remember the department superintendent that I hold mostly responsible for unionizing the mill. I can remember him forbidding me and kicking me out of the department. . . . But that was typical of that guy. . . . It was *his* empire and if . . . that paper was ok, what the hell did you know!
>
> —Howard Reiche Jr., interview

There was no systematic approach to how supervision was performed—not surprising given a complete lack of training. Foremen learned their way on the job, and the personnel department had little involvement with shop-floor relations.[49] Once workers were hired, personnel managed paychecks and benefits and left all other matters to department superintendents and their supervisory staff.

Then there was the maze of payment.[50] The mill had long maintained a complex system of bonus rates on various machines and other labor processes. Calling it a system is too generous. It was plagued by two problems. For one, the ability of workers to influence productivity varied, and over time, workers often found themselves on jobs where they little influence over productivity but still had their payment based on the end product of their work. Paper machines were notorious. They were the heart of the moneymaking, and we've described how workers on the machines worked hardest when the process broke down; most of the time that didn't happen, and they otherwise couldn't make a difference on what the machine produced.

Worse, in some departments, notoriously in finishing, one job might pay three times what a nearby job paid if one was willing to sacrifice one's body. For example, young men on guillotine presses—large, sharp-bladed machines that cut large piles of paper to custom size—worked furiously with a dramatic motion where they pulled down a wide bar from above their heads to their waists. Huge paychecks were apparently sufficient to induce manic work effort but left men permanently impaired by age forty.[51] Mill chief production manager

Karl Dornish recalled that the bonus system "really doesn't make sense in a lot of places—the wage rates were really screwed up." At the time the mill unionized, he "did a big study on our incentive system, and I said it really doesn't make sense in a lot of places where they don't have any control of [their productivity]." At that point, he was ready to see it end:

> I would have got rid of it then, probably. Because, it's very, very, very hard, to make a fair bonus system, that really measures how much work, people put into stuff. On the manual stuff, like in the finishing depart-ment, you have to estimate how hard a guy is working, and that's nor-mal. Ok, so anything he does over that, he ought to get paid money for. And, that is a very subjective evaluation. And it is hard to do. I put all these industrial engineers through school, and all of that, still, I never— we weren't bad, but we weren't, it wasn't good.[52]

However, the bonus system was so ingrained that it would take more than a de-cade before the union and company decided to abolish it altogether.

An added factor to the tangle of pay rates was the frequent need for workers to do an extra. With absenteeism widespread, and the absolute need for machines and processes to be tended to, supervisors would have to tap workers on the job to stay on for an additional six or eight hours. For the willing, frequent extras could also add a great deal to the paycheck. As with the high bonus, extras were for some a blessing, and for others a curse. The power to assign high bonus jobs and extras gave supervisors tremendous scope in awarding high pay to those they favored. And by all accounts, abuse of their free hand appeared to be something close to the rule.[53]

What did supervision look like? With a complete lack of formal guidelines or procedures, each department superintendent and his underlings were free to op-erate in whatever manner best suited them. For instance, within the finishing de-partment, the two side-by-side rooms had polar-opposite atmospheres, the one harsh and no-nonsense, the other convivial and festive.[54] Mae Bachelor and her niece recalled the homey atmosphere in their smaller and easy-going paper in-spection and counting department, overseen by the "wonderful" "Poppa" Gory; regular breaks were taken for birthday celebrations, and women raised money to help their sisters who had to miss work and income when having a child.[55] They were even unaware that they were on bonus with little pressure on the speed at which they worked beyond meeting a basic standard. They at the same time feared transfer to the "big room" where supervisors insisted on workers meeting a rig-orous and exhausting bonus standard, and the mood was no-nonsense and su-pervisors impatient and exacting.

Department superintendents believed that their departments were "empire(s) separate from the rest of the mill," and often failed to cooperate with each other when pride stood in the way, sometimes resulting in the spoiling of entire runs of paper (which were then sold to jobbers at a loss).[56] As Howard Reiche put it: "the principal operations—the pulp mill, power generation, paper machines, maintenance, finishing, and specialty coating—were kind of managed and viewed as different businesses."[57] Without unionized seniority protections, foremen controlled access to specific jobs and had the right to send workers home without pay if they deemed a worker's effort or behavior problematic. Phil Lestage was critical of how nepotism resulted in shop-floor workers getting promoted to supervisory roles that they were not necessarily prepared for: "But I know some of those guys who were foreman didn't know nothing about the machines. They got there through relatives, really. Some of their relatives were higher up. And they made them foreman—I just couldn't understand how they could, you know, run their household let alone run a machine. I mean they were numb."[58]

Robert Burton was a typical skilled paper worker promoted to foreman off the work floor. He describes his foreman training from the early 1950s this way: "Yeah, the guy handed me a wrench, and said 'you do this and this and this" and go to work. [Laughs] I did train with another foreman for about a week, but I was doing it all in a couple of weeks." Dornish said about foremen: "as far as supervising skills, they weren't really given much of any thing."[59] Functionally, they were in charge of coordinating production on one or several machines or operations, and they or their direct superiors generally had a free hand in allocating workers to job openings, overtime assignments, and the like.

Familiarity and informality cut both ways. Many foremen were respectful. They were invariably recruited off of the shop floor and often had strong connections with their relatives and neighbors who remained in production. So, some groups of workers were spared the worst because a supervisor might be a decent guy (women were virtually never promoted to supervisory jobs) or a close friend or relative. But too often this was not the case, as supervisors and foremen took advantage of the lack of oversight or company-wide policies on pay and promotion. Given the idiosyncrasies of pay under their watches, they could reward or punish workers with substantial increases or decreases in weekly pay on a whim, or most likely, to reward family members.

In addition to the Harvard Business School's copious ethnography of the mill, we benefit from the insider perspective of Karl Dornish and Howard Reiche.[60] Dornish and Reiche were astute observers. Reiche characterized bad actor foremen as abusing their "enormous power" to either send a worker home without pay or by allocating overtime "because this person might be a son of a friend of theirs that was a first hand on a machine." He cited the paper mill department supervisor as the worst actor, a "real asshole" who screamed at workers all the time, whose behavior was so erratic and awful that, at a later date, he would have "been committed" to psychiatric care. Asked if the mill's management made any effort to train or constrain the power of foremen, Reiche responded by saying: "Absolutely not, absolutely not." Dornish conveyed a similar image:

> The guys that ran the departments were, for the most part, pretty powerful individuals, or at least they thought they were. And it worked that way from before my time; I didn't invent this thing. It was just the way things worked. . . . We had guys doing their own thing. And some of the guys were really bad.

Asked if the mill manager's open-door policy was a route for shop-floor workers to redress abuse or unfairness, Dornish replied "no, not for . . . that."

Workers who lived through this era recalled that favoritism was rampant, based largely on nepotism. With extended families strewn throughout the mill, opportunities to reward the cousin, nephew, or sister were widespread. One problem was the mill's longstanding view of Franco-American workers as a lesser group deserving the dirtiest and least paid jobs.[61] Phil Lestage, a second-generation French-Canadian worked with his six brothers and father. As a Franco, managers subjected him and others to the raw end of this stick: "a lot of people were getting screwed over. . . . Of course, there was a lot of favoritism back then. . . . If you got on the wrong side of one of the foreman, they wouldn't give you any extras unless they couldn't fill it." Failing in several attempts to get a better job, Howard Parkhurst expressed bitterness about being blocked for years prior to unionization to get a long-desired job: "I could have gone into the pipe shop two or three times, but back then, this is prior to the union, if you didn't know anybody, or you wasn't [sic] a suckass, you could go over and stay second-class until the day you retired." And Clyde Harriman, a key member of the United Paper and Paperworkers organizing team, and briefly a union president in the late 1960s, recalled: "it naturally developed that people throughout the mill, you know, those in control, the superintendents and that, had these little sweetheart deals so there was no, there was really no conformity to regulations or how things should be done."[62]

Favoritism intersected with sexual harassment for the hundreds of women in the finishing department. Shirley Lally remembered that, "If you were a sweetheart or pretty, you would be given a prized bonus job." Dan Parks, who became a shop steward in the finishing department shortly after unionization recalls: "women got jobs by giving sexual favors to foremen." Women who refused "had the shittiest jobs," and received "the worst treatment." Women were also treated like a contingent workforce. Women with ten to twenty years of seniority were laid off in favor of men with only a few years' tenure when work slowed down. As we noted in chapter 2, Mae Bachelor had short, unpaid maternity leaves when she had each of her four children, and her seniority was reset to zero each time.[63]

The mill also had categorized jobs into heavy and light work. The so-called heavy jobs were, of course, better paid; women were denied access to these jobs. Through seniority, after unionization, many women gained access to formerly heavy jobs on the paper machines and driving transport vehicles.[64]

Reiche and Dornish, as we've seen, were shocked and disgusted by frontline supervisors' behavior. Over their first fifteen years, they moved around the mill's production operations and witnessed widespread abuses first-hand.[65] By 1970, they had reached the top two management positions—mill manager and chief production manager—and embraced the new unions as collaborators in creating a fair and more modern workplace. For them, creating job allocation rules based on seniority were a huge and effective upgrade of practices under the pre-union supervisory era. Reiche couldn't have been more emphatic: "I had the interesting experience of working in a facility that was nonunion, and a facility that then *became* union. . . . If I had a choice, I'd pick the union. It was easier. It was fairer—much fairer. I mean, your heart goes out to some hourly person who was mistreated, particularly a person who was defenseless in the sense that they, if they came back [at their supervisors], they'd lose their job. Under unionism, they could have a grievance."

Unionizing Mother Warren

They couldn't hide it any more, the little foremen that were dictators in their own section of the mill. All of a sudden they lost that power [about] what they did or said because they knew it would be heard upstairs [through the grievance procedure].

—Bill Carver, Local 1069 president from 1980–91

A new round of organizing emerged in the 1960s. The small maintenance unions of skilled electricians, pipefitters, and machinists won a National Labor Relations Board (NLRB) election in 1963, but the company aggressively challenged the election in court and dragged the matter out until late 1965 when federal courts upheld the vote. Out of legal options, S. D. Warren signed a first contract covering approximately four hundred skilled workers in the middle of the following year.[66]

The unionization campaign for the 80 percent of production workers began in 1964, and would take three years to complete. Joe Jensen and Clyde Harriman were two of the three principal leaders (with Bob Charest) of the organizing committee that began in 1964, working with the United Papermakers and Paperworkers, and International Brotherhood of Pulp, Sulfite, and Paper Mill unions in a coordinated campaign.[67] The very fact that this drive started three years before Scott Paper purchased the company, and made much progress in the intervening three years, undermines any notion that it was only the purchase by Scott that sparked unionization.

The key to this renewed effort was moving beyond crude attacks on Warren. In the year or two before the organizing team emerged, representatives from the two major paper unions distributed flyers at the mill's gates.

> One afternoon I went to work . . . and I had seen it a couple of times, the representatives of the international paper union would pass out these flyers . . . outside the gates, and they really didn't tell you anything. It was more directed with calling Mother Warren an over-bearing paper baron and things like that. Real childish stuff, I thought. And I never gave it any thought.
>
> —Clyde Harriman, interview

The following year, Harriman expressed pointedly to international representatives that unionizing Warren would take a different approach, based on building relationships slowly in small meetings and by addressing substantive problems workers had, without the "childish stuff" denigrating the company as a whole. Harriman's direct reaction to professional organizers' lame exhortations led to his recruitment to help lead the organizing effort, effecting a shift to the hands of Warren employees who better understood the landscape. Harriman emphasized reaching out to Warren's large female workforce:

> So I got involved with them in a big way, and it took us two years to organize. And the way we did it was to have breakfast parties. You know, let the union spend a couple of bucks on coffee and donuts, and whatever, and to have it at a central place where a maximum number of *women* could come, so that they could address them and tell them what unions are all about and hopefully the things that could do as a union to help them and make their place of work a better place of work.
>
> Because women, it seemed to me, you can convince them, being the second bread-winner, some of them being *the* bread-winner, probably had lost their husband, were looking for stability and security in their

job. And I mean, those things just don't come along, and nobody grants those things.[68]

As noted below, women's role in securing the home front gave them a powerful voice. And, many were motivated by a protofeminist sensibility that their thoroughly second-class treatment by the mill needed addressing.

Joe Jensen joined the core organizing committee at the same time. One thing the internationals did bring in was perspective on the wage and benefits situation. Jensen and others discovered that despite the wage premium they earned compared to some local employers, Warren workers had fallen behind others in the Northeastern paper industry. The organizing team simply passed out contract booklets from unionized paper mills showing higher wages and especially much more solid benefits. Organizers emphasized the need to upgrade from the mill's hit-or-miss and antiquated benefits to more regularized, especially for when workers got hurt (for which they got an uncertain level of mill relief) and when they retired (when they would get very modest pensions determined by the company without worker input).

Organizers made clear the benefits of unionization. Of course, they emphasized grievance mechanisms backing contract provisions defining sacrosanct lines of progression and seniority-based distribution of extras would effectively end widespread favoritism. They also addressed women's circumstances in the mill.[69] Women lost seniority when they were frequently laid off—they served as a buffer that allowed men to keep their jobs when work was slow.[70] Women also suffered a huge wage disparity working in light women's jobs that paid much less than men's heavy jobs—and they received shorter vacations. Sixty-six women were laid off during a slowdown a year before the union vote; led by Shirley Lally, an active group of ten women went to union leadership shortly after unionization. Dan Parks and other male union leaders pushed hard to reinstate at least some of the sixty-six and to put an end to treating women as a supplemental workforce that could be used to insulate male workers from layoffs. Health insurance copayments had recently jumped dramatically when the mill switched from Blue Cross-Blue Shield, sparking another area of dissatisfaction that union collective bargaining could address. Safety was also a motivating factor. There had been four deaths on site in past fifteen years, including the dramatic 1966 explosion in the pulp mill's solvent coater operation, which killed two workers and deeply disfigured others.[71] The accident prompted surviving workers to walk out until safety concerns were adequately addressed.[72] Finally, the union would put an end to the widespread practices of favoritism and supervisory abuse.

In fall 1967, production workers voted in favor of union representation by the United Papermakers and Paperworkers and the International Brotherhood of

Pulp, Sulfite, and Paper Mill Workers; over 60 percent of the 1647 workers who voted approved union representation.[73] The NLRB counted votes on site, and the company accepted the results, despite years of advice and legal stratagems from union-avoidance lawyers hired by the company. A young man named John Nee distributing a well-argued address to workers laying out the argument for voting for the union.[74] Nee drove a small vehicle moving semi-finished product across a number of departments, allowing him to covertly and widely deliver the letter. Marv Ewing, active in the unionization effort, had this remembrance:

> It was to the effect: "Do you really think you wouldn't be better off with . . . Would you *not* . . . How could you possibly not be better off with a union than you are?" It was basically that. But it was so well written. . . . The guy really had a gift . . . he put down the words that a lot of people thought, obviously. . . . [It got to people] who were really on the fence.[75]

Finally, the sale of Warren to Scott spurred broader support. For many workers, it crystallized the need to address the deep underside to S. D. Warren Company's ostensibly happy industrial community. The Westbrook mill was Mother Warren no longer, and the sense that a beneficent company could be fully relied on to solve or salve daily problems was replaced by a new era of collective bargaining and shop-floor activism.

Local 1069 and the Emergence of Workplace Contractualism

> We had people . . . and, back in them days, people were more . . . they seemed very *enthusiastic* about things. . . . There was always enough people that were enthusiastic. . . . The company would do something they didn't like and there'd be grievances and people would approach it from an angle there . . . we can resolve problems [but] we're going to have to fight for it. . . . I think that somewhat surprised the company—that, you know, for so many years, you know, people were dormant. . . . Maybe they complained, but that would only go so far and then they'd say, "Oh, the heck with it. It won't do us any good anyway!" When the strike came up, they were *totally shocked* that these people were going to do this.
>
> —Marv Ewing, UPIU, Local 1069 president, 1970–79, interview

Local 1069, working in concert with Local 404, which it absorbed in a mid–1970s' merger,[76] emerged as a powerful force reshaping the mill's structure and procedures in the decade after unionization.[77] With an independent voice and backlog of burning issues, it quickly found its legs. It had a large, active membership, and a skilled, aggressive leadership. Its transformation into powerhouse came in several steps. First, it benefited from the rise of a seasoned, politically ambitious leadership. Local 1069's leaders sought to transform both the mill and the city, had little difficulty cultivating active participation from rank and file, and built contracts and procedures that aimed to address the cumulative unfairness of shop-floor life. And when it came time to stand up for its new demands, it did so firmly. It won a major six-week strike in 1977, followed by another in 1983. Above all, its exercise of workplace contractualism through frequent grievances gave it a prime role in the all-important process of allocating lucrative job assignments. This effectively put an end to favoritism. Shop stewards made managers and the company pay dearly for failure to follow seniority rules in allocating work.

Once unionized, the mill signed initial contracts with the new locals. Local 1069 held a huge meeting in the midst of 1969 contract negotiations; it took an overwhelming strike organization vote with more than one thousand in attendance at Westbrook High School.[78] Local 1069 used this significant leverage to gain a strong first contract. The first contract brought wage increases, a cooperative effort led by Karl Dornish on management's side to address illegal wage discrimination against women workers, and a modernized benefit system. Local 1069 also worked to get many of the sixty-six laid off women reinstated the following year.

In 1970, Local 1069 of the Papermakers elected new leadership, with firebrand Marv Ewing becoming president.[79] Ewing was a New Jersey transplant. Prior to coming to Maine in 1966, he had been groomed as a union militant organizer and union leader, first as a teamster and then at a New Jersey paper mill in his late twenties, helping to lead a strike at a mill there. Marriage to a young woman from Westbrook brought him to S. D. Warren in the mid-1960s. His consigliore was Arthur Gordon, who took various positions on the local's executive committee. Gordon was a small, bird-like man with an air of intellectuality and a modest manner that belied his penchant for starting strip clubs in a rough neighborhood in nearby Portland.

Gordon was the key behind-the-scenes strategist for 1069. He envisioned Local 1069, which would become one of the state's largest locals with nearly two thousand members, as a political powerhouse in waiting. He first engineered a union takeover of Westbrook's political offices in 1968 and 1970, first being elected a city counselor and then to the Maine state senate. A piece of Warren's historic paternalism was that mill management kept the small city of Westbrook Republican and effectively ran its own machine by placing senior managers in positions from city council up through state legislators and the all-powerful governor's council. Gordon recruited candidates from the union to run as Democrats, and he engineered voter registration efforts. Democratic Party registration indeed jumped significantly after unionization, growing from 34 percent of Westbrook registered voters in 1960 to over 54 percent in 1976.[80] Crucially, Gordon's efforts quickly overturned the long pattern of senior mill managers in offices and Republican dominance of voter rolls. He later cofounded the Maine Labor Group on Health, a statewide advocacy group organizing for workers injured on the job. He became, for a time, an influential state senator—a status of such little import to him that the author only found this out from other sources.

Gordon promoted Ewing from the get-go. He first supported his candidacy to head Local 1069. Later, he talked Ewing into running for the AFL-CIO Maine state federation vice-presidency, a position Ewing won handily in 1975, holding the position until 1979. Gordon saw Bath Iron Works' International Association of Machinists Local 6 as Local 1069's main rival for power within the state [AFL-CIO] fed. Gordon unsuccessfully attempted to get Ewing elected AFL-CIO Maine state president in 1979.

Perhaps their biggest accomplishment came in the successful 1977 strike. The strike was over the union's proposal to create mill-wide seniority. Previously, with department seniority, layoffs were spread across departments, regardless of the comparative seniority found of the total workforce. With weaker seniority regimes, some workers with only one year of tenure would escape layoffs, while others with ten to twenty years were laid off. The problems stemming from department seniority were driven home by major layoffs during the 1973–75 recession. The 1977 strike lasted for six weeks, with enthusiastic picket line participation. Scott gave in, and mill seniority was established. The new contract also significantly improved the terms of health insurance, finally reducing enormous copayments. Local 1069 struck two negotiating rounds later, when Scott asked for concessions on health care costs. The strike was unexpected, as a corporate level Scott negotiator insulted 1069's leader, which Reiche found embarrassing. Lasting only a few days, the strike reinforced the local's tough style and proved it could take and win confrontations.

Ewing left the mill when prolabor Democrat Joe Brennan was elected in 1978. Brennan oversaw a great move of union officials into state government office, and Ewing became director of the Bureau of Labor Standards, eventually heading the Unemployment Insurance Commission. While Local 1069 president, he, Gordon, and others groomed a younger generation of leadership schooled in an aggressive and manly defense of the contract. This was reflected in how Local 1069 approached negotiations; Local 1069's leaders routinely choreographed negotiating room dramatics. These included verbal outbursts and table pounding intended to express the importance to the local of a particular demand or issue. Management brought a diverse group to bargaining procedures. Mill manager Reiche could be tough on issues, but he was a conciliator and union leaders trusted him. Scott, however brought in "union-haters" who were disrespectful toward Local 1069 and the mill's maintenance union leaders.[81]

Senior production managers were a bit bewildered by union leaders' emotion and theatrics. Trained in engineering, they approached matters by being rational and impersonal, in contrast to Local 1069 leaders' more personal and emotional style:

> You'd have some very stone-faced looking managers sitting across from some folks that—had a lot of emotion on their face. [They] were used to dealing with each other on a one-on-one basis like that, on a very personal [level]. . . . We don't really do that as managers. It's [a] very objective . . . fairly unattached way of dealing with work, [with] a lot of [management] people coming out of engineering backgrounds.[82]

Between 1967 and the 1980s, Local 1069 had come to emulate similar large paper worker locals around the state. It attracted hard-nosed leadership, increasingly independent of international union bureaucrats who often sought avoid conflict and strikes and cut deals above the heads of local leaders. Statewide, the UPIU was led by two strong officials in George Lamberson and Gary Cook, who acted as a buffer between Maine paper workers and the international leadership—identifying with local unions against UPIU's national leadership and supporting the growing militancy of UPIU unions in Maine.[83]

Meanwhile, overturning the legacy of favoritism took on a life of its own. An asymmetry emerged. Union officials, particular the local shop stewards who were the first involved in these matters, were aggressive, often zealous, in defense of the contract's rules about job allocation. Pursuit of extras was especially important. A former manager observed:

> Discipline was always grieved. Pay issues, overtime pay, who has got the right extra. Filling extras is a big bone of contention—in fact most of the grievances were related to filling extras. They had a very complex, convoluted system, with many pages of details of how you do it, don't do it.[84]

Frontline managers would make mistakes in allocating extras, and would then lose in grievances. To them, it was infuriating. One factor in this circumstance was the proliferation of memorandums of agreement specifying job allocation rules and exceptions to these rules. Managers overseeing specific machines or products, unchecked by human resource managers, had great autonomy in signing these agreements, which were often later added into the mill-wide contract. "The more complex the contract is, the more pages it has, the more opportunity to find out where you're wrong." Another manager summed up the resulting frustration:

> [There were] people who would spend all their free time, which they had lots of, trying to think of a way of getting money by analyzing the contract and see where management was going wrong. . . . And I think for some folks, it was a kind of a game. Because we had an enormous number of grievances and they were focused on getting people more money. Free money, for doing nothing.[85]

Undoubtedly, there was a competitive aspect to it. The manly bearing of the shop-floor worker, elected as steward to stand up to bosses on workers' behalf, fueled litigiousness. The typical and frequent outcome would be the company paying twice for an extra—once for the worker chosen ad hoc and the eight hours' pay who went to the worker who was *supposed* to get the extra if procedure had been followed. While this "money for no work" phenomenon infuriated the direct managers, mill manager Reiche saw it as small potatoes that didn't undermine the mills' profitability: "No. It was the old something for nothing—it made all the supervisors mad, because somebody was getting something for nothing. But in terms of dollars, it was a drop in the bucket."[86]

Conclusion

Warren's newly unionized workforce after 1967 practiced job control unionism with vigor. Constant litigation of contract protections became central to the daily life of the union. Across Maine, workers struck often and could count many improvements in their contracts and pay as a result. Worker pride in knowing how to make the world's best paper now extended to being zealous guardians of shop-floor rights. Moreover, as a democratic institution, a wide array of workers came forward to staff the unions' lower levels, where building the contract and defending its use was a serious business. As we'll see, Warren was not unique.[85]

MADAWASKA REBELLION

Four years after S. D. Warren unionized, workers at Fraser Paper Company, some 350 miles to the north, struck. Local French-speaking Acadians revolted against an English management regime that for three years had forced speed-up, reneged on employment promises, and denigrated both union leaders and shop-floor workers. Workers, their families, and community members fought back, using civil disobedience that spiraled into a violent confrontation with mill leaders and state and local police.

The same growing pressures that faced Warren impacted Fraser Paper, and disrupted mill relations. Like Warren, Fraser was initially run by a tightknit group comprised of the founders and their sons, along with a stable cadre of professional executives who joined Fraser beginning in 1932. In 1966 and 1967, the company ran into new headwinds—greater competition that ate into its profitability, and it faced two hostile takeover threats.[1] To secure its future, the owners brought in hard-charging John "Pete" Heuer, formerly an executive at Great Northern Paper (GNP), and gambled on a huge capital expansion in hopes of leapfrogging its competition and restoring sufficient profitability to keep the company independent. Upon being introduced in April 1968 to shareholders as the new president and chief executive office, Heuer declared: "I know Fraser has problems and decisions to make, and they will be made. We will work out our problems ourselves, and not by the merger."[2]

Heuer cut a powerful figure. Physically, he towered over others, chain-smoking nonfilter cigarettes while projecting great certainty in his master plan to revive the company.[3] Within weeks, he cleaned house, appointing a new senior mill management comprised mostly of outsiders, many who had worked with him at GNP.[4] Heuer and his new group of managers, led by production head Martin Roach, introduced a harsh management approach and were quick to battle with the mill's unions. They first extracted major pay concessions in 1968. The mill's unions agreed to major pay concessions in exchange for the promise of a huge increase in hiring to staff the larger facilities.[5] Workers would soon find out, however, that Heuer and Roach aimed to get the existing workforce to do more work each shift rather than hire new workers. Heuer's gambit to increase productivity without hiring new workers meant speed-up, accomplished by heavy application of time-work studies. The omnipresent man in a white suit with a stopwatch and a clipboard symbolized new shop-floor oppression, and a direct violation of the unions' contracts.

Workers' militant response was shaped through two lenses—the norms of workplace contractualism and a remarkable local Francophone (French speaking) culture. Madawaska is part of the Upper St. John Valley, on a river forming the border of northernmost Maine and New Brunswick, Canada. Locals were bilingual Acadian and Quebecois descendants. On the U.S. side (a separate pulp mill was located across the river in Edmundston), the location of the 1971 strike, workers and their families had faced decades of oppression of their language and culture. This carried over to the mill, with its English-French divide between Fraser's managers and workers. When Heuer arrived, workers readily framed conflict as resistance to the English. Acadians' communal culture gave impetus to a powerful solidarity—a fight for French Power, if you will—that fueled an audacious uprising.

Historical Antecedents: The Mill and Its Unions

Fraser's paper mill is located on the banks of the Saint John River in Madawaska, Maine's northernmost town. The Upper St. John River Valley straddles the Canadian border for some seventy miles, home to roughly 50,000 people.[6] The valley, in local vernacular, is a geographically and culturally distinct region: a cross-border society composed of Franco-American and French-speaking Canadians. Madawaska forms the valley's midpoint. The valley is also at Maine's northernmost border. Madawaska's population peaked at about 5,000 at the time of the strike, and has ebbed only slightly since.[7] Fraser hired workers from both sides of border and river.

Fraser's constructed its works between 1917 and 1925. From its inception, it has been the Saint John Valley's largest employer. For most of its history, Fraser employed as many as 1,100 each in the Madawaska paper mill and its pulp mill across the river in Edmundston, New Brunswick. The mill's location was in many ways ideal. Fraser's lumber holdings already relied on Madawaska-Edmundston as a headquarters.[8] An unusual feature of the mill was location of the pulp mill in Canada, where pulp has been pumped ever since 1925 through huge conduits across the Saint John River to the Maine paper production complex. It could thus export pulp duty-free to its Maine mill that, combined with the weak Canadian dollar, gave Fraser a huge competitive advantage over U.S.-based mills in U.S. markets; the dollar differential often amounted to a 40 percent discount on pulp costs.[9] The Madawaska paper mill could then produce and ship high-quality specialty papers by rail to Northeastern U.S. printing and publishing markets with the benefit this enormous cost advantage.

In its earliest years, the company secured lucrative, long-term contracts to supply catalog paper first to Sears, Roebuck and Company and then Western Electric.[10] Focusing on high-end specialty papers and eschewing the commodity newsprint business shielded Fraser from devastating Canadian competition in newsprint that plagued the U.S. industry after 1910. Like many Maine mills, Fraser was highly profitable when the economy was strong, and had a well-earned a reputation for being technologically progressive, aggressive in its capital investments, and well managed.[11] Also, unlike some Maine paper mills, such as those owned by Scott Paper and International Paper Companies, Fraser had only one production site—making Madawaska the singular focus of its investment in final paper product, a circumstance that made constant upgrading of equipment, technology, and management techniques even more imperative.[12] Fraser's single-mill structure thus both enhanced its Chandlerian orientation *and* also made it more vulnerable to a strike.[13]

Scottish immigrants from the Fraser, Matheson, and Brebner families, and their descendants, originally opened logging camps and sawmills in New Brunswick and eastern Quebec in the late nineteenth century.[14] Subsequently, the founders decided to expand into more lucrative paper manufacturing. These original owners were self-made captains of industry in lumber production, but they were not paper making experts. When founder and first president Donald Fraser Sr. dropped dead in the early 1930s at age sixty-two on a hunting trip, the other owners reorganized top management, bringing in high-powered professional paper executive K. S. MacLachlan to run the company.[15] Here, as at S. D. Warren, GNP, and Oxford Paper, founding owners turned to industry professionals, with backgrounds in paper engineering or other aspects of the business, to manage facilities and sales forces and to set investment strategy. In the ensuing years, they progressively brought on more and more paper industry insiders with paper engineering and marketing backgrounds. The founding families remained prominent after 1932, but these new insiders took over the combined role of company president and mill manager.[16]

This structure of close ownership and a stable management regime persisted until the 1960s. By then, the company faced increased competition and takeover threats. This set the stage for the move to bring in Heuer and finance a massive capital expansion.

The International Brotherhood of Pulp, Sulfite, and Paper Mill Workers first organized Fraser in 1938–39.[17] Separate union contracts at both the Edmundston and Madawaska sites brought steady improvement of wages and benefits that typified postwar Maine mills, and there were no strikes at the twin mills a prior to the 1960s. Over time, the one Madawaska local morphed into four, one each for the two parts of the paper mills (paper and calendar), a skilled maintenance local, and an office workers' unit. Contracts featured careful job definitions and lines of progression based on seniority. Bargaining at the Edmundston and Madawaska mills remained entirely separate, and it appears that there was little in the way of coordination between the two.[18]

Fraser's long-term labor relations' ethos had been quite different, framed by the sharp ethnic divide between managers, who were Anglophones from elsewhere in the United States and Canada, and local Acadian/French workers. Rather than a fatherly, "like a family" paternalism, the availability of steady industrial work at far higher wages than other local pursuits anchored employee commitment. The driving motivation of these French Catholic workers was to earn wages sufficient to maintain large families.[19]

Indeed, for Fraser's Catholic workforce, up to and including at the time of the strike, a male worker and his wife having six to twelve children was the norm, and some families had twenty or more.[20] This made the notion of a family wage an exceptionally powerful component of collective bargaining with Fraser.[21] In socially conservative, heavily Catholic Maine mill towns, the idea of good wages was synonymous with the male head of household earning enough wages to support a family. Traditionally, the family wage norm obscured the contributions of women's labor, both in the home and in the workplace; but in the valley, boys and girls were trained to work from a very early age, and hard work by all was respected, regardless of gender. Indeed, some valley women describe their roles in family decision making as first among equals.[22] And, like other Maine paper mills, plenty of local women worked in either the office or finishing department. In the valley, the fight for better wages and *more* employment (for close relatives and neighbors) made the family wage central to both the motivation to strike and to the specifics of how it was conducted.

The Advent of the Big Thrust—Speed-Up and Failed Job Promises

Relations between Heuer's team and local workers soured quickly. The *Maine Sunday Telegram* noted in 1971 that "relations between Fraser and its workers, local sources say, were good up until three years ago when new management took over in the company."[23] A "veteran Fraser worker" quoted in the article stated: "This is a rough, tough new set of bosses. . . . They think they know everything. They don't listen to you, and believe me, with their attitude they are running the mill right into the ground."[24] Local historian Nicole Lang, who interviewed many Edmundston workers from that era, recalls: "What they hated about that period, is that they were under the microscope constantly." The "microscope" here was work efficiency studies that were used to justify increased workloads. Lang notes that "the workers really hated it."[25] Lucien Mazzerolle remembered the feeling workers had shortly after Heuer and his team arrived: "There was a feeling amongst the worker[s] that these two individuals . . . were coming from another town, from downstate, [and they] were not here to look after the best interests of the people."[26]

Heuer and Roach aimed to transform the mill. This transformation included new investment and a work reorganization program designed to transform the Fraser mill's product lines and reduce production costs. While competitive pressures on prices were beginning to eat into profits, it was still an era where sellers dictated prices to buyers, and competition was mostly over quality and ability to deliver.[27] Thus, adding more efficient and larger machines was the key to warding off competition. Early in 1969, Heuer rolled out its new capital drive called the Big Thrust to great local fanfare (and no apparent irony).[28] The Big Thrust came amid several corporate takeover attempts in the late 1960s; ownership sought to rebuff these challenges from a position of strength.[29]

Heuer's first move in 1968 was to exact a quid pro quo with the mill's unions. He gained two tough concessions: a three-year wage freeze, and regular Sunday production for the first time. It would be hard to say which concession was most resented, though the issue of Sunday work had long been a fundamental bone of contention for paper workers across the United States and Canada. This was especially true among Fraser's singularly Catholic workforce, which had successfully resisted the advent of Sunday work for decades with the backing of local priests.[30] From the company perspective, the economics were obvious—idling a huge capital plant weekly was very costly and ate into profits. For the workers, the sacrifices required to do shift work, with little rest between rotating weekly across the three shifts, were already great; retaining their religious Sabbath was a dear matter. Nonetheless, Heuer pushed successfully for these concessions, promising in exchange significant new employment as new machines were added, to the tune of four hundred to five hundred more jobs—nearly a 50 percent employment increase. In the unions' reckoning, this was an acceptable quid pro quo.[31] Nonetheless, Sunday work and the wage freeze were bitter pills.

Heuer's management regime quickly took shape with speed-up the order of the day. This precipitated a battle perennial in the history of factories: company efforts to lower costs by having the same workforce do more—workers recognize speed-up as an enemy to resist.[32] The motivation to resist is obvious: speed-up is physically exhausting, causes more injuries, and effectively cuts workers' wages and employment. This conflict has prompted strikes throughout the history of modern capitalism, and it did here in Madawaska.[33]

The problems workers had with Heuer were not just about speed-up. Workers took concessions expecting hundreds of new jobs—more paychecks to feed large families. It quickly became clear as new machines were added in 1969 and 1970 that the new jobs Heuer promised were nowhere to be seen. It was all quid, and no quo. A crisis of legitimation ensued, leading to rowdier and more disruptive protest. For these reasons, once the Big Thrust materialized, workers rejected it.[34]

The $60 million machine-building campaign commenced in 1969 and took two years. During that time, one new major paper machine was installed while two other machines were extensively rebuilt. The all-important boiler plant was rebuilt to effect a shift from coal to oil fuel, and the rest of the mill's equipment underwent a thorough rebuild, notable for adding the first computer-quality controls and monitors on older machines. Buildings were added, the company's two other Canadian pulp mills were similarly upgraded, and the company also financed a shift from river drives to trucking to deliver pulpwood to the mill.[35]

As Fraser installed new machinery, staffing and work issues became obvious. Armed with stopwatches, Heuer's underlings led by Marty Roach defined new jobs so the least-sized group of workers would handle the increased workload. When necessary, the company added hours, not new hires. Camille Bernier recalls workers assigned to get the new machines up and running required to put in seventy to eighty hours a week, as the company didn't want to incur the increased benefit costs associated with hiring new workers. Bernier went on to note that many of his fellow workers voted in the 1971 strike to have a break from the grueling hours. He noted, "Some of these guys were working seventy-five to eighty hours a week, and they were burnt. I had one old guy tell me that 'the reason I am going on strike is that I need a rest.'"[36]

Workers began to speak of the morale problem, asking their union leaders to demand that Fraser to make good on failed promises. Company managers rebuffed the unions at every turn. As a result, workers shut down the mill in an illegal wildcat in 1970, and they subsequently girded for a possible strike in 1971 when the contract ran out—at which point conducting a strike would be legal. As the confrontation grew, younger rank-and-file workers were especially willing to take extraordinary measures to resist. By the time of the 1971 negotiations, workers were bitter, organized, and interpreted the threat to their union's protections and their families' living standard as existential.[37]

Heuer and Roach then upped the ante. The failure to create new jobs as promised was a violation of manning letters—specific agreements in the 1968 contract that defined the relationship between new required work and work assignments. In spring 1971, as negotiations for a new contract were underway, Heuer then went a step further, demanding that manning letters be ditched completely. They were to be replaced in the proposed new contract by a management letter that gave production managers the right to assign work and workers as they saw fit.[38]

The management letter demand was, perhaps, a final straw. Or, perhaps not. The entire regime had already come to be seen as an imperialist invasion. The Big Thrust was not just an attack by aggressive bosses. These bosses were English, and the oppression of the French by the English was interpreted as the latest in a long history of cultural and political subjugation. Reaction to this subjugation was thus mediated by Acadian solidarity. Fighting back against betrayals of promises made in 1968 meant establishing a level of respect for French power from the outside world.[39]

The Acadians of the St. John Valley: French Identity and Conflict with the English

Scots-Irish, English, Yankees, and Swedes are considered by Maine Acadians to be collectively English. . . . Disdain for these neighboring groups arose during the long period of their political and economic domination over Maine Acadians and is sustained by the continuing prejudice encountered by the French outside the valley.[40]

The valley is known for its Acadian heritage and close ties between the French-speaking communities on both sides of the border. Heritage and memory are strong features of the area's culture to this day, and pride in the accomplishments and the distinctiveness of the area's Francophone identity frames memories of the past.

French Acadians initially settled the valley in 1785. British forces violently expelled Acadian French from what became Nova Scotia in 1755, an event remembered as the Debacle or *le grand derangement*.[41] Descendants of that diaspora in New Brunswick, as locals recall it, were further chased by the Canadian British; some eighty-five Acadian families, seeking a promised land, settled in the valley a generation later. These original Acadians commingled with other French Canadian strains over the next century, and the move of the original Acadians immigrants was not directly from Nova Scotia.[42] Nonetheless, locals think of themselves as being part of the Acadian diaspora forced on their ancestors by hostile British oppressors. This identity is nested in a set of collective memories that has come to define the region's self-understanding.[43] Acadians on the American side of the border identify themselves as part of the cross-border French-speaking community. Since the imposition of the United States-Canadian border in 1842, easy movement across the border for visits and shopping, cross-border jobs, intermarriage, and families that hail that from both sides of the border, has together kept valley Acadians closely integrated.[44]

The history of the American Saint John Valley Acadians took on a distinct twist when Maine authorities passed a 1919 law forbidding the use of non-English languages in school instruction. This law was generated by the activist xenophobia of Maine's strong Ku Klux Klan movement. The presence of large Franco-American populations in New England mills towns stoked anti-French activism; the persistence of French language up to the time of the Klan and the xenophobia that swept the United States after World War I made Franco-Americans a singular target in Maine and other New England states.[45] As portrayed in the documentary *Réveil: Wake Up French*, 1919 and the years shortly thereafter were marked by "the rise of the KKK, their campaign of terror against the French, and its psychological effect on the French community resulting in invisibility and language loss."[46]

Thus, the history of language on the U.S. side of the valley is a sore spot and at the center of the sense of contention and grievance between the English and the French. The 1919 law prohibited speaking French at school, even in the playground:

> Teachers, often themselves native French speakers, were required to punish children who spoke French at school. [Local historian] Guy Dubay reports that he was made to stay after school and write hundreds of lines of "I will not speak French at school." In high school, students who spoke the Valley variety of French were ridiculed by teachers of "standard" French because of their accents, choice of words, or syntax.[47]

Valley residents frequently bring up a personal version of this story.[48] This signifier serves as a marker of English oppression at the heart of community-wide discussions of the past.

Despite this quasicolonial imposition of English language, locals continued to use French as their primary daily language, not only through the time of the strike but also into the twenty-first century. The twentieth and twenty-first century American Acadians are fluently bilingual, and continued use of French is a source of pride and identity. Valley Acadians also see themselves as a separate local culture from the Franco-Americans of the rest of New England. In short, memories of brutal eviction by the British and Maine's forceful imposition of English language instruction defined the valley Acadian as subjects of a persistent English cultural imperialism.[49]

Maine Acadians have a strong communitarian streak. Tightknit closeness and putting community first was typical of U.S. immigrant communities of a century ago, but white American culture since World War II has become both more homogenous and individualistic.[50] Maine Acadians draw on a communally oriented Catholicism and a deep orientation toward family, hard work, and hospitality to neighbors and outsiders. To folklorist Lise Pelletier, valley Acadians are French Catholics who "preach the good of all before self," where it is "better to work for the community" than for one's self.[51]

Strong family identity is also key. "'Home and family is everything,' say many [valley] Acadians."[52] Family remains the primary source of personal and cultural identity. Sense of family is reinforced by the predominance of about a dozen family names—a glance at the local phonebook reveals a hundred or more entries associated with a particular surname. In an apt joke, union and Democratic Party activist Paul Cyr quipped "there are more Cyrs here than there are people."[53] As noted by *Acadian Culture in Maine*:

> A relatively small number of family names are shared by a great many . . . Interest in genealogy is widespread, and the practice of producing commemorative volumes featuring old photographs, documents, and oral history is popular among families, as well as community institutions.[54]

Maine Acadians' communal, participatory culture was further embedded through union membership and Democratic Party identification. Workers viewed their unions as a voice for workers at the mill, and they equally valued their local Democratic Party as a political voice in a traditionally Republican state.[55] Support for and identification with union and Democratic Party membership separated Fraser's Acadian workers from Yankee loggers and farmers who predominate the rest of Aroostook's population, who were distinctly Republican, individualistic, and antiunion.[56]

Paul Cyr recalls the importance and pride associated with union membership and the high degree of participation of the rank and file in union affairs through attendance at monthly meetings:

> Yes, it was a very big thing at that time, people were very proud of the fact that they were in a union. It's a small community . . . so I think that was part of the glue that held that together . . . [The union was] very strong . . . very many people involved in the union meetings—[there was] strong support from the membership at union meetings. . . . I remember we used to meet in the basement of the elementary school many times—it's a huge basement—and it was packed.[57]

Jerry Cyr (no relation) declared:

> Being a union member was at one time a respectable job. You went into the mill [and] you were expected to join union. It carried a lot of weight, you could use it if you needed it, and they protected you in case people tried to bump you in case of favoritism. It was a good thing to join at the time.[58]

Valley residents, and especially Fraser workers, were also part of a vibrant local Democratic Party. Paul Cyr recalls the high degree of energy around building the party and using the region's voting impact to help the state's labor movement leverage voting power to press state reform on workers' issues like improvements in workers' and unemployment compensation.[59] The net impact of this organizing, further stoked by the outcome of the 1971 struggle, was an impressive jump in Democratic Party membership; the percentage of registered democrats in Madawaska grew sharply from 61.5 percent to 84.2 percent between 1960 and 1976.[60]

Finally, another important source of the Democrats' appeal was toleration of ethnic difference—most closely linked in Maine specifically to acceptance of Franco-Americans.[61] This was especially true in Aroostook County, where Republicans were closely identified with Yankee oppressors.

Seeing the New Management Regime as English

From its founding, Fraser managers were Canadian English who were not from the valley.[62] Language was a prime barrier; the mills' and company's business at the senior management level was conducted in English, fully excluding workers from Edmundston and, to a lesser extent, Madawaska, from becoming managers. Regardless of language ability, Fraser's managers did not see local workers as candidates for middle or senior management. According to historian Nicole Lang, Aubrey Crabtree, who headed the mill from 1941 to 1962, "kept on saying—as long as he was president, no Francophone would have a top job in that company."[63] Former Fraser worker Ron Albert recalls: "Every time they wanted a foreman, they hired somebody on the outside—English. They would never hire . . . local personnel."[64] For a company that was headquartered in Toronto, such a practice was not surprising, and it followed a pattern found throughout Quebec and New Brunswick paper and logging mills. Prior to the 1960s, Fraser workers also often lacked the requisite degree of education, as many left school by eighth grade. As Lang notes: "Every time they wanted a foreman, they hired somebody on the outside—[managers who were] English. They would never hire . . . local personnel. They had to be English; if you spoke French, they wanted no part of you." Lang recalls that growing up in Edmundston in the 1960s, Acadian locals had little interaction with the families of English managers, who had their own section of town, a separate golf course, and who left the area permanently after their stints were complete. It bears note that mill managers elsewhere in Maine settled in among their fellow Americans, retiring in the mill's area, often with a grand house on a company-owned lake.[65]

Perceptions of these managers were squarely framed in terms of Acadian Fraser workers' shared memory English oppression. What is noteworthy is not the fact that the valley's Acadians recall both the harsh Heuer regime and that the regime's harshness was bound up with their Englishness. It is how they put their memories together.[66] The strike, as we'll explore below, is remembered as both a moment of standing up to the English and at the same time a shocking and, to some, traumatic, moment for the community. As Heuer and his new managers bore down on Fraser's workers, the Acadian workers erupted.

The 1970 Wildcat

Tensions boiled over in a weeklong wildcat—an illegal strike.[67] The wildcat prefigured the 1971 strike in several ways. Workers and their union leaders were fed up by the unending management efforts to impose new arrangements that violated both the union contract and traditional practices. The strike was specifically triggered by a change in the boiler house's technology that left fewer workers doing more work. The walkout began with twelve steam plant workers, and it quickly metastasized into a mill-wide strike; Pulp and Sulfite Local 365, which represented the boiler workers who conducted the initial walkout, set up a picket line. Workers in other parts of the mill, and temporary unionized contract workers building new paper machines, honored the picket.[68] Foreshadowing the 1971 strike, workers made violent efforts to turn away managers trying to enter the mill, while the mill tried to restart production by using managers. Public statements by the company and Local 365 made clear the sizeable gap in sentiment and outlook that also characterized the 1971 strike.[69]

The walkout began early on Saturday night, September 26, 1970. Union leaders told the press that week that "the walk off was due to the loss of jobs and increased work load in the steam plant that led to the steam plant crew requesting wage adjustment to compensate for these changes."[70] The increased workload came about when the mill converted from coal to modern oil boilers. Workers walked off when ongoing talks between Fraser and Local 365—the company was refusing to budge on the union's demand of wage increases for the boiler room workers—hit a wall that Saturday afternoon. Twelve workers, including Lucien Mazzerolle and Ron Chasse, proceeded to shut the boilers down. Mazzerolle and Chasse recall proudly being labeled "the dirty dozen" by the company.[71] The company fired the twelve; Local 365's leaders then pulled the rest of its workers from the mill and set up picket lines; other mill locals joined the line. The mill halted production for over one week, imposing significant costs on the mill. Boilers are essential to paper production. As Paul Cyr recalls: shut down the boilers, and entire paper mill goes down.[72]

The company sought to keep some workers on the job, preventing them from leaving the mill during the stoppage.[73] Yet, solidarity was high as Local 365 first walked out as a group; maintenance workers were then joined by paper machine workers, and even outside contractors refused to cross the picket line.[74]

Tough behavior on the picket line augured events next year. Picketers used nails to stop management cars crossing the picket line and also defaced the mill manager's car with paint. They stopped management workers' vehicles and sent home workers that managers were trying to smuggle in to restart the boilers. The local also ignored entreaties from the international to end the stoppage.[75]

The local's leaders laid out its account of why the strike happened in a letter to the *Saint John Valley Times*.[76] It centers directly on the 1968 contract's job promises. Local 365 stated that by 1970, not only had one hundred promised new boiler jobs fail to materialize but that an additional seventy-five jobs had also been eliminated through retrenchment enabled by speed-up. The letter also cites the violation of a separate memorandum of agreement between the mill and Local 365 on staffing and the union's complaint that some workers had been compelled to work on July 4 rather than relying on volunteers, which had been the mill's traditional practice. Union efforts to address these concerns had been rebuffed by local managers, and an effort to reach out to the company's Connecticut corporate headquarters had been similarly ignored. The letter concludes by saying, "We want better communication with the company . . . because we feel lack of communications was one of the principal reasons the men went on strike." Union leaders had lost faith in the ability to communicate with Heuer and the mill's other managers, and were looking to appeal to the company's top owners.

In the end, workers returned without full resolution of the issues that sparked the walkout. Union members did stay out until the dirty dozen were rehired, though the fragility of the situation was evident in the fact that an agreement to rehire the twelve fell through several times before the company finally acceded. Part of the agreement was that the twelve workers were furloughed without pay for thirty days; Local 365 replaced their lost salary in an act of solidarity.[77] It was thus clear that Fraser workers were ready to take powerful actions to maintain solidarity and to achieve workers' goals. The lack of resolution set the stage for the more dramatic events of 1971.

The Strike of 1971: Issues and Battle Lines

> Yeah, the strike of 71. Everybody had it in their minds that while the management was pushing, pushing, pushing, and no wage increases, the consensus was that everybody wanted us to work for the same wages, no benefits, no long-term pensions or anything, so we were just being pushed against the wall, so we just walked out.
>
> —Bob Gogan, interview

In 1971, the companies' proposition to junk the manning letters for a management letter was the last straw for Fraser's workers. Adding fuel to the fire, Heuer and Roach fired some twenty Acadian lower-level supervisors, whose loyalties were suspect.[78] Together, failure to deliver on promised new jobs, the firing of local supervisors, and the cumulative anger over speed-up and shop-floor slights—and then the company's insistence that remaining union job protections would be overturned via a new management letter—were joined in a larger narrative: Fraser had run roughshod over workers, betraying the trust and faith workers invested to save the company through huge concessions in the 1968 union contract.[79]

At the ground level, this was experienced as ethnic exploitation, prosecuted by Heuer's team since its 1968 arrival. Ron Albert recalls: "Yeah, with Recor, and Heuer and those people. They were English. [These managers said] 'the less we give those Frenchmen, the more money we make, and they're stupid, they'll do it.' And the word got around."[80] Albert goes on to note: "We all knew in the background that the leadership that we had there, and . . . [they] did not respect French people, they bordered [looking on] us as being slaves." And Phil Dubois:

And what had happened at that time, prior to the strike, the people that had moved in—English people that moved into the mill, I mean. There was a fellow by the name of Marty Roach. Apparently, and pardon my language, he was an asshole, and he fired a lot of management people, and he was very hard on the union, and he basically was a union buster.[81]

In a high-profile, full-page advertisement in the *St. John Valley Times* at the beginning of the strike, striking locals emphasized their experience of betrayal in direct, bold, language; while not explicit, the perception of disrespect for the French by the English outsiders lays just below the surface:

"HOW DOES A COMPANY WHO TREATS ITS PEOPLE LIKE THIS EVEN DARE ASK FOR COOPERATION?

"The *present management* has never heard of human dignity and it does not seem as if they want to learn. . . .

"If the management of Fraser companies wants cooperation from their employees, they should learn to respect them as human beings by giving cooperation themselves. The survival of this company could be made possible."[82]

The Strike: Beginnings, Blocking the Tracks

In early July, the mill's four locals voted to go on strike, and the strike commenced at noon, Friday, July 9, 1971, with the Knights of Columbus hall serving as strike headquarters. The international unions approved twenty-eight dollars per week in strike benefits; workers had saved money, and many got other jobs in farming and construction to tide them through the strike. According to the strike leaders, "Local members are taking to the picket lines and doing duties at strike headquarters with the highest morale."[83] Paul Cyr recalls the pickets as being effective: "And pretty much nothing moved in and out of the mill, except for the management people."[84]

Several weeks after the strike began, the strikers confronted the company three times between August 5 and August 9, 1971. Strikers were well aware that the mill had a produce a substantial stockpile of extra paper prior to the strike. They also knew that managers were at work in the mill packaging this paper for shipment since the strike began on July 9.[85] Incredibly, the company announced on August 5 that it was going to attempt to move that paper, as well as its intentions to forcibly go after strikers who picketed illegally. In a full-page ad in the *St. John Valley Times*, the company asked provocatively: "What Does It Take To Move a

Mountain?—a mountain of paper that is." It goes on: 'Today, Fraser has a mountain of paper waiting to be moved to its customers. Sometime shortly, this paper
will be moved and we hope with the cooperation of the strikers. Our customers
need this paper. We fully intend to keep our customers happy." The company then
threatened that anything other than informational picketing was a violation of
the law and that strikers violating the law would be subject to prosecution, civil
damages, and dismissal from the company.[86]

Participants recall a fierce determination to resist:

> The big contention . . . the big confrontation that came during that strike when
> company attempted on a couple of occasions to move a trainload out of the yard
> at the mill and onto the railroad tracks for shipment to its customers. . . . But
> the unions were well prepared, and they were adamant—there's no paper, no
> paper cars with paper that's leaving the premises, and nothing left.
>
> —Paul Cyr, interview

Strikers prepared to block the tracks and prevent the mill from moving out the
paper. They first confronted the company when it tried to move twenty-seven boxcars of finished paper on August 5, the very day that its advertisement announced
its plan to do so.[87]

Workers took advantage of the mill's reliance on rail to ship paper. Fraser relied on two sets of railroad tracks that connected to the Bangor and Aroostook
Railroad (BAR). Madawaska's location was distant from the U.S. markets served
by the plant. The nearest major U.S. population center—Bangor, Maine—is two
hundred miles away, and there was no convenient highway access to the southern part of the state or beyond the state's borders to major U.S. markets.[88]

Strikers developed a precise plan to ensure that the company could not ship
its paper. It is likely that these plans had been developed prior to the mills' August 5 announcement; workers and union leaders knew the mill had stockpiled a
significant amount of paper, and they were tipped off by friendly managers that
the mill was preparing to ship the paper soon.[89] Workers recall that moving the
paper would likely have cost the workers the strike. Their calculus: with such a
large shipment of paper, the company would certainly be able to hold out for
many more months, positioning it to wear out strikers and thus gain an upper
hand. Bob Gogan recalls: "They could have held us for a long time, by selling the
paper at the warehouses. [So] we got together and so we say that they can't ship
any paper, we've got to stop the train from shipping any paper."[90]

On August 5 and 6, Fraser had the BAR bring in engines staffed by railroad
managers (unionized rail workers would not have crossed the picketline) and then
attempted to move the twenty-seven cars filled with paper.[91] Good-sized crowds

of strikers—estimated to be in the hundreds—confronted and turned back the trains. Strikers physically blocked the tracts, faced down armed company security, and put pulpwood on the tracks to ensure the trains had no possibility of moving out. They also ignored threats by police and the town manager to stop their illegal behavior. On August 6, the *Portland Press Herald* noted that:

> Large crowds started milling around the mill's siding gate early. The engine again arrived from Fort Kent, coupled on the freight cars and started moving toward the security gate. Police, using bullhorns, urged the crowd to disperse, but to no avail. They were warned that they were subject to arrest on charges of trespassing but the answer was loud catcalls and boos. No attempt was made to move the freight cars beyond the gate.[92]

Local police then decided to nix efforts to move the train. On August 6, following these confrontations, the call went out to the state police—whose numbers were augmented by local sheriffs' officers.[93]

Madawaska's Birmingham Moment

The arrival of state troopers marked an escalation in the battle. Strikers were ready. They had devised an elaborate plan to step up nonviolent civil disobedience in order to confront the company and armed state troopers.[94] Workers planned to bring their families—"men, women, and children"—to the confrontation. The tactic: have children actually lay on the track with their mothers. The strategy echoed the historic events in 1963 in Birmingham, Alabama, at the height of the civil rights movement, when young African American children faced Bull Connor's and the Birmingham, Alabama, police's fire hoses and police dogs. Under the leadership of the Southern Christian Leadership Council, participants in Birmingham were, however, far more disciplined in their commitment to nonviolence.[95] The Madawaska effort initially featured aggressive but nonviolent civil disobedience. But events there ultimately followed a quite different script than Birmingham. First, the strike had a familial aspect, emphasizing the presence of all members in the act of disobedience as a unit, understood as a defense of the family wage. Secondly, strikers were quick to abandon passive resistance for confrontation, resisting violent police efforts to remove them with even greater aggression. Finally, confrontation came within a hair of even more serious violence. According to many participants, strikers were willing *and* prepared to go even further to use violent means to prevent the trains from moving. Recalled Ron Albert and Paul Cyr:

If the train got through one side or the other end, they were pulling out the rails. And a little further down, if the rails didn't come off, there was dynamite to blow them off the rails. But we never had to do that, never.

—Ron Albert, interview

It could have been a lot worse than it was. Even if the railroad locomotives had left the company, with the boxcars, they would not have made it out of the town. There was [sic] allegedly explosives planted; it could have been really, really bad. I don't have first-hand knowledge, but I have good second-hand knowledge. There were guns involved on both sides. I know there were police sharp shooters on the roof of the mill. So, it wasn't pretty, and it was really serious.

—Paul Cyr, interview

As Ron Albert's and Paul Cyr's observations convey, the strikers' plans to stop the train were extensive and precise, showing a willingness to escalate as far as was needed to prevent the loaded train from leaving Madawaska. It is likely that these plans had been developed prior to the mills' August 5 announcement; as noted, workers and union leaders knew the mill had a significant amount of paper and that mill managers had been packaging paper to ship it. Had the paper been successfully moved, the Fraser workers' struggle would be cast over a precipice.

In the early morning hours of Monday, August 9, young male strikers acted to prevent any efforts to move the train out in the middle of the night. A young Bob Gogan recalled: "[at] like three o'clock in the morning, we took some rails out and they had to have a crew put the rails back in so that the train could pass, and bought us some time."[96]

The plan to pull up rails, as well as other aspects of their plan to block the trains, were developed separate from union leadership in order to allow elected union officials plausible deniability for the illegal actions to follow.[97] Camille Bernier, president of Local 247 at the time of the strike, when asked what he remembers about the militant actions that began on August 5, stated: "Very little, because we were definitely being advised to stay away from the radical stuff, to stay away from there. None of the officers were allowed to go nowhere [near]."[98] According to Paul Cyr: "The union leaders distanced themselves from that kind of activity. And, I think that was both a smart move and a legal move, because they couldn't be associated in any kind of activities that were borderline, or actually illegal. And a lot of things happened, in retrospect, [that] were probably very illegal."[99]

Pulling out the rails delayed the BAR from being able to move the train until daylight—when workers and their families would be able to make a large show of force on the tracks. Then, the advanced crew that had pulled up rails went to the fire station to pull a fire alarm that could be heard throughout the town.

According to Bob Gogan—"So it ended up that . . . around five, five-thirty. . . . There was light, and when the horn let go, the siren let go, everybody got up and went down to the tracks. . . . It was well planned, we were working together; it was like a big team." Entire families streamed down to what was then the Acadia School, near the train tracks, and once assembled, moved to the tracks and prepared yet again to block the tracks.[100]

At least three hundred, and likely more, strikers and family members gathered initially.[101] Even at the low end, the size of the crowd sitting on narrow train tracks—many times that of the forty police and sheriff's deputies—meant that the police could not overwhelm the strikers physically, short of acts of aggression such as wielding tear gas or weapons.

By the time the company tried to move the train, resistance had grown into a spectacle. Women and children sat down (literally) on the tracks to prevent it from moving forward.[102] According to the *Portland Press Herald,* "Women and children—in some cases, accompanied by their pet dogs—were in the forefront of the demonstration."[103] The state police were there, some recall in a wedge, and attempted to move the women and children off the tracks—in vain as the wives and sons and daughters of strikers immediately moved back onto the tracks. Others recall the train moving forward slowly and almost running the women and children over. From there, workers recall a series of events that quickly escalated into a violent confrontation.

As initial efforts to dislodge the protesters failed, state troopers responded by firing teargas into the crowd.[104] This police action provoked the ensuing violence. The strikers, sometimes organized as families, answered the teargas by throwing rocks and other missiles at the police. Bob Gogan recalled someone simply yelled "rocks"—hinting at premeditation once teargassed. Phil Dubois, a teenager at the time, recalls the moment when strikers and their families turned on the troopers: "I could remember a black cloud of rocks, and . . . they could have killed us with the teargas canisters if it would have landed on anybody's head."[105] For good measure, strikers again piled some "ten, twenty chords of four-foot pulpwood" on the tracks.[106]

Strikers chased down the police and, in some cases, beat them. Three troopers were trapped in a police car. A group of men bashed pulpwood through the rear window and then overturned the car with the police trapped inside. One of these police was hospitalized in serious condition. One bit of lore is that strikers stripped an entire uniform off one of the policemen and collected a number of police hats kept as trophies.[107] The final act was to then disable the train engine. Paul Cyr recalls: "When locomotives finally did show up . . . the workers simply climbed up on the locomotive ordered all of the locomotive engineers off and simply destroyed the train, just trashed it."[108] Phil Dubois: "And the rail cars never did move, they never did ship their paper."[109]

This denouement was fortunate for at least one reason: it avoided more consequential violence waiting for the train on the edge of the town. After the rout, a newspaper helicopter caught the end result of the mayhem on a dramatic photo, showing hundreds milling around what had become a battlefield.[110]

The Strike Ends—and Its Fallout

After the confrontation, Fraser abandoned further efforts to move paper out of the mill. Maine's young liberal Democratic governor Kenneth Curtis immediately called off the state troopers. Negotiations resumed on August 10, led by Governor Curtis, who flew up on August 9 to Madawaska to restart negotiations.[111] Curtis's chief aid, Neil Rolde, accompanied Curtis and was present for the deliberations, which took place in a local school. Rolde remembers hot tempers on both sides, and arrogance on the part of the company's negotiators:

> NEIL ROLDE: We met first [with] the workers [who were], if I remember, very fired up, I mean, they were very upset. . . . They were upset about the company trying to move their stuff, trying to freeze them out, and then the violence. I mean, these were very hotheaded people. And they were really—Ken [Curtis] was trying to calm them down. And then on the other side, it was just the same, you know. . . . There was one guy—I can't remember his name—and he was a loudmouth son of a gun, and he was, "you've got to stomp on these people, and you've got to force them to do what we want."
>
> MICHAEL HILLARD: Turning back to the company and its attitude toward the strike—you went there and you actually heard from the company that they wanted you to put down the strike, and use the militia?
>
> NEIL ROLDE: Oh absolutely, yeah, as I remember he [Fraser executive] was saying "you've got to call out the National Guard."[112]

Curtis got negotiations rolling, but they struggled initially.[113] The company still dug in its heels; it offered only three additional cents to the package, while refusing to budge on the issue of the manning letter. The company continued to insist on eliminating the manning letter and substituting the management functions letter.[114] Further confusing matters, President Richard M. Nixon announced his historic ninety-day wage and price controls on August 15, which prohibited union-negotiated wage increases during the ninety-day period.[115] The Nixon administration also asserted that it had the authority to insist that striking workers had to go back to work, but striking workers throughout Maine (including grocery workers in Bangor and paper workers in Waterville as well as the Fraser strikers) ignored this entreaty.[116] When the new contract offer was put in front of workers on August 21st, the four locals rejected it by an overwhelming 591 to 48 margin.[117]

Talks continued into early September. The company finally backed off its drive to get vastly more control over the workplace through the management letter. It agreed to retain manning letters and added two cents to its earlier bump of three cents per hour on the compensation package. In an intriguing development, Local 365—the union that started the wildcat in 1970 came a single vote short of unanimously in rejecting the company's first offer initially refused to go back to work.[118] The St. John Valley Times said that "the union wanted to continue the strike on its own, but because the other unions had accepted the contract it became effective and continuing to strike would be illegal. One union spokesman said that, in protest, no member of No. 365 signed the contract, but that it was one of the international representatives who signed it for them."[119]

While the overall increase in compensation was ultimately 96.5 cents per hour by the contract's end in 1974, workers recalled that they returned for a nickel. From newspaper accounts, it is evident that Fraser only raised its initial offer by five cents an hour.[120] The unions did win the crucial point that manning letters would be retained, thus rebuffing the company's proposal for a carte blanche management letter. Given the sentiments that fueled both strikes, this was a major victory in and of itself. In the ensuing years, management also would remind former strikers, particularly union officials—clearly for purposes of intimidation—that it had photographs of workers taken during the August 9 confrontation that could be used to prosecute them.[121] On the whole, while the strike left a bitter taste in many workers' mouths, they evinced pride in standing up to the English regime of Heuer and finding justice in retaining key job protections in their union contracts.[122]

The longer-term fallout was positive for the strikers. Heuer and Roach were let go soon after the strike—Heuer in fact passed away in early 1972. Within a few years, the mill brought on a mill manager in Bill LaFramboise, who is remembered fondly and who reduced the mill's ethnic divide through respectful treatment of the workers and also by opening up far more management jobs to local Acadians.[123]

The strike was also a turning point in that the union locals were able to gain much more at the bargaining table in subsequent contracts, beginning in 1974. Jerry Cyr recalled: "Maybe that was a turning point for Frazier, because . . . after that we started getting better contracts. I mean, when we started saying we were unhappy with the contracts, we were listened to, which was a move forward. A very bad experience, but not a bad result from it."[124] Another worker observed: "The union was very, very strong and we got 5 or 6 contracts in a row that were outstanding and brought Fraser up to par with the rest of the paper industry."[125] At the next round of negotiations in June and July 1974, all four locals turned down an initial contract offer, subsequently winning much higher wage increases than in the 1971 contract, along with substantial vacation pay increases. The new owner, Noranda Mines Limited, conveyed to workers a different, less hostile intent that the Heuer-Roach regime three years earlier.[126] Later management, in a move common to other mills around Maine, promoted a number of union leaders into management—and pursued others—both as a way to weaken the unions but also to improve understanding between management and the union locals.[127] The strike also further boosted the valley's political independence as a Democratic-voting oasis in a heavily Republican region. As noted, Paul Cyr recalls young activists raising voter participation levels in the valley through voter registration drives, and his father became Madawaska's town manager after being fired from his supervisor's position at Fraser.[128] Many of the younger strikers later became union leaders and retained a sense of separation from the union officialdom of the United Paperworkers International Union (UPIU) and its tendency to cut deals with the company.[129] It was just this tension that emerged sharply in the International Paper Strike in 1987–88.

Though not clear at the time of the strike, the events that unfolded in the following years arguably made the strike a material success, adding to the moral victory and vindication of identity that the strike's confrontations represented.

Epilogue: Memory and Meaning after the 1971 Strike

An important feature of memory about the strike is the centrality of women and children and their role in the strike's epic action on August 9. It figures into the story of what was being fought for and who was doing the fighting. Repeated efforts by the author to find an adult woman who participated in the action or deliberations about it were not successful. Participants who were teens at the time remember winding up at the school and then on tracks, and were thrilled when recalling stoning the police.[130] Thus, it remains a mystery as to who hatched the plan to use children and women to participate in blocking trains, especially putting them on the tracks in front of the train, risking life and limb in a confrontation with armed troopers and a determined company.

One plausible explanation of this reticence is fear of prosecution. From the moment of the August 9 confrontation onward, the company made credible threats to prosecute workers and family members for their actions. The company told union leaders and other workers that they had photographs of participants in the August 9 confrontation, and still could take militants to court. Paul Cyr recalled being told: "The statute of limitations still hasn't run out, Paul, and you should remember that."[131] Forty years later, retired workers who had participated in the strike's most aggressive actions were reluctant to identify who actually organized and conceived of the elaborate tactics and the overall plan to win the confrontation on the tracks. In such a tight-knit community, it is evident that a very large swath of the community knew of essentially secret plans to take these actions, and also that planners responded to the two prior confrontations beginning on August 5 with an escalation of tactics. Some recall "people just knew what to do," but it challenges credulity to believe that such elaborate actions were simply spontaneous.[132]

The clearest narrative in remembering the strike is that of the role and meaning of having entire families participate in the civil disobedience on the tracks. There are several possible and complementary interpretations for this emphasis: that the workers' family wage was on the line; workers made sense of the participation of the whole family as part of their family-centric Acadian communal culture; and the fact that contemporaneous accounts in newspapers emphasized the participation of women and children. The shock of the overall confrontation must have entered the community's lore from the time of the strike, and has been digested and reaffirmed ever since.

> MICHAEL HILLARD: State police were armed—did you fear for your safety?
> JERRY CYR: No, I don't think so—I think the idea that your protecting your family more than yourself. And I don't know why you want to put state police up against people—*I mean women and children, that was ridiculous, on the state's part.* [speakers' emphasis]
> MICHAEL HILLARD: What was the thinking on the part of the strikers of bringing out women and children the whole community came?
> JERRY CYR: Yeah, women and children—they were all involved in this. The strike affected the whole family. It was not just a workers' strike, this was the whole family—you're involving in your family here.[133]

There is also little doubt that women played a central role in the strike, both on August 9 and in the decision to conduct the strike in the first place. Locals recall that valley Acadians' families were matriarchal. Former state senator and valley community leader Judy Paradis framed it this way: with a strike placing the well-being of a large family in such jeopardy, and with the monumental economic task of simply feeding so many children, women's voices were undoubtedly central in the decision to strike, and likely the thinking about tactics as well. She put it this way: "the men would not have wildcatted on their wives."[134]

More broadly, the strike represents a chapter in the Saint John Valley's Acadian legend. Historically, the valley's collective memory and identity is a two-edged sword, with great ethnic pride but also and a lingering sense of being viewed, incorrectly, as a lesser people. In this context, their ability to stand up to an offensive by an English oppressor in the form of Fraser's management, and also to state police forces who had "come to teach the French a lesson," is very much embedded in the area's larger historical identity.[135] From its low point in the early to mid-twentieth century when the state of Maine punished locals for speaking French at school, the people of the valley have made a strong and steady climb to reclaim their heritage and establish definitively a proud place in the world. Remembering the strike, and the ingenuity and success of its people in standing up to an English oppressor, has certainly been an ingredient in sharpening the region's mythology and identity.

What distinguishes Madawaska and the valley from other struggles in Maine in this period? The communal solidarity and identity of valley Acadians were, at the time of the 1971 strike, a throwback to an earlier era before 1950.[136] A key aspect of post-World War II corporate strategies was a combination of investment and location strategies and internal labor relations' efforts designed to strike down the connections between unions and workers in order to solve what was, for employers, the plague of strikes and militancy that interfered with management's "right to manage."[137] Not yet the suburbanized factory worker, or the post-melting-pot ethnic integrated into English-speaking, consumption-centered U.S. culture, Madawaska workers and the broader valley Fraser workforce mobilized their Frenchness to resist Fraser.[138] At the same time, as a paper company seeking a transformation to meet the financial demands of a new era, it was new "forces acting upon workers" that precipitated a remarkable example of this era's growing working class rebellion.[139] Unfortunately for Heuer and his team, they picked a fight they couldn't win.

CUTTING OFF THE CANADIANS

The same pressures that sparked the fall of Mother Warren and the Madawaska rebellion were being felt acutely in the woods.[1] For the first time in a generation, sporadic actions by local Maine woodcutters began in the early 1970s and evolved into a movement by 1975. This movement erupted in protest in October 1975, when hundreds of Maine's woodcutters picketed at mills across the state, and many more attended meetings and protested hosted by the newly formed Maine Woodmen's Association (MWA).[2] Labor historian Leon Fink correctly characterizes it as "one of the more exotic examples of the mid-seventies upsurge in labor activism" then sweeping the United States.[3] It was especially exotic because the majority of the protesters were conservative former farmers, mostly of Yankee stock, who had little interest in and no history of unionization; other logging regions in the United States had long histories of labor militancy and unionization.[4] These Mainers saw themselves largely as their employers did: as independent businessmen, hired as contractors with perhaps one or two employees with whom they shared both labor and modest incomes. The MWA pressed paper companies for redress of low and infrequent pay, and the consequent worsening of the pulp peonage that stressed debt-laden small contractors beyond the breaking point. The MWA action grew out of a hothouse atmosphere of wide frustration by Maine citizen loggers, where spontaneous pickets evolved into a gambit to thwart paper production across the state and force the companies to bargain over a host of issues, with barring Canadian guest workers at the top of a long list. The protest effort did disrupt production at some mills and thoroughly grabbed the state's attention as Maine's Governor Longley intervened directly to bring about an end to the attempted strike.[5] For over two weeks, protests, negotiations, and acts of sabotage dominated the headlines of Maine's newspapers. While it had great energy, and brought to surface the deep struggles faced by thousands of Maine Yankee woodcutters, it quickly foundered. The MWA action was encumbered by companies' refusal to negotiate, companies' successful efforts in court to get injunctions restricting pickets, and especially by divisions between protesting Yankees, large contractors with differing circumstances and attitudes who had no interest in joining the protest, and the large workforce of Canadians who were the target of the action. To boot, the United Paperworkers International Union (UPIU) not only didn't support the MWA but viewed it as a threat to paper mill employment. Against these odds, the protest crumbled after two weeks.

Leadership Emerges

If the movement had a singular leader, it was Wayne Birmingham of Patton, Maine, who helped found and then became the president of the upstart MWA. Birmingham was a tall, burly man who grew up in the 1940s and 1950s in the southwest corner of "the county"—that is, the vast expanse that is Aroostook County. The area is a lush center for hunters and hikers, with the majestic mountains of Maine's Baxter State Park in view. Underneath this appealing veneer was the reality of a long economic decline of local agriculture that began in the 1920s.[6] Patton itself, when the author visited for three days in 2004, was largely a collection of white clapboard buildings reminiscent of Depression-era Dorothea Lang photos. It was a typical rural center with a local mix of declining farms, seasonal logging, hunting lodges, and small lumber mills, and was home to woodcutters like Birmingham. Locals honored the region's logging legacy by creating the Patten Lumbermans' Museum in 1963. Town folk were intimate and shared their successes and hardships; families dependent on woods work lived close to the economic margin. Wayne's wife Barbara Birmingham recalled the necessity of going months without income during each mud season—spring's enforced hiatus from logging.[7] Canning sixty quarts of green beans late each summer, in addition to other garden vegetables and fruits, and the previous fall's hunting bounty of venison and bear meat, were essential to getting the Birminghams through the mud season.

The one obvious alternative to grinding out such a marginal existence was lucrative factory work in Connecticut. A steady migration of mid and northern Mainers to high-paying unionized positions began in World War II and continued at least into the 1980s.[8] Claire Bolduc recalled this as a widespread: "There was a hard-core bunch that didn't leave for Connecticut, when everybody else did. So, people in my generation . . . from the valley, from Elliot, went to Connecticut. Sikorsky, Napier Jewelers, Acme Tire, those kinds of places."[9] Jon Falk remembered encountering three woodcutters who had worked as lathe operators on a specific shift at Pratt and Whitney, perhaps the biggest employer of Maine migrants—"That whole plant, I guess, was Maine people." For many, factory life in Connecticut didn't suit them, especially homesick married men who left wives and children behind. Falk again: "They didn't like it. . . . They liked the money, [but] they didn't like anything else about it, really. It wasn't home.[10]

Birmingham and his close friend and workmate Larry Palmer (also from Patton) came of age joining their fathers learning the ropes in the woods. Like many, they quickly joined the exodus of rural Mainers seeking better money in southern New England factories. Birmingham and Palmer toughed out seven years in a unionized Connecticut tire factory before homesickness and a desire to escape their factory's hot drudgery brought them back to Patton in 1974. Carroll Gerow, a friend and neighbor, hired them to cut wood. While leaving behind the fumes, dirt, and stress of a hot tire mill, they did bring something back that was foreign to most of Aroostook—union consciousness. While in Connecticut, they were indelibly impressed by a United Rubber Workers business agent with known communist politics who handled grievances and negotiations at the plant. The agent regularly dressed down factory managers in front of workers, a direct challenge of economic authority that to these Pattonites was as novel as it was thrilling. It was this image of what a union could do that inspired Birmingham, Palmer, and Gerow to begin to organize fellow woodcutter-contractors upon their return.[11]

Birmingham was joined by antiwar and civil rights activists with experience from student unrest at Maine universities, and by out-of-state, leftish "back-to-landers." Among the MWA's leadership were a number of such movement women and men. Jonathan Falk, Peter Hagerty, Claire Bolduc, and Don and Cecile Fontaine joined Birmingham and Palmer in building the woodcutters' movement. Hagerty was an Ivy League educated activist from away (not Maine)—a gifted, politically hard-core civil rights and antiwar activist who counted the Black Panthers among his influences. Falk was a college educated local who, after the strike, got a graduate degree from Yale's forestry school and was a keen analyst of the economic vice paper companies wielded over local contractors, as well as an MWA leader.[12] Don Fontaine, a legal aid attorney employed by Pine Tree Legal was Franco-American, and his wife Cecile and Bolduc were Maine-raised Acadian French from the upper St. John Valley. As we learned in chapter 4, Maine Acadians were likely to be Democrats, pro-union, and economic progressives with a communal ethos; the leap to movement activism was a small one. As a group, these organizer-leaders brought the political sensibility of the national New Left along with strategies and tactics employed in the civil rights and anti-Vietnam War movements.[13]

Under Don Fontaine's direction, his wife Cecile and Claire Bolduc spent several years documenting the terrible conditions, impoverishment, and exploitation of county loggers in the early 1970s. Bolduc heard complaints and frustrations about frequent bouts of unemployment (with no support income), injuries that led directly to poverty because workers' compensation was unavailable, and the persistent struggle to make payment on equipment loans. Many injured or unemployed woodcutters came to Pine Tree Legal—often meeting with Bolduc—when faced with abject hunger because they had nowhere else to turn. Inspired and supported by Bolduc's organizing efforts, these downtrodden woodcutters formed the St. John Valley Woodmen's Association in 1972. This group worked with attorney Fontaine to challenge the companies' illegal refusal to hire citizen loggers for work in favor of Canadian guest workers.[14]

Hagerty was a gifted, politically hard-core civil rights and antiwar activist who counted the Black Panthers among his influences. Falk had been trained at Yale's Forestry School and became a keen analyst.

Finally, Yankee locals Mel Ames and Bill Butler were leaders who more closely represented the experience and sense of independence held by the small contractors and their employees who made up the base of the MWA movement. Ames was a farm owner from Dexter, a small mill town in central Maine, and also a college-educated forester who specialized early on in sustainable harvesting. He identified with his neighbors who were struggling under the weight of pulp peonage.[15] Bill Butler was perhaps one of a kind. A college educated engineer from away, he settled in far Downeast Maine after World War II and found a vocation in logging, joining the ranks of contractors like many others when logging was at its most lucrative in the late 1950s. Butler was an iconoclast who bridled at the plantation sensibility he encountered in company foresters, and, like Ames, increasingly became a critic of unsustainable forestry practices.[16] Butler and Ames would join Birmingham, Bolduc, and the others in helping Maine woodcutters to frame and organize a response to deepening economic distress.

Pulpwood Peonage

We see the price of everything else going up and up—food, clothes for kids, gas for the car. But the price of pulpwood? Well, that just seems to stay the same. Oh, maybe they'll add $1 here or 75 cents there, but if you make your living off the stuff, then that doesn't mean much. It's not right. Our costs have gone way up and the mills know it. We work longer and hard to make the same we did five years ago and then that doesn't go very far.

—Independent contractor, 1974

But I think they [the paper companies] were in a position of tremendous power from the beginning, because they owned everything. It's the only place in the country with this type of ownership. They owned the woods, they owned the mills, they owned the roads.

—Jon Falk, interview

Circumstances faced by small contractors after 1965 precipitated the uprising. It is worthwhile to put this in fuller context of the postwar pulpwood procurement system. As early as 1939, companies no longer wanted citizen loggers on their payroll. At that time, newly implemented New Deal laws, especially social security and unemployment insurance, added direct and substantial payroll costs for companies directly employing woodcutters. Immediately, paper companies ceased hiring locals as waged workers and instead employed them as independent contractors; they later worked successfully in state and federal legislatures to ensure companies were free of any legal liability for loggers if employed as contractors. When they could, companies relied on Canadian guest workers, still employing many as direct employees. For citizen loggers and the companies, new technology—chainsaws, skidders, and hydraulic loaders that put logs onto trucks with ease—combined with steady wood prices offered a strong annual income for a time that lasted into the 1960s (see figure 5.1).[17] For companies, the shift from river drives to trucking, and the use of these new technologies, delivered better quality and lower cost wood to mills throughout the year rather, than just each spring.[18] Productivity grew dramatically, nominal wood prices (the piece rate paid to loggers) held constant, and small contractors could now log up to ten months with the new equipment versus the previous four to five month season. Median income for full time Maine loggers thus doubled from 1950 to 1970, and logger income relative to manufacturing rose from 62 to 76 percent.[19] This drew many Mainers from farming and other pursuits into full-time logging work.

Beneath this average, though, were a great range of circumstances in which some more favored contractors, or those lucky enough to get a great chance, or the most skilled, would make significantly more than this prosperous average. But just as many or more deeply struggled, even when work was steady.[20] Crucially, as contractors and not employees, all of the risk and insecurity fell on their own shoulders. Weather varied dramatically, and woodcutters could be forced to waste many hours digging down to tree bases when snow was especially deep.[21]

The work was dangerous; in a given year, one in eight loggers suffered work-inhibiting injuries that put woodcutters out of work for on average half a year.[22] Loggers died in significant numbers each year, in grisly accidents that included being crushed by trees and bleeding to death from chainsaw accidents.[23] Chainsaw operator's mortality rates were astronomical.[24]

FIGURE 5.1 Chainsaw cutting, which peaked between the 1950s and early 1980s, was one of the most dangerous occupations in U.S. industrial history, with up to twenty Maine woodcutter deaths a year caused by chainsaw kickbacks and falling trees. Pictured here is Leslie Pepper, using a chainsaw to delimb a tree in central Maine, in a recent photo. Safety equipment like Pepper's helmet with visor and ear protection was atypical during the peak years of hand crews using chainsaws. Linda Coan O'Kresik, *Bangor Daily News.*

Equipment difficulties were endemic. Contractors often missed regular workdays to malfunctions and spent most weekend time off working hard to keep equipment repaired. Company foresters could and often did dole out a poor chance—a chance being the plot of woods a company would assign—to the contractor and his crew. It is little surprise that, in 1970, the rate of poverty for full-time loggers was 25 percent, four times the national average.[25] As real earnings began at that point to decline in the late 1960s, the piece rate system effected what scholar David Vail called "the invisible foreman"—a self-imposed pressure to speed up, exacerbating injuries of all types.[26] Having a shot at making a decent living required working sun up to sundown, up to eighty hours a week when sunlight permitted.[27]

These difficult circumstances, and the weak leverage contractors had in negotiating with company foresters, was due in part their exclusion from most labor laws and income security programs. Maine's paper companies waged a successful campaign after World War II to ensure that companies would have no legal obligations to contractors.[28] Led by Great Northern Paper (GNP), lawyers for

Maine's companies trained their efforts on escaping liability for contractors and their employees.[29] In the immediate postwar years, GNP's legal department had a great deal of internal correspondence and also exchanges with state and federal labor regulators over how to draw lines that would relieve companies of obligations to its woodcutters.[30] In 1950, at the behest of Maine paper company lobbyists, Congress passed an amendment to the Fair Labor Standards Act (FLSA) that exempted pulpwood contractors employing fewer than twelve workers exempt from the minimum wage and overtime provisions.[31] In the 1950s, the state also exempted small contractors with four or fewer employees from responsibility for workmen's compensation coverage of their employees; as a result, by 1960, 75 percent of Maine loggers were not covered by workers' compensation.[32] Finally, small woodcutting contractors frequently subcontracted to, rather than formally hired, their cutting crews to ensure all were free of regulation and taxes on labor. Trucking crews also consisted of just one or two drivers and were also separate contractors. Not surprisingly, the percentage of pulpwood cut by employees fell from 75 percent at the end of World War II to less than 20 percent by the late 1960s.[33] Altogether, a key part of the rise of the small contractor in the postwar era was the success large companies had in remaking the workforce into contingent labor almost entirely free of modern labor standards.[34]

Perennial complaints came to the fore in the deteriorating conditions leading up to the protest. In small woodcutters' experiences, facing just two or three local wood procurers meant low wood prices/piece rates; loggers believed companies colluded on prices paid for wood. Carroll Gerow, looking back in 2004 on decades in the woods, paints this picture of his lack of market power, echoed by many his peers:

> MICHAEL: So, were you able to get a good price for your wood?
> CARROLL GEROW: The price? No. The price was normal. And you didn't get as much price as you thought you should have. No!
> MICHAEL: But they pretty much gave you a take-it-or-leave-it" price?
> CARROLL GEROW: Yeah, they always did, they always did. They did that. Because, because, they did a lot of, I guess I could call it today—price-fixing.[35]

Landowner dominance also came in the form of stumpage and scaling. Contractors had to pay coming and going; that is, they were charged a fee per cord to cut wood on lands owned by others—so-called stumpage—as well as covering all of their equipment costs. Stumpage fees were on the rise after the late 1960. And the one steady landowners' representative on a woodcutting site was the infamous scaler. The scaler measured the cut wood that had been skidded to a central yard to be loaded on to trucks and delivered to the mill. Needless to say, underscaling wood (first measured by the inches/length at a log's base, or butt, and then later by weight measure) was a sore spot. Complaints of unfair scaling was long a major frustration for woodcutters, one that dated back generations but still very much a concern in this era.[36]

Companies began to squeeze the contractors in the late 1960s. Piece rates were held nominally constant at seven dollars a cord at a time of high inflation; the consumer price index rose 61 percent from 1967 to 1975.[37] Thus, from the mid-1960s to the time of the protest, woodcutters suffered a 40 percent drop in value of their piece-rate.[38] In addition, companies suspended wood purchases more frequently, as the United States had two recessions between 1969 and 1975.[39] Woodcutters were given contracts to deliver wood at the start of each season, but these contracts could and often were cancelled at the companies' whims.[40]

For many small contractors and their employees/coworkers, these conditions added up to a state of "pulp peonage."[41] To maintain their incomes, they had to purchase larger and more expensive equipment—larger skidders (tractor-like devices that hauled logs out of the woods) and better chain saws—all on credit;[42] woodcutters mainly financed these purchases with loans from local banks. Interest rates were volatile between 1965 and 1975, and more than doubled from 1972 to 1974 to nearly 12 percent.[43]

A small contractor's only route to cope with this financial stress was to speed up: work faster and for longer hours in order to try and cut even more wood per week. With financial exigency rather than a human supervision pushing them to their limit, exhaustion and accidents were inevitable. One estimate put the number of annual deaths while logging in the Maine woods each year at twenty.[44] And the lack of any social safety net meant personal catastrophe. As Bolduc recalls:

> The workers' comp was really not what it was today. Many of these men were not covered by workers' compensation, and ended up on what was then AFDC [family welfare] if they were injured. If they were injured, they were done. They were so history. And their families suffered, because income from welfare was never going to equal a weekly paycheck. As meager as that might be, it was more than welfare.[45]

Frustrations by citizen loggers over the use of Canadian guest workers would become the focus of the MWA struggle. In northern and eastern Maine, the legacy workforce was a combination of local Mainers and nearby Canadians, farmer stock equally skilled from generations of woods work. Whether objective circumstances, or company strategy, or domestic xenophobia, Yankee woodcutters perceived that the companies' extensive hiring of Canadians denied them work and depressed wages.[46]

Canadian loggers' legal status as guest workers gave them no leverage with employers.[47] Already very skilled at woods work, Canadian loggers' employment status meant they could be pushed to their limit.

Each Canadian worker was colloquially called a bond, named for the money a firm would have to put up to guarantee that the guest worker would work only for them, and to ensure the worker's return to Canada at the end of a six-month contract. Officially, this was supposed to be a bulwark against Canadians remaining in the United States illegally and pursuing other jobs.[48] Because Canadian bonds were not allowed to switch employers, they were effectively indentured to their employers. Dating to the nineteenth century, loggers' only way of protesting bad conditions was to vote with their feet—quitting one bad situation (poor pay or food being the key complaints) and searching about a better situation.[49] This classic practice, known as jumping, was foreclosed for Canadian guest workers. These Canadians faced high unemployment in their home provinces, and their equipment (chainsaws and skidders) was subsidized by the Canadian government as well as the provision of national health insurance.[50] As historian William Parenteau describes, they aimed for a set amount of annual income and not a particularly wage rate. David Vail observed that:

> Court testimony shows bonds to have been largely ignorant of their rights. Desperate for work, they tolerated practices which exploited them, and indirectly, Maine loggers. They worked 50 to 60 hour weeks while accepting pay for forty hours. They neglected to file insurance claims for many injuries and accepted the corporations' demands that they supply their own saws and skidders. They also tolerated crowded and unhealthy camp conditions.[51]

For locals, frustration was perhaps deepest over the how chances were allocated—the moniker for the plots of forest where loggers were assigned to cut by company foresters. Larry Palmer describes pointedly the power of this tool: "Ninety-five percent of the difference in output was the quality of the chance, not skill."[52] In both in the 1950s and 1970s protests, Maine woodcutters complained that companies favored Canadians with superior patches of woods. As David Lutes stated boldly to Maine's governor during a spontaneous sit-down strike several months before the fall MWA protest:

> They [the paper companies] hire Americans and put them in mud holes. When Americans quit, it is because they are lazy. They don't want to work in mud holes.
> They're experts in divide and conquer. They pick out a few influential men in the area and give them plumb jobs and contracts. They can

keep the rest quiet. They're fat . . . it's all designed to keep most Americans away. Canadians can work cheaper and under scale and they won't squawk.[53]

A crucial moment came in the early 1950s. In 1952 and 1953, Maine companies led by GNP succeeded in staffing their woodlands only with Canadian bonds, reaching a total of eight thousand guest workers for the state at that time (and had done this once before in 1943), radically reducing employment opportunities for Maine loggers. This pivotal event produced huge protests when Yankee woodcutters found themselves unable to get any woods work for those two years. They marched on the Maine state house in 1954 and 1955, securing a U.S. Senate hearing in the latter year; subsequently, tighter enforcement of restrictions on the use of guest workers dropped their numbers to two thousand to three thousand. This new status quo for the next twenty years represented roughly one-third of the woods labor force.[54]

Memory of displacement was thus seared in local woodcutters' minds. Combined with the issue of favoritism in the allocation of chances, and chronic difficulties some Maine loggers faced in getting woods work, "cutting off the Canadians" became Maine's Yankee contractors' prime aim.[55] For them, eliminating guest workers was a potential panacea: more and steady work, higher piece rates, and better chances.

The MWA Protest

The rumblings began long before 1975. Maine woodcutters boycotted International Paper and Oxford Paper in western Maine in 1970, followed by sporadic protests and sabotage over the use of bonded labor in the northwest Allagash region between 1972 and 1974. In northern Aroostook, Claire Bolduc's organizing led to the formation of the St. John Valley Woodmen's Association.[56] The key was the provision of an organizer. Says Donald Fontaine: "They just needed someone to give them the time, and make some calls, they needed someone to do the legwork. It [the organizing] went very fast."[57] In the summer of 1975 the well-publicized, spontaneous sit-down strike by contractors occurred at a remote Irving camp in protest of two American woodcutters' arrests for trespassing; the passions inspiring this action were captured in David Lutes's unhappy description of their lousy chances. Anger underlying the protest was squared directly at Canadians getting better chances. The wildcat was settled directly by Maine's governor, James Longley, and led to a reinstatement of the loggers.[58]

By early 1975, activists were organizing in each of the state's various regions, and eventually several local organizations merged into the MWA, officially formed in spring 1975. A series of MWA meetings, held primarily in centrally located Bangor—the largest municipality in the heart of Maine's forestlands—attracted growing numbers. In September, political luminaries Senator Edmund Muskie and Representative William Cohen spoke at an MWA meeting, giving the organization instant credibility.[59] In an early October MWA meeting attended by over two hundred, passions boiled over. As one logger after another gave testimony, the talk quickly turned to bringing their protest directly to the mills.

MWA organizer/activist Claire Bolduc describes the mood at that moment:

> And then in October, it was '75, there was a problem with, again, *the Americans objected to the bringing in of bonded labor, when they didn't have work.* And, still, nothing had been done [about it]. And they had spoken to all the candidates . . . politicians and their representatives . . . and nothing had come of it. So there was no regulation of the wood measurement. *Mills were not giving tickets—it was October. That was their winter money, you know.* . . .
>
> And so the MWA said: *"we can't take this, we're going out."* And they decided quite quickly, and it was like this [snaps her finger]—it was overnight. So overnight, the workers stayed out of work.[60]

The MWA had been in existence for only a few months, its official membership having grown from a few dozen to a few hundred. Creating a statewide organization became a vehicle for the discovery of shared grievances. At the same time, there had been virtually no time for the leadership to reconcile ideological differences or build a disciplined organization. Early membership represented perhaps 5 percent of the citizen woods workforce of roughly seven thousand. Accumulated resentments and frustration were evidently very high—Larry Palmer noted that loggers across the state "had the same complaints."[61] But a strategy to maintain solidarity, overcome legal barriers, and develop a shared vision of organization or goals had not yet been developed when the protest began in early October.[62]

MWA leader Peter Hagerty's description of the reasons why Maine loggers joined the protest indicates the mood and outlook that fueled the sudden action:

> For some people, bonded labor was a huge issue. And they felt that this new generation of loggers was being given the raspberry patch, and the French-Canadian cutters were given the best wood. . . . And some people were angry because the technology that was being introduced was out of their reach. They just saw what was coming around the corner that they weren't going to be able to finance and purchase the kind of equipment they needed, and that they saw an era was closing, and they needed

to blame somebody, so they blamed the French-Canadian workers and the bonded labor program. Other people just wanted more money per cord, for their wood.[63]

The protest erupted on Monday, October 6, 1975, as a limited action meant to protest a new law that effectively reduced wood truckers' legal load by four cords, reducing their pay in the piece-rate system.[64] The initial plan, devised at that large Bangor meeting which included both MWA members and woodcutters who had not yet joined, was to focus on stopping wood deliveries at a single mill, St. Regis Paper in Bucksport, Maine. The MWA at the time had also been meeting with Governor James Longley over the Canadian labor issue, and at the beginning of the protest, MWA President Birmingham was still praising Longley's responsiveness on the issue. Dozens of picketers showed up at the Bucksport St. Regis mill that Monday morning, but they were rebuffed by a clever ploy by the company: managers their claimed that a pending National Labor Relations Board (NLRB) action with its own workers prevented it from legally meeting with the MWA. The picketers then decided to travel thirty miles north to the Diamond International plant in Old Town. There, a truck loaded with critical chemicals was stopped when the driver honored the picket line, leading to a shutdown of a mill that otherwise had a very ample reserve of pulpwood on site. Within a day, pickets showed up at a number of paper and lumber mills around the state, including plants in Sherman, East Millinocket, Costigan, and Winslow.[65] As the *Portland Press Herald* noted on October 19: "Association members began their work stoppage in response to a truck weight law they viewed as restrictive. The issue instantly became submerged in the woodsman's string of economic grievances, topped by the basic complaint that low pulpwood prices make it impossible to earn a decent living."[66] In addition to low prices, inconsistent work, and their animosity toward the perceived effects of Canadian guest workers, MWA loggers also complained about the combination of accidents and injuries in the absence of workers' compensation protection, and especially their long-held perspective that companies cheated contractors when weighing their wood for payment.

Following the Old Town/Diamond International incident, regional MWA leaders held mass meetings that typically produced pickets at mills around the state. The Old Town scenario, with slight variations, repeated itself at other mills. For example, a MWA picketer at Scott's Winslow mill cut brake lines on a truck. As the truck was leaving the mill, its brakes locked and its tires caught fire. This event made television news across the state and created a lot of excitement and momentum. Much of this activity moved forward in environment of permissiveness created by sympathetic state police. According to MWA leader Hagerty:

A lot of the brothers and sisters of the state police all worked in the woods, *and they allowed a certain environment to be created. An environment of hope, and belief this could work.* I think if [Governor] Longley had stepped in sooner, and come down harder, and dragged people off to jail [the protest] might have not taken off.[67]

Woodcutters around the state who might otherwise have been hesitant to join the MWA quickly decided that it was better to be part of the action than to be left behind. Says Hagerty: "And then people started thinking—'If I'm not part of the bandwagon, maybe I'm not going to get a piece of the action.' So I think more people got on board then."[68] At S. D. Warren's home Westbrook mill, three chemists honored a picket line; a mill in Costigan shut down when railway workers refused to cross a picket line to deliver chemicals; and the Diamond Old Town facility shut down briefly. Historian William Parenteau summed up the peak of the protest this way:

> By the end of the second week the pulpwood boycott was noticeably affecting the operation of paper mills around the state. St. Regis, for example, was forced to close their chip mill and lay off seventy employees. Other companies such as Scott, Great Northern, and Diamond Int'l remained in production but at significantly lower production rates.[69]

Numerous press reports cited acts of sabotage (for example, the destruction of railroad tracks carrying pulpwood to mills) and threats by members of the MWA protest against contractors still attempting to cut and deliver wood to the mills.[70]

The role of Maine's eccentric one-term independent governor, James Longley, is worthy of brief mention. Longley, who is credited for having little sense of how to govern on many fronts during his one term, simultaneously took the MWA protest as a personal affront worthy of crushing, while personally acting as a mediator between paper companies and the MWA throughout the two-week upheaval.[71] MWA leader Bill Butler recalls:

> But he was very much against us—Longley was Governor—he hated us. And he—[thought we were] 'disorderly on his watch,' I guess, and so they brought the full power of the state into oppose us, and I sat through that [the court proceedings] for several days.[72]

A week into the protest, Longley interrupted a courtroom proceeding in process by a phone call, and asked to speak to Attorney Fontaine. Fontaine's description of the Governor's blunt imperative:

> Hello—is this Fontaine? Is this Fontaine? . . . I'm not blaming you for all of this, but let me get something really clear to you and the people

you are representing there. This strike better end, and end quickly. Right away today. This better end, or I'm going to bring 5,000 Canadians across the border to do this work.[73]

Toward the end of the protest, Longley aggressively sought to shut the action down—telling one gathering of MWA protest to go back work lest he "fill the [Maine] woods with Canadians," but his indecisiveness early in the protest contributed to its initial momentum.[74]

As the protest wore on, the combination of internal disarray, increasingly powerful court injunctions, company and public backlash from reported sabotage efforts, and a fracturing of leadership wore down protesters' efforts. In the wake of the paper companies' decisive, concerted effort to use the courts to stop the pickets and declare the strike illegal, and the Governor's adamant opposition, effectively halted the MWA's action, and 750 MWA activists called an end to their strike action on Sunday, October 19, 1975.[75]

Why the Strike Failed and the Successes Hidden in Failure

A number of factors limited the MWA's effectiveness in waging a strike or in building either permanent organization or a larger solidarity with organized labor in the paper plantation. During the brief fall 1975 upsurge, the widespread sense of shared grievance created a commonality that briefly swelled the MWA's numbers. The extent of participation is hard to establish and a matter of some dispute, but notably around six hundred participated in an MWA march of the state capitol, 750 attended a Bangor meeting to vote to end the strike, and the MWA itself claimed as many as three thousand participated in one way or another, while one protagonist from company side of the dispute contended that the organization and participants in the protest were far fewer.[76] From these numbers, it is likely that one thousand or more may have participated in meetings at one point or another, though perhaps not all who did favored striking.

The MWA's leadership had no time to form a coherent vision or agenda for reform, and its muddled legal standing meant that a demand for collective bargaining was easily thwarted as injunctions were quickly handed down. As historian William Parenteau notes, the MWA leadership neither organized the attempted strike nor exercised effective control over it once it started. "While MWA officials traveled throughout the state attempting to organize the strike, they did so without a clear purpose."[77] Even the leadership of the strike lacked coherence. In the middle of the protest, Governor Longley got President Birmingham alone on a small plane from Augusta (the state capitol) to Millinocket and, through threats and cajoling, got Birmingham to announce a halt to the strike. Other MWA leaders and rank-and-file picketers promptly ignored the MWA president's pronouncement.

The strike thus happened before the formation of a shared understanding of common class circumstances or anything other than a momentary solidarity among a large subset of Yankee small contractors. Differences abounded at all levels. The MWA leadership itself contained at least three distinct perspectives. Birmingham and his fellow Patton loggers sought to create a nonradical working-class movement to collectively bargain as workers with paper companies. Jon Falk, Claire Bolduc, and especially Peter Hagerty viewed the strike as a mass uprising of the oppressed against the corporate rulers of Maine's paper plantation, and as a movement that paralleled the urban and student unrest of the 1960s. They also were at odds in the desire by others to cut off the Canadians. Bill Butler and Mel Ames fully shared the rank-and-file woodcutters' consciousness of themselves as individual businessmen looking for a better deal. Neither these differences, nor opposing views of how to view and what to do about the division between Maine contractors and Canadian bonds, were addressed or resolved prior to or during the strike.[78]

A central factor limiting the MWA's success was the nativism and individualism of Maine loggers. With the exception of bilingual Acadian/Franco-Americans from northernmost Aroostook County, language and cultural barriers in tandem with hostility toward Canadians foreclosed a more inclusive strategy. Given more time, the Acadian French of Aroostook County might have helped the MWA bridge the gap between Yankee contractors and Canadian bonds. Indeed, as we learned in chapter 4, Aroostook French exercised surprising militancy and solidarity in the 1971 Fraser strike. Bolduc, Falk, and Hagerty all saw this as the attempted strikes greatest missed opportunity. The Canadian loggers themselves were already participants in union organizations; had MWA leaders and the rank and file been open to including them in their struggle, they would likely have been met with enthusiasm. In June 1975, Hagerty and Falk traveled to Quebec to meet with members of L'Association des Forestiers de Sud-Est, a union-like labor association that included many of the Canadian bonds working in Maine. The Canadian loggers expressed a willingness to join the MWA, despite the animosity they were used to contending with.[79] But given the antipathy toward Canadians of both rank-and-file MWA members and key leaders such as Birmingham, Butler, and Mel Ames, building bridges with these French-speaking guest workers was at odds with their diagnosis of the source of their problems.

It would be easy to blame the dominant faction of the MWA for being nativist. As we saw in the Frasier strike, non-Franco Mainers had a long history of racism toward French Canadians, evidenced in part by widespread participation in the Klan in the 1920s.[80] Arguably, the MWA would have been a fairer and more just organization had it heeded historian Parenteau's observation that: "While Canadian bonded workers played a major role in the degradation of native woodsmen, they were victims rather than perpetrators of the system."[81]

However, the MWA was correct in its assertion that guest workers were present in violation of federal law. That law proscribed hiring guest workers when such an added workforce depressed domestic wages and were correct in contending that, other things being equal, restriction or elimination of guest workers would improve the MWA members' bargaining power, create employment, and likely raise earnings. For several years leading up to the protest, legal aid lawyer and MWA attorney Don Fontaine organized investigations that definitively demonstrated that paper companies did not widely advertise for, nor were willing to hire, Maine woodcutters for jobs that practically had been reserved for French-Canadian bonds. MWA members looked hard to find advertisements for job openings (these were rare), and when openings could be identified, applied for them. The MWA tested the law and company practices aggressively over several years by having Maine woodcutters apply in large numbers for minimally advertised jobs, and they concluded that such jobs were largely chimeras.[82] When the loggers showed up, they would not be hired, or they were invited to move on to a remote worksite only to find they weren't needed when they arrived there. This was a direct violation of the terms of the H2 immigration program governing the use of bonded guest workers.[83]

Agency capture undergirded this long-term problem for Maine loggers. Maine officials responsible for regulating the use of guest workers acted more like a service agency to companies than an independent regulatory agency representing the interests of Maine workers and the public.[84] According to Fontaine, the nonenforcement of protections against replacing citizen workers stemmed from:

> bureaucrats upon whom no pressure was being put. They take the line of least resistance. All the pressure and contacts from the Department of Labor come from the paper companies. They're attorneys, professional HR people, and they'd say: "There's no one up here who really want to do this work. Americans are getting out of this, everyone wants to go to college." And they wouldn't hear anything from the other side because, as is so typical of our society, the poor and the working class are underrepresented. . . . Part of it's the pressure coming from the one side [paper companies], and the lack of pressure from the other side [local woodcutters].[85]

It was only blowback on the order of a statewide protest that moved the needle on enforcement.

Moreover, the companies had long been explicit in enunciating their threat to replace Maine loggers with Canadians. For instance, Bill Butler recalls St. Regis Paper forcing him in the early 1960s to abandon lucrative "high-grading" of valuable saw logs for local wood mills in favor of cutting three thousand cords of pulpwood per year at a price that barely covered operating costs. When he balked, a company forester told him: "'We know there isn't enough money in the price, but you do it for that, or we'll replace you with Canadians.' It was an overt threat."[86] Longley's threats to fill the woods with five thousand Canadians drew on a longer practice of company threats to use Canadians as job-breakers.

While the actions undertaken by the MWA were militant, its rhetoric and outlook was not an example of working-class radicalism. The laser focus on ending the guest worker program, and calls for fairness in prices and allocation of chances, differed dramatically from either working-class radicalism rooted in leftist ideology or from traditional business unionism practiced by the paper worker unions. Rather, contractors wanted to be able to survive by earning enough income that would also reasonably cover their debt obligations. Thus, their conception of fairness was not a working-class one of obtaining fair wage increases commensurate with productivity growth; rather, they thought of themselves as businessmen seeking a better deal on the commodities they were selling. And while they focused on piece-rates and the allocation of chances, and the strategy that cutting off the Canadians would correct these in their favor, in the end the focus was on achieving a livable income.

The narrow focus on expelling Canadians overlapped with the independence, individualism, and generally antiunion sentiment of rank-and-file Yankee woodcutters. The unsupervised workers' control woodcutters exercised in their isolated labor process was a powerful compensation for low pay and frequent injury. A love of being in nature—virtually all loggers were also hunters, and many were professional hunting guides—combined with a manly pride in doing difficult and complex work in the worst of elements. Working by themselves or on tiny crews of relatives and neighbors contrasted with paper workers sharing massive workplaces and tight-knit mill town life. Indeed, woodcutters typically had little experience with organization beyond town civic organizations—Claire Bolduc noted "most of them didn't have any experience with being in a group and tolerating democracy."[87] This combined with antipathy toward unions fueled by animosity toward the mill towns heavily comprised of descendants of Catholic immigrants were where Maine's unions were concentrated. For instance, Hagerty recalls: "for them, I think, I'm not sure they ever saw it as a union movement, they just saw it as a way to better their situation, but I don't think they ever saw it in the larger context." He goes on to give this frank assessment: "The MWA membership, if you probably looked at it hard and cold, probably would not have been pro-union. They don't want to be told, by anybody, when to do, what to do, or when.[88] Bill Butler on the level of interest in unionization in his area: "It wasn't in the cultural make-up of my neighbors. . . . Well, we all thought we were independent."[89]

The physical demands of their work left little energy for organizing, particularly sustained participation in an organization of geographically dispersed workers. Bolduc goes on to say:

> I mean, basically, these guys work ten to twelve hours per day, they go home and eat; they sleep. On the weekends, they drink, go boating, snowmobiling—that's it. . . . You get to eat at night—that's it, it puts your body to sleep. It is so depleted of everything. So it's tough, tough, tough stuff.[90]

Cecile Fontaine saw the same life:

> Work consumed your whole life, spent trying to do all of that work. Always fixing machines when not in forest. Families were constantly worried about their loggers getting injured. . . . [They were] isolated, working seventy hours a week and going home exhausted, and having to get up at 4 a.m. Not much time to start thinking about procedural issues or organizing one's self.[91]

Maine's paper workers and their unions were an unrivaled economic and political working-class force. As the woodcutters' movement arose, Maine's paper workers and woodcutters remained ethnically and occupationally divided, despite being effectively employed by the same entity. Indeed, a UPIU business agent took the dramatic step of driving a truck through an MWA picket (making a delivery of raw materials) to symbolize the UPIU's aggressive stance against the attempted strike.[92] This starkly antagonistic relationship between the MWA and Maine's established labor unions demonstrated the underlying class and cultural antagonism between loggers and mill workers. The two groups were part of the same industry and often lived nearby if not literally side-by-side; proximity brewed resentment hardened over generations.[93] The unions representing paper mill workers had long been disinterested in organizing woodcutters. From its 1930s' origins, the national union leaders of these top-down unions bought into companies' focus on keeping mills profitable and running without labor interruption; organizing woodcutters was at furthest remove from this intent.[94] The principal paper workers' unions reacted to the formation of the MWA and its strike effort as a direct threat to the stability of paper mill employment and the interests of union members.[95]

In the 1977, Eldon Hebert testified at the U.S. Senate hearing in Bangor, Maine on Maine logging. The UPIU started a campaign to unionize company logging crews in late 1975. Hebert was its organizing director. The UPIU sought, at least in part, to channel pro-MWA sentiment into organizations under its purview. In his testimony, Hebert discounted all of the MWA's allegations of adverse impacts from Canadian labor in the Maine woods. In addition, he stressed the likelihood that a cut-off of Canadian labor would shut down the state's paper and woods products industries, where sixteen thousand out of twenty-three thousand workers were UPIU members.[96] In all, the UPIU's organizing of hundreds of woodcutters in company crews did not constitute a more deep-rooted alliance between the opposed groups.

Even before the protest ended, both the MWA's leadership split and the movement created by the strike effort receded. At the same time, the MWA itself survived as a smaller organization, one that organizers felt had been created, not destroyed by the protest. Former leaders recall a hardy group of four hundred to five hundred members in the ensuing years.[97] MWA activists continued to picket, leaflet, lobby the legislature, conduct border roadblocks and sit-ins at the Maine Employment Security Commission, and got the state's U.S. senators to hold a Bangor hearing in 1977. If small in number, the attempted strike gained the MWA a measure of credibility and influence for what had been a voiceless group.[98]

The MWA's actions aimed to cut off the Canadians; in this, the smaller MWA actions, combined with the turmoil of the 1975 protest itself, played a contributing role in the industry's move away from reliance on Canadian woodcutters. After major protests against Canadian labor in 1954 and 1955, between 2,500 and 3,000 Canadian workers still worked in the Maine woods. As recently as 1967, the figure was still over three thousand. During the 1970s, numbers declined, but estimates of their numbers were highly contested, as companies and sympathetic economists continued to claim that bonds were only being hired near the Canadian border and that their presence had little impact of Mainers' job opportunities.[99] In 1977, MWA leaders claimed over two thousand Canadians were at work in the Maine woods, while paper companies and Maine Department of Labor (MDOL) officials claimed a figure in the hundreds. MDOL data indicates that in the years leading up to the 1975 MWA protest, nearly two thousand Canadians were authorized to work in Maine under the bond system alone, with an additional smaller number in Maine on regular visas. With slack work in late 1975, and under increased public pressure on the issue thereafter, the number of bonds authorized dropped by 1977 to under one thousand. By 1980, the number had fallen to around five hundred.[100]

As for the MWA, entropy set in within a few years. The organization was especially damaged when two leaders entered a Canadian-staffed logging camp, destroyed equipment and other property, and terrorized the loggers living in the camp. A lengthy and costly court case ensued, draining the organization's meager coffers and sapping the group's energy. Most of all, companies moved aggressively to recruit new labor supplies and replaced contractors with expanded company crews where possible.[101] Thus, the MWA was as a shell of organization by 1980 and went out of existence shortly thereafter.[102]

For former MWA leaders and activists, the MWA was not, in hindsight, either a failure or of no consequence, as some scholars and certainly former company executives have said.[103] Certainly, its aim of direct improvements for Maine contractors—steady work, fair prices, and fair scaling—was only modestly achieved, and only for a relatively short period of time. But the very fact of the event and its extensive participation, public recognition, and scope was in many respects a complete surprise to its core of leaders and members. Butler recalls: "So, they were surprised, [and] we were surprised." And also: "We had made a statement, we made a show." To the MWA, the strike effort *initiated* their statewide organization—that it was a beginning, not an end point—and they could proudly point to having a significant impact on the industry.[104] Besides efforts to cut off the Canadians, the state legislature passed a fair scaling law, and an expansion of workers' compensation that quickly covered most of the woods workforce.[105]

The MWA protest also led to a modest level of legitimate unionization, a rarity in the long history of Maine logging. There is no doubt that this unionization would not have occurred in the absence of the MWA protests of October 1975. Even before the end of the protest, Wayne Birmingham sought to affiliate MWA members with the International Brotherhood of Carpenters and Joiners, but he did so without the assent of other MWA leaders.[106] These organizing efforts bore little fruit. Meanwhile, the UPIU, which had opposed the MWA strike effort and earned the enmity of the MWA leadership, viewed the MWA as a threat to its members and its general control of Maine's labor turf. Somewhat ironically, the UPIU immediately began conducting organizing campaigns in the fall of 1975, focusing on company crews. The motivation was to bring at least some of the woodcutters under the UPIU's tent, reducing the likelihood of future wildcat disruptions of paper operations.[107] By the late 1970s, it had succeeded in organizing 40 percent of woodcutters on company and large contractor operations.[108] At companies like GNP, St. Regis, and Georgia Pacific, unionization led to better pay and benefits for woodcutters. But less than one thousand such woodcutters, mostly on new mechanized crews, would benefit from unionization, and they would be laid off a mere decade later.[109]

Restructuring Post-1975

Globally, a second wave of postwar mechanization developed in the 1960s. Scandinavian and U.S. logging machine suppliers invented various vehicles, led by the feller-buncher (see figure 5.2), to replace the backbreaking and life-threatening work of chainsaw hand-cutting. Accompanying the feller-bunchers were more powerful skidders, truck loaders, and onsite wood-chipping machines. In the feller-buncher, a worker would sit in the cab of a machine that was similar in size and appearance to a construction crane. He could drive the harvester up to a tree and grasp the tree at mid-height, cut the tree at its base with a large circular saw, and send up another cutting device that delimbed the tree. Compared to chainsaws, these powerful devices could cut six times more timber per hour. Operators sat in a protected, air-conditioned or heated cab, which made cutting work drastically safer, not to mention vastly more comfortable, than working with chainsaws.[110]

Two developments spurred an acceleration of efforts to mechanize. First was the MWA protest and its fallout, particularly the curtailment of the Canadian guest workforce.[111] The MWA uprising exacerbated political instability associated with

FIGURE 5.2 Feller-buncher—the mainstay of modern mechanized wood harvesting. Mechanical harvesters first entered the Maine woods in 1966 and became the standard technology for wood harvesting over the 1970s and 1980s. Building up the necessary skills and adapting the technology to Maine conditions required over a decade of experimenting to be successful (iStock photos).

the guest worker program; one forester recalled his woodlands managers asking every year how many bonds the company had, and he pressed forestry managers to cut down on their use.[112] Another observed "better to be away from it, and we did."[113] At the same time, a spruce budworm epidemic that killed trees in a huge stretch of Maine's industrial forests took root in the remote locations owned by the three companies that had led the way in developing mechanized operations. Expanded used of mechanized harvesters allowed companies to clear-cut—the term for simply mowing down an entire section of forest, fully denuding the landscape of trees. Chainsaw cutting of these trees, many small, was uneconomical at existing piece rates. Thus, companies purchased more mechanical harvesters and used them in salvage operations. Using mechanized harvesting meant cutting millions of acres of wood that otherwise would have been a total loss.[114]

While it took nearly fifteen years to fully adapt the machines to the Maine woods, and to train both operators and mechanics to repair the complex machines, by the early 1980s the companies had overcome these challenges.[115] It gave the companies leading this effort—Georgia Pacific, Scott, and GNP—the chance to recruit a new workforce to replace Canadian guest workers and the traditional Maine woodcutting force.[116] A woodlands manager recalled: "And there were lots of fine young men available, all up and down Route 11 and elsewhere, that wanted to get into our training programs [on how to] run mechanized equipment, and did—it was a very successful program."[117] For those companies undertaking mechanization, the promise of success was cutting even more wood with a new, much smaller, stable, and docile workforce. While gearing up these operations, the companies relied on direct employees—many benefitting from new unionization—to staff the new mechanized crews.[118]

As the companies began to master the technology and create a new skill base, they turned to diffusing the new mechanized technology to a new set of contractors. These new contractors and their employees had little personal connection to the MWA; the paper companies selectively targeted the best of these contractors and financially supported them in acquiring mechanical harvesting equipment.[119]

By the late 1980s a solid and growing fleet of contractors had thus mastered mechanized cutting. Over the following decade, the majority of contractors still in business adopted the technology. By 1999, the Maine Department of Labor estimated that 65 percent of contractors were mechanized.

By the 1990s, paper companies used their dominant role over the contractors and their mechanized operations to radically reduce their incomes. Whereas real wages rose for mechanized harvester operators between 1974 to 1986 by 30 percent, they in turn dropped by 61 percent in the following thirteen years.[120]

Productivity gains were striking. The woodcutting workforce fell by roughly 75 percent the twenty-five years following the MWA protest to 2,500.[121] This much smaller group of woodcutters doubled wood production.[122] The relatively small number of bonds—remaining steady at roughly five hundred (with several hundred more Canadians in the woods on visas)—went from being a marginal to an important part of the workforce.

By the end of the twentieth century, a highly-mechanized Maine woods industry continued to cut ever-increasing amounts of wood with a sharply reduced labor force. For woodcutters, mechanization removed the harshest features of woods work, but earnings returned to the lower end of blue–collar work in Maine.[123]

Maine citizen loggers have continued activism over the twinned issues of bargaining rights and Canadian labor up to the present. In 2019, Maine's woodcutters earned a surprising victory in 2019 when Maine's Governor Janet Mills signed a new law authorizing logging contractors to unionize.[124]

The historic disconnect between paper mills workers and their unions, on the one hand, and citizen woodcutters, on the other, removed what might have been a more powerful double alliance during the upsurge of worker resistance in the 1980s.[125] While both workforces felt violated by new pressures from above in the 1960s and 1970s and reacted with agency, the long, nonunion legacy of woods workers in Maine and defeat of the MWA meant loggers would not join the larger struggles that emerged after 1980.

Part 3

FINANCIALIZATION, RESISTANCE, AND FOLK POLITICAL ECONOMY

6

FEAR AND LOATHING ON THE LOW AND HIGH ROADS

By the mid-1980s, workers, unions, and companies alike faced a new, existential threat. National and international competition was eroding companies' pricing power and market shares. Corporate leaders were forced by Wall Street to answer to much greater expectations for profit performance. Employers, academic experts, journalists—citing examples of dramatic job losses in domestic manufacturing such auto and steel—instructed that without fundamental change, workers in a mature industrial state like Maine could expect to see their paper industry jobs disappear as production moved overseas and work was automated at home and abroad. In response, the national companies that now owned Maine's mills made radical demands on workers and attacked traditional union contracts outright. The result was a wild and damaging drama that went far beyond what any of its participants could have anticipated.[1]

In 1986 and 1987, Boise Cascade and International Paper Company (IP) provoked strikes by making extreme, untenable demands on workers in their Rumford and Jay, Maine, mills. Workers walked out in protest, and the two companies each executed well-laid plans to fire the striking workers and permanently replaced them with nonunion workers (scabs, in union parlance) recruited from across the United States. More than 1,500 striking workers at these two mills lost their jobs, traumatizing their communities.[2] Across others of the state's mills, these strike defeats yielded to a more complex story of competing visions of corporate restructuring.[3]

The union-busting campaigns conducted by these two companies defined what economists and others now call the low road—clobbering workers in the quest to quickly raise profits.[4] A more intriguing development also entered the stage—the so-called high road. High road employers eschewed clobbering workers. Rather, firms offered a win-win; in exchange for keeping their jobs (and perhaps gaining additional income), workers would have to learn new skills and, most importantly, work cooperatively with their bosses to create a new ways of doing work. For those workers not directly challenged by unthinkable concessions and permanent replacement during strikes, wasn't the necessity for change obvious—given a stark contrast between the high and low roads? Why resist a better offer? But, the high road was also tough sell. Some of Maine's paper workers did buy into the vision of a win-win outcome. But the real story here is how—and, crucially, why—Maine's paper workers built a radical movement statewide that resisted high road proposals, notably because much of the high road's day-to-day substance was a Trojan horse, which companies unwittingly commingled with heinous acts of union busting.

When the high road appeared after the Rumford and Jay strikes, Maine's unionized paper workers, for good reasons, did not see the high and low as being so different. Indeed, they appeared as two faces of a singular class war waged against Maine's paper workers. And even where high road cooperation took root, success took on a pyrrhic quality.

The New Forces Acting upon Workers in the 1980s: The Case of Paper

Workers' fears were realized when [Great Northern] President Bartlett announced on January 31, 1985, that the company was in financial jeopardy. Besides the job cuts, he said that the unions would have to compromise away many of their hard-won work rules that Bartlett characterized as costly and archaic. He said Great Northern must, like competitors, move to greater labor efficiencies through multi-craft, team concepts and flexible work assignments to reduce the labor costs of producing paper. Bartlett said Great Northern's man-hours per ton was 5.8 in 1985, compared to 5 for Quebec, 4 for the U.S. South, and 3.7 for Finland. "With salaries and wages comprising 40 percent of all our costs, there is no way we can survive unless we address this problem," he said.[5]

Throughout the United States, paper companies were asking workers to agree to embrace the growing sea change toward team-based work sweeping American industry.[6] Entering that decade, paper was still one of the United States' most unionized industries. The steadfast commitment of Maine paper workers to workplace contractualism augured a head-on collision with the new team concept. To Maine's paper workers, agreeing to such changes meant accepting the destruction of their workplace rights. Any changes to well-established job definitions and lines of progression meant toppling the very edifice upon which fair workplace treatment rested.[7]

In many ways, paper embodied the transformation of industrial relations going on in traditionally unionized industries. Industrial corporations' existence was now challenged as never before by heightened competition and new financial demands from Wall Street. This meant either "forcing" or "fostering" this transformation, to use the parlance of labor relations experts.[8] What models could companies draw on? Prior to 1980, the low road was exemplified by the likes of union-busting Midwestern companies such as Kohler and Perfect Circle, as well as RCA. RCA repeatedly uprooted production in search of nonunion areas—creating so-called runaway shops whose major operations left Camden, New Jersey, beginning in the 1950s, moving first to the Midwest and South, and then finally to Mexico.[9] At the other end of the spectrum was the accommodating approach found in automobile and paper industries. Like the big four auto companies, paper companies conducted a postwar capital-labor accord of sorts, insofar as companies in both industries found tolerating the presence of unionism prudent. Both industries shifted heavily into new southern plants after World War II and concluded that accepting unions in their new plants worthwhile as a concession to keep their Northern union locals from being on the warpath.[10]

In the 1970s and early into the 1980s, United Paperworkers International Union (UPIU) nationwide became increasingly aggressive about using strikes to gain leverage in negotiations. This aggressiveness reflected the same forces sweeping Maine mills and U.S. manufacturing; because the UPIU was decentralized, and its locals democratic, militant workers were able to take a measure of control away from the international and thus contradict the UPIU's historic sensibility of cutting deals with companies over the locals' heads.[11] With more militant elements and sensibilities arriving from warfronts and other countercultural locales, and less patient national-level UPIU leaders, workers in Maine and elsewhere fought for more, or for better, or—as in the case of Frasier—rebuffed speed-up efforts.[12] The need of paper companies to run their mills at over 90 percent capacity to be highly profitable, and the crucial role of operator knowledge and skill, led paper companies to avoid strikes and generally concede significant bargaining power to its unions, at least on economic issues, given the residual ability pass on higher labor costs to customers.[13] Consequently, compensation in paper grew more rapidly than in other industries, with the ratio of average hourly earnings in paper to all U.S. manufacturing rising from 1.16 in 1960 to 1.56 in 1986.[14] This generous pattern was especially pronounced in first half of the period from 1976–86, when compensation awards in paper raced far ahead of manufacturing and other comparable unionized industries.[15]

By 1980, paper companies began to push back. Seismic change in labor relations nationally burst into public view first with the near bankruptcy of Chrysler in 1979 and contemporaneous, extensive layoffs in the iconic U.S. steel mills. Both instances imposed huge job losses while setting the tone for the 1980s with huge wage and benefit concessions. Then in 1981, President Ronald Reagan fired and replaced eleven thousand striking air traffic controllers, members of the Professional Air Traffic Controllers Organizations (PATCO).[16] In this one act, Reagan made PATCO a household name (at least for unionized workers) and redefined the norms of labor relations. Whereas President Franklin Roosevelt ushered in an ethos of accommodation and union legitimacy in 1933, Reagan now legitimized open confrontation by employers seeking either dramatic concessions or outright destruction of their workers' unions.[17]

Prior to PATCO, several paper companies won strikes by successfully using temporary strike replacement workers. These examples shifted industry thinking about its strategic options in collective bargaining. The PATCO strike, and aggressive national concessions movement commencing in the 1981–82 national recession, deepened this new thinking.[18] Specifically, the management perception that strikes were costly and to be avoided went by the wayside, and aggressive bargaining became the norm. For the first time, paper companies began to see the strike as a tool of the employer, not unions. The emergence since 1960 of a significant nonunion sector in Southern, so-called greenfield (i.e., newly built) plants, was also a factor. Mead-Stevenson, with its "socio-technical job design," and Procter and Gamble, with its "technician system" at Charmin tissue plants, built new paper mills that were not only union-free but were also showcases for early versions of the new flexible workplace organizations that paper managers increasingly desired. Growing competition from such nonunion mills also spurred paper companies' increasingly hard-nosed bargaining approach.[19]

Weak profit performance drove paper companies' new labor relations strategy.[20] "Restrictive work rules and other productivity impediments ranked even higher as an irritant within the industry" than high wages.[21] Thus, management saw job control unionism as the major barrier to restoring higher profitability. By 1985, it was clear that CEOs that didn't force radical changes on workers to raise profits would be ousted;[22] Chandlerian independence was dead. A seminal study of this era's labor relations described paper companies' new "management agenda": ". . . operating managers thought that their highly structured [work] systems used only a portion of their employees' skills, and they knew that most employees were discouraged from pooling their skills and ideas both by work rules and by long traditions of managerial control and adversarial relations."[23]

In addition to prying unions away from traditional work organization, even before the events described here in Maine beginning in 1986, paper companies aimed to roll back economic gains made by its unions in the previous decade and longstanding costly pay practices, especially double-time wages for Sunday work.[24] Even without firing striking workers, paper industry wage increases quickly shrank after 1980, and by 1987–89 were about zero. By 1987, paper was now falling below average wage increases for all manufacturing.[25] But wage cuts were not the heart of the matter; CEOs needed to speed up work, and they were trying to sell their local workers and union representatives that the team concept was an offer that workers hoping to keep jobs could not refuse.[26]

Strategic Change Comes to Maine

In the parlance of business leaders and academic experts, the push back against paper unions was part of a larger path of strategic change in U.S. manufacturing. "Strategic" in the 1980s meant putting every aspect of business operations on the table.[27] In relations with workers, it meant closing some mills, radically redefining traditional ways of doing business in mills that remained, and refashioning labor relations through aggressive implementation of either the low and high roads. On the one hand, companies engaged in outright union busting, or sought to introduce ostensibly cooperative and radical work reorganization. Crucially, at times companies did so in combination.

As time went on, companies were pressured to embrace shareholder maximization strategies based on financial engineering.[28] This so-called engineering was most typically radical downsizing—closing factories and laying off workers and managers by the thousands.[29] Companies could thereby be made lean.[30] Laid off workers and whole communities suffered; those who kept their jobs had to take on the work of those who left, resulting in speed-up. All the while, financial engineering meant stock prices would soar (or recover), and wealthy investors would get a huge financial windfall. In the process, vestiges of Chandlerian management would be isolated and starved, or simply cut out, as more traditional managers left the field of a losing battle.[31] Chandlerian managers at Maine mills increasingly now headed to the exit after a decade of losing arguments about local reinvestment and long-run strategizing for their mills with their national corporate overseers.

These and other elements of roiling change in U.S. manufacturing sparked a national debate over strategic restructuring. The premise for this debate was the belief that the survival or decline of U.S. manufacturing enterprises was still a contingent matter, in which successful strategies might rescue enterprises and their workers while inertia would lead to demise. Experts declared that the cause of this existential threat was a new era of global competition where Japanese, German, and other advanced nations deployed better technologies and marketing acumen, stressing once unrivaled American industrial giants in a new economic war. U.S. manufacturers were already suffering heavy losses in both domestic and foreign markets to the likes of Sony, Volkswagen, and Nippon Steel. The language of being globally competitive or just competitive—spread to policy discussions of schooling, basic research and development, training, and government policies impacting industry.[32]

Advocates of strategic change hailed from many quarters, including corporate and union leaders, and academic business and labor relations experts. Support for union-management collaboration and reorganization of work into teams was paramount for liberal commentators, who were especially concerned about the fate of workers as global competition seemed to be an attack on the American middle class. Boosterish writing by popular writers Lester Thurow and Robert Reich, and the hortatory if wonkish, *Thinking for a Living* by former U.S. Secretary of Labor Ray Marshall, brought attention to these ideas.[33] They called for industrial policy—targeted government support for research and development and training for specific industries, cooperative relations with unions (while expecting unions to give up traditional protections), while instituting managed trade of the mercantilist sort practiced then by Japan. Business gurus like Michael Porter, Peter Drucker, and Peter Senge called for a new science of benchmarking against the globe's best-practice companies and implementing strategic change that brought US companies up to these best practices.[34] This version of strategic change required radical shifts in the nature of work. Workers and frontline management would form teams that scaled up to entire learning organizations. Japanese corporate workplace practices held a special mystique, as their version of a system called Total Quality Management became the centerpiece of building new team-based work organization. Economists Michael Piore and Charles Sabel announced the arrival of nothing less than a second industrial divide—the end of leading industrial nations' ability to succeed using mass production techniques that could not withstand low wage competition or rapidly changing consumer tastes.[35] To these writers, only a radically reconceived set of work and marketing practices—in service of high-quality products that could rapidly move into niches—would save U.S. manufacturing. At the core of these appeals was the promise that workers would have more power over their jobs, reducing the drudgery of factory work as they took on more responsibilities, added skills, and were empowered to make decisions once the province of foreman and supervisors.

Studious thinking on the subject emanated from labor relations experts like Eileen Applebaum, Rosemary Batt, Thomas Kochan, and Paul Osterman, all of whom had a hand in spreading the term "high-performance work systems" (HPWS).[36] These thinkers noted compelling reasons why unionized workers might resist change. While still acting as strong advocates, as early as 1999 Paul Osterman was discovering that while HPWS spread, two upsides supposed to support workers failed to materialize, namely job security or a share in economic gains produced in HPWS.[37] Secondly, financial downsize and divest strategies or general corporate indifference meant that even successful HPWS were often fleeting entities. For example, Thomas Kochan and Saul Rubinstein wrote an insightful account of Saturn automobile's impressive success as a paragon of the high road, with workers equally involved in workplace and even marketing strategies.[38] And while their *Learning From Saturn* published in 2001 offered a road map to other employers considering the benefits and challenges of the high road, Saturn itself was already languishing as a bastard division disliked by GM headquarters. If a second edition had been published a decade later, the only noise a reader could hear would be the doors of Saturn's famed plant being shuttered.

Playing up best practice cases, high road advocates saw the HPWS as an escape route from deindustrialization. If successful, it could solve, or at least abate, the host of threats facing American manufacturers. The high road was thus a responsible alternative to a low road structural change already ravishing workers and communities across the United States. They noted that achieving HPWS was an uphill battle, requiring deep cultural changes from unionized workers accustomed to job control unionism. These changes would only be possible if employers stayed the course long enough to build credibility, most importantly by eschewing low road practices. They identified financial engineering as the biggest potential threat to high road efforts, a concern that proved prescient. But if achieved, high road companies could preserve many of the type of unionized well-paying jobs that Maine's paper industry typified.[39]

Another pole of the debate came from financialization proponents. Economist Michael Jensen writings propagandized in the late 1970s and 1980s a call for a new shareholder value movement. Anticipating the fictional Gordon Gekko's famous "greed is good" slogan,[40] business CEOs ruthlessly responsive only to shareholders would remake a better capitalism for all because it would enhance value throughout the economy. Jensen's proposed financial engineering went way beyond low road labor practices; firms were best thought of as bundles of assets to be blown up, reconfigured, put to death for tax advantages, or heavily financed if sufficiently promising.[41] A version of this approach to running corporations had emerged from business consultants some fifteen years earlier—then focused on conglomerate mergers.[42] But Jensen and his acolytes propagated a more searing vision that bolstered a turn toward financial innovation goosed by Reagan-era deregulation of Wall Street. This thinking made its way into the paper industry

between 1985 and 1995. In the words of some academic critics, these theories became "performative," as corporate actors came to embody the new theories of
how to restructure corporations in a hostile financial world.[43]

Maine's paper industry had always, as noted in chapter 2, pushed out of its mills
a widely eclectic range of papers, but coated publication papers and newspaper
print always led the way. It had mainly faced domestic competition (except in
newspaper print) until the 1970s when Canadian and Scandinavian companies
entered the field. So what was new? Declining profitability stood out the most.
Maintaining profitability of Maine's mostly older mills became more challeng-
ing. New foreign and domestic competition from more efficient plants, and growing overcapacity, limited pricing power.[44] Strategic change was now the order of
the day.

Many experiments and new strategies came to the fore. As national paper companies, including IP, Boise Cascade, Champion, and Scott, turned increasingly
to strategic action in the 1980s, Maine's paper industry became a hothouse of labor
relations' initiatives. Threats to fire and permanently replace workers, and entreaties to improve labor-management collaboration and raise mills' efficiency, were
enacted in Maine mills side by side.[45] The industry's historic geographic concentration in locales such as Maine and Wisconsin would make these side-by-side
initiatives a kind of Pandora's box. To Maine paper workers, the full import of
now being ruled by distant, out-of-state corporate ownership and control materialized in an increasingly ugly reality.

The story of how these corporate strategies coursed through Maine's labor relations is an instructive case study for the fate of the high and low roads. At least
in the case of the IP strike, Jay demonstrated the outsized costs for corporations
of pursuing the low road.[46] With this contrast in mind, why would rational stakeholders, particularly workers and their unions, refuse to embrace high performance work systems? Industrial relations experts acknowledged deep cultural
reasons why unionized workers were suspicious of high road proposals but ultimately implied this: Who could disagree (rationally) with a win-win outcome?
Unionized workplaces that did embrace change were held up as exemplars by these
experts, hoping to sell a broader audience of workers on the concept. Yet, given the
way events unfolded in Maine, it turned out that this resistance to HPWS was indeed rational. Much of the post-2000 recognition of HPWS's flaws by scholars
and promoters of HPWS were well understood before 1995 by Maine workers.

In this chapter and chapter 7, we have a ground-level view of why this strong
corporate reform movement floundered. We also see how financialization was a
key reason why these initiatives were ultimately destined to fail; Jensenite corporate owners had little patience for high road reforms with upfront costs and an
uncertain longer run payoff. Moreover, poor corporate strategy issuing from this

so-called shareholder value movement gratuitously accelerated decline by under-mining production and marketing competencies.[47] Maine's paper workers and their union leaders—and many local managers as well—were particularly astute in grasping this reality, which informed much of their resistance and disgust.

To see how this played out in Maine, we begin with the advent of the low road. Two key events loomed large just when paper companies across the board were asking workers in Maine mills to submit to work reorganization. The timing and character of these events had much to do with subsequent problems on the high road.

Lowering the Boom: The Low Road in Rumford and Jay

Out of the gate, the most visible strategic change was union busting. In Maine, Boise Cascade and IP followed a clear formula established in other industries in the preceding five years: propose terrible contract terms intended to provoke a strike, then follow through on carefully made plans to hire permanent replace-ments.[48] These replacements, with the help of managers who returned to the shop floor, many of whom were imported from other mills, would acquire sufficient skills to maintain production and would leave management a completely free hand to reorganize work in a way that speed up work and lower labor costs. With time, the replacement workers would vote out the union. Management gained unilateral control of production, and could squeeze workers at will.[49]

This new tactic made its first appearance at the historic Rumford Oxford plant. Boise Cascade purchased the mill in 1976 from Ethyl Corporation. Workers and union leaders detected the arrival of a harsher attitude when Boise took posses-sion of the mill in 1976, and the company was well poised to effect a strategic up-heaval. It had used permanent replacements in a 1983 strike at one of its Southern mills, and it took 2,500 applications across the country before the strike at Rum-ford commenced.[50] In 1986 negotiations, the company asked for huge wage cuts and the elimination of a plethora of work rules; 94 percent of UPIU Local 900 members voted to reject the contract and go on strike on June 29.[51] Over the fol-lowing eleven weeks, the company kept the mill running while steadily bringing in more permanent replacement workers—reaching a total of 342 positions in the 1,200 worker facility.[52] The company announced in September that it would also move to wholly subcontract maintenance work to nonunion outfits while continuing to hire and retain permanent replacements.[53] Union leaders at that point recognized that continuing the strike would lead to all of its members los-ing their jobs. Facing this threat, Local 900 of the UPIU reconsidered, and voted

2-1 to return in September, accepting Boise's original proposal.[54] For Boise management, the biggest prize gained was a vast expansion of management discretion. Notes historian Timothy Minchin, the "concessionary contract, includ[ed] the flexibility provisions many had so vehemently opposed, which gave the company wide latitude to re-assign workers in a job area as well as to alter its promotion and overtime policies."[55]

IP followed suit in nearby Jay, Maine in a strike that began June 15, 1987. The strike was to become a national cause célèbre, joined by two other mills elsewhere in the country and a fourth mill where the company locked out its workforce. At this point, the national union-busting wave was already more than a half-decade old. Like Boise in Rumford, IP had carefully prepared to rout striking workers. It built new fences around the mill while creating temporary housing inside the mill for strikebreakers. It brought in sizeable private security forces, and it publicly contracted a notorious southern firm, B. E. and K., that specialized in providing skilled strikebreakers who knew how to maintain paper mills.

Paper workers at Rumford and Jay believed their mastery of the finicky processes required to profitably make their high-quality publication papers protected them from worst-case scenarios seen in the PATCO and Hormel Meatpacking strikes.[56] For workers at both plants, this turned out to be false. Business was strong and profits were up (thanks mainly to a national economic boom).[57] Paper workers and their union leaders saw these new attacks as the gratuitous pursuit of higher profit and counted on the companies to recognize that using replacement workers and managers to run the mill would be too financially ruinous. Workers saw themselves as ethically in the right—the companies' bargaining stances reflected corporate greed—and practically they believed the company was going to feel the hurt before workers did.[58]

IP's proposal to UPIU Local 14 and two small craft unions in maintenance, like those of Boise to UPIU Local 900, was loaded with specific symbolic content designed to enrage. Asking for a wage cut of more than 10 percent at a time of record profits begged the question, for workers, of why IP was asking for concessions in the first place, other an unjust greed. IP asked for the right to subcontract skilled maintenance work. In the union's estimation, this would have cost 350 unionized jobs, nearly 30 percent of the mill's workforce. "Project Productivity"—work reorganization schemes that workers saw as speed-up— would have cost another 150 jobs. What union would agree to the (unnecessary) loss of 40 percent of its members' jobs and still be a representative of the workers' interests?[59]

Crucially, IP viscerally aimed at a deeply prized benefit: double pay for Sunday work, and the Christmas shutdown.[60] For paper workers in Maine and elsewhere, Sunday work had been a deeply contentious issue dating from the 1800s. Across dozens of interviews, workers talked of being particularly vexed by years of missing church and especially key events in the lives of their children. Being compensated very well by a doubling of one's hourly wage made these sacrifices palatable, but always with a sense of caveat. As for the end to the Christmas shutdown, closing the "one holiday a year to be with your family" was equally resented.

On the day the strike began, the author called Bill Meserve, president of the UPIU Local 14 at Jay, with the aim of being prepared for a live television interview that evening. Meserve spoke precisely, with passion and at length, about how Local 14 had made its deal over Sunday work in 1948. He also discussed the loss of jobs and income that would result from accepting IP's contract offer, but the Sunday pay issue was in the forefront.[61]

IP also managed to firmly tie the symbolism of key features of the supposed high road to its scorched earth low road assault. Specifically, IP initiated project productivity in the year prior to the strike. The project was a mix of typical high-performance work schemes. Creating teams was high on the list, but IP added other unusual features, like having workers writing detailed job descriptions that could become a manual for training replacement workers. IP was following Boise Cascade's successful effort in Rumford to have its workers write the manuals prior to the strike; Local 900 strike leaders contended that the company had used worker-compiled manuals to train their permanent replacements once union workers struck.[62]

These harsh and unprecedented demands were merely a pretext to push workers into striking. Officially, IP followed Boise Cascade in asking for the concessions sufficient to raise profitability to a level satisfactory to the Wall Street markets. Despite unionized workers' sense that they held enough cards to rebuff concessions, Boise and IP had made careful preparations to hire replacement workers months before strike votes. Both companies planned to push workers to strike so the company could hire a new and compliant labor force. Following the low road formula, once IP's new nonunion workforce was in place, wages and benefits were immediately screwed down, and work was reorganized along company's preferred lines. In Jay scabs then voted to oust the union in 1991 under NLRB supervision. While IP's workers waged a historic and remarkable struggle to win their strike, their effort failed by the fall of 1988, most of the workers lost their jobs, and their union was decertified a few years later.

The IP strike differed from Boise in two respects. First, Boise was satisfied to replace only one-fourth of the strikers as long as Local 900 fully capitulated. IP clearly planned to completely replace its workforce. Secondly, as superbly told by Julius Getman in his account of the strike, IP's workers and their UPIU Local 14 built a powerful campaign to win the strike. Led by longtime movement radical Peter Kellman, then under the employ of the state's AFL-CIO organization, Jay's UPIU Local 14 spent a year preparing its workers to not only resist concessionary demands in bargaining with the company but to directly resist on the mill floor the efforts by IP management to reorganize work. By the time the strike began, Local 14 had mobilized a national strategy, held weekly rallies in the Jay high school gym of 1,000–1,500 people from all over Maine and the country, including notable political and union leaders, and spread out across the region to educate other paper workers about their cause and the need for them to join a broad solidarity effort to support the strikers. Local 14 mixed 1960s civil rights movement practices and ethos with a contemporary corporate campaign that pressured financial companies with ties to IP. Along with a similar campaign by Local P-9 of the United Food and Commercial Workers in a strike against Hormel in Austin, Minnesota, Kellman, Meserve, and a sophisticated rank and file sought to build an effective counterstrategy that could turn the tables against the national attack on unionized labor.[63]

Strike support and involvement from other Maine mills would link IP's struggles into one overriding politics of resistance across the state.[64] Unfortunately for Jay's strikers, they faced not just the harsh attack from IP but also a rearguard resistance from the international UPIU officers and a shift in the application of labor law that provided no succor to embattled unions, especially those who attempted to strike.[65] The ultimate loss of the strike was a severe blow to their community, destroyed their union, and meant abrupt downward mobility for paper workers and their families accustomed to high wages.[66] In a poignant vein, many of the strikers, and the town of Jay itself, were transformed. A number of rank-and-file strike leaders were elected to the Maine legislature, and they built an influential labor caucus there that persisted into the 2000s. A slate of Jay strikers fully took over local government, imposing high taxes and vigorous environmental regulations, costing the mill millions of dollars annually. Embracing an environmental politics was one sign of how radicalized Jay's workers became during the strike.[67]

Strikes are complex acts, and the scale and character of the Jay strike illustrates the diverse and far-reaching fallout of their remarkable effort. But in the end, they, along with Rumford workers, were on the wrong end of a furious low road effort, and the ledger for the event weighs heavily toward extreme income loss, loss of economic security, and deep trauma of such a huge and adverse event.

Spillover Effects from the IP Strike in Maine: A Movement Culture and Seeing HPWS as Part of the Low Road

Jay strikers spent the sixteen-month strike building a grassroots campaign. Caravans of rank-and-file strikers fanned out to union halls, college campuses, and community centers, across Maine and beyond, bringing a movement message that was explicitly modeled on the civil rights movement of the 1950s and 1960s. Paper workers at other Maine mills were recruited to be part of the struggle. Paper workers and other union members traveled to Jay each week to join in the Wednesday night revival meetings and a number of large protest marches; dues assessments and plant-gate collections to support Local 14's strike fund complemented well-attended meetings of other mill/locals.[68]

Across the state, the strike's impact on the thinking of rank-and-file and union leaders alike was transformational. The Jay strikers' motto—Stop Corporate Greed—became the Maine labor movement's slogan, showing up in picket lines and protests even fifteen years after the Jay strike ended. Most transformational was Jesse Jackson's October 1987 speech to more than 3,500 in Jay. In a stirring call to arms, Jackson argued that workers needed to see the strike as part of a brewing class war declared by corporate America, and to especially turn focus away from punishing scabs to mobilizing against not just IP but corporate leaders associated with IP.[69] Maine union activists subsequently flocked to Jackson's 1988 presidential bid, propelling Jackson to a strong second-place showing in Maine's Democratic caucuses—all the more remarkable given that Maine, at that time, was the second whitest state in the United States. Jackson's speech and subsequent presidential campaign infused a movement mentality, getting paper workers involved in electoral politics at an unprecedented level. Republican moderate Congresswoman Olympia Snowe barely scraped to victory in a 1990 reelection campaign with less than 50 percent of the popular vote, for the only time in her lengthy political career. The Jay strike labor movement took some credit for this close scare and the fact that, subsequently, Snowe was more aware of and supportive of taking positions of interest to organized labor. For example, she heartily opposed NAFTA in 1993 and voted to override a policy by President George W. Bush's administration to deny overtime pay to 5 million workers.[70]

Most important was the impact Jay strikers had while working at other paper mills, and other major industrial employers such as Bath, Maine, Iron Works during the strike. Jay strike leader Ray Pineau describes the response of fellow workers when he was briefly at the S. D. Warren Westbrook mill:

> Well, it was outstanding. We would . . . present ourselves as strikers from Jay to the members of the local. . . . The workers would come over to us and ask us what it was like. . . . The reason that they would indicate such a strong support is that they knew there was no doubt that what happened in Jay would be directly reflected in what was going to happen in Westbrook. . . . But the fight was so long lasting, so intense, and it involved so many people from across the country, not just in the area. And I think that probably they sensed that, and they were a big part of it.[71]

Peter Kellman recalls:

> At the union hall at Jay, during and after the strike, when these [Jay workers] . . . were working (in other) paper mills would come back . . . they would talk about the conditions at these different places, and what the people were talking about, and how they were proselytizing, how they were constantly talking to people about what's going on. And they were seen as leaders in those mills—people looked to them—but it was also, to me, it was gratifying to know that when you go through a strike, they become very political, and very conscious of themselves as workers.[72]

Tying the High Road to the Low Road: Manuals and the Attack on Workplace Contractualism

Late in the Jay strike, UPIU leaders across Maine adopted a position that since workers could no longer effectively strike, that they had to find ways of resisting within plants. The question was: What in-plant resistance would workers focus on? Jay strikers emphasized their struggle to resist to the team concept. What made high road experiments elsewhere in Maine radioactive was the practice of having workers develop manuals describing their jobs for training purposes. In preparing for the strike, Jay workers resisted this practice after being tipped off by union leaders in nearby Rumford.[73] Ray Pineau, both a rank-and-file strike leader and a worker who did brief work stints in several other paper mills helped shape workers' thinking about the significance of the team concept:

> And so one of the things . . . clearly was this writing manuals. And this was where they took a strong stand, in the mill, you know, before the strike. The lines were drawn, and that whole notion of class solidarity begins to develop around writing manuals. And this was where they took a stand, in the mill, you know, before the strike.[74]

Wittingly or unwittingly, companies like Scott trying to build worker support for work reorganization inserted this toxic practice into their menu of initiatives. Thus, company initiatives attached this piecemeal practice to the broader notion that the high road was equally part of the brewing class war perpetrated by the paper companies.[75]

The organizing and fallout of Jay strike activism created what historian Lawrence Goodwyn calls a "movement culture."[76] Statewide, paper workers supported Jay strikers and embraced the corporate greed frame for characterizing the motives of the large corporate employers in the paper industry. Because of the near impossibility of winning a strike, Maine UPIU leaders and activists saw in-plant resistance as the new tactic to resisting corporate demands. And, it made resistance to new HPWS projects the focus of its struggle in the class war between paper workers and new corporate owners. The movement was a Maine movement; paper workers and their unions elsewhere, even among those in states like New York and Pennsylvania who had been visited by the Jay caravans, did not necessarily share this perspective and strategy.[77]

Maine paper workers read proposals for strategic change in class war terms when mills around the state, including Fraser and Champion, saw their companies' owners precede contract negotiations by deploying the same threatening optics IP brought to Jay: new fences around the mills, installing houses on mill sites for strikebreakers, and hiring notorious strikebreaker company, B. E. and K. So, companies other than IP dared unions to refuse major concessions on work rules, go on strike, and very likely lose their jobs.[78] Great Northern, still the largest paper employer in the state, didn't use the same atmospherics but concentrated their workers' attention with the layoff of more than one thousand workers just prior to 1986 negotiations.[79]

It was in this context that Scott Paper, the leading company trying to implement the high road in the wake of the IP strike, contended with the forces unleashed by the strike in Jay. Scott's executives sought to radically dissociate itself with IP's forcing tactics, and it embraced the idea of high road win-win outcomes, which was theoretically the opposite of class warfare. While Scott was to have success in many locations across the United States, it confronted a tumultuous environment in Maine.

THE HIGH ROAD COMETH

Look, sometimes you [i.e., Scott Paper] will give us people to work with that are pretty honorable people. And they work here for a few months, and then they're gone. "Corporate" sends him somewhere else, and a new face shows up—we don't get along with that person too well. And he may not be too trustworthy. Now, how the hell are we going to have good faith that you're always going to give us somebody who's going to be reputable to deal with?

And if it doesn't work out, a year, two years down the road—you say: "Hey, the process is over." We look at our contract, and our contract's been torn apart, we can't get that back without negotiating it back. And I think once it's gone, it's going to be awful hard to get it back, because you guys could be gone tomorrow. All of you sittin' here could be gone tomorrow. Then, we're dealing with a bunch of bastards that are not willing to give us anything back, and they're going to hold our feet to the fire on what's left of the contract. So, we're not willing to do that.

—Bill Carver, President, UPIU Local 1069, Scott's S. D. Warren Westbrook mill

In 1988, Scott Paper executives and United Paperworkers International Union (UPIU) national leaders were both anxious to avoid a scrum like Jay, especially given rumors of huge economic losses for International Paper (IP) as a result of the strike. In a bold strategic move, Scott's senior management, led by Labor Relations vice president John Nee, a former UPIU local union president, initiated a new program of labor management cooperation in 1988 dubbed Jointness.[1] Jointness was a far-reaching gamble on a high road solution to Scott's decade-long underperformance. Scott would avail itself of labor relations best practices—building so-called High Performance Work Systems (HPWS), create win-win solutions with employees and other stakeholders, and join the ranks of companies seeking a progressive alternative to the painful low road debacles like Jay.[2]

Each side faced challenges. Corporate leaders had to sustain an honest, expensive, and long-term commitment to a project with slow and uncertain results.

CEOs like Scott's then chief Phil Lippencott had to stave off the wolf at the door—hostile financial markets unsympathetic to HPWS projects. Sluggish profits during the years it took to implement new work practices often cost top managers their jobs.[3] Scott's unionized workers, local union leaders, and local supervisors all had to buy in to a vast change in the usual ways of doing the daily business of supervision and work.[4] For union leaders and members whose identities and sense of workplace justice were built into traditional job structures, rules, and seniority-based lines of promotion, reorganizing work meant giving up huge swaths of contracts protecting standard practice.[5]

Carver's concerns were paramount. Full HPWS offered to traditional factory workers a chance to overcome assembly line drudgery and expand employee voice. But Maine's paper workers already had a big voice in the actual production process. They had good reason for perceiving work reorganization as a gambit to take away organized workers' most important tools for achieving fairness. There was also an implicit threat: this might just be their last chance of saving their jobs and the middle-class life that went with it. Painted this way, opposition by workers—at least from experts' perspectives—was irrational and self-destructive.[6]

With all of this in mind, the story of Scott Paper's sincere and far-reaching campaign to implement the high road illustrates the difficulties, messiness, and ill-fated prospects for this ambitious project. Credit is due to Scott's strategy and commitment. Its leaders were sincere, sophisticated, and fully committed to a strategy that would take years to unfold. Scott was willing to give their workers wins while avoiding the low road where possible—a rarity at this moment, all the while hoping to retain not only business but also workers' jobs and thus their economic welfare. In the event, Scott did succeed in transforming several of its sixteen U.S mills to the HPWS model.

Scott Paper had three Maine mills—Winslow, Westbrook, and Hinckley (the latter two in the S. D. Warren division). Here, Maine's anticorporate movement culture inspired by the Jay strike was in full force. As we'll see, many local managers were dubious as well. Remarkably, union leaders at Winslow decided to embrace Jointness because of extraordinary commitments Scott made to reinvigorate an old mill. At Hinckley and Westbrook, the opposite was true. Thanks to the toxic practice of having workers write manuals, Maine paper workers identified Jointness as a Trojan horse for sneaking in the low road. Scott and the UPIU leaders, in the end, failed to make a successful case that would overcome these fears.

Arguably, however, we'll see that this opposition was not only rational but also compelling and, to a degree, inevitable, given the proximity of Maine mills and the Jay-inspired movement culture. Events would show that advantages gained by implementing the HPWS had little to do with the long-run success or failure of those mills that had adopted it. In the case of Hinckley, a simple fact that corporate leaders had just invested in the highest technology and best capital equipment was sufficient to retain jobs and keep workers engaged. Ultimately, Wall Street would have the last word.

Proposing Jointness

Beginning in the fall of 1988, John Nee and UPIU officials began appearing at Scott's sixteen mills across the United States to outline Jointness to local managers and union leaders. The first step was establishing labor-management cooperation committees at each mill. These committees engaged in trust-building exercises with the assistance of consultants and then commenced work redesign. In theory, work processes would now emphasize greater use of employees' skills, skill development, flexible work design, and continuous improvement, especially in waste reduction and in the improvement of product quality. These steps would take years to implement.

Jointness was certainly a reaction to perceived lessons of the IP strike, but it grew out of a corporate strategy developed in the mid-1980s to improve Scott's lackluster earnings and overall performance, prior to the IP strike. Top Scott executives analyzed the areas of competitive advantage held by Scott and its competitors. They concluded Scott had none. Procter and Gamble, a direct competitor of Scott in the tissue business and a superior performer, had numerous areas of advantage.[7] At a moment where Wall Street had yet to start regularly sacking underperforming CEOs, there was still room for a leader like CEO Phil Lippencott to pursue a long-term strategy to build competitive advantage. In opposition to shareholderism, Scott pursued an updated version of Chandlerian strategy by improving relations with Scott's stakeholders—customers, suppliers, and most importantly, employees and their unions. But unlike pursuing such a strategy in the 1920s or 1950s, Lippencott and his team were now on a very short leash. Other than a remarkable profit turnaround, being deposed by investors was a proximate threat.[8]

Scott had been the most struck company since 1970. This legacy of conflict was the chief impediment to cooperating on changes in work design.[9] Executives took the bold view that the company needed to strengthen, not weaken, union leaders in order to build a foundation of trust. Scott's leadership hoped that union leaders might be able to bring along their members if they were able to win things of value at the bargaining table. Thus, in contract negotiations in 1988 and 1989, Scott notably eschewed asking for an end to Sunday premium pay, then all the rage. Scott executives made it clear that "we're not going to . . . run roughshod over them and take away all their benefits and all the things they worked for over the years."[10] The company took the unusual step of appearing to make *management* concessions to their unions at the bargaining table at the very moment that low road employers took the opposite tack.

UPIU's national leadership quickly embraced Jointness. For them, accepting Scott's initiative was a profound act of pragmatism, a way for the union to ally with progressive companies to stick it to low road companies. Prior to Scott's proposal, UPIU leadership aggressively opposed the team concept (as HPWS was called at the time). This antipathy was in accord with the union's tradition of workplace contractualism; HPWS called first and foremost for relinquishing the work rules UPIU and other unions had spent decades fighting for. Notably, the national union had conducted anti-HPWS education with union locals across the country in the mid-1980s. Locals fully embraced the message.[11]

Explaining this sudden and abrupt embrace of Jointness to union locals was a tall order. UPIU official John Beck recalls the international's pitch as a recasting of the union's fighting image: mobilizing workers to either "boycott the boss, you know, march through the center of Livermore Falls . . . or to put the shoulder to the wheel with the boss, to try to beat the competition, and to try keeping the plants open."[12] Beck recalls Maine UPIU Locals' initial, somewhat crude, response: "How can you tell us that this guy is an asshole one day, and then, in a little bit, you're going 'no, you know, that other guy is a asshole but [Scott] *isn't* a asshole, this guy is our buddy,' and all of sudden—'you can't do that.'"

The greatest challenge for Jointness was selling the plan to local leaders on both the management and union sides. A Scott executive recalls deep-seated resistance from mill manager down to the rank and file, noting: "Their whole career, they were brought up to be adversarial with each other, and now all of a sudden, we wanted to change that. And that's a hard thing for a lot of people to do."[13]

The varied circumstances of mills, idiosyncrasies of mill managers, local union leaders, and specific labor relations' histories led to very different outcomes. Typical problems came to the fore. Any deviation of commitment by the company in its efforts to create wins for workers and the UPIU could and often did sink years of work; Scott, following new rules laid down by its financial vice president, began to treat specific work processes, such a single paper machine, as assets or profit centers; in some cases this led to shutdowns and layoffs in particular parts of mills. When this happened frequently, or at the wrong time, layoffs could be enough to sink reform efforts in some mills.[14] Moreover, HPWS designs typically reduced or eliminated the need for direct supervisors. As in other industries, frontline supervisors can and did drag their feet; they had the most to lose.[15] Perhaps more than anything, though, was the challenge of overcoming shop-floor skepticism that promised job and income gains—the "quo" in the quid pro quo—would actually materialize.[16] The asymmetry of timing was a problem. Jointness asked union locals to relax (give up) existing job rules in exchange for benefits down the road. Cooperation required a huge act of faith on the part of workers.

On the company side, the growing influence of Wall Street analysts brought the same skepticism. That is, HPWS require a variety of immediate investments: consultants and training, certain kinds of pay increases, and of course foregone concessions, with the returns likely to come no earlier than three to five years earlier. Industrial relations scholars Thomas Kochan and Paul Osterman noted that the eyes of stock analysts—whose assessments can easily sink a company in this era—would glaze over when hearing corporate presentations about plans to building HPWS. In practice, such strategies founded on stakeholderism constituted for the financially minded institutional investor a misuse of funds unless they could miraculously increase short-run profits.[17]

The decades-long shift in the character of mill management was also a problem. Local 1069 leader Bill Carver shined a light on how newer managers lacked the ability to maintain the constructive problem-solving ethos that he had obtained earlier in his tenure. Before the 1980s, managers came up through the ranks, knew the hardships, sacrifice, and commitment of workers, and were able to act cooperatively to solve production problems or personnel issues.[18] New outsiders lacked these traits:

> And then . . . they were bringing in these people from outside the mill to take these jobs—foreman and department supers—and I'm not saying these were dumb people—they were very smart people, they'd been to college and they studied paper making, and that sort of thing, manufacturing. . . . But they were clueless as far as what the problems really were. I mean, they knew how to be a manager, they knew probably the technical end of it, but the really everyday, down-to-earth, problems, they didn't understand. And when you would talk to them on it, they'd just take a hard, fast position on something and stick to it. And in a lot of cases, it wasn't even good for the mill.[19]

This perspective was shared by some longtime managers. Patrick Peoples, a senior research scientist in the technology center recalled that a new company policy in the 1980s requiring foremen to have college degrees backfired: "That just doesn't work. They didn't know what they were doing. They didn't have the depth of experience. And they hadn't developed the skills you need to be the manager of a production unit."[20] Undoubtedly, memory of this aspect of past culture of production at Warren stood in contrast to the new "white hats" who came in from outside.[21]

There was also an asymmetry between fresher faces on the management side and the long tenures of workers and union leaders. In contrast to management at many levels, local and national union leaders had long tenures, and consequently institutional memories, that ran into the decades. Past fights for a better shift schedule or mill-wide seniority, and the turnstile of new managers who neither knew this history nor respected it, heightened skepticism.[22] Even if they trusted current managers, the shortening tenures and outsider origins of local managers meant that current collaborators could and often were replaced by newcomers who ignored past understandings and accommodations.[23] Local labor relations managers were either pushed aside or their role minimized when the brass came in. For example, Curtis Pease had arisen from the shop floor to union official, and then was hired into management by the astute Howard Reiche to help manage relations with the mill's unions. In a 2001 interview, the mention of Scott Jointness leader John Nee provoked Pease's rage, who asked me to turn off his recording equipment for several minutes until he could regain his composure.[24] There was also a split between Scott and S. D. Warren divisions. Warren's mill and sales force managers remained tight-knit after Warren merged with Scott in 1967, and remained so for a long time after. Scott executives who later moved into the division were perceived as outsiders who lacked respect or appreciation for Warren's culture.[25]

These challenges to Jointness' success were exemplary of case-study analysis of the HPWS movement at the time by dispassionate analysts and advocates of the high road.[26] What's different here is that resistance emerged specifically out of Maine's movement culture sparked by the Jay strike. Maine workers and local union activists and leaders saw past the ultimately very sincere efforts by Scott to see a larger picture: those paper company executives already listening to Wall Street patrons were adopting harsh attacks on unions and that even goodwill of the kind being extended by Scott's corporate attack was unlikely to be authentic or sustained.[27] Why the skepticism? Too much of Maine paper workers' lived experience contradicted the happy talk and aspirations of the proposed high road.

In the end, the resistance of Maine's paper workers to the high road reflected an astute assessment of this version of strategic change. The rank and file confronted the existential threat this way: Would corporate leaders put their money where their mouth was through visible signs of long-term capital investments in particular mills, combined with the appearance or retaining of Chandlerian managers? And even if such a thing was established, would the leaders of Scott or other paper companies remain in place to see through the high road over the longer run? Scott did have success in some of its sites, including Scott's Winslow, Maine mill.[28] But ten years later, the skepticism of local leaders like Bill Carver would prove to be prescient.

The remainder of the chapter describes how Scott and UPIU leadership, deeply and skillfully committed to the high road, met with some success, including an exceptional case in Maine. We also learn how the statewide movement culture thickened within the Maine S. D. Warren mills and thwarted cooperation over the high road. Finally, we see the overwhelming force of hostile financial interests taking control of Scott in 1994, bringing ruin to Scott's Jointness program and wreaking havoc on the lives of paper workers in Maine and elsewhere. We see especially how and why Maine union leaders came to define HPWS initiatives as corporate attacks on workers that differed little with IP-style low road onslaught, save for tactics. To offer a full picture, we begin with a look at two of Jointness' successes.

When Things Go Right: Mobile, Alabama, and Winslow, Maine

Scott Paper's Mobile plant was huge: it had three major operations with a total of three thousand employees, including a pulp mill and power generation facility; a Scott tissue and towel mill; and an S. D. Warren division mill.[29] It had had four strikes in the preceding two decades, two in the 1980s. The 1986 strike, waged partly over the company's demands to relax work rules and widen job classifications, was the longest, and it ended when employees returned after Scott threatened to permanently replace striking workers.

In 1988, local management, with the help of John Nee, initiated its Jointness effort. In Mobile, Nee's strategy was able to take root. Trust-building exercises proved successful, and Scott replaced a contentious mill manager with one who was able to win trust from the unions.

In the early 1990s, Scott-Mobile established a joint management-labor leadership team comprised of an equal number of union and management representatives who operated via consensus decision making. This model was attempted in many Scott sites, including Winslow, Maine. The leadership team was able to move forward quickly in work redesign, creating asset teams of cross-trained workers responsible for entire processes. Absenteeism and safety quickly improved, and by 1994, productivity and quality had improved dramatically. For example, the mill was able to achieve top ranking out of 171 major pulp mills worldwide in its digester output, raising output from 800 to 1,150 tons per day.[30]

Scott's Winslow, Maine, mill, the former anchor of Hollingsworth and Whitney Company, was a smaller and older facility founded in the nineteenth century, with eight hundred employees in the late 1980s. It produced a variety of products—

including tissues, paper towels, Cut-Rite plastic wrap, and S. D. Warren publication papers—on mostly older machines. The only capital investments in the previous generation was a retrofitting of two paper machines to make the S. D. Warren papers and plastic wrap in the late 1970s. Local labor relations were contentious, including a 1980 strike over a demand by Scott to eliminate mill-wide seniority.[31]

Jointness efforts gained momentum after 1990. First was the advent of new union leadership who represented a break with the sensibility, if not philosophy, of prior union leadership.[32] Perhaps most crucial: Scott persuaded local leaders that it was committed to Winslow over the long term as a key regional producer of commercial tissue and towel products. Scott offered to keep Winslow open as a modestly downsized mill, focused on a core business, with a long-term future *if* Winslow workers embraced HPWS.[33] Other Maine UPIU leaders adamantly opposed to team concept recognized that as a small, older mill facing likely closure, it made sense for Winslow's union leaders to strike this type of deal. Senior Scott executives regularly visited Winslow to reassure workers that the mill had a future. On the union side, UPIU vice president Jimmy DiNardo and local business agent Gordon Roderick were also a reassuring presence.[34]

The most important event was the advent of a new mill manager, Fred Boyd, in 1991. Boyd had been a senior manager at Winslow, highly trusted by Winslow union leaders and workers, who had joined Scott's senior management in Philadelphia. Boyd convinced Scott's brass to bet on Winslow and then returned to implement the new plan. His stature was that of a respected mill manager from the industry's paternal era.

Boyd helped found the new joint mill leadership team, using consensus decision making to plan out and implement major changes in mill operations. Here was Scott's Jointness plan at its best—fully including union leaders in mill management and establishing what in Germany is known as codetermination. Management shared all financial data with union leaders; UPIU locals brought in their own accountant to teach them the relevant accounting and verify the data's authenticity. Union leaders also credit the lead consultant for being effective in a variety of ways—sharing insider Scott information with them, being willing to criticize Scott managers, assisting the local union leaders in developing leadership skills, and helping them to understand the perspective of Nee and other corporate leaders of the Jointness effort. Under new conditions, Scott made good on the promise of creating Chandlerian stability just when shareholderism was gaining full force.[35]

Winslow's leaders and Scott negotiated a difficult development—the announcement that Scott would shut down all noncommercial tissue and towel operations, resulting in the loss of 250 jobs. Union leadership made the company's handling of the layoffs a test, asking for generous severances and a promise of no future layoffs. Scott responded by granting the union's wishes in full.[36]

The period between 1992 and 1994 saw significant progress. While only about 20 percent of workers initially participated in training required to get pay-for-knowledge advancement in the new technician system, by 1994, 80 percent were participating. Thus, most of the workforce achieved the top technician three status—meaning they had acquire both new people skills for working in teams and business skills required for statistically-based quality improvement practices. This training took about eighteen months to complete, and workers were rewarded with substantial pay raises. Scott made significant capital improvements, completing a major rebuild of a paper machine, installing new testing and computer monitoring equipment, and heavily automating the finishing department. In a few years, overall costs had steadily declined while quality improved, raising profit margins. Many of the cost improvements came not just on the shop floor but also from efficiencies in purchasing raw materials and machine parts identified by hourly worker teams. Along with Mobile, Winslow had become a model for the rest of Scott. Both were among national HPWS experts' favorite demonstration cases.[37]

Failure at S. D. Warren

After its 1967 purchase of S. D. Warren, Scott made a major commitment to Warren's product niche by building a massive new, technologically advanced $1.5 billion mill to produce Warren standard grades. Located in Hinckley, Maine, and known as its Somerset mill (for the county its located in), some eighty-eight miles north of Westbrook, it was remarkably the only major new mill opened in the Northeast United States after 1970. By the mid-1980s, it had a pulp mill, two huge paper machines (and was completing a third), and was further advantaged by being located much nearer to Scott's Maine woodlands. Workers were initially recruited from Scott's nearby Winslow mill. Somerset eventually employed about one thousand workers, and at the time of this book's writing is the one remaining paper mill in the state still near its peak employment level.[38]

Scott and UPIU leadership's efforts to implement Jointness at Westbrook and Somerset met huge headwinds and ultimately failed. Union leaders and rank and file in both locations were deeply tied into the Jay movement, which reinforced local cultures antithetical to Scott's quest to implement the high road.

Even if it hadn't been stoked by the Jay movement, Somerset union workers would probably not have embraced Jointness. Following common industry practice, Scott recruited its core workforce from the Winslow facility, which was only twelve miles away. Scott agreed to union representation in order to avoid conflict at Winslow, and until 1985, UPIU Locals 431 and 911—founded in Winslow in the 1940s—also represented workers at Somerset. Thus, while a new mill, Somerset carried over the legacy and style of bargaining that had existed at Winslow.[39]

Karl Dornish came to the mill from Westbrook in the early 1980s as a senior manager. He was immediately confronted with the mill's tough relations, with hard attitudes on both sides. According to Dornish, his fellow managers told him: "What I had heard . . . is, 'we're up here from Winslow, and we've got the worst contract in the world out of Winslow, the unions really killed us, and we're not going to give them anything. . . .' And so they really would go overboard to knock the union back, and as a result the union was very obstreperous."[40]

The principal union leader in the decade between the mill's initial construction and the arrival of Jointness was Frank Poulin. Poulin began as president of Local 911 at Winslow, led negotiations at both mills for nearly a decade, and finally led newly separate UPIU Local 9 at Somerset in its first two years (1985–87) as a separate entity. Poulin was a notorious, pugnacious fist pounder (see anecdote in chapter 3). Like Marv Ewing at Westbrook, Poulin stamped the traditional sensibilities of manly union leadership in defense of job control unionism onto the culture of subsequent leaders of Local 9.[41]

For Poulin, any HPWS proposals that asked union men and women to be responsible for disciplining team members was simply unacceptable. In discussing his rejection of Jointness, one traditional concept was sacrosanct: the division in responsibilities between management and hourly. He made this point:

> I don't believe there's [any place] between a management or a union person. . . . You can't be both. And this self-management, personally, I'm against it. What they're trying to do . . . is to put the responsibility on the worker's shoulders. That's not what I'm hired for. I was hired to do a pipefitting job, he's hired probably to be a machine tender, or whatever, and the supervisor should be doing their job. One of these days there's going to be friction, it's going to hit him right back between the eyes. And the reason I say that is, when you have this joint concept, so to speak, a crew leader—you're going to vote who is in your crew and who isn't. That's a management function. Not a union function. And discipline. They always say: "you don't have to discipline." Well I don't believe that either. When a problem comes, and arises, with the company, they'll call you in to testify.
>
> So, no, you can't serve two masters. You're either union, or your management. You can't change it.[42]

Grudges and memories stood at the ready any time bargaining took place. Somerset workers conducted an unusually successful three-week strike in 1985; Local 9 won its bid to move to a thirty-six-hour work week, three-days on, three-days off, with twelve-hour shifts. The new schedule gave workers more time off per se, and it allowed workers to recover better from night shift work. Starkly, this was perhaps the only successful offensive paper mill strike in the 1980s.[43]

When Jointness was presented to managers and union leaders at Somerset, interest was weak on both sides. For management, it represented a Scott overture, something the S. D. Warren managers viewed with disdain. Karl Dornish spoke with derision about Scott corporate officials' presentation of Jointness: "Scott, I always thought, was great at fads. That's a great concept, if you can do it, but those aren't the guys to do it, [laughs] because they can't stay at it. So, yeah, I went to the meetings where Phil [CEO Lippencott], Dick Layman and all of the Scott brass would come to, and *ply the platitudes.*"[44]

One remarkable development feeding resistance came from a training session organized by Somerset union leaders, led by Local 9 president Carl Turner, in fall 1988. The session featured Jane Slaughter of *Labor Notes.* At the time, Slaughter and her frequent coauthor, Mike Parker, were the labor movement's most vociferous critics of 1980s' labor-management cooperation, quality circles, and other variations of the team concept.[45] The *Labor Notes* perspective was that high road initiatives were Trojan horse measures aimed at undermining union strength. Slaughter recalls her standard presentation from that time:

> And we would have talked about, explicitly, some of the dangers in these programs, ranging from making the union irrelevant, to swamping the union leadership because they are going to all these other meetings, to speed-up itself, to dividing the union among people who think this is great versus the people who don't—calling each other the dinosaurs or the sucks.[46]

Local 9, with the support of UPIU international representative Gary Cook, who also serviced Westbrook's UPIU Local 1069, invited not only the Maine Scott council but also leaders of other Maine UPIU locals at other companies to the training. It is notable that such an event—bringing in a radical critic at the beginning of an important international initiative, might not have been tolerated in other, more centralized unions. But with the support of Cook, who embraced the class warfare perspective of the Maine paper workers' movement culture, Local 9's leadership felt comfortable asserting their independence, and fortifying their views. Slaughter recalls from this training that "they were already in resistance mode; they were just looking for more information, ways to fight, things like that."[47]

To leaders at both S. D. Warren mills, Slaughter's critique of Jointness simply rang true. If the union bought into the proposal, seniority would be undermined and workers would be required to discipline peers. Jointness's brand of HPWS meant, in their eyes, a radical loss of union locals' ability to protect workers via exercising the contract, especially seniority–based progression.[48]

At Somerset, Local 9's leaders were also convinced that their new mill's superior competitive position put them in a strong position to resist. Turner stated: "We've got a new mill . . . we've got a contract; they're not going to shut the place down, so we're not going to need this Jointness." Moreover, Turner and others saw great advantage in being free-riders: they got the benefits of Scott's swearing off of aggressive concessionary demands as part of its Jointness campaign. Whether a local Scott mill ultimately bought into Jointness, all were saved from demands to end Sunday premium pay. Hinckley workers were thus able to maintain traditional job protections, grievance and arbitration rights, and other provisions that Jointness was perceived to threaten. Local 9 felt like it didn't have to go along, so it didn't.[49]

Westbrook's Local 1069 and Jointness: "The Toughest Local This Side of the Mississippi"

> And then, there was Westbrook.
>
> —Former Scott executive, interview

> We question authority at all times. . . . John Nee had labeled us the *toughest local this side of the Mississippi River* . . . and [with] the tenaciousness of a pit bull we . . . won't let them destroy our contract.
>
> —Tom Lestage, UPIU Local 1069, interview

Without a doubt, UPIU Local 1069 at S. D. Warren's historic Westbrook became the vanguard of resisting Jointness. It leadership fully embraced the Jay movement. Local 1069's leadership and political culture was shaped indelibly by its recent militant legacy and deep commitment to workplace contractualism.

Local 1069 formed a close relationship with Jay strikers in 1987 and 1988. Like Somerset's Local 9, it raised money through regular membership collections to help pay the Jay workers' strike benefits, hosted strikers for local forums on the strike, and both leaders and rank and file made the seventy-mile trip to Jay to join demonstrations against IP. And like most large industrial workplaces in Maine, a number of Jay strikers took jobs at S. D. Warren.[50]

Coming out of the Jay strike, paper worker union leaders and activists began to speak of the no-strike rule. But this didn't put an end to resistance to the paper companies' class war. Because resistance to high road initiatives could be legally prosecuted through existing contract mechanisms, along with shop floor resistance, the struggle moved to this terrain. Just as Jesse Jackson had helped frame radical response to union busting, Jane Slaughter provided a radical analysis of HPWS initiatives.[51]

A national UPIU staffer working on Jointness recalled of these Maine workers: "*Their fear of being co-opted, in these programs, you could cut it with a knife. And . . . even if they had never read a line of Marx, you know, [they had a] very, very strong kind of local, nascent Marxist (view), in terms of their class analysis.*"[52] Carver, the UPIU official, and others all recall that only recently UPIU trainings provided by the international had attacked the team concept, and were now trying to sell a "complete 180."[53]

Remarkably, Westbrook's management first wanted workers to develop training manuals on their own jobs, a red flag in the wake of Rumford and Jay. Some local managers seemed truly unaware of the connection their workers were making. For management, it was an efficiency question. A former manager described how highly skilled first and second hands "would all have their unique way of running operations, which they weren't willing to share." He attributed their recalcitrance to a desire to make themselves irreplaceable. Warren management seemed not to get union trepidation when the IP strike strengthened the issue as a point of contention with the union: "I remember one time, they [the union] wanted to have total control over all of the training documents. So, if there was a strike they could walk away with them, which was just garbage."[54]

It was in this setting that Scott Paper initiated Jointness at Westbrook in 1989. Between 1989 and 1994 these negotiations went through several phases. The first was an effort to increase general labor-management cooperation. Jointness was succeeded in the early 1990s by enabling, under which the mill and its unions developed pilot total quality management (TQM) projects, such as a waste/cost-reduction committee as well as a renewed focus on safety. Finally, the company sought acceptance of a plant-wide work redesign in negotiations during 1993–94. Rank-and-file members of Local 1069 ultimately rejected the proposal negotiated by union and management.[55]

As with Somerset, local managers as well union leaders at Westbrook saw Jointness as a dictate from corporate, and neither side rushed to embrace this new cooperation initiative. One former manager put it this way: "Both parties didn't come to the table with the best of intents. Or with the belief that it was going anywhere, or that it was a valuable use of time."[56] While management perceived the union as recalcitrant, it also admitted that their side also was slow to put aside older ways of doing things. Early on, managers continued to take unilateral actions that conflicted with Jointness' goals:

> What usually got in the way, was . . . the need to manage back at home in the same old way. You might jointly, within that meeting, talk about areas of cooperation, but you might walk out of there, and you might give that person a suspension. . . . You might, look at the workforce and see that you have too many workers and downsize.[57]

Both sides were also unimpressed by the Scott executives who met with and presented the program to management and union officials in Westbrook.[58] Nonetheless, management officials recognized that the mill's age, and the increased competitive pressures it faced, necessitated efficiency efforts, and therefore that the mill's long-term survival depended on the mill redesigning its work processes, at least to a degree. Current managers maintained their hard-nosed attitude but still sought to get the unions to agree to change its contract and participate in work redesign.[59]

Turning to Local 1069, UPIU's earlier critiques of HPWS resonated with the local's leaders. President Carver: "In fact, the international warned us . . . to watch out for this Jointness stuff. It's just a way of stealing language and worker's rights, away from you, under the pretense that they are going to be your friends."[60]

That Local 1069 resisted is unsurprising. Leadership also saw the new work practices as solving a problem that did not exist; namely, in the mill's craft and collaborative tradition, workers on particular processes, engineers from the technology center, and supervisors had long worked together to solve production and quality problems.[61] As Carver put it: "I told John Nee and all of the rest of them: 'You guys don't really know that we resolve thousands of problems every year. This isn't nothing new as far as solving problems—we've been doing it. It's an ongoing thing.' The company comes to the union, with a situation that's going on in the plant that's not good, to keep jobs. The union got involved with them to straighten that problem out."[62]

Moreover, they saw Nee's initiative in terms framed by Slaughter: it was a project to weaken if not destroy the union altogether. Carver was emphatic on this point:

> They had these little key words—Jointness, flexibility. *I mean, what the hell is flexibility?* . . . I was no college graduate, but it didn't take me too long to realize just what the hell was up—*the company wanted the workers here in Westbrook to pretty much give up most of their rights under the contract, just under good faith.* . . . The thing we won't do, is give them everything we've negotiated over the years. I mean, if you do that, you might as well decertify, and get the union out of there, and let the company do what they want.[63]

Despite its hard, initial stance, Local 1069 nonetheless participated in five years of negotiations and projects. Throughout, the union executive board debated seriously over the company's proposals, with some leaders expressing interest or support. There was also turnover within the union's leadership, with later leaders taking less of a hard line. And, the union fully participated in several pilot projects. One project supported by the local was a major waste reduction project, largely viewed as a success. Both sides were enthusiastic about the results. In the rare cases during this period where a new production process was created within the mill, the union also acquiesced to management's desire to organize work along high performance lines.[64]

However, new managers soured the atmosphere. Howard Reiche retired in 1988. After Reiche, Scott brought in a series of mill managers whose tenures were brief, and in the case of one manager, disruptive, and who further lacked credibility because he came from the auto parts industry and knew little of the technology or culture of a paper mill.[65] In 1991, this widely disliked mill manager gathered the entire workforce, surprising even the management, for a meeting that backfired. The mill manager stated, "All assets in the mill were 'under review'"; employees were asked to find ways to save money or expect parts of the mill to be shut down.[66]

David Martin, a third-generation paper maker who came up through the ranks into supervision, recounts how management training in cooperative leadership foundered and stood in poor contrast to the generous touch of Warren's traditional paternalistic culture. He and other front-line supervisors were sent to Philadelphia headquarters for such training. Martin already prided himself in having long practiced the new philosophy being presented to them. In his own prior application of the Mother Warren ethos, he had a bargain with his crews—leniency and respect in exchange for a willingness to work extra hard when needed. Here Martin cites the culture of what economists call gift exchange that was the heart of the Mother Warren tradition.[67] Martin was called on the carpet by the new mill manager for not disciplining a worker who, in violation of a contract provision, had a third absence within a three-month period. This absence was to attend the worker's uncle's funeral; this uncle had raised the man, and "was like a father." Martin both knew this man to be a good and committed worker and truly understood how close this family relationship was to him. Disciplining the worker under these circumstances was an act of aggression, and the supervisor refused to do—the matter was taken out of his hands resolved by a higher level of management according to mill managers' wishes. Martin wondered out loud why the top mill management had not been trained in the same new philosophy.[68]

Another critical event was the shutdown, announced in late 1992, of the mill's finishing operation. Union leaders claim that management had made a verbal promise that the operation would be retained if a joint, local cost-cutting committee—a typical HPWS venture—could reduce the overall cost per ton in this area by $100 per ton; the committee's final recommendations claimed a $110 per ton reduction. Scott still shut down the operation, moving the work to a green-field, nonunion facility in Pennsylvania. This resulted in the loss of over two hundred production jobs at a time that the mill's overall employment had recently dropped to 1,500 from over 2,000 in the late 1980s.[69]

The signal case was the proposal to reorganize workers across the mill into cross-trained teams that rotated jobs. The union's reaction to this proposal was equivocal; some of Local 1069's leadership viewed positively certain aspects of job rotation. For example, job rotation reduced repetitive motion injuries, and it was thought that reduced hierarchy could improve solidarity amongst the rank and file.[70]

Still, both the union's leaders and its rank and file had major problems with reorganizing work in this fashion. Paper had been made effectively for genera-tions with work organized in the familiar hierarchy where workers rose from fifth up to first hand. One issue was how pay rates would be equalized within teams. In the company's proposal, an employee who was initially at a lower place on the line of progression—for example, a fourth hand—would get their fourth-hand's pay plus up to $1.83 per hour of "pay for knowledge." Many of the younger rank and file felt that if they were going to be trained to a first-hand level, they should be paid accordingly. More senior workers were also unhappy with job rotation. Having paid your dues doing the intense physical labor characteristic of lower jobs, seniority-based promotion relieved older workers of heavy physical labor. Job rotation meant the end of that benefit.[71]

In 1992, management and union leaders traveled to A. O. Smith, a Milwau-kee auto parts plant that Scott's consultant had worked for earlier and consid-ered a benchmark example of HPWS. The consultant considered it a role model because union and management were able to cooperate and implement an HPWS, despite enormous layoffs. Scott's managers were approving: "Their union president talked like he was in management. . . . They had job rotation, and those workers who didn't want to cooperate feel the heat from their union leadership."[72]

Local 1069's leaders recalled the trip in almost exactly the same detail but with a different interpretation of the meaning of what they learned. Carver, like Som-erset's Frank Poulin, was horrified that union officials and members were required to discipline fellow workers, crossing the sacrosanct line between union and man-agement. Carver was repulsed: "After being there for about two hours, you couldn't tell the union officials from our managers here at the mill."[73] Lestage con-curred: "And so they were doing the company's bidding, and that was very dis-tasteful to us." For Lestage, Carver, and other Local 1069 members along for the trip, the consultant's utopia symbolized a nightmare. On the spot, Carver exercised a contract provision giving either side the right to unilaterally fire the consultant. "If you think that piece of shit that you just showed us is something that we want, I got a surprise for you. Because there's no way I'm going to let the union treat our members the way that these union officials are treating theirs."[74]

In 1994, Local 1069's executive board recommended the work redesign to its membership and put it up for a vote, despite their serious reservations. Scott had moved significantly on one issue by offering large buyouts to injured workers unable to rotate. The surprising willingness of these leaders to recommend (though half-heartedly) a version of the work redesign reflected an assessment of how weak their position was.[75] As Carver notes:

> Our concern was we had a contract coming up within the next six . . . or eight months, and . . . in that high time of no strikes, you're kind of [committing] political suicide to think about asking for a strike vote or anything. So, we recommended it because we feared that they would force it down our throat anyway—either you get paid for it and take the buck-eighty . . . or you'd get it come next fall and you wouldn't get a nickel for it, they'll just put it in, and you ain't gonna walk because of it. . . . It failed anyway. It didn't pass.[76]

Ironically, if Local 1069's membership had voted for the HPWS proposal, they would have seen it nullified within months. The leader of a sister S. D. Warren mill in Muskeegon, Michigan said in 2003 that his union had voted for the work redesign, and he and his members had later regretted it for the same reasons articulated by Carver.[77] Shareholderism, for Westbrook, Winslow, Mobile, and other Scott-owned plants, would have the last word on these mills' fates.

Epilogue: Chainsaw Al and the Destruction of Scott

Jointness came to an abrupt end during "Chainsaw" Al Dunlap's brief CEO reign at Scott during 1994–95. Dunlap's dramatic tenure became a leading parable of how financial engineering on behalf of shareholders—divest and distribute—can be brilliantly lucrative. The Scott/Dunlap episode was featured in a Harvard Business School (HBS) case and received even more attention as the lead chapter in a heralded 1998 HBS conference and book that summoned the best of business academia and the corporate world to debate shareholderist and stakeholder models of corporate transformation. Scott's place in the book couldn't be more prominent; Harvard scholars Beer and Nohria use it as their first and fully archetypal downsize and distribute shareholder strategy—featuring Chainsaw Al's disman-tling of Scott.[78] But success for shareholders meant devastation for workers and communities, and it negated the progress that Jointness program had achieved. Within some eighteen months, a third of Scott's twenty-five thousand employees lost their jobs. Dunlap then oversaw the sale of remaining operations to two competitors—Kimberly Clark Corporation and South African Pulp and Paper In-dustries (SAPPI). Dunlap's moves netted shareholders a nifty $6.3 billion-dollar windfall. Dunlap himself got a stunning $120 million, mostly from stock options but also a $20 million noncompete bonus for agreeing to not work for another paper company for five years.[79] Dunlap's actions cost over eleven thousand work-ers their jobs. Despite a booming economy, most of these workers in Maine and elsewhere typically saw their income drop by half—with the attendant loss of homes, marriages, and shorter life spans.[80] Dunlap then moved on to consumer product manufacturer Sunbeam, notably inducing major layoffs including in sev-eral Maine facilities before his unscrupulous accounting methods effectively ended his career. He was permanently banned by the Securities and Exchange Commission from heading public companies.[81]

Scott Paper's story illustrates the state of the struggle between shareholderism and HPWS in the late 1980s and 1990s. The center of ultimate power lay with Wall Street and its complex of investors, financiers, stock analysts, and other mem-bers of the financial coalition. This coalition used control over institutional funds to fire underperforming CEOs and ensure that financial engineering took precedence over long run strategies such as HPWS. Indeed, the core financial strategy was huge layoffs (and thus speed-up of the remaining workforce), plant closures that came with tax benefits, and then sale of remaining operations to leveraged buyers who would load up the remaining company(s) with debt burdens.[82]

Dunlap's ascent to Scott's CEO chair was at the expense of long-time chief Phil-lip Lippencott. Lippencott's top corporate advisors (largely Scott executive vice presidents) had initially sold him on the stakeholder approach and ultimately the Jointness effort.[83] In a different era, or in another nation with a patient institu-tional financial system, the two choices such a leadership would face would be a HPWS project like Jointness or business as usual.[84] But by 1990 in the United States, structural change was imperative, either through a program like Jointness or financial engineering. Stakeholder strategies like Jointness were on a very short leash.

Even in the early stages of Jointness, Wall Street's wolves were bearing down on Lippencott. Per se, major U.S. paper companies had felt this heat for at least a decade, and Scott's record in the 1980s as a subpar performer (profitable, but below the targets that Wall Street stock analysts describe as adequate) meant that business as usual was a prescription for rapid decline and failure.[85] But just as Jointness was getting underway in the late 1980s, Scott's executive vice president for finance acted as the Charlie McCarthy to the Edgar Bergen of the stock analysts' assessment of Scott's performance. Scott's senior vice president who led Jointness recalled the advent of these wolves. By 1989, stakeholder efforts had made some progress and Jointness was well underway. Before the 1990–91 recession, Scott's financial performance improved significantly due to these efforts. Despite this, Scott's finance vice president began demanding that the company's operational managers suddenly start squeezing workers, suppliers, frontline management ranks in order to effect a quick further increase in profitability. He recalls: "our vice-president of finance got up basically and said: 'all we got to do is increase our margins a couple of percent and reduce our turnover—our assets to sales, basically by 10 or 20 percent, and the numbers work out. So that's all you've got to do.'" Doing so through improved productivity was totally unrealistic. "Trying to increase margins 2 percent on a business is a *tremendous amount of increase*. And, you work like hell to get a 1 percent margin increase. When you're running around 5 or 6, to go to 8 is 25 percent increase in the profit of the business. *And it just didn't make any sense.*"[86]

At the very moment that Jointness was beginning to have a real impact, Lippencott had clearly turned toward shareholderism. The context was a short recession in 1990 and 1991, predictably depressing business not just for Scott Paper but the entire industry. The leveraged buyout procedure used to seize control of underperforming companies was on what would be a short hiatus after a recent financial crisis, but the corporate world was well aware that shareholderism was waiting on the doorstep for companies like Scott. This Scott vice president describes what happened as a lament:

> Sometime around the early nineties, 91, 92, Phil [Lippencott] got off of [stakeholderism] and got refocused on the shareholder is the most important stakeholder, and we've got to cut cost and make money for the shareholder. And as soon as that shift started to take place, Scott went right down the hill. . . . Everybody at that point started to get treated differently, and over a longer period of time that became a serious problem, to the point that it ruined Scott, I really believe that.[87]

The bottom line on Scott's high road efforts is that it did improve the economic performance of some of its mills. But this came to a sharp end once Dunlap took over in early 1994. Dunlap immediately implemented radical cuts in middle management, ended safety efforts and laid off safety staff. Jointness was abolished soon thereafter.

It is worth recounting the fate of the four Scott operations described in this chapter in the wake of Dunlap's moves. The new Somerset S. D. Warren mill did little in the way of adopting new work schemes or abandoning traditional job control unionism. Notably, it has remained a successful mill in the subsequent twenty years because of its modern equipment and technology and traditional workforce skills.[88] For the historic Westbrook facility, it is obvious that if it had adopted full work redesign in 1994, its HPWS would have been stillborn as Dunlap came in and scuttled such efforts. With the economy strong, Westbrook maintained its employment and production levels until 1999. Sharp downsizing then ensued.[89] As we'll see in chapter 8, other options were on the table in Westbrook that might have altered its fate.

The fallout from the turbulent change in Scott's governance for Mobile and Winslow was much more severe. Scott's actions under Dunlap resulted in these two showcase mills' closures. At Winslow, Dunlap's executive team reneged on the previous no lay-off commitment. Union-management codetermination and further investments in the project were immediately halted. At the end of 1995, the traditional part of Scott was sold to Kimberly-Clark, a direct competitor in the tissue and towel business. Kimberly-Clark shut down the Winslow mill in 1998.[90] Former union leaders there are still convinced that their mill's productivity and quality was superior to that of Kimberly-Clark's competing facilities.[91] Kimberly-Clark's strategy fit that of many companies at the time that sought to acquire facilities for the sole purpose of closing them in order to restrict industry supply and raise prices.[92]

Mobile's facilities were broken up when Dunlap sold the S. D. Warren division to SAPPI in 1995. The S. D. Warren coated paper mill went with SAPPI, while the tissue mill and pulp mill stayed with Scott. The synergies that came from the cheap pulp and energy that advantaged the two paper mills on site were lost when the company was broken up.[93] Within a few years, the two paper mills were buying pulp and energy on the open market, with the pulp and energy facilities closed. Eventually, the cost advantages once enjoyed were lost. SAPPI closed its Mobile facility permanently in 2001.

While many factors contributed to the fate of these two shuttered mills, the fundamental question of corporate governance looms large. As we saw in chapter 6, corporate leaders responded to pressures from low-profit performance and the enhanced power of Wall Street by attacking and sometimes eliminating their unions. Here, we've considered the more optimistic and constructive high road strategy during its day in the sun. Like Saturn, which languished and then closed in the 2000s, the days of HPWS in the paper industry were numbered. While there are legitimate questions about the wisdom of Westbrook's UPIU Local 1069's absolute resistance to Jointness, Carver's prescience was uncanny, particularly when considering the fate of the Mobile and Winslow plants. Defending job control unionism at Westbrook may have been fighting last year's war, and in and of itself resistance would not forestall the gale of creative destruction coming at U.S. paper manufacturing. But retaining its protections and forms of workplace justice continued to be valid. For the workers at S. D. Warren Westbrook, the class war unfolding in Maine in 1987 and 1988 made any other path seem foolish.

8

MEMORY, ENTERPRISE CONSCIOUSNESS, AND HISTORICAL PERSPECTIVE AMONG MAINE'S PAPER WORKERS

As the 1990s and 2000s wore on, Maine's once great mills hemorrhaged jobs. The historic Westbrook mill contracted from over two thousand jobs to several hundred in the early 2000s. Employment at Great Northern Paper Company's three mills shrank by two thirds over the same period. By 2000, frequent layoffs hollowed out once great institutions and the way of life described over the course of this book. A number of the historic mills—including those in Madawaska, Jay, Bucksport, Rumford, Old Town, and Lincoln hung on after 2000 as private equity companies swooped in, bought the mills using highly leveraged sources of credit, sought and received huge concessions from unionized workers, and kept a few specific paper machines and products running with vastly reduced workforces (most in the range of two hundred to six hundred) and for the most part had at best medium-range business strategies. Many fully closed within a decade, damaged especially by the deep 2007–09 recession, the now well-established influx of paper imports from advanced mills subsidized by governments (especially but not only China, which receive permanent trade status with the United States in 2000) and the shrinking markets for publication papers as the digital reading became widespread. By 2017, only seven major Maine mills remained open with an average of five hundred employees each (see figure 8.1).[1]

Not surprisingly, the loss of the last, large, well-paid source of rural employment (outside of health care), sparked a progressive depopulation of rural towns in Maine, leaving a population that is mostly over fifty and soaring rates of hunger and drug addiction.

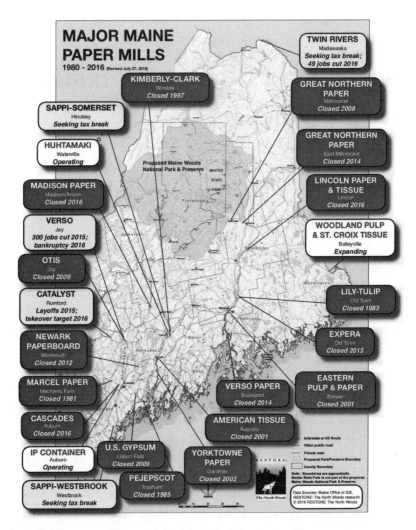

FIGURE 8.1 Map of Maine paper mill closings, 1980–2016. Seventeen major paper operations permanently closed in Maine between 1980 and 2016, leaving only seven major facilities operating with vastly reduced workforces (RESTORE: The North Woods).

But rather than ending on the familiar note of economic and social loss to deindustrialization, let's consider the agency of paper workers. At the heart of their agency was the creation of a radicalized criticism of paper companies that included an implicit history of capitalism—a folk political economy. This history of capitalism contrasted corporate governance and labor relations in the Chandlerian and shareholderism eras. For them, the transition from one to the other was at the center of why companies had gone into decline.[2] The Jay inspired movement culture targeted a new corporate greed, one that encapsulated the attacks companies waged against unions in the 1980s and 1990s, growing managerial incompetence, and declining capital investment.

This folk political economy is evident in the recollections of former workers from the historic S. D. Warren mill in Westbrook. Asked about how they came to terms with class war against Maine paper workers, and their unfortunate encounter with a rapacious shareholderism, workers wove together their rich description of life during the Mother Warren era with their critiques of how their company and the economy had changed since that era.[3] Notably, they also acted on their critique, seeking to purchase and run the mill themselves.[4]

Historian and oral history maven Alessandro Portelli reminds us that community memory is a complex act of construction.[5] Memory in this light is not a literal reconstruction of the past and should not be evaluated on how true it is to specific events and items of fact from the past. Community memory does do two things: convey meanings communities develop that transcend any specific accounting of specific past events, while responding to the needs of the present. For Warren workers who lived in or near Westbrook, the period after 1985 was marked by the cumulative trauma of deindustrialization. This trauma stemmed from the initial assaults on their union contracts; an alienating turnstile of mill managers with little sense, in the workers' eyes, of how to run their historic mill; the death by a thousand cuts by means of frequent small layoffs and several large ones—one Local 1069 leader referred to the multitude of layoffs as "like cutting the dog's tale off, one inch at a time";[6] and the progressive abandonment by distant owner-investors of their cherished enterprise. Overall, Warren's workers thought the decline of their mill was not inevitable.

The famed Mother Warren labor relations legacy was an intriguing and contradictory mix. On the one hand, older workers maintained and passed on a memory of its pre-union years—the legendary extraordinary kindness and generosity of Warren's local managers and owners. Memories of shop floor problems overlapped with sunny recollections of the Warren family's generosity. Workers who lived through the late pre-union years of the 1950s and 1960s recalled favoritism and nepotism and the company's failure to stay current with unionized mills in providing workplace fairness, health and retirement benefits, and seniority protections.

As we've learned, UPIU Local 1069 responded to this aspect of the past by developing a militant workplace contractualism, where the workers themselves for the first time became responsible, through the creation and enforcement of union contracts, for the employment outcomes they once experienced as a guarantee from their kindly bosses. As this doctrine's fiercest advocate, Local 1069 went on to play a key role in the movement culture sparked by the Jay strike. The Jay movement, and the insights of radicals Jesse Jackson and Jane Slaughter, helped Westbrook workers develop a radical critique of what they perceived as class war perpetrated by heartless out-of-state corporations. As we learned in chapter 7, this included a perceptive grasp of how financialization and shareholderism made high road offers a dubious gambit not to be trusted; subsequent events confirmed their skepticism.

Let's explore what Warren workers remembered. When asked about the past, they invoked Mother Warren as a guarantor of the worker and his or her family's economic security. Mill managers, and some supervisors, were remembered for their deep personal care for and interest in workers and their family's well-being. Job security was multigenerational. When asked about a family's employment history, workers responded with some version of "first my grandfather got in, then, my father, then my mother, and *I* got in. There were cousins, uncles . . ."[7] The mill's safety net extended to the mill's weakest: the injured, the alcoholic, and the sick were supported, rehabilitated, and tolerated, but never fired.

Central was Mother Warren's ubiquitous provision of security. Rescue stories feature prominently—workers in financial or health troubles could count on the mill manager directly producing a loan, to be paid back by deducting "a dollar out your check" for as long as it took to repay the loan.[8]

At the very heart of the narrative was filiopietism—a worshiping of the founding father Samuel Dennis Warren, who was repeatedly invoked by name. Warren and his managers built what was once the largest paper mill in the world, and they endowed the company with its technological prowess, recognized as the font of a prosperity shared by all. Warren and his descendants were remembered as guarantors of a cradle-to-grave economic security, and they embodied the powerful paternalism of direct contact, acknowledgement of, and care for each worker. Not surprisingly, the widespread trope of "like a family" was a thick sinew in workers' stories. A typical recollection: that Samuel Dennis Warren himself would bail you out—"if a worker ran out of coal, he'd come to your house and give you coal, whatever you needed."[9] Joseph Jensen, whose thirty-year span in the mill included first being a member of the in-plant union organizing team from 1965–67, and then many years as a production manager, recalled: "It was a kind of a close *family*-run type of a thing, it was that atmosphere inside. . . . The mill manager lived right here on the mill property. . . . He lived right on the site, came through the mill, and walked through the mill, talked to people on the floor, a lot people's family came into the mill, a guy's sons or daughters would come work at the mill, so, it was kind of a close-knit, family type of a thing."[10]

In 2000, Chris Murray, a young electrician, had recently taken a job elsewhere shortly ahead of a huge 1999 layoff in which he would have certainly lost his job. Born shortly after the Warren era ended in 1967, he nonetheless excavated a deep knowledge of the mill founder. He had collected a century's accumulation of local hagiographies of the founder and subsequent Warrens as a way of coming to terms with his and the mill's circumstances.[11] When the author began to interview Murray, he plopped down a pile of dusty manuscripts and a sheaf of old newspaper clippings. When I asked how he came to study Warren, he said:

> I started doing research on him myself. . . . There is so much out there on him, and what he did, and what his family did for the community. I mean, I live in Westbrook, and half that city, he might have owned it, *but he gave it back*. He built schools. He built churches and parsonages, and ball fields, and swimming pools, and he gave it, and housing, and gave it to the people of Westbrook. Now, don't get me wrong, I'm sure *he* was making a lot of money at the time, but, the stuff he did, *he* didn't have to do. *He* didn't have to build the city church—I think *he* gave half of it to the old church that was on the corner there. It's unreal. It really is. I mean, I know that it doesn't appear to happen today at all. But what a great thing back then.[12]

Knowing that his father's and mother's generation made constant reference to S. D. Warren, Murray made sense of loss by reaching back to learn of Warren's beneficence, and he concluded that Warren, if alive in 2000, would have been disgusted.[13]

Notable is the sense of class justice.[14] Warren clearly was a wealthy capitalist, cashing in on the company's powerful economic position, but he is remembered equally for sharing the mill's profits with the community and its workers. Part of workers' sense of their role in their industrial community was a keen sense that the company's profit be used wisely. This could take two forms; for example, by investing in new machinery or paying for research and development and sales efforts that secured the company's and workers' economic futures, *or* if profit was shared with workers and community as an extra reward.

Shirley Lally, who inspected paper and counted reams of paper by hand for four decades, described how she understood the shift when Scott purchased the mill. "I felt it wasn't *family* any more. That it was from out of town. I really, I know the Warren family was from Massachusetts, originally, so that's out of town too, but no, I felt, no I felt that we'd been sold down the river. I wasn't too happy."[15] I asked if she thought Scott treated the mill and Westbrook workers differently than the owners from the Warren era. She said unequivocally: "*They used us. They used us*. . . . They just milked us, I thought. Maybe it would have happened anyway—I don't know. But, they cut the trees down. I mean, they weren't careful. They didn't care about Westbrook. They really didn't. They just wanted to make the money, and then sell it piece-by-piece. And get out. It's even worse now than it ever was." In the end, she said, "it didn't feel like *family*. It was different. Just different."[16]

Thus, the owners' family blended into workers' families, perhaps the dominant trope of the paternalistic mill employers throughout U.S. industrial history.[17] The remembered mill founder was a double signifier: the benevolent owner who cared about, and cared for, the workers and their families. And secondly, they were an emblematic part of a producerism;[18] in this instance, it was the shared skill and technology prowess of the workers who made the paper, the engineers who built great machines and invented new products in adjacent labs, and the senior managers that secured massive accounts with leading New York publishers and dozens of accounts with midsized printers that together contributed to Warren's long record of success. The founding fathers' credibility as rulers (however beneficent) was especially rooted in their superior entrepreneurial capacities. They were construed to be true captains of industry and fellow and honored members of a producer class of paper makers.[19]

This sensibility is illustrated by the remembrances of novelist and memoirist Monica Wood. Wood grew up in Mexico, Maine—part of the Mexico-Rumford community home to Oxford Paper. Her best-selling memoir, *When We Were the Kennedys*, recounts what she characterizes as an oft-repeated geography lesson that features the story of Hugh Chisholm, founder of both International Paper and Oxford Paper, where Wood's father worked.[20] Chisholm was a childhood friend of Thomas Edison, and Wood recalls her third grade nun and teacher's lush parable about how Chisholm was a brilliant entrepreneurial talent superior to the nation's greatest inventor. The teacher placed this parable alongside tales of great explorers and discoverers like Christopher Columbus and "all those brazen men from Spain and Portugal . . . [and] their intrepid forays to convert the heathen masses."[21] This veneration of the founders' brilliance was a signifier for the collective pride in the industry's success—due in no small part to the equal talent of the machine hands who had made the nation's highest quality paper. To use the formal language of business, these employers were corporate governors of a special kind, progenitors of a fair and just industrial community.

As we'll see, the workers' folk political economy saw decline as stemming from the shift from Chandlerian to financialized corporate governance. These workers had inherited a deeply productive organization, reliant on the skills of machine tenders, paper inspectors, technology center chemists and engineers, and those who maintained the company's long successful marketing and sales strategy. Even a fifth hand winding rolls of paper and female paper inspectors had a critical role in ensuring paper quality and company profitability. In economists' language, these were organizational capabilities and core competencies.[22] As we'll see, when financialization made its presence in the 1980s and early 1990s, Westbrook workers could account in detail how these capabilities/competencies were gratuitously (or "endogenously") destroyed.

Paper mill and forestry managers, as a group, had a different perspective.[23] Managers cited objective economic trends as the causes of paper industry retrenchment. They noted the impact of new technologies that automated production and sharply reduced labor requirements; the advent of new competition from plants in the U.S. South, Canada, Scandinavia, and Asia; and, after 1990, the problem of endemic overcapacity within the United States and abroad as the paper industry sales flattened and then started to decline.[24] In a similar vein, forestry managers present during the Maine Woodsmen's Association strike saw the restructuring of pulpwood production, especially mechanization, as a response to objective labor trends (declining labor supply), the need to use new technology to renew productivity growth, and the problems of the budworm, while minimizing the role of protesting woodcutters in the companies' new emphasis on expensive mechanization.[25] These causal factors, in economists' language, were exogenous—factors outside the firm. Labor relations was a variable but mainly as a negative—as in Maine's contentious workers and unions discouraged continued investment in Maine.[26] Workers saw the causes of decline as internal, in terms of relationships, and the subjective agency of their employers. Whether it was the demand for concessions at a time of record profitability (e.g., at Jay and Rumford), or the abrupt closure of International Paper's Mobile, Alabama mill in 2001, the deep belief in their skills and the viability of a profitable paper mill, company leaders were betraying their side of a relationship that *should* and once *was* about mutual obligation. In historian Timothy Minchin's study of the Mobile plant's closure, the workers felt that "the company should not have closed a profitable mill with such dedicated employees."[27]

Thus, memory of Mother Warren was a belief system that valued the enterprise its workers and past owners had built. Workers celebrated the Warren family's class justice—particularly the owners' extensive distribution of company profits in community public works. They dwelled on the how the kind of economic security Warren offered that was vastly at odds with the market realities faced by other workers in Maine at the time, or Maine paper workers per se after the 1980s.[28] They celebrated the communal values that were insinuated in the company's paternalistic culture. And they insinuated the craft pride of workers into the legendary prowess of their founders.

In turn, the loss of local, family ownership is invoked in describing the shift in corporate governance. "Out of state" was a loose signifier for the changing types and behaviors of the national companies that became owners of Maine's historic mills from the 1960s on. Continued survival of these mills under difficult circumstances required two elements that progressively slipped away: sufficient capital investments, and use of and investment in the local talent built up over generations. The question became: How to bring this about?

Buy the Mill?

Scott Paper executives contended that the Westbrook mill was losing its competitiveness. Nonetheless, Westbrook's workers and managers continued to see their mill as a flagship operation, with many advantages over other S. D. Warren division mills and other companies in their market. This thinking was not far-fetched: Scott's S. D. Warren division was the largest publication paper producer in the United States in the early 1990s. At the time, industry analysts still saw the Westbrook mill as a viable enterprise with a future.[29] In the midst of Scott's Jointness initiative, Scott brought in new outside managers that plied workers with the financial language of assets that came from economist Michael Jensen.[30] That is, each component of the mill was conceived of as separate assets, to be evaluated separately, then shut down, reinvested in, or even sold off. Then, on 1991, Scott announced that the mill as a whole was being put up for sale altogether.

Union leaders were more than dubious of the depiction of the mill as a collection of assets. This brash new company narrative furthered the sense that corporate owners had lost all commitment to the mill. Longtime mill manager Howard Reiche retired in 1988, followed by a quick succession of three mill managers, including one who had never worked in the paper industry.[31] This deepened the sense that the mill's fate was in the hand of senior executives with little facility for running the mill effectively. As the top hollowed out, they began to see the eclipse of their enterprise. In their political economy, Mother Warren was an enterprise that deserved, both economically and morally, to be governed by competent and committed stewards. The more they looked at it, the more they decided that the best stewards might just be themselves. If they couldn't exactly recreate the Warren era by bringing back now dead benefactors, worker ownership would be a feasible alternative.[32]

And so, the mill's unions took up the project of making an offer to purchase the mill, led by UPIU Local 1069. For them, the mill's decline could be attributed to changes in corporate governance that replaced the previous era legitimate owners—for instance, the loss of a Chandlerian ethos shaped by a once local ownership. In creating a contrast between two historical eras, each with their own institutional characteristics, effects on prosperity, and ethical norms, they were able to confront the new threats to their enterprise with a coherent analysis.[33]

As noted, Westbrook was the original Warren mill, with a rich past and culture. Locals had a strong identity based on confidence in workers' and engineers' skills, the status of their mill's products as industry leaders, the importance of Maine's high-quality industrial forests for providing the pulp needed for high-end paper products, and especially the ability of its technology center to generate new products and product improvement. At the time in the early 1990s, the technology center had recently invented and patented a new Ultracast process for making paper molds for auto seats, synthetic leather, and a variety of other products.[34] It had also developed new pressure sensitive products such as peel-and-stick labels. At the same time, during the previous thirty years, Scott diverted the mill's profits to other mills for a variety of reasons, including the militancy of the mill's union locals, the more efficient layout of the Hinckley mill, and the access of the other S. D. Warren mills to regional markets outside of the Northeast.[35] Despite the advantages of these new locations, Westbrook's workers were at a loss—perhaps beyond recognition of the consequences of the workers' union strength—to understand why grades and investment would be moved elsewhere. Regardless, its workers had confidence in the mill's future, a sentiment shared by paper workers at other Maine mills, along with Wall Street analysts.[36]

Discussing the mill's viability in retrospect, Tom Lestage argued:

> [We had] the world-renowned, best quality coated paper in the world. We had the market cornered on Utracast products . . . the Ultracast products, it was just a money pit. . . . So even through this whole dark cloud [time frame], we were being the top initiatives in the company, creating brand new products, successful products. I mean [our machines] were one hundred years old, [and] we were still breaking records in our facility; we were famous for that throughout the chain. If you couldn't run it, bring it to Westbrook and we could run it. And that's where the grade development, that's where the technology center was recognized, and was put here. [Westbrook was where] . . . the complete knowledge, the complete dedication to process from our guys, and girls.[37]

David Martin, a third-generation paper maker, put it eloquently:

> Westbrook had a world-wide reputation of making some of the best paper in the world, and we always prided ourselves on that. But as they began merging with these bigger companies, and more mills became part of the chain, they started taking our grades of paper and tried to make them in other mills, and they just couldn't make 'em like we did. And the quality suffered immensely, and eventually business got so bad for those particular grades that they just took them off the market, they

disappeared. And I felt real bad about that, because we used to make some beautiful, beautiful paper. And when they found it wouldn't work some other place, why they never brought it back, I don't know. That's one of the problems with making decisions in Philadelphia for a mill that's in Westbrook, Maine.[38]

Indeed, as workers explored making a buyout offer with Wall Street consultants, they got a firm impression that the mill would continue to be a very profitable operation. A Wall Street analyst observed that "I don't see why [the workers] wouldn't want to buy the plant. . . . As economic conditions improve [the Westbrook S. D. Warren plant] could be a very interesting purchase."[39] Workers believed that "the mill appears to have been doing well with its expensive and lucrative pressure sensitive papers . . . [and release papers] . . . [and] workers say executives have told them at periodic plant updates that the mill is profitable."[40] Overall, S. D. Warren workers had great confidence in the ability of their enterprise to prosper given competent management and financial commitment.

This contrasted with Scott's announced strategy of putting the mill up for sale. Scott saw the mill's future as limited, in the narrow segments of its newest specialty products (pressure sensitive and Ultracast products), and it downplayed the future of its coated publication papers despite pronouncements by analysts that Westbrook's sales in the grades would be strong as the economy rebounded from the 1991–1992 recession.[41] In 1992, Scott began to ship existing publication grades to other mills within the S. D. Warren division. This was taken badly by the Westbrook workers, who saw this as poorly conceived action that would accelerate the deterioration in Warren grades' reputation and further the mill's decline.[42]

As workers saw representatives of prospective buyers tour the mill, they embraced the idea that they should buy the mill themselves. It became evident that Scott was having a hard time attracting a buyer, which further clouded the mill's future. The local buyout effort was initiated and led by Local 1069. In December 1991, the unions announced that it was hiring Wall Street consultants to explore the company's financials and help them construct a realistic offer. Tom Lestage recalled that former mill manager Howard Reiche was willing to invest in the buyout and possibly return to help oversee a new management structure.[43]

After identifying various sources of financing, the workers offered $147 million to purchase the mill in 1992. In November 1992, Scott announced that it was refusing the offer because it was roughly $40 million less than what it was seeking, and it took the mill off the market. Union leaders found this deeply frustrating because it cut short any attempt at further negotiations on price.[44]

The moral of this story is how memory was used to construct a folk political economy and how its critique of modern owners blended with the belief that the workers themselves could become the kinds of stewards that had existed during the Mother Warren era. They appropriated a different sensibility about the nature of moral and effective corporate governance from this remembered past. Like workers elsewhere faced with the mean taskmaster of creative destruction, they sharpened their belief in the enterprise as a community institution whose true constituents—stakeholders, in business language—were the workers and the locals who depended on the mill's prosperity. Core to their political economy was a consciousness of enterprise that stood at odds with modern theories of the capitalist enterprise that underlay shareholderism.

The S. D. Warren case is also, in one respect, distinct from similar cases of resistance to creative destruction—for example, the celebrated struggles of Youngstown steel workers where workers also sought to save their mills through worker buyouts and developed a belief in community property rights over local industrial enterprises.[45] The difference in context is that Maine workers were reacting to shareholderism; from their encounters with new corporate rulers in the 1980s and 1990s, they fashioned sharp distinctions in the historical forms of corporate governance and how these shaped their enterprises' prosperity or lack thereof. Worker and community ownership was not so much a property right as an effective proposal to reinstate the conditions for their employer's success.

In their 2003 edited volume, *Beyond the Ruins*, Historians Jefferson Cowie and Joseph Heathcott offered the most notable recent intervention on the experience of U.S. industrial decline.[46] They begin with the important point that while creative destruction is an inevitable part of capitalism, it nevertheless comes as a shock to those who suffer its consequences. They note that "to many workers who walked out of the factory gates for the last time . . . it must have felt like an occupying force had destroyed their way of life."[47] Like the essays on memory in their volume, Maine's paper workers also "reveal a powerful sense of moral economy that they believe their employers violated"; and their celebration of a legacy of skill and achievement permitted them to escape "portray[ing] themselves as simple victims."[48] Cowie and Heathcott go on to argue that learning from this history, and workers' engagement with it, is most useful if used to recast "capital in terms of stewardship, democracy, and prosperity broadly shared" in a manner that requires "writ[i]ng new rules."[49]

Maine paper workers, responding to disruption and decline, especially in the 1980s and 1990s, generated a folk political economy that argued for such new rules. Either by building a statewide movement to protest International Paper's union busting, in their disgust with mismanagement by new outside managers, or in seeking to become the mill's owners at S. D. Warren, Maine's paper workers were willing to fight for a capitalism with values. This is their contribution to the conversation about how to write new rules in a twenty-first century political economy.

Epilogue

PAPER WORKERS' FOLK POLITICAL ECONOMY VERSUS NEOLIBERALISM

Since the 1990s, class resistance in Maine's paper industry has waned—and with it, the movement culture that shaped and sustained it. The folk political economy described here also had its moment, as many of those who held it have moved on or passed away. But its narrative and economic imagination has resonance for Mainers and is a cultural artifact that can be joined in a critique of neoliberal capitalism.[1] Read closely in the state and quite evidently nationwide, there is widespread antipathy to key features of the neoliberal era: especially the loss of local ownership and control of enterprises and the replacement of Chandlerian stability with the fierce and ugly rationalization imposed by financial investors. Overall, this antipathy is aimed at neoliberalism's assumption that only unfettered private markets provide good economic outcomes.

Maine's paper workers' folk political economy can be an important resource in sharpening a critical discussion about Maine's economic future and by extension the nations. Most importantly, it offers two alternatives to financialized corporate governance: a return to traditional Chandlerian practices or worker ownership. These views are grounded in a historical memory of good and bad capitalisms in the past century. Their local provenance makes it more likely to find traction in a broader discussion of economic alternatives than the abstract arguments proffered by academic experts in the neoliberal camp.[2]

Since 2000, Mainers of all political stripes regularly embraced a role for the state in preserving important local enterprises. For instance, in 2005, local workers learned that Maine's second-largest industrial facility, the U.S. Department of Defense-owned Portsmouth Naval Shipyard (PNS), with over four thousand highly paid, unionized employees, would soon lose their jobs, thanks to a decision by the federal Base Realignment and Closure Commission (BRAC) to put it on the newest list of military facilities slated for closure. Union and community activists joined Maine and New Hampshire's Congressional legislators who took up the fight to keep the base open. With Republican Maine U.S. Senator Susan Collins in the lead, Mainers flooded local hearings, sent twenty busloads of locals to Washington D.C. for a protest, and set to work marshaling evidence that the PNS was a cost-effective, highly efficient, and modern enterprise. In Senate hearings and in the press, Collins acted like the lead defense attorney. Protesters and local politicians recognized that the facility's fate was under the control of the democratically elected branches of the federal government, and that the decision to keep open or close this huge, public, industrial facility lay within the purview of leaders accountable to the public. The ensuing and effective campaign resulted in PNS being removed from the list of facilities slated for closure.[3] Over a decade later, it thrives, with PNS increasing employment by over two thousand, a nearly 50 percent increase in a major expansion in the late 2010s.[4] Without much critical reflection by the participants, it is nonetheless clear that the enterprise consciousness associated with the PNS is at odds with neoliberal norms that eschew a central role for the state in adjudicating the rights of a local community over an industrial enterprise.

Moreover, Democratic governor John Baldacci (2002–10) and Republican Tea Party Governor Paul LePage (2010–18) repeatedly mobilized in a similar fashion each time a Maine paper mill was slated for closure by its owners.[5] Here the rules are somewhat different: while these campaigns are similar, elected leaders rely on finding new private investors to purchase mills and keep them running. With technical and strategic help from the principal paper workers' union, now part of the United Steel Workers, these local alliances have succeeded in reopening mills for a time—though often with far fewer employees—at Fraser in Madawaska, the former Great Northern Paper (GNP) mills in Millinocket and East Millinocket, Lincoln Paper, and the Old Town's former Georgia Pacific mill, among others.[6] Following the example of local buyouts in the 1990s—including Hathaway Shirt in Winslow, Maine, and Biddeford Textile—these politician-led efforts have focused on finding new investors (local if possible) and salving difficult competitive circumstances with aggressive local economic development packages typically featuring extensive tax breaks and state-supported financing. At one point in Millinocket, the former home of GNP, locals called for taking over one of the former mills through eminent domain.[7]

These events are evidence that Mainers across the political terrain see major industrial enterprises as community institutions, not simply privately owned assets. This is at odds with the prevailing neoliberal wisdom that shareholders or private equity investors are the only valid residual claimants.[8] And perhaps the best way to validate this enterprise consciousness is to tap into paper workers' critique of the flawed corporate governance that comes from out of state corporations characteristic of this era of shareholderism.

A number of sentiments and developments drive this thinking. First the contrast between financial vulture capitalists and the traditional corporate governance has become ever sharper. For aficionados of the topic, there is even the case of a Koch Brothers financial fund that bought a Maine paper mill, dithered with it for a couple of years, and then shut it down.[9] And the idea that workers or the community might possibly follow Westbrook's example and publicly own and reopen mills sprouted elsewhere in the state.[10]

These views suggest a narrowing gap between common thinking in Maine and the increasingly and fundamentally critical views of our political economy among wide swaths of the U.S. public. New thinking has emerged about an "America beyond Capitalism," to use the apt title of Gar Alperovitz's popular book. These works explore cooperative economic practices, including worker ownership, and are part of new economic imaginaries—literally what people consider to be possible economic institutions and practices.[11] If individual cases like PNS or the attempted buyout of S. D. Warren are valid, why not worker ownership as a more systematic alternative to financialized corporate governance?

A related, instructive discussion is to ask: Was the death or truncation of Maine's great paper enterprises the inexorable outcome of iron laws of capitalism? Or, are there, among the varieties of capitalism across U.S. history and across national boundaries conditions under which creative destruction could have been managed in a way that preserved, at least to a greater degree, industrial prosperity in paper and similar industries?[12]

The necessity of destruction of what workers themselves believe are viable enterprises and livelihoods, one can argue, is far from a settled matter. Most economists would tell the public that there are objective rules of competition and capital markets, and when the time comes that an enterprise is losing out in competition, or if it generates profits below the cost of capital, deindustrialization is inevitable and contributes to the social good. This is certainly what happens under current institutional arrangements, especially given the power and practices of Wall Street financial institutions.[13]

The Maine folk political economy described here takes issue with this way of thinking. Maine's paper workers' and managers' experience of financialized corporate governance was that it contributed directly to industrial decline. Their insight is that decline was exacerbated by endogenous (or internal) causes: managerial instability, poor decision making, neglect and other fallout from financial engineering, and rapid ownership turnover. It also celebrated the values of reciprocity, class justice, economic security, and what may be viewed as a so-cial democratic ethos associated with the Chandlerian enterprise.[14] Remembered is a form of corporate governance that had room for these values to be embed-ded in an industrial community that could still meet the demands of a national marketplace. Indeed, financialization was antithetical to competing in the mar-ketplace to the extent that it destroyed organizational capabilities built up over years.

Judith Stein reintroduced a topic abandoned twenty years ago—the case for a U.S. industrial policy. Her *Pivotal Decade: How the US Traded Factories for Finance in the Seventies* describes how from the 1970s onward, both liberal and conserva-tive political leaders blocked serious consideration of industrial policy while em-bracing financial and other forms of deregulation that, along with new attacks on unionized labor and free trade policies, ushered in the neoliberal era.[15] By con-trast, since the 1950s, industrial enterprises in nations like Germany, Japan, and France, and more recently Asian behemoths like China, benefitted from national policies and institutions more supportive of Chandlerian practices. These included financial institutions that permit industrial enterprises focusing on the long-term; a range of subsidies including publicly funded research and development; and di-rect, mercantilist forms of managed trade that block import competition and enhance companies' abilities to succeed in international markets. The German model—built on the pillars of patient finance, meaningful worker representation on corporate boards, and a two-track system for worker voice (unions and works councils)—fully addressed the concerns raised here about financially driven in-dustrial decline.[16]

To see what industrial policy in the paper industry might look like, consider Chinese policy since 2000. Fine-coated publication grades that were pioneered and long produced in Maine are now being manufactured in China. The Chinese government poured $22 billion into paper production technology between 2001 and 2011; a significant part of these monies went into designing methods for turn-ing recycled paper from the United States into coated publication papers.[17] While Chinese labor costs are clearly an advantage, arguably the technology in-vestments and currency manipulation are as if not more important in Chinese enterprises displacing those in the United States.

On a final note, the 2016 election of Trump, who is popular in Maine's rural areas where paper mills are now mainly shuttered, shows a missed opportunity for this kind of discussion worth taking up now. The Trump phenomenon is com-plex, binding identity issues and an amorphous economic populism. But one key thread is how Trump garnered broad political support opposed to the neoliber-alism of the Obama-Clinton wing of the Democratic Party and the deregulatory neoliberalism of establishment Republicanism (as did Bernie Sanders). As George

Packer noted in fall 2015, Trump's sudden salience was deeply rooted in his willingness to use (or signal an intention to use) the U.S. government to promote American working-class interests (though squarely aimed at white working-class Americans), through an evinced commitment to maintaining Social Security, restricting low-wage labor supply through his famed border wall, but especially an aggressive trade policy.[18] Practically, there is little to recommend in Trump's actual performance—for example, imposing tariffs at this late stage by itself cannot turn the clock back on the creative destruction that decimated paper employment in recent decades. But it shows a broad political appetite for overturning the conventions of the version of U.S. and global capitalism that prevailed since the 1980s.

As of this writing (2019), one insightful presidential candidate, Massachusetts Senator Elizabeth Warren, has proposed changing corporate governance structures in the United States. Her Accountable Capitalism Act would give worker representatives both 40 percent representation on corporate boards, and, importantly, effective veto power over corporate policies decided by boards of directors. This is a proposal that aims not to end capitalism but to reconfigure its institutional structure to tame the deeply antiworker practices that neoliberalism and financialization ushered in. Lest anyone consider this radical, it is important to remember that it is based on the capitalist institutional structure that has operated in Germany for nearly fifty years.[19]

The folk political economy of Maine's paper workers celebrates an economic life that matches effective production for markets with an extra-market morality at odds with the ruthless version of capitalism that overtook their community institutions. Before concluding, it is important to acknowledge the limits of the political economy these workers remember. Because of the arc of creative destruction, tying social democracy to capitalist enterprises, rather than the society as a whole—usually comes with an expiration date. Post 1970s deindustrialization, for example, has meant the loss of access to health insurance and adequate retirement for the large part of the workforce who once worked for Chandlerian companies overtaken by financialization since the 1980s.[20] So a simple restoration the Chandlerian era would leave in place the long-run structural flaws that come with relying on private institutions to be the sole provider of economic security.

Nevertheless, overturning financialization to put in place better corporate governance would be a radical change to U.S. and global capitalism. It would help address, but not by itself solve, economic inequality and economic insecurity, including but not only the downward mobility of displaced manufacturing workers. A decade of popular rage against Wall Street institutions and practices since the 2008 financial crisis has certainly put such structural changes in U.S. capitalism on the agenda. A majority of Americans now recognize that the private sector, even a reformed one, may still not deliver the goods under present economic arrangements. In 2019, strong majorities in national polls support Medicare for all, a wealth tax on households with more than $50 million in assets, and free tuition at public two- and four-year colleges.[21] In the end, the conversation of our time, and the lessons of capitalist history embedded in stories like the rise and fall of Maine's paper industry, asks that we draw on the best features of our economic past and recognize the urgency of a necessary rebalancing of social outcomes and the market that four decades of financialization and neoliberalism has made urgent for working-class Americans.

Notes

PREFACE

1. Bob Gogan interview, St. David, Maine, July 8, 2008.

2. Phil Dubois interview, Madawaska, Maine, May 5, 2012; Jerry LaPointe, quoted from "Madawaska Rebellion," Podcast audio. Michael Hillard and Gabriel Grabin, producers, first airdate, September 4, 2016, Maine Public Radio. https://beta.prx.org/stories /194809.

3. William Osborne, *The Paper Plantation: Ralph Nader's Study Group Report on the Pulp and Paper Industry in Maine*. (New York: Grossman Publishers, Viking Press, 1974), 133–55.

4. Donald Fontaine, interview with author, Portland, Maine, July 15, 2004.

5. The heart of this movement was a major strike against International Paper in Jay, Maine. Chapter 7 tells the story in detail.

INTRODUCTION

1. See David C. Smith, *History of Papermaking in the United States:1691–1969* (New York: Lockwood Publishing, 1971) for what is still the best source on the industry's rise, including the centrality of Maine and Wisconsin. Besides Smith's important, early book, one can point to only five books in recent decades on the business and labor history of the U.S. paper industry: Robert Zeiger, *Rebuilding the Pulp and Paper Workers Union, 1933–1941* (Knoxville: University of Tennessee Press, 1984); Julius Getman, *The Betrayal of Local 14: Paperworkers, Politics, and Personal Replacements* (Ithaca, NY: Cornell University Press, 1998); Timothy Minchin, *The Color of Work: The Struggle for Civil Rights in the Southern Paper Industry, 1945–1980* (Chapel Hill: University of North Carolina Press, 2003); Peter Kellman, *Divided We Fall: The Story of the Paperworkers' Union and the Future of Labor* (New York: The Apex Press, 2004); and Jamie Sayen, *You Had a Job for Life: Story of a Company Town* (Lebanon, NH: University Press of New England, 2018). In Maine, Pauleena MacDougall and Amy Stevens contributed a number of articles about the business and labor history of Eastern Fine Paper Company of Brewer, Maine. See Pauleena McDougall and Amy Stevens, "The Power of Place in Memory: An Oral History of the Eastern Corporation in Brewer Maine," *Maine History* 45, no. 1 (2009): 4–13; Amy Stevens, "'I've Got a Million of These Stories'; Workers' Perspectives at the Eastern Fine Paper Corporation, 1960–2004," *Maine History* 45, no. 1 (2009):15–36; and Pauleena MacDougall, "Oral History, Working Class Culture, and Local Control: A Case Study from Brewer, Maine," *Oral History Forum d'histoire orale* 33 (2013):1–21.

2. This moniker is taken from William Osborne's 1974 expose of Maine's paper industry, focused largely on environmental degradation, mistreatment of loggers, and undue political power. William Osborne, *The Paper Plantation: Ralph Nadar's Study Group Report on the Pulp and Paper Industry in Maine* (New York: Viking Press, 1974). This author does not necessarily share the pejorative inflection of the term but rather sees it as a metaphor of the scope and depth of the industry's domination of Maine's economy, local cultures, and state politics.

3. These areas contain four hundred townships with impersonal designations like T23 R4 and still account for over one half of Maine's land mass. In 2016, year-round residents

in these territories numbered a mere nine thousand. Notably, thirty-four localities have names that include "plantation," such as Cary Plantation. "Unorganized Territory," Maine Revenue Services, accessed July 14, 2016, http://www.maine.gov/revenue/propertytax/unor ganizedterritory/unorganized.htm.

Maine forestry economist and historian Lloyd Irland has chronicled the history of Maine's forests and forest economy in a number of places, including Lloyd Irland, "Maine Lumber Production, 1839–1997: A Statistical Overview," *Maine History* 45, no. 1 (2009): 36–49; and Irland, *Maine's Forest Industry: Essays in Economic History* (Wayne, ME: unpublished manuscript, 2007, 281 pages).

4. Lloyd Irland, *Maine's Forest Industry: Essays in Economic History* (Wayne, ME: unpublished manuscript, 2007, 281 pages), 43; and Maine Department of Labor, Center for Workforce Research and Information, accessed March 17, 2020, https://www.maine .gov/labor/cwri/qcew.html. Employment peaked in 1967, and remained about the same into the 1980s; the comparison date for the late number in second quarter of 2019.

5. Karl Marx, *Capital*, vol. 1 (New York: Penguin Press, 1977).

6. Joseph Schumpeter, *Capitalism, Socialism, and Democracy* (New York: Harper and Brothers, 1942).

7. See Louis Hyman, *Debtor Nation: The History of America in Red Ink* (Princeton, NJ: Princeton University Press, 2011); Louis Hyman, *Temp: How American Work, American Business, and the American Dream Became Temporary* (New York: Viking, 2018); Nelson Lichtenstein, *The Retail Revolution: How Wal-Mart Created a Brave New World of Business* (New York: Henry Holt, 2009); Bethany Moreton, *To Serve God and Wal-Mart: The Making of Christian Free Enterprise* (Cambridge, MA: Harvard University Press, 2009); Julia Ott, *When Wall Street Met Main Street: The Quest for an Investor's Democracy* (Cambridge, MA: Harvard University Press, 2011); and Daniel Sidorick, *Condensed Capitalism: Campbell Soup and the Pursuit of Cheap Production in the Twentieth Century* (Ithaca, NY: Cornell University Press, 2000). A fine branch of this work not directly relevant here focuses on the rise of U.S. and global capitalism, with a special emphasis on slavery as a foundation for industrial capitalism. See, for example, Sven Beckert, *Empire of Cotton: A Global History* (New York: Knopf, 2014).

8. Chapters 7 and 8 present this story in more detail.

9. In addition to chapter 3, the author's audio documentary "Remembering Mother Warren" provides the listener a thick description of Warren's paternalistic system and community memory that built up during the years of conflict and decline that started with the sale of the company to Scott Paper in 1967. See https://beta.prx.org/stories/2734.

10. There was one unsuccessful strike by part of Warren's workforce in 1916; the strike provoked the takeover of mill management by non-Warrens and pushed the mill to be even more generous to its workers. More on this in chapter 2.

11. Chris Murray, interview with the author, Portland, Maine, September 7, 2000.

12. My thinking about community memory and industrial decline is shaped by a number of classic treatments, especially Alessandro Portelli's pathbreaking 1991 book, *The Death of Luigi Trastulli and Other Stories* (Albany: State University of New York Press, 1991).

13. For background on the industry's Maine origins, David Smith's history in unequalled in its authority. In addition, I draw on Lloyd Irland, Maine's foremost expert on the industry's history and economics. Lloyd Irland, interview with author, Wayne, Maine, August 9, 2011, and Irland, *Maine's Forest Industry*.

14. Smith, *History of Papermaking*, 49–71, 305.

15. See Smith. *History of Papermaking*, 130–36 and A. J. Valente, *Rag Paper Manufacture in the United Sates, 1801:1900: A History, With Directories of Mills and Owners*, (Jefferson, NC: McFarland, 2010), 153–62.

16. This expression is a widely used colloquialism in paper mill communities through Maine and U.S. paper mills. See no author, "Environmental Ordinance—Jay," *Institute for Self Reliance*, accessed March 17, 2020, https://ilsr.org/rule/devolution-and-preemption /2163-2/; Milton P. Dentch, *The ISO 14001:2015 Implementation Handbook: Using the Process Approach to Build on Environmental Management System* (Milwaukee, WI: American Society for Quality, 2016), 1; John Henry, "Smell of Money Will Linger: International Paper Says Pine Bluff Will Be Sold, Not Shuttered," *Arkansas Business* 22, no. 34 (August 29, 2005): 1; Susan E. Dick and Mandi Johnson, "The Smell of Money: The Pulp and Paper-Making Industry in Savannah, 1931–1947," *George Historical Quarterly* 84, no. 2, (2000): 308–23.

17. Jason Newton, "Forging Titans: The Rise of Industrial Capitalism in the Northern Forest, 1850–1950" (Unpublished PhD diss., Syracuse University, 2018).

18. Lloyd Irland interview, and Irland, e-mail communication with the author, July 28, 2018.

19. See Irland, *Maine's Forest Industry*; and Hannes Toivanan, "Waves of Technological Innovation: The Evolution of the US Pulp and Paper Industry, 1860–2000," in *The Evolution of Global Paper Industry, 1800–2050, A Comparative Analysis*, ed. by J.A. Lamberg et.al. (New York: Springer Dordrecht Heidelberg, 2012), 49–80.

20. Two former Maine paper mill managers who headed mills in the 1970s and 1980s each described having fought a losing battle for investment in Maine mills, and the general loss of local autonomy that resulted from being recently merged with large national companies. Howard Reiche Jr., interview with the author, Harpswell, Maine, August 8, 2001, and anonymous interview with former paper mill manager, Portland, Maine, June, 28, 2006. Strikes in both Maine mills and throughout the U.S. hit a high–water mark for the postwar era between the early 1960s and mid-1970s. See Jefferson Cowie, *Stayin' Alive: The 1970s and the Last Days of the Working Class* (New York, NY: New Press, 2012), 1–10, 21–74; Nelson Lichtenstein, *State of the Union: A Century of American Labor* (Princeton, NJ: Princeton University Press, 2002), 98–140; and Nicola Pizzolato, "Strikes in the United States Since World War II," in *The Encyclopedia of Strikes in American History*, eds., Aaron Brenner, Benjamin Day, and Immanuel Ness (Armonk, NY: M.E. Sharpe, 2009), 226–38. Chapters 3 to 5 of this volume provide three case studies of this development in Maine's paper industry.

21. See Adrienne Birecree, "Corporate Development, Structural Change, and Strategic Choice: Bargaining at International Paper Company in the 1980s," *Industrial Relations* 32, no. 3 (Fall 1993): 343–66; Julius Getman, *The Betrayal of Local 14: Paperworkers, Politics, and Permanent Replacements* (Ithaca, NY: Cornell University Press, 1998); and Bruce Kaufman, "The Emergence and Growth of A Non-Union Sector in the Southern Paper Industry," in *Southern Labor in Transition 1940–1995*, ed. Robert Zeiger (Knoxville, TN: University of Tennessee Press, 1997), 295–330.

22. Two qualifications. The U.S. South, and people of color and many women were largely excluded from the early prosperity of the early New Deal era. Also, while private sector nonagricultural union density approached 40 percent during the 1950s, it was the spillover to nonunionized companies such as IBM that carried the higher wage and benefit standards to another third of the U.S. workforce.

23. Popular economic writing includes work by Robert Reich and others who decried the shift of blue collar work in the 1980s to low income nations. See Robert B. Reich, *The Next American Frontier* (Danvers, MA: Crown, 1983). Much of this writing was framed by Michael Piore and Charles Sabel in their influential *The Second Industrial Divide: Possibilities for Prosperity* (New York, NY: Basic Books, 1984), which made the case that a new labor and technology model was essential for the U.S. to be able to keep some good blue collar work given that standardized assembly line work was already flowing to low wage

nations. Progressive writers especially pointed to the rise of the multinational corporation as the villain; see William Greider, *One World: Ready or Not: The Manic Logic of Global Capitalism* (New York, NY: Simon and Schuster, 1998).

24. Modern thinking on corporate governance commenced with Adoph Berle and Gardiner Means's seminal *The Modern Corporation and Private Property* (New York: MacMillan Press, 1932). Michael Jensen and William Meckling's consequential 1976 article quickly became the basis for a new era of financialization, often characterized as the shareholder value movement. Jensen and Meckling, "Theory of the Firm: Managerial Behavior, Agency Costs, and Ownership Structure," *Journal of Financial Economics* 3, no. 4 (1976): 305–60.

On changing corporate governance during the period covered in this book, see Michael Beer and Nitkin Nohria, *Breaking the Code of Change* (Boston: Harvard Business School Press, 2000); Adrienne, M. Birecree, "Corporate Development, Structural Change, and Strategic Choice: Bargaining at International Paper Company in the 1980s," *Industrial Relations* 32 no. 3 (1993): 343–66; Ewald Engelen, "Corporate Governance, Property and Democracy: A Conceptual Critique of Shareholder Ideology," *Economy and Society* 31, no. 3 (2002): 391–413; Justin Fox, *The Myth of the Rational Market: A History of Risk, Reward, and Delusion on Wall Street* (New York: Harper Business, 2011); Sanford Jacoby, "Finance and Labor: Perspectives on Risk, Inequality and Democracy," *Comparative Labor Law and Policy Journal* 30, no. 1 (2008): 17–66; William Lazonick, *Business Organization and the Myth of the Market Economy* (New York, NY: Cambridge University Press, 1992); William Lazonick, *Sustainable Prosperity in the New Economy? Business Organization and High Tech Employment in the United States* (Kalamazoo, MI: W. E. Upjohn Institute, 2009); William Lazonick and Mary O'Sullivan, "Maximizing Shareholder Value: A New Ideology for Corporate Governance," *Economy and Society* 29, no. 2 (2000): 13–35; Paul Osterman, *Securing Prosperity: The American Labor Market: How It Has Changed and What to Do about It.* (Princeton, NJ: Princeton University Press, 1999), 148–62. An important updating of this phenomenon focusing explicitly on the private equity industry is Eileen Appelbaum and Rosemary Batt, *Private Equity at Work: When Wall Street Manages Main Street* (New York: Russell Sage, 2014).

25. Two important examples are the insertion by IP of a Wall Street friendly CEO John Georges in the early 1980s, who developed a low road strategy to devastate union contracts and to outright bust unions in the companies mills, leading to the 1987–88 IP strike (see Getman, 1998), and insertion of "Chainsaw Al" Dunlap at Scott Paper Company in 1994—Dunlap laid off nearly 40 percent of the companies' workers in a two year period, and then sold off the company in parts, netting Scott shareholders a $6 billion windfall; see Stephen Greenhouse, *The Big Squeeze: Tough Times for the American Worker* (New York, NY: Anchor Books, 2008), 83–87.

26. Greenhouse, *The Big Squeeze*, 83–87, and anonymous author, "The Scott Paper Company, Case 9-296-048" (Boston, MA: Harvard Business School, 1997).

27. Chapter 3 recounts this history. For a brief period in the 1910s, a stronger flavor of unions took hold in Maine and national papermills, but were largely crushed in the 1920s. Kellman, *Divided We Fall* and Zeiger, *Rebuilding the Pulp and Paper Workers Union* are the best accounts of this earlier historical chapter.

28. David Harvey, *A Brief History of Neoliberalism* (Ithaca, NY: Cornell University Press, 2005).

29. Many characterize the postwar (1946–73) era as a golden age of shared prosperity, evident in income compression between the wealthy and the working class, a reduction in wealth disparity, and a doubling of median real wages during this period. It was also the era of the greatest expansion of the social wage—public provision through education and social insurance. See Lawrence Mishel, Josh Bivens, Elise Gould, and Heidi Shierholz,

State of Working America, 12th ed. (Ithaca, NY: Cornell University Press, 2012); and Osterman, *Securing Prosperity*. This stylized view of the period overstates the case, as African Americans, women, and many working-class people were either left out or saw few of these benefits until later in this period.

At the same time, the observation of a certain stability in some unionized relations comes with an important qualification—recent scholarship shows that leaders of major industrial corporations developed a multifaceted ideological and strategic effort to undermine unions' place in the American landscape. This long-term effort set the stage for the neoliberal turn in U.S. labor relations in the 1980s, which paper companies joined even if they were not leaders in the New Deal era efforts to attack the premises of unionized labor relations. Lichtenstein, *State of the Union* offers the most comprehensive treatment of this history. For a critical review of the postwar era golden age see Richard McIntyre and Michael Hillard, "Capitalist Class Agency and the New Deal Order: Against the Notion of a Capital-Labor Accord," *Review of Radical Political Economics* 45, no. 2 (2013): 129–48.

30. Leon Fink, "The Great Escape: How a Field Survived Hard Times," *Labor: Studies in the Working Class History of the Americas* 8, no. 1 (2011): 112.

31. Economists Bluestone and Harrison captured the beginnings of the crisis faced by unionized manufacturing workers in the U.S. in the 1980s in their benchmark book, *The Deindustrializtion of America* (New York: Basic Books, 1982).

32. The most important contemporary analysis of this development is Thomas Kochan, Harry Katz, and Robert McKersie, *The Transformation of Industrial Relations* (Ithaca, NY: Cornell University Press, 1994) which first appeared in 1986.

33. See notes 20 and 21 above.

1. A RAGS TO RICHES STORY

1. The U.S. government began to collect solid statistics on literacy in 1870. At that time 88.5 percent of white Americans over the age of fourteen were literate, with a bit higher rate for citizens and bit lower rate for immigrants. African Americans were mostly illiterate, with only about 20 percent literacy rate. During the first decades of the twentieth century, white illiteracy fell to the low single digits and black literacy grew dramatically to nearly 85 percent by 1940. Source: National Center for Education Statistics, "National Assessment of Adult Literacy: 120 Years of Literacy," accessed June 29, 2018, https://nces.ed.gov/naal/lit_history.asp.

2. U.S Census Bureau, *Measuring America: The Decennial Censuses From 1790 and 2000* (Washington D.C: U.S. Department of Commerce, September 2002), Appendix A-1.

3. And grew still further to 570 pounds by 1970. David C. Smith, *History of Papermaking in the United States:1691–1969* (New York: Lockwood Publishing, 1971), 662.

4. Smith, *History of Papermaking*, 662.

5. Adam Smith, *An Inquiry into the Nature and Causes of the Wealth of Nations*, ebook version, Project Gutenberg, Chapter 3 Title; release date February 8, 2009, updated September 7, 2019, accessed March 18, 2020, https://www.gutenberg.org/files/3300/3300-h/3300-h.htm.

6. Richard Nelson and Sidney Winter, "The Rise and Fall of American Technological Leadership," *Journal of Economics Literature* 30, no. 4 (1992): 1931–64; 1939.

7. There is a wide literature on the story of the United States' second industrial revolution. Notable works include: Alfred Chandler, *The Visible Hand: The Managerial Revolution in American Business* (Cambridge, MA: Belknap Press, 1977); Daniel Nelson, *Managers and Workers: Origins of the Factory System in the United States, 1880–1920* (Madison: University of Wisconsin Press, 1975); Michael Piore and Charles Sable, *The Second Industrial Divide: Possibilities for Prosperity* (New York City: Basic Books, 1984); and

David Hounshell, *From the American System to Mass Production, 1800–1932* (Baltimore, MD: Johns Hopkins University Press, 1984).

8. Smith, History of Papermaking, 189–218; and A. J. Valente, *Rag Paper Manufacture in the United States, 1801–1900: A History, with Directories of Mills and Owners* (Jefferson, NC: McFarland Press, 2010), 3–152.

9. Robert Zeiger, *Rebuilding the Pulp and Paper Workers Union, 1933–1941* (Knoxville: University of Tennessee Press, 1984), 19.

10. A. J. Valente, *Rag Paper*, 5.

11. Smith, *History of Papermaking*, 17–48.

12. Smith, *History of Papermaking*, 81–120.

13. See Paul E. Rivard, *Made in Maine: From Home and Workshop, to Mill and Factory* (Charleston, SC: The History Press, 2007); and Bruce Laurie, *Artisans into Workers: Labor in Nineteenth-Century America* (New York: The Noonday Press, 1989), 28–31.

14. Nelson and Wright, "The Rise and Fall," 1937–1941.

15. Valente, *Rag Paper*, 89–102.

16. This paragraph is based on Smith, *History of Papermaking*, 81–152 and Valente, *Rag Paper*, 3–88.

17. This paragraph is based on Smith, *History of Papermaking*, 130–36 and Valente, *Rag Paper*, 153–62.

18. Smith, *History of Papermaking*, 136.

19. Smith, *History of Papermaking*, 152.

20. Poplar would not be the prime tree source for Maine paper mills over the long run. S. D. Warren Company, the first large scale Maine paper company, heavily used poplar in its early soda production pulping process, especially in its Yarmouth, Maine mill, acquired in 1874. Warren phased out use of poplar after 1930. See Yarmouth Historical Society, "Poplar, Forest Paper Co.," *Maine Memory Network* (website), accessed September 2, 2019, https://www.mainememory.net/artifact/67525#artifact-67525; and S. D. Warren Company, *A Hundred Years of S. D. Warren Company* (Westbrook, ME: S. D. Warren Company, 1954), 41–44, 113.

21. Smith, *History of Papermaking*, 152.

22. Valente, *Rag Paper*, 160.

23. It is common to think of a clean, one-step leap forming the industrial revolution—from self-sufficient family farms to full-blow factories. Instead, U.S. farm households in the eighteenth and nineteenth centuries were a mix of agricultural and hand manufacturing production, with many households boarding outsiders (often women) who worked in household workshops making a variety of commodities, either for local barter or to sell to merchants for cash income. The result is that those on the farm prior to 1870 were part of a multigenerational tradition of making things and working with tools and machines. By the 1840s, the hundreds of small mills and shops making traditional goods (grist mills, saw mills, and small paper-making operations) using Maine's water power were joined by modern textile mills, and a burgeoning machine-making industry, which began with the building of the machines for Saco and Biddeford textile mills but grew to include tool and die shops and then becoming a major producer of train engines. By 1850, Maine had well over one thousand machinists. Rivard, *Made in Maine*, 13–38 and 115–49; and Laurie, *Artisans into Workers*, 15–45.

24. Smith, *History of Papermaking*, 81–120.

25. Smith, *History of Papermaking*, 163; Kenneth Root and Rosemarie Park, *Surviving Job Loss: Papermakers in Maine and Minnesota* (Kalamazoo, MN: W. E. Upjohn Institute, 2016), 7.

26. Originally named S. D. Warren and Companies, upon Warren's death in 1888 the company was renamed "S. D. Warren Company."

27. Smith, *A History of Papermaking*, 170.

28. International Paper Company, "A Short History of International Paper Company," *Forestry History Today* (1998): 29–34.

29. Smith, *History of Papermaking*, 189–218; and John L. Leane, *The Oxford Story: A History of the Oxford Paper Company, 1847–1958* (Rumford, ME: Oxford Paper Company, 1958).

30. David C. Smith, *A History of Lumbering in Maine, 1861–1960* (Orono, ME: University of Maine Press, 1972), 189–218.

31. Oxford Paper Company and its workers were located in two adjacent townships, Rumford and Mexico.

32. John L. Leane, *The Oxford Story: A History of the Oxford Paper Company, 1847–1958* (Rumford, ME: Oxford Paper Company, 1958), 6–7.

33. Monica Wood, *When We Were the Kennedys: A Memoir from Mexico, Maine* (Boston: Mariner Press, 2012), 59.

34. Smith, *History of Papermaking*, 169–70.

35. Smith, *History of Papermaking*, 153–218.

36. Chandler, *Visible Hand*, 316–31.

37. Smith, *History of Papermaking*, 153–188.

38. Leane, *The Oxford Story*, 6–19.

39. Smith, *History of Papermaking*, 153–188.

40. Smith, *History of Papermaking*, 173.

41. In the early 2000s, private equity companies (PECs) bought up many Maine mills, and in some instances created funds that financed the PECs' profits up front, driving the enterprise into bankruptcy only to set up another fund to purchase the mill out of bankruptcies for pennies on the dollar. Jackie Farwell, "Paper Money: Private Equity Firms Own Six of Maine's Major Paper Mills, For Better or Worse," *Mainebiz*, May 16, 2011, accessed March 19, 2020, https://www.mainebiz.biz/article/paper-money-private-equity-firms-own-six-of-maines-major-paper-mills-for-better-or-for.

42. One million board feet of spruce or pine weighs approximately two million pounds.

43. David Smith, *A History of Lumbering in Maine, 1861–1960* (Orono: University of Maine Press, 1972).

44. Andrew Barton, Alan White, and Charles Cogbill, *The Changing Nature of the Maine Woods* (Durham: University of New Hampshire Press, 2012), 141.

45. Smith, *History of Lumbering*.

46. Smith, *History of Lumbering*, 200–203.

47. Smith, *History of Papermaking*; and John McLeod, *The Northern: The Way I Remember It* (Bangor, ME: Great Northern Paper Company, 1974).

48. MacLeod, *The Great Northern*.

49. Rumford typified the diverse ethnicity of remote paper town industrial recruits. In 1910, 22 percent of the people in Rumford were U.S. born; 23 percent were French Canadian; and 47 percent were either English, Scottish, Italian, Irish, German, Danish, Swedish, French, Turkish, Norwegian, Russian, Lithuanian, Polish, or Latvian. Nearby Livermore Falls' ethnic distribution was less diverse, though 46 percent were French Canadian or children of French Canadians. Anders Larson, "Franco-Americans and the International Paper Company Strike of 1910," *Maine History* 33 no. 1 (1993): 40–60; 46–51. GNP's initial workforce similarly included French-Canadian and Scot-Irish-English from eastern Canadian provinces, and there were new immigrants from Eastern and Central Europe: Poland, Latvia, Lithuania, Estonia, Russia, Germany, and Austria. Greeks, Albanians, and Lebanese came from the near East. Dorothy Laverty, *Millinocket, Magic City in the Wilderness* (Freeport, ME: Bond Wheelwright, 1973), 15.

The most homogeneous paper mill community would be Fraser Paper Company in Madawaska—nearly all its blue-collar workforce were local Acadian French (split about 50–50 between U.S. and Canadian citizens); managers there were anglophones from Canada and the United States. See Nicole Lang interview, Edmundston, New Brunswick, May 8, 2012, and *Acadian Culture in Maine*, Acadian Archives, (Fort Kent, ME: University of Maine-Fort Kent), http://acim.umfk.maine.edu/.

50. Jason Newton, "'A drunk, a woodsman, a lousy woodsman': Free Labor, Class Formation, and the Spatiality of Production and Consumption in the Hinterland, 1870–1950" (unpublished essay, Syracuse University, 2016); and "'Consult the teamster, the farmer, the woodchopper' Antimodernist Anxiety and Rural Working Class Hegemony" (unpublished essay, Syracuse University, 2016).

51. Smith, *History of Lumbering*, 200–203.

52. There were mechanized vehicles for skidding felled trees from the early twentieth century on, and even small tractors in use in the 1950s, but it was only with the arrival of the skidder in the late 1950s that tree hauling would become widely mechanized. Until the advent of usable chainsaws in the 1950s, the actual cutting and trimming of trees was done with hand tools.

53. David Weil, *The Fissured Workplace: Why Work Became so Bad for so Many and What Can Be Done to Improve It* (Cambridge, MA: Harvard University Press, 2014).

54. Chandler, *Visible Hand*.

55. David Vail, "The Internal Conflict: Contract Logging, Chainsaws, and Clear-cuts in Maine Forestry," in *Who Will Save the Forests? Knowledge, Power, and Environmental Destruction*, eds. T. Banuri and F. A. Marglin (London: Zed Books, 1993), 142–89; and Jason Newton, "Forging Titans: The Rise of Industrial Capitalism in the Northern Forest, 1850–1950" (Unpublished PhD diss., Syracuse University, 2018).

56. Newton, "Forging Titans."

57. This freedom long persisted for many locals, especially those who remained outside of the web of direct company employment. This is not to take away from the incredibly harsh nature of the work, but it is more a testament to ways that woodcutters exploited their nominal independence and the comparative grind of traditional farm work. Newton, "Forging Titans."

58. Newton, "Forging Titans."

59. "Satisficing" is an economics term for settling for enough rather than straining for the maximum.

60. Newton, "'A drunk, a woodsman, a lousy woodsman.'"

61. See chapter 4 in this volume.

62. Smith, *History of Papermaking*, 164.

63. Vail, "The Internal Conflict."

64. Chandler, *Visible Hand*; Alfred Chandler and Takashi Hikino, *Scale and Scope: The Dynamics of Industrial Capitalism* (Cambridge, MA: Belknap Press, 1990); Alfred Chandler, "Organizational Capabilities and the Economic History of the Industrial Enterprise, *Journal of Economic Perspectives* 6, no. 2 (1992): 79–100; William Lazonick, *Business Organization and the Myth of Market Economy* (New York: Cambridge University Press, 1991); David Teece, "The Dynamics of Industrial Capitalism: Perspectives on Alfred Chandler's *Scale and Scope*," *Journal of Economic Literature* 31, no. 1 (1993): 199–225; William Lazonick and David Teece, eds., *Management Innovation: Essays in the Spirit of Alfred D. Chander* (New York: Oxford University Press, 2012).

65. Chandler, *Visible Hand* and *Scale and Scope*; Lazonick, *Business Organization*; Teece, "The Dynamics of Industrial Capitalism."

66. Imagine a "J" slanted to the right. See Theodore Levitt, "Exploit the Product Life Cycle," *Harvard Business Review*, November 1965, accessed March 19, 2020,

https://hbr.org/1965/11/exploit-the-product-life-cycle; and R. D. Norton, "Industrial Policy and American Renewal," *Journal of Economic Literature* 24, no. 1 (1986): 1–40.

67. In addition to Chandler's very readable work, Lazonick's writings offer the best single source on this huge topic. See Lazonick, *Business Organization* and *Sustainable Prosperity in the New Economy? Business Organization and High-Tech Employment in the United States* (Kalamazoo, MI: W. E. Upjohn Institute, 2009). Also, See Hannes Toivanan, "Waves of Technological Innovation: The Evolution of the US Pulp and Paper Industry, 1860–2000," in *The Evolution of Global Paper Industry, 1800–2050, A Comparative Analysis,* ed. J. A. Lamberg et al. (New York: Springer Dordrecht Heidelberg, 2012), 49–80

68. See Adoph Berle and Gardiner Means's seminal *The Modern Corporation and Private Property* (New York: MacMillan Press, 1932); Chandler, *The Visible Hand;* and Lazonick, *Business Organization.*

69. Chandler, *Visible Hand;* Lazonick, *Business Organization.*

70. S. D. Warren Company, *A Hundred Years,* 90–92; James Madden, *A History of the Hollingsworth and Whitney Company, 1862–1954* (Boston, MA: Hollingsworth and Whitney, 1954), 1.

71. Berle and Means, *The Modern Corporation.*

72. Companies like U.S. Steel were originally ruled by Wall Street financiers who could closely hold control of the company with as little as 10 or 20 percent of total shares. Over several decades, control by these financiers would wane, shifting to top management.

73. S. D. Warren, *A Hundred Years;* Madden, *History of Hollingsworth and Whitney;* MacLeod, *The Great Northern;* Leane, *The Oxford Story;* Smith, *History of Papermaking.*

74. S. D. Warren, *A Hundred Years;* Madden, *History of Hollingsworth and Whitney.*

75. Thomas Beckley, "Pluralism by Default: Community Power in a Paper Milltown," *Forest Science* 42, no. 1 (1993): 35–45; S. D. Warren Company, *A Hundred Years.*

76. See Berle and Means, *The Modern Corporation;* John Kenneth Galbraith, *The New Industrial State* (Princeton, NJ: Princeton University Press 2007); and Nelson Lichtenstein, *A Contest of Ideas: Capital, Politics, and Labor* (Urbana, IL: University of Illinois Press, 2013), especially Chapter 4, "Tribunes of the Shareholder Class," 47–55.

77. Julia C. Ott, *When Wall Street Met Main Street: The Quest for an Investor's Democracy* (Cambridge, MA: Harvard University Press, 2011), 185–88; and Marco Becht and J. Bradford DeLong, "Why Has There Been So Little Blockholding in America," in *A History of Corporate Governance Around the World: Family Business Groups to Professional Managers,* ed. Randall Morck (Chicago, IL: University of Chicago Press, 2005), 613–66.

78. Economists, led by Frank Knight, Henry Simons, and later Oliver Williamson, focused intensely on this question, seeing it as exemplifying a principal-agent problem to which a financialized firm aggressively attacking slack and firing managers with this sensibility was seen as solving a problem and advancing capitalism. A useful review is found in Oliver Williamson and Sydney Winter, eds., *The Nature of the Firm: Origins, Evolution, and Development* (New York: Oxford University Press, 1991); see also Lazonick, *Sustainable Prosperity?* 200–215—for a critical perspective shared by the author.

79. Sanford Jacoby, *Modern Manors: Welfare Capitalism Since the New Deal* (Princeton, NJ: Princeton University Press, 1997), 34.

80. See discussion of indulgency pattern in chapter 2.

81. James Shaffer, interview with author, Portland, Maine, April 19, 2013.

82. See note 24 in the Introduction.

83. Kochan and Osterman quote a CEO of a large U.S. corporation saying this: "When I brief Wall Street analysts on our current earnings, sale projections, downsizing program, and capital spending plans they busily punch all these numbers right into their laptops as I speak. When I start telling them about our plans to invest in training and reform the workplace, they sit back in their chairs and their eyes glaze over." Thomas Kochan and Paul

Osterman, *The Mutual Gains Enterprise: Forging a Winning Partnership among Labor, Management, and Government* (Boston: Harvard Business School Press, 1994), 114.

84. Paul Osterman, *Securing Prosperity: The American Labor Market: How It Has Changed and What to Do about It* (Princeton, NJ: Princeton University Press, 1999), 151.

85. Michael Beer and Nitkin Nohria, *Breaking the Code of Change* (Boston: Harvard Business School Press, 2000); Adrienne M. Birecree, "Corporate Development, Structural Change, and Strategic Choice: Bargaining at International Paper Company in the 1980s," *Industrial Relations* 32, no. 3 (1993): 343–66; Justin Fox, *The Myth of the Rational Market: A History of Risk, Reward, and Delusion on Wall Street* (New York: Harper Business, 2011); and William Lazonick and Mary O'Sullivan, "Maximizing Shareholder Value: A New Ideology for Corporate Governance," *Economy and Society* 29, no. 2 (2000): 13–35.

86. Zeiger, *Rebuilding*, 15–24; Toivanan, "Waves of Technological Innovation," 51–55, 65–66.

87. Toivanan, "Waves of Technological Innovation," 62–63.

88. Toivanan, "Waves of Technological Innovation," 65.

89. Quint Randle, "A Historical Overview of the Effects of New Mass Media Introductions on Magazine Publishing in the Twentieth Century," *First Monday* 9, no. 3 (2001), accessed July 17, 2016, http://firstmonday.org/article/view/885/794#4.

90. Toivanan, "Waves of Technological Innovation," 62–63.

91. Theodore Peterson, *Magazines in the Twentieth Century* (Urbana: University of Illinois Press, 1956), 54–55.

92. Toivanan, "Waves of Technological Innovation," 63–64. The calculation here is derived from Toivanan's Tables 3.5 and 3.6.

93. Madden, *Hollingsworth and Whitney*, 12–13.

94. S. D. Warren Company, *A Hundred Years*, 79–84, 90–94,108–9; Howard Reiche Jr., interview with author, Harpswell, Maine, August 8, 2001.

95. I first gleaned this term from former mill manager Howard Reiche Jr. Reiche interview with author.

96. This story is told in Martin Green, *The Mt. Vernon Street Warrens: A Boston Story, 1860–1910* (New York: Charles Scribner Sons, 1989). Green's book offers a rich account of the lives of the first two generations of both rich and poor Warrens, centered on a controversy among the founder's heirs—the five rich Warrens of Boston, several of who were in their own right historical figures—in which a dramatic row led to a high-profile lawsuit against S. D. Warren II, whose siblings accused him of stealing company wealth at their expense that culminated with Warren Junior committing suicide the day before he was about to lose his legal battle. Green offers this portrait of the earliest days of the Warren empire:

> Charles Fairchild, Mr. Warren's partner in the 1870s, was appalled by what he called the company's "rank nepotism." In that decade, George Warren Hammond was agent of the mills; his brother Billie looked after the shipping; his sister Mary's husband, William Longley, was superintendent; Bert Warren (son of Mr. Warren's brother Jonathan) was in charge of the shops; John E. Warren (son of Joseph) was all around man and later agent; Henry Merriam (son of Mary Warren) ran the Copsecook Mill; Kit Blasland (grandson of Anna Warren Hammond) ran transportation. At the end of the decade, Mortimer Mason, son of Sarah Warren and John Mason, became partner. Green, *The Mt. Vernon Street Warrens*, 21.

97. This is the core story portrayed by Green, *The Mt. Vernon Street Warrens*.

98. Charles Scontras, "A Non-Adversarial Labor Relations in Nineteenth Century Maine: The S. D. Warren Company," *Maine History* 37 (1997): 2–29.

99. Scontras, "Non-Adversarial Labor Relations," 24–26, and "12-Day S. D. Warren Strike in 1916 Idled 600 Workers," *Portland Press Herald*, December 19, 1962.

100. Howard Reiche Jr., interview with author, Harspwell, Maine, August 8, 2001; and S. D. Warren Company, *A Hundred Years*, 91–93.

101. Howard Reiche, interview. Here is one of Reiche's stronger recollections of Olmstead, Fick, and Hyde's move to reorganize leadership of the company:

> They went to the Warren family and said: "What you're doing isn't right, and the mill can't continue to exist," and it came out in the form of an ultimatum that "We're not going to keep working here unless we can have control of the mill." At this point the mill passed out of the hands of the Warren family, and into the hands of these people. . . . And then those people . . . were in the mill, and their sons and . . . some of their daughter's husbands—they were in the mill right through, or in sales, right up through the late 1970s.

102. The ensuing description comes from S. D. Warren Company, *A Hundred Years*, 71–73.

103. S. D. Warren Company, *A Hundred Years*, 73.

104. Howard Reiche, interview; and S. D. Warren Company, *A Hundred Years*, 108–14.

105. S. D. Warren Company, *A Hundred Years*, 118; Smith, *History of Papermaking*, 153–218; Stuart Gilson and Jeremy Cott, "The Scott Paper Company, Case 9-296-048" (Boston, MA: Harvard Business School, 1997), 2.

106. Karl Dornish, interview.

107. Lloyd Irland, *Maine's Forest Industry: Essays in Economic History* (Wayne, ME: unpublished manuscript, 2007), 37, 43.

108. Paul McCann, *Timber! The Fall of Maine's Paper Giant* (Ellsworth, ME: Ellsworth American, 1994), 9.

109. Smith, *History of Papermaking*, 531–592.

110. Toivanan, "Waves of Technological Innovation," 67–68.

111. Based on Census of Manufacturers data, in 1947, 84 percent of book paper, 95 percent of writing paper, and 87 percent of tissue paper was produced in the Northeast and Midwest. Helen Hunter, "Innovation, Competition, and Locational Changes in the Pulp and Paper Industry: 1880–1950," *Land Economics* 31, no. 4 (1955): 314–27, 323. This advantage quickly eroded in the next two decades.

112. Toivanan, "Waves of Technological Innovation," 74.

113. S. D. Warren Company, *A Hundred Years*, 105–6; Howard Reiche, interview; Madden, *Hollingsworth and Whitney*.

114. Thomas Beckley, "Pluralism by default: community power in a paper milltown." *Forest Science* 42, no. 1 (1996): 43.

115. Paul McCann, *Timber! The Fall of Maine's Paper Giant* (Ellsworth, ME: Ellsworth American, 1994).

116. Madden, *Hollingsworth and Whitney*; Karl Dornish, interview with author, Waterville, Maine, March 20, 2003; and Howard Reiche, interview.

117. Dornish interview; Michael Hamel interview, Winslow, Maine July 23, 2003; Frank Poulin, interview with author, Oakland, Maine, June 12, 2003.

2. THE PARADOXES OF PAPER MILL EMPLOYMENT

1. Some of this chapter's content first appeared in Michael G. Hillard, "Labor at Mother Warren: Paternalism, Welfarism, and Dissent at S.D. Warren, 1854–1967," *Labor History* 45, no. 1 (2004): 37–60, used here by permission of Informa UK Limited, trading as Taylor & Francis Group, www.tandfonline.com.

2. S. D. Warren Company had three shifts per day from 1903 (advent of their eight-hour day) through the mill's current operation in the twenty-first century, with the exception

of a twenty-year period beginning in 1932 when the company created a four six-hour shift arrangement to spread work in the Great Depression.

By the author's count, over two-thirds of the interviewees who worked directly for paper mills (not true of loggers, mostly) were of retirement age or older and had worked most or all of their lives at Warren. Younger former workers were either still in their careers, or had been retrenched in the rapid downsizing that began in the 1990s. A suggestive sample of interviewees with their ages at the time of interview who worked their entire adult lives at Warren are: Mae Bachelor and Margaret Lowell, interview with author (conducted together), Westbrook, Maine, June 25, 2003 (roughly age 83 and 72 respectively); Oscar Fick Jr., interview with author, Westbrook, Maine, February 25, 2003 (age 93); Shirley Lally, interview with author, Westbrook, Maine, October 27, 2000 (early 70s); Arthur Gordon, interview with author, Westbrook, Maine, June 30, 2000. (late 70s); Phil Lestage, interview with author, Westbrook, Maine, August 29, 2001 (late 60s); Phil LaViolette, interview with author, Westbrook, Maine, July 8, 2003 (mid 70s); Howard Parkhurst, interview with author, Westbrook, Maine, June 14, 2001 (late 60s); Howard Reiche, interview with author, Harpswell, Maine, August 8, 2001 (late 60s).

3. Barry Kenney, interview with author, Portland, Maine, August 15, 2000.

4. Mae Bachelor, interview with author, Westbrook, Maine, June 25, 2003. All quotes from Mae Bachelor in this section are from this interview.

5. This is found in any of the modern plethora of nearly identical principles text books, for example, Paul Krugman and Robin Wells, *Economics* (New York, NY: MacMillan, 2018).

6. A useful survey on such scholars includes: John Budd, *The Thought of Work* (Ithaca, NY: Cornell University Press, 2011); David Gordon, Richard Edwards, and Michael Reich, *Segmented Work, Divided Workers: The Historical Transformation of Labor in the United States* (Cambridge, MA: Cambridge University Press, 1982); Bruce Kaufman, *The Origins and Evolution of the Field of Industrial Relations in the United States* (Ithaca, NY: Cornell University Press, 1992); Bruce Pietkowski, *Work* (Boston, MA: Polity, 2019); and Paul Thompson and Kirsty Newsome, "Labor Process Theory, Work, and The Employment Relation," in *Theoretical Perspectives on Work and the Employment Relationship*, ed. Bruce Kaufman (Urbana, IL: IRRA Series, 2004), 133–62.

7. See Richard Freeman and James Medoff, *What Do Unions Do?* (New York: Basic Books, 1984), 10–11; Kaufman, *Origins and Evolution*, 19–43; and Karl Marx, *Capital*, vol. 1 (New York: Penguin Press, 1977), 270–81.

8. The ensuing passage on scientific management, the drive system, and Fordism draws on a vast literature. Key texts include: Huw Benyon and Theo Nichols, eds., *The Fordism of Ford and Modern Management: Fordism and Post-Fordism*, vols. 1 and 2. (Northampton, MA: Elgar, 2006); Harry Braverman, *Labor and Monopoly Capital* (New York: Monthly Review Press, 1974); Daniel Nelson, *Managers and Workers: Origins of the Factory System in the United States, 1880–1920* (Madison: University of Wisconsin Press, 1975); and Kaufman, *The Origins*, 19–43. See also Sanford Jacoby, *Employing Bureaucracy: Managers, Unions, and the Transformation of Work in the 20th Century* (Mahwah, NJ: Lawrence Erlbaum, 2004); Bruce Kaufman, *The Origins and Evolution of the Field of Industrial Relations in the United States* (Ithaca, NY: Cornell University Press, 1992); David Montgomery, *Workers' Control in America: Studies in the History of Work, Technology, and Labor Struggles* (New York: Cambridge University Press, 1979); Nelson, *Managers and Workers*; and Paul Thompson and Kirsten Newsome, "Labor Process Theory, Work, and the Employment Relation," in *Theoretical Perspectives on Work and the Employment Relationship*, ed. Bruce Kaufman (Urbana, IL: Industrial Relations Research Association, 2004), 133–62.

9. The analysis of how work standardization produced these skills and work intensity effects is derived originally from Karl Marx, *Capital*, vol. 1 (Boston, MA: Digireads.Com

Publishing), 265–459; extensively developed by Harry Braverman in *Labor and Monopoly Capita: The Degradation of Work in the 20th Century* (New York, NY: Monthly Review Press, 1974); and described at length in surveys of modern U.S. labor history such as Nelson Lichtenstein, *State of the Union: A Century of American Labor* (Princeton, NJ: Princeton University Press, 2002).

10. For example, Andrew Zimbalist, ed., *Case Studies in the Labor Process* (New York, NY: Monthly Review Press, 1979).

11. David Montgomery first made this criticism in *Workers' Control in America: Studies in the History of Work, Technology, and Labor Struggles* (Cambridge, UK: Cambridge University Press, 1979). Ensuing work is summarized well in Thompson and Newsome, "Labor Process Theory."

12. Stanley Mathewson, *Restriction of Output Among Unorganized Workers* (New York, NY: Viking Press, 1931) provided an early wealth of primary data on this phenomenon; Montgomery's *Workers' Control in America* further developed this analysis followed by other studies, notably Rik Fantasia, *Cultures of Solidarity* (Berkeley, CA: University of California Press, 1989). Tom Juravich's *Chaos on the Shop Floor: A Worker's View of Quality, Productivity, and Management* (Philadelphia, PA: Temple University Press, 1985), added an important twist—the notion that the sharp conflict top down work organization provoked undermined the ability to produce quality production.

13. Sanford Jacoby, *Modern Manors: Welfare Capitalism Since the New Deal* (Princeton, NJ: Princeton University Press, 1997).

14. Michael Piore and Charles Sabel, *The Second Industrial Divide: Possibilities for Prosperity* (New York, NY: Basic Books, 1984).

15. Kaufman, *The Origins*, 24–25.

16. Philip Scranton, "Varieties of Paternalism: Industrial Structures and the Social Relations of Production in American Textiles," *American Quarterly* 36, no. 2 (1984): 235–57.

17. Jacoby, *Modern Manors*.

18. Jacoby, *Modern Manors*.

19. See Kaufman, *Origins and Evolution* (1992), 21–29; and Chris Nyland and Kyle Bruce, "Democracy or Seduction? The Demonization of Scientific Management and the Deification of Human Relations," in *The Right and Labor in American Politics, Ideology and Imagination*, eds, Nelson Lichtenstein and Elizabeth Shermer (Philadelphia, PA: University of Pennsylvania Press, 2012), 42–76.

20. The first significant use of corporate welfare practices—weak, impermanent, and mainly in the most prosperous large producers—occurred in the 1920s. David C. Smith, *History of Papermaking in the United States:1691–1969* (New York: Lockwood Publishing, 1971), 593–603; and Robert Zeiger, *Rebuilding the Pulp and Paper Workers Union, 1933–1941* (Knoxville: University of Tennessee Press, 1984), 39–40.

21. John D. Glower and Ralph M. Hower, *The Administrator: Cases on Human Relations in Business*, 1st ed. (Homewood IL: R. D. Irwin, 1949) and 3rd ed. (Homewood IL: R. D. Irwin, 1957), 397.

22. The classic treatment of the idea of partial gift exchange between employers and employees is G. A. Akerlof, "Labor Contracts as Partial Gift Exchange," *Quarterly Journal of Economics* 97, no. 4 (1982): 543–69.

23. John Budd, *The Thought of Work* (Ithaca, NY: Cornell University Press, 2011). Budd artfully identifies a broad set of meanings for work, as: "a curse, freedom, commodity, disutility, social relation, personal fulfilment, occupational citizenship, caring for others, identity, and service," Budd, 14. Two meanings from Budd's list that fit the Warren story closely are occupational citizenship and work as a social relation, in addition to Jacoby's notion of membership in an industrial community, or gemeinschaft. Jacoby, *Modern Manors*, 40–41.

24. This is broadly true of the work experience; in Budd's (2011) formulation, the meanings of work he describe including "curse, freedom, occupational citizenship, personal fulfillment, a social relation, caring for others," and the ultimate "identity" are at work for most workers, and certainly here, as evidenced in the self–interpretation of Mae Bachelor. As I spell out below, the moniker "Mother Warren" for these workers acted as a signifier not just for who these workers worked for, but also for the workers themselves as part of an industrial community inscribed by skill, pride, and reciprocity. The formation of community memory is also a dimension, and was especially evident in my interviews with S. D. Warren company workers cited here and in chapters 3 and 8.

25. Sociologist Alvin Gouldner coined this term in his *Patterns of Industrial Democracy* (Glencoe, IL: Free Press, 1954). I'm indebted to Sanford Jacoby for this insight.

26. Dornish and Reiche Jr., interviews.

27. Glower and Hower, *The Administrator*.

28. David Martin, interview with author, Westbrook, Maine, July 18, 2003.

29. The titles of machine tender and paper machine "first-hand" were equivalents, but one or the other prevailed at various times and across the nation's hundreds of mills. In the years before 1920, machine tenders had their own union—the International Brotherhood of Paper Makers—and often directly hired their own crews.

30. Glower and Hower, *The Administrator* (1949 and 1957).

31. Glower and Hower, *The Administrator* (1957), 354; emphasis added.

32. Glower and Hower, *The Administrator* (1949), 406.

33. Jerry Cyr, interview with author, St. Francis, Maine, July 8, 2008.

34. Glower and Hower, *The Administrator* (1957), 354.

35. Glower and Hower, *The Administrator* (1949), 398.

36. Shoshana Zuboff, *In the Age of the Smart Machine: The Future of Work and Power* (New York: Basic Books, 1988), 60; Zuboff, 62.

37. See Fantasia, *Cultures of Solidarity*; Mathewson, *Restriction of Output*; Montgomery, *Workers' Control in America*; Thompson and Newsome, "Labor Process Theory."

38. Glower and Hower *The Administrator* (1949 and 1957).

39. Jerry Cyr, interview, interview with author, St. Francis, Maine, July 8, 2008.

40. Jerry Cyr, interview.

41. Howard Reiche, interview; S. D. Warren Company, *A Hundred Years of S. D. Warren Company* (Westbrook, ME: S.D. Warren Company, 1954), 22.

42. Glower and Hower, *The Administrator* (1949).

43. Howard Reiche, interview.

44. Frank Jewitt interview, Buxton, Maine, July 20, 2001, and Dornish and Reiche interviews.

45. Pulp created by dedicated pulp mills and sold to all segments of paper mills was a commonplace from the advent of modern pulp production in the 1880s. Pulp would be made into sheets and dried, and then packaged into bales for shipment to paper mills. Scandinavian pulp exports grew in the early twentieth century up through the Great Depression; S. D. Warren Company and a great many companies in states like New York that saw pulpwood supplies erode by the 1920s relied on imported Scandinavian pulp. See Helen Hunter, "Innovation, Competition, and Locational Changes in the Pulp and Paper Industry: 1880–1950," *Land Economics* 31, no. 4 (1955): 314–27.

46. Glower and Hower, *The Administrator* (1949), 355–56.

47. Dornish and Reiche interviews.

48. A pseudonym.

49. Glower and Hower, *The Administrator* (1949), 347–48.

50. Dornish and Reiche interviews.

51. Glower and Hower, *The Administrator* (1949 and 1957), and Dornish and Reiche interviews.

52. Glower and Hower, *The Administrator* (1949), 392.

53. Glower and Hower, *The Administrator* (1949), 371.

54. Glower and Hower, *The Administrator* (1949), 345–57; and Karl Dornish, interview.

55. Glower and Hower, *The Administrator* (1949), 383.

56. Glower and Hower, *The Administrator* (1949).

57. By this calculation: from the 1920s–1960s, the mill ran fourteen paper machines. They were typical staffed by five-man crews, or seventy hands per shift. From the 1930s into the 1950s, the mill ran four shifts, rendering 280 paper machine hands at a time when the mill employed just under three thousand. Glower and Hower, *The Administrator* (1949).

58. Glower and Hower, *The Administrator* (1957), 361.

59. Robert Dorr, interview with author, Portland, Maine, July 11, 2000.

60. Tom Lestage, interview with author, Westbrook, Maine July 20, 2000.

61. Tom Lestage interview, July 20, 2000.

62. Glower and Hower, *The Administrator* (1957), 364.

63. Phil Lestage, interview with author, Westbrook, Maine, August 29, 2001, Robert Dorr interview, Barry Kenney interview, Howard Reiche interview, Tom Lestage interview, July 20, 2001.

64. Barry Kenney, interview.

65. Barry Kenney, interview; Jack Jensen, interview with author, Portland, Maine, July 28, 2000.

66. Phil Lestage, interview with author, Westbrook, Maine, August 29, 2001.

67. Mae Bachelor and Margaret Lowell, interview with author (conducted together), Westbrook, Maine, June 25, 2003.

68. Shirley Lally, interview with author, Westbrook, Maine, October 27, 2000.

69. Estelle Maelot, interview with author, Westbrook, Maine, July, 2003.

70. Arthur Gordon, interview.

71. Howard Parkhurst, interview with author, Westbrook, Maine, June 14, 2001.

72. Tom Lestage, interview.

73. Timothy Minchin, *The Color of Work: The Struggle For Civil Rights in the Southern Paper Industry, 1945–1980* (Chapel Hill: University of North Carolina Press, 2003), 36–37.

74. Tom Lestage, interview.

75. S. D. Warren Company, *A Hundred Years*, 67.

76. Peter Kellman, *Divided We Fall: The Story of the Paperworkers' Union and the Future of Labor* (New York: Apex Press, 2004), 27.

77. Robert Dorr, interview.

78. Arthur Gordon, interview.

79. Robert Dorr, interview.

80. In 1909, the Maine commissioner of industrial and labor statistics was officially charged with counting deaths and injuries in Maine factories, counting forty-one deaths between April 1 and December 1 of that year—certainly many would have been in Maine paper mills. The report noted two paper mill deaths that echoed similar stories I heard from more recent years:

> [A worker] employed as a second hand on a machine . . . was caught between the first dryer roll and dry felt and was drawn under the roll. . . . His head and chest were crushed and his right arm badly burned. . . . The body stopped the machinery. He was scarcely 18 years old.

[A worker] was caught by the driving shaft beneath calendar number 22 at the paper mills at three o'clock this morning and was instantly killed. He was assisting in replacing a belt and the revolving shaft, and in an instant his body was thrown around the pulley and hurled with tremendous force against the iron rods which controlled the breaks. The machinery was stopped as soon as possible and when the body was removed it was found that one leg and one arm was torn from the body. . . . He was but 19 years of age.

Maine Bureau of Labor, *Report of Industrial and Labor Statistics* (Waterville, ME: Sentinel Publishing, 1909), cited in Kellman, *Divided We Fall*, 31–32.

81. Barry Kenney, Robert Dorr, Phil Lestage, and Tom Lestage, interviews; Oscar Fick Jr., interview with author, Westbrook, Maine, February 25, 2003.

82. Dave Martin, interview with author, Westbrook, Maine, July 18, 2003.

83. Jeffrey Haydu, "Two Logics of Class Formation? Collective Identities among Proprietary Employers, 1880–1900," *Politics and Society* 27, no. 4 (1999): 507–27; Sanford Jacoby, "American Exceptionalism Revisited the Importance of Management," in *Masters to Managers: Historical and Comparative Perspectives on American Labor* (New York: Columbia Press, 1991), 173–200; and Nelson Lichtenstein, *State of the Union*, 106–7.

84. Gerald Mayer, "Union Membership Trends in the United States," *Congressional Research Service, CRS Report for Congress*, August 21, 2004, Figure 1, p. 11, accessed March 21, 2020, https://digitalcommons.ilr.cornell.edu/cgi/viewcontent.cgi?article=1176&context=key_workplace.

85. Kellman, *Divided We Fall*, 107–8; Zeiger, *Rebuilding the Pulp*, 127–67.

86. *Committee of the Senate upon the Relations between Labor and Capital*, 48th Congress, volume 3 (Washington: Government Printing Office, 1885), 383; (testimony of Samuel D. Warren, founder of S. D. Warren Company; and Charles Scontras, "A Non-Adversarial Labor Relations in Nineteenth Century Maine: The S.D. Warren Company," *Maine History* 37 (1997): 2–29.

87. Glower and Hower, *The Administrator* (1949), 409.

88. Dana Babb, interview with author, Westbrook, Maine, February 21, 2003; and Glower and Hower, *The Administrator* (1949), 304. On the spillover effect, see Paul Osterman, *Securing Prosperity: The American Labor Market: How It Has Changed and What to Do about It* (Princeton, NJ: Princeton University Press), 28. The *Harvard study* observed: "For many years it had been Mr. [Hyde's] policy to keep the mill 'out in front' of other New England paper mills in the wages paid the employees." Glower and Hower, *The Administrator* (1949), 304.

89. Parts of the content of this section, and short passages, first appeared in Michael Hillard, "Labor at Mother Warren: Paternalism, Welfarism, and Dissent, 1854–1967," *Labor History* 45, no. 1 (2004): 37–60. Reuse/reprinted by permission of Informa UK Limited, trading as Taylor & Francis Group, www.tandfonline.com.

90. *S. D. Warren: A Tribute from the People of Cumberland Mills* (Cambridge, MA: Riverside Press, 1888).

91. Howard Reiche had by far the deepest and most erudite knowledge of company history of any of my interviewees. He had read both the company history and the two editions of the *Harvard study*—indeed, I first learned of this study from him, but he especially had absorbed what proved to be an accurately received oral history within the firm from the likes of George Olmstead, Junior, Oscar Fick, Junior, and Rudy Greep who themselves came of age under the management leaders who took control of the company in the 1920s. See also Harry Foote, interview with author Portland, Maine, July 10, 2002; Frank Jewitt, interview with author, Buxton, Maine, July 20, 2001; Curtis Pease, interview with author, Gorham, Maine, August 1, 2001; Ron Usher, Westbrook, Maine, August 2,

2001; Jan Usher, interview with author, Westbrook, Maine, June 19, 2003; and Tom Lestage, Arthur Gordon, Shirley Lally, Mae Bachelor, Karl Dornish, Phil Lestage, Karl Dornish, and Howard Reiche, interviews.

92. Martin Green, *The Mt. Vernon Street Warrens: A Boston Story, 1860–1910* (New York, NY: Charles Scribner Sons, 1989), 21. S. D. Warren, *A Memorial Tribute* (Cambridge, MA: Riverside Press, 1888); Scontras, "A Non-Adversarial Labor Relations."

93. S. D. Warren Company, *A Hundred Years*, 22.

94. S. D. Warren Company, *A Hundred Years*, 61.

95. S. D. Warren Company, *A Hundred Years*, 64.

96. Frank Jewitt, interview.

97. Martin Green, *The Mount Vernon Street Warrens: A Boston Story, 1860–1910* (New York: Charles Scribner's Sons, 1989); *S. D. Warren: A Tribute*; Scontras, "A Non-Adversarial Labor Relations"; *Committee of the Senate*.

98. This paragraph draws on these sources: Green, *The Mount Vernon Street Warrens*, 13–36; and Scontras, "A Non-Adversarial Labor Relations," 6–26.

99. Green, *The Mount Vernon Street Warrens*, 14.

100. Quoted in Scontras, "A Non-Adversarial Labor Relations," 9.

101. Green, *The Mount Vernon Street Warrens*, 26.

102. Green, *The Mount Vernon Street Warrens*, 26.

103. Scranton, "Varieties of Paternalism." An important, indeed crucial, caveat is that there is no record in these sources of the workers' experience or attitudes about Warren's paternalism other than journalistic depictions of worker protest during a 1916 union struggle. At that time, workers were deeply frustrated by the loss of Johnny Warren (who died the year before) as a trusted mill leader who the men could appeal to about frustrations on the shop floor. Beyond Scranton, the literature on paternalism is extensive. I am most influenced by David Flamming, *Creating the Modern South: Millhands and Managers in Dalton, Georgia, 1884–1984* (Chapel Hill: University of North Carolina Press, 1992); and Jacquelyn Dowd Hall, Robert Korstad, and James Deloudis, "Cotton Mill People: Work, Community, and Protest in the Textile South, 1880–1940," *American Historical Review* 91, no. 2 (1986): 245–86.

104. Scranton, "Varieties of Paternalism," 235–57.

105. See S. D. Warren Company, *A Hundred Years*, 28.

106. Laurie, *Artisans into Workers*, 127–28.

107. Dan Parks, interview with author, Portland, Maine, June 13, 2001; Curtis Pease, interview with author, Gorham, Maine, August 1, 2001; Howard Parkhurst, interview with author, Westbrook, Maine June 14, 2001; and Phil Lestage, interview.

108. See S. D. Warren Company, *A Hundred Years*, 30; and Scontras, "A Non-Adversarial Labor Relations," 9.

109. Green, *The Mount Vernon Street Warrens*, 26; S. D. Warren Company, *A Hundred Years*, 68, puts the date at 1874; Scontras, "A Non-Adversarial Labor Relations," 11, dates its founding to 1882.

110. S. D. Warren, *A Hundred Years*, 68–69; and Scontras, "A Non-Adversarial Labor Relations," 10–11.

111. Scontras, "A Non-Adversarial Labor Relations," 22.

112. Portland *Sunday Times*, "800 of Paper Mill Workers Attend the Mass Meeting in Cumberland Hall," reprinted in the *Paper Makers Journal*, April (1916), 4–8.

113. See Phil LaViolette, interview, and Ernest R. and Marian B. Rowe, *Highlights of Westbrook History* (Westbrook, ME: Westbrook Women's Club, 1952), 83–84.

114. Martin Green, *The Mount Vernon Street Warrens*, 25; Howard Levy, "Worker Housing in Westbrook, Maine, 1820–1890" (Portland, ME: unpublished paper, 2000); Scontras, "A Non-Adversarial Labor," 9.

115. Scontras, "A Non-Adversarial Labor," 9.

116. Scontras, "A Non-Adversarial Labor," 22–23.

117. Scranton, "Varieties of Paternalism."

118. Scranton, "Varieties of Paternalism."

119. S. D. Warren, *A Hundred Years*, Graph 1, 117.

120. The most authoritative study of twentieth-century U.S. welfare capitalism is Sanford Jacoby's *Modern Manors*. See also Stuart Brandes, *American Welfare Capitalism: 1880–1940* (Chicago: University of Chicago Press, 1970); H. M. Gitelman, "Welfare Capitalism Reconsidered," *Labor History* 33, no. 2 (1992): 5–31; Walter Licht, "Fringe Benefits: A Review Essay on the American Workplace," *International Labor and Working Class History* 53 (1998): 164–78; Andrea Tone, *The Business of Benevolence: Industrial Paternalism in Progressive America* (Ithaca, NY: Cornell University Press, 1997); and Gerald Zahavi, *Workers, Managers, and Welfare Capitalism: The Shoeworkers and Tanners of Endicott Johnson, 1890–1950* (Urbana, IL: University of Illinois Press, 1988).

121. S. D. Warren Company, *A Hundred Years* mentions that some elderly mill employees including Civil War veterans, and/or their wives, were granted pensions in the late nineteenth century. No estimate or figure is made either about the amount of the pension or how many employees received it. Also, after the 1916 strike, Joseph A. Warren announced in a newsletter posted in the mill that:

> Pensions have given in many instances as a natural impulse to recognize long terms of service. Those who have been working for us uninterruptedly for a considerable term are entitled to customary recognition. In the cases of those re-employed . . . there will be no provision for pensions. (Cited in Mathew J. Burns, "History of the Papermakers Union," [Unpublished manuscript, 1922], 183.)

122. *Report of Industrial and Labor Statistics* (Augusta, ME: Maine Bureau of Labor, 1901), 98.

123. Kellman, *Divided We Fall*, 36, 47.

124. S. D. Warren Company, *A Hundred Years*, 65–68; and Anastasia Wiegle, *A Presence in the Community: The Warren Family Legacy* (Westbrook, ME: Warren Memorial Foundation and Cornelia Warren Community Foundation, 2000), 10–17.

125. Howard Reiche noted that during his reign as mill manager from 1970 through 1988—firmly in the era after Scott Paper Company had absorbed Warren as division—he was able to maintain an annual giving fund for Westbrook, comanaged by union leaders, that reached $350,000 per year. Howard Reiche, interview.

126. Wiegle, *A Presence in the Community*, 13–21; S. D. Warren Company, *A Hundred Years*, 102–3.

127. Dana Babb and Howard Reiche interviews.

128. Charles Scontras, *Labor in Maine: Building the Arsenal of Democracy and Resisting Reaction at Home, 1939–1952* (Orono, ME: Bureau of Labor Education, 2006).

129. This was mentioned in a variety of interviews—see especially Shirley Lally, Frank Jewitt.

130. Phil LaViolette, interview.

131. S. D. Warren Company, *A Hundred Years*, 30.

132. See S. D. Warren Company, *A Hundred Years*, 77; this practice was continued after the 1930s. Many retirees who worked at the mill during the 1940s–1960s period report that many six-hour shifts or tour jobs worked seven days a week. Mae Bachelor, interview; Karl Dornish, interview; Phil LaViolette, interview; Dan Parks, interview; and Howard Reiche, interview.

133. Howard Reiche, interview.

134. Howard Reiche, interview.

135. Marv Ewing, interview with author, Yarmouth, Maine, July 20, 2000; Clyde Harriman interview, Portland, Maine, July 24, 2002; Joe Jensen, interview with author, Westbrook, Maine, June 20, 2002; and Phil Lestage and Howard Reiche, interviews.

136. David Martin, interview with author, Westbrook, Maine, July 18, 2003; Mae Bachelor, interview; Harley Lord, interview with author, Windham, Maine, June 6, 2003; and Estelle Maelot, interview with author, Westbrook, Maine, May 29, 2003.

137. Shirley Lally, Phil Laviolette, Tom Lestage, Phil Lestage, Dan Parks, and Curtis Pease, interviews.

138. S. D. Warren Company, *A Hundred Years*, 119 notes the male worker minimum wage was $1.40 per hour; the U.S. federal minimum wage at that time was $0.75 per hour. U.S. Department of Labor, "History of Federal Minimum Wage Rates Under the Fair Labor Standards Act, 1938–2009," U.S. Department of Labor Wages and Hour Division. Accessed March 20, 2020, https://www.dol.gov/agencies/whd/minimum-wage/history/chart.

139. Phil LaViolette, interview.

140. Phil LaViolette, interview

141. Phil LaViolette, interview.

142. S. D. Warren Company, *A Hundred Years*, 65; Arthur Gordon and Howard Reiche, interviews

143. Karl Dornish and Howard Reiche, interviews.

144. S. D. Warren Company, *A Hundred Years*, 65.

145. Arthur Gordon, Ron Usher, interviews.

146. William Osborne, *The Paper Plantation: Ralph Nadar's Study Group Report on the Pulp and Paper Industry in Maine* (New York: Grossman Publishers 1974), 227–39; Howard Reiche, interview.

147. Italicized words in quotations from oral history reflect the interviewee's emphasis. The manager quoted here is Howard Reiche, who is described and quoted extensively below.

148. Osborne, *Paper Plantation*, 256–57.

149. Glower and Hower, *The Administrator* (1949).

150. Robert Burton interview, Westbrook, Maine, July 9, 2002.

151. Oscar Fick interview, Westbrook, Maine February 25, 2003

152. Karl Dornish, interview.

153. Dana Babb, Howard Reiche, interviews.

154. Glower and Hower, *The Administrator* (1949), 346–47; author's emphasis.

155. The author encountered references to this in many conversations and interviews over the years. In a personal communication, leading local expert on Maine's forestry and paper industry, Lloyd Irland, confirmed that this was true in his fifty years of field experience. In particular, he recalled that: "Paper companies . . . offered leases . . . to workers, local neighbors, [and] perhaps there was favoritism to the powerful and influential. . . . Many of the paper companies' leases were formally year to year, but people ignored that, and put foundations in, then year round homes. . . . In the late 70's, early 80's there were folks who had leased lots on beautiful, largely wild lakes for $100 per year!" Email communication with author, March 21, 2020.

156. Chapter 4 develops the story of Fraser's employment bargain.

157. I am indebted to Sanford Jacoby for this insight. See Gouldner, *Patterns of Industrial Bureaucracy*, 49–66. The notion of a gift exchange comes from the labor economics literature on efficiency wages. See, especially, G. A. Akerlof, "Labor Contracts as Partial Gift Exchange," *Quarterly Journal of Economics* 97 (1982): 543–69.

158. Oxford Paper Company, *Papermaking at Oxford: More than Fifty Years in the Manufacture of Fine Quality Book and Specialty Papers in Rumford, Maine*" (Rumford, ME: Oxford Paper Company, 1954), 3.

159. Smith, *History of Papermaking*; Daniel Corcoran, interview with author, Millinocket, Maine, June 22, 2006.

160. Recent, gigantic machines are capable of over 6,000 feet per minute, or 580 miles of paper in one eight-hour shift.

161. Barry Kenney, interview.

3. THE FALL OF MOTHER WARREN

1. Lloyd Irland, *Maine's Forest Industry: Essays in Economic History* (Wayne, ME: unpublished manuscript, 2007), 37–43.

2. Claire Bolduc, interview with author, July 7, 2004; Jerry Cyr interview with author, St. David, Maine, July 8, 2008; Paul Cyr, interview with author, St. David, Maine, July 8, 2008; Marv Ewing, interview with author, Yarmouth, Maine, July 20, 2000; Jonathan Falk, interview with author, Carmel, Maine, July 24, 2004; Cecile Fontaine, interview with author, Portland, Maine, July 16, 2004; Donald Fontaine, interview with author, Portland, Maine, July 15, 2004; Peter Hagerty, interview with author, Portland, Maine, August 8, 2004; and Larry Palmer, interview with author, Patton, Maine, July 10, 2004.

3. Charles Scontras, *Organized Labor in Maine: War, Reaction, Depression, and the Rise of the CIO, 1914–1943* (Orono, ME: Bureau of Labor Education, 2006); and Charles Scontras, *Labor in Maine: Building the Arsenal of Democracy and Resisting Reaction at Home, 1939–1952* (Orono, ME: Bureau of Labor Education, 2006). Great Northern Paper was the exception—it unionized in the 1910s and remained unionized through the 1920s and early 1930s when other upstart unions in Maine mills were crushed. McLeod, *The Northern*.

4. For the lay reader, the nomenclature for unions distinguish the national organization and local organizations using the terms "International" and "local." The "international" is typically a nationwide, U.S. based organization that includes some Canadian locals, hence "International."

5. Peter Kellman, *Divided We Fall: The Story of the Paperworkers' Union and the Future of Labor* (New York: Apex Press, 2004) 25–90; and Robert Zeiger, *Rebuilding the Pulp and Paper Workers Union, 1933–1941* (Knoxville: University of Tennessee Press, 1984).

6. David Brody, *Working in Industrial America: Essays on 20th Century Struggle* (New York: Oxford University Press, 1980), 173.

7. A comprehensive picture of U.S. union density trends is found in Stephanie Luce and Ruth Milkman, "Labor Unions and the Great Recession," *RSF: The Russell Sage Foundation Journal of the Social Sciences* 3, no. 3 (2017): 147. Harvard labor economist Richard Freeman estimated that private, nonagricultural sector workers covered by union contracts reached a historical peak of 39 percent in 1954. Richard Freeman, personal communication with the author, June 12, 2009. See also Richard Freeman, "Contraction and Expansion: The Divergence of Private and Public Sector Unionism in the United States," *Journal of Economic Perspectives* 2, no. 2 (1988): 63–68, especially exhibit 1.

8. Zeiger, *Rebuilding*, 95–112.

9. Zeiger, *Rebuilding*, 11–13.

10. Kellman, *Divided We Fall*, 107.

11. Zeiger, *Rebuilding*, 188.

12. Zeiger, *Rebuilding*, 218. While Zeiger makes clear that this reputation was specifically acute in Southern U.S. mills, his entire book makes the case that the International Brotherhood of Pulp, Sulfite and Paper Mill Workers suffered from these flaws throughout the United States. One result was the wholesale secession of the Western paper worker union locals who formed a new international union in 1964.

13. The International Brotherhood of Papermakers merged with a small CIO upstart called the United Paper Makers in 1957 to form the United Papermakers and Paperworkers Union which then merged with the Pulp and Sulphite union in 1972 to form the UPIU. On the make up of union locals at a typical paper mill, see Adrienne Eaton and Jill Kriesky, "Collective Bargaining in the Paper Industry: Developments Since 1979," in *Contemporary Collective Bargaining in the Private Sector*, ed. Paula Voos (Madison, WI: Industrial Relations Research Association, 1994), 25–62; Adrienne Eaton and Jill Kriesky, "Decentralization of the Bargaining Structure: Four Cases From the U.S. Paper Industry," *Relations Industrielles* 5, no. 2 (1998): 486–516; Minchin, *Color of Work*, 25–28; and Zeiger, *Rebuilding*, 25.

14. IP was exceptional in having two large bargaining pools with negotiations covering over ten mills each. IP dismantled these pools in the 1970s and 1980s to gain more leverage over its unions. See Michael Hillard, "An Analysis and Perspective on the International Paper/Jay Strike," *Maine Business Indicators* 33, no. 3 (1988): 1–3.

15. Kellman, *Divided We Fall*; Julius Getman, *The Betrayal of Local 14: Paperworkers, Politics, and Personal Replacements*. (Ithaca, NY: Cornell University Press, 1998); and Zeiger, *Rebuilding*.

16. See Thomas Kochan, Harry Katz, and Robert McKersie, *The Transformation of American Industrial Relations* (Ithaca, NY: Cornell University Press, 1994), 28–29 for a formal definition. The skill/physicality trade-off that improves up a job ladder is a common feature of industrial job ladders. See, for example, Ruth Milkman, *Farewell to the Factory: Autoworkers in the Late 20th Century* (Berkeley: University of California Press, 1997).

17. Karl Dornish, interview with author, Waterville, Maine, March 20, 2003; Arthur Gordon, interview with author, Westbrook, Maine, June 30, 2000; and Howard Reiche, interview with author, Harpswell, Maine, August 9, 2001.

18. Getman, *The Betrayal of Local 14*; Kellman, *Divided We Fall*; Paul Cyr, interview with author, St. David, Maine, July 8, 2008; William Carver interview, Westbrook, Maine, December 9, 2001; Gary Cook interview, Augusta, Maine, March 4, 2003; Marv Ewing, interview with author, Yarmouth, Maine, July 14, 2000; Bob Gogan interview, St. David, Maine, July 8, 2008; Arthur Gordon interview, Westbrook, Maine, June 30, 2000; Peter Kellman interview, Portland, Maine, February 13, 2003; Tom Lestage, interviews with author, Westbrook, Maine, July 20, 23, and 24, 2000; Raymond Pineau, interview with author, Augusta, Maine, March 3, 2003; and Frank Poulin, interview with author, Oakland, Maine, June 12, 2003.

19. David Brody, "Workplace Contractualism in Comparative Perspective," in *Industrial Democracy in America: The Ambiguous Prospect*, ed. Nelson Lichtenstein and Howell John Harris (New York: Cambridge University Press, 1993), 176–205.

20. Historian Staughton Lynd leads a school of thought critical of workplace contractualism. Lynd argued that grievance-based union contracts were a repressive force aimed at tamping down shop-floor rebellion in the 1940s; companies welcomed a process that ended the widespread practice of brief wildcat strikes (note: wildcat strikes are strikes unauthorized by union locals or internationals), and work slowdowns that workers used to challenge and reshape supervision and work practices; archetypally, this would express itself as resistance to management efforts to speed up work. See Staughton Lynd, introduction to *We Are All Leaders: The Alternative Unionism of the Early 1930s*, ed. Staughton Lynd (Urbana: University of Illinois Press, 1996), 1–26. For mass-production industries in the 1940s, the grievance mechanism individualized shop-floor complaints and helped employers reassert the right to manage. See Howell John Harris, *The Right to Manage: Industrial Relations Policies of American Business in the 1940s* (Madison: University of Wisconsin Press, 1982). But this critique Brody's argument is not compelling here because

there was no tradition of sit-down strikes and local wildcats in paper mills. In Maine, defense of the contract became the wellspring for the new militancy during the post-1960 era. In short, the daily practice of seeking and enforcing workplace justice laid a foundation for the upsurge of strikes beginning in the late 1960s and lasting through the 1980s.

21. Frank Poulin, interview.

22. Tom Lestage, interview with author, Westbrook, Maine, July 20, 2000.

23. The first strike of the era was a six-week affair at Oxford in 1964. Timothy Minchin, "Broken Spirits: Permanent Replacements and the Rumford Strike of 1986," *New England Quarterly* 74, no. 1 (2001): 5–31; 30 and Monica Wood, *When We Were the Kennedys: A Memoir from Mexico, Maine* (Boston: Mariner Press, 2012).

24. Paul Cyr, interview; William Carver, interview; Gary Cook interview, Augusta, Maine, March 4, 2003; Marv Ewing, interview; Bob Gogan, interview; Arthur Gordon, interview; Peter Kellman, interview, February 13, 2003; Tom Lestage, interview; and Raymond Pineau, interview.

25. Getman, *Betrayal of Local 14*, 20–24, Peter Kellman, interview, February 13, 2003; Timothy Minchin, "Permanent Replacements and the Rumford Strike of 1986," *New England Quarterly* 74, no. 2 (2001): 5–31.

26. Eaton and Kriesky, "Collective Bargaining in the Paper Industry," and "Decentralization of the Bargaining Structure"; Getman, *Betrayal of Local 14*; and Peter Kellman, interview, February 13, 2003. Also see Chapters 6 and 7.

27. Bureau of Labor Statistics, cited in Rich Exner, "Major Work Stoppages up in 2011, but Far below Historical Levels," Cleveland.com, February 12, 2012, http://www.cleveland.com/datacentral/index.ssf/2012/02/major_work_stoppages_up_in_201.html.

28. See Adrienne Eaton and Jill Kriesky, "Collective Bargaining in the Paper Industry," 25–62; Bruce Kaufman, "The Emergence and Growth of a Non-Union Sector in the Southern Paper Industry," in *Southern Labor in Transition, 1940–1995*, ed. Robert Zeiger (Knoxville: University of Tennessee Press, 1997), 295–330; Timothy Minchin, *The Color of Work: The Struggle For Civil Rights in the Southern Paper Industry, 1945–1980* (Chapel Hill: University of North Carolina Press, 2003); and Minchin, "Broken Spirits."

29. A term with great import in economic theory, it defines a company owner's objective as something other than maximizing profit returns to shareholders. In Chandlerian firms of the managerial era that stretched from 1900 into the 1960s and 1970s, companies could sacrifice some profits for greater costs that promised longer-term stability. This including extravagant spending on wining and dining key customers, higher labor costs that ensured greater worker productivity, commitment, and product quality, and patient investments in production, marketing, and especially research and development. See Herbert A. Simon, "Rational Decision Making in Business Organizations," *American Economic Review* 69, no. 4 (1979): 419–513.

30. Gary Cook, interview; Paul Cyr, interview; Arthur Gordon, interview; David Martin, interview with author, Westbrook, Maine, July 18, 2003; and Frank Poulin, interview.

31. Chapter 4 provides a detailed case study of this, telling the story of the lead up the the Fraser Paper Company strike in 1971. See Arthur Gordon, interview, and Tom Lestage, interviews, July 23 and 24, 2000.

32. Chapter 5 explores this.

33. John Beck interview (phone), January 29, 2003; Howard Reiche, interview; Karl Dornish, interview; and anonymous interview with former Scott executive, June 17, 2003.

34. On the S. D. Warren developments, see the remainder of this chapter; on Boise Cascade, see Thomas Beckley, "Pluralism by default: community power in a paper mill-town," *Forest Science* 42, no. 1 (1993): 35–45, and Monica Wood, *When We Were the Kennedys: A Memoir from Mexico, Maine* (Boston, MA; Houghton, Mifflin, and Harcourt,

2012); on GNP see "GNP Workers Vote Tonight On New Offer," *Portland Press Herald*, June 30, 1978; "Labor: Unions Are Split," *Maine Times*, July 21, 1978; "Great Northern to Sue Unions if Strike Goes On," *Portland Press Herald*, August 1, 1978; "Great Northern Strikers Still at Impasse on Rules," *Portland Press Herald*, August 2, 1978; "Great Northern: Paperworkers Sign Contract," *Portland Press Herald*, August 4, 1978; "Great Northern: No Progress Yet In Paper Strike," *Portland Press Herald*, August 6, 1978; "Labor: Paper Impasse," *Maine Times*, August 18, 1978; "Great Northern Seeks Compromise in Seven-Week-Old Mill Walkout," *Portland Press Herald*, August 21, 1978; "Governor Tries Negotiation Hand," *Portland Press Herald*, August 23, 1978; "Paperworkers to Vote Monday," *Portland Press Herald*, August 25, 1978; "Workers End Great Northern Strike," *Portland Press Herald*, August 29, 1978; "Strike: Paper Rolls Again," *Maine Times*, September 8, 1978; on Fraser, see Chapter 4; and on Pejepscot, see John Newton, interview with author, Portland, Maine, December 5, 2012.

35. The migration of union militants and radicals leading to organizing is one the most enduring features of labor history, and it is evident in the turn in labor relations that began in Maine in the 1960s. See Jefferson Cowie, *Capital Moves: RCA's 70-Year Quest for Cheap Labor* (Ithaca, NY: Cornell University Press), 63–72; and extensive work by labor geographers—see especially Andrew Herod, "The Spatiality of Labor Unionism: A Review Essay," in *Organizing the Landscape: Geographical Perspectives on Labor Unionism* (Minneapolis: University of Minnesota Press, 1998), 1–36; and Jane Wills, "Space, Place, and Tradition in Working-Class Organization," in *Organizing the Landscape*, 129–58.

36. Ron Usher, interview with author, Westbrook, Maine, August 2, 2001.

37. Joe Jensen, interview with author, Westbrook, Maine, June 20, 2002. Jensen recalled a significant, well-organized work slowdown in the mill's finishing department over piece rates in the early 1960s.

38. Maine labor historian Charlie Scontras documents four unsuccessful organizing drives by the International Brotherhood of Pulp, Sulfite and Paper Mill Workers in 1938, 1941, 1948, and 1950. Scontras, *Labor in Maine*, 201–3.

39. "800 Paper Mill Workers Attend the Mass Meeting in Cumberland Hall," *Portland Sunday Times*, reprinted in the *Paper Makers' Journal*, April 2016, 4–8; "12 Day S. D. Warren Strike in 1916 Idled 600 Workers," *Portland Press Herald*, December 19, 1962.

40. See Alvin Gouldner, *Patterns of Industrial Bureaucracy* (New York: Free Press, 1954).

41. Howard Parkhurst among others had vivid recollections of on-the-job drunks. Parkhurst began in 1961 in a brutal job maneuvering coal during winters from railroad cars through a hopper that fed the coal to the mill's boilers. His work partner his first winter needed a six-pack of beer on the job to "get going," and would often disappear midshift to renew his supply. Howard Parkhurst, interview with author, Windham, Maine, June 14, 2001.

42. Howard Reiche, interview, and Karl Dornish, interview.

43. As previously noted, the Papermakers union absorbed the previously separate CIO union, known as the United Papermakers of America, to become the United Papermakers and Paperworkers union during the period of 1957 to 1972. Zeiger, *Rebuilding*, 219.

44. Clyde Harriman, interview with author, Portland, Maine, July 24, 2002.

45. William Carver, interview; Karl Dornish, interview; Arthur Gordon, interview; Joe Jensen, interview; Shirley Lally, interview; and Dan Parks, interview.

46. John D. Glower and Ralph M. Hower, *The Administrator: Cases on Human Relations in Business*, 1st ed. (Homewood, IL: R. D. Irwin, 1949), 387.

47. Glower and Hower, *The Administrator* (1949 and 1957).

48. Karl Dornish, interview.

49. Robert Burton, interview with author, Westbrook, Maine, July 9, 2002; and Howard Reiche and Karl Dornish, interviews.

50. This paragraph is derived from dozens of interviews of former S. D. Warren Company workers and managers; see especially Karl Dornish, interview; Arthur Gordon, interview; and Howard Reiche, interview.

51. Arthur Gordon, interview.

52. Karl Dornish, interview.

53. William Carver, interview; Karl Dornish, interview; Marv Ewing, interview; Shirley Lally, interview; Howard Reiche, interview; and Dan Parks, interview.

54. "Marshall Company (MR₃)" in Glower and Hower, *The Administrator* (1957), 389–404.

55. Mae Bachelor and Margaret Lowell, interview with author (conducted together), Westbrook, Maine, June 25, 2003.

56. William Carver interview; and Howard Reiche, interview; and Glower and Hower, *The Administrator* (1949 and 1957), xx.

57. Howard Reiche, interview.

58. Phil Lestage, interview with author, Westbrook, ME, August 29, 2001.

59. Robert Burton, interview with author, Westbrook, Maine, July 9, 2002; and Karl Dornish, interview.

60. Karl Dornish, interview; and Howard Reiche, interview.

61. "My father said in the old days, if you were French, you would get the shitty jobs. You didn't get the good jobs. You got the ones like my father, you got the wood yard and out in the pulp mill . . . real bad jobs [that] nobody wanted. So, that did happen. If you was [sic] French back then, you was, you got the shit jobs." Phil Lestage, interview.

62. Clyde Harriman, Phil Lestage, and Howard Parkhurst, interviews.

63. Shirley Lally, interview with author, Westbrook, Maine, October 27, 2000; Dan Parks, interview with author, Portland, Maine, June 12, 2001; and Mae Bachelor, interview.

64. Karl Dornish, interview; Shirley Lally, interview; Dan Parks, interview; and Clyde Harriman, interview.

65. Karl Dornish, interview; and Howard Reiche, interview.

66. "Unions Resume Drive to Organize 2600 S. D. Warren Production Workers, *Portland Press Herald*, August 16, 1962; "S. D. Warren Company to Fight Union's original Bid," *Portland Evening Express*, December 18, 1962; "Legal Battle by Four Crafts Unions to Fight Union's Original Bid," *Portland Evening Express*, December 19, 1962; "Warren Tells Workers Few Could Close Mill," *Portland Press Herald*, January 4, 1963; "Unions—S. D. Warren Hearing to Resume Tomorrow," *Portland Evening Express*, January 7, 1963; "Mill Union to File Briefs as NLRB Hearing Ends," *Portland Press Herald*, January 24, 1963; "Labor Panel Orders Election at Warren. Westbrook Firm to Appeal Ruling," *Portland Evening Express*, April 5, 1963; "S. D. Warren To Challenge Craft Union Vote Ruling," *Portland Press Herald*, April 6, 1963; "Upholds Ruling For Separate Voting By Maintenance Unit," *Portland Press Herald*, August 26, 1963; "Unions Seen Victor In Warren Mill Vote," *Portland Press Herald*, September 13, 1963; "S. D. Warren Will Take Union Battle to Courts," *Portland Evening Express*, September 16, 1963; "Unions Win at S. D. Warren; Company Will Try to Appeal," *Portland Evening Express*, October 9, 1963; "S. D. Warren Asks National Labor Board to Review Ruling on Labor Unions," *Portland Evening Express*, October 28, 1963; "S. D. Warren To Take NLRB Rule To Court," *Portland Evening Express*, December 6, 1963; "S. D. Warren Found Guilty of Failure to Bargain," *Portland Evening Express*, December 18, 1964; "Court Direct S. D. Warren To Bargain With Union, *Portland Press Herald*, November 9, 1965; and "Mediator Session Called Thursday In Warren Strike," *Portland Press Herald*, July 4, 1967.

67. Clyde Harriman, interview; and Joe Jensen, interview.

68. Clyde Harriman, interview; and Joe Jensen, interview.

69. Clyde Harriman, interview; and Joe Jensen, interview.

70. Mae Bachelor, interview; Shirley Lally, interview; Phil Lestage, interview; and Dan Parks, interview.

71. Mae Bachelor, interview; Karl Dornish, interview; Marv Ewing, interview; Oscar Fick, interview; Phil Lestage, interview; and Howard Reiche, interview.

72. Marv Ewing, interview.

73. "Union Wins NLRB Election At Warren," *Portland Press Herald*, October 18, 1967; Marv Ewing, interview; Arthur Gordon, interview; and Ron Usher, interview.

74. Marv Ewing, interview. John Nee later became Scott's vice president of labor relations and led a work reorganization effort in the late 1980s that figures prominently in chapters 6 and 7.

75. Marv Ewing, interview.

76. Local 1069 was originally chartered by the United Papermakers and Paperworkers, and Local 404 was a branch of the International Brotherhood of Pulp, Sulfite, and Paper Mill Workers. The two national unions merged in 1972 to become the UPIU; initially the two locals remained separate as UPIU locals. After a couple of one–year contracts, they began to bargain in concert in 1970. In the mid–1970s, the much larger Local 1069 absorbed Local 404 and the combined local continued under President Marv Ewing's leadership. See note 66 on sources for this history.

77. Sources for the ensuing narrative about labor relations at S. D. Warren Company through the 1970s and early 1980s are: William Carver, interview, Karl Dornish, interview; Arthur Gordon interview; Shirley Lally, interview; Clyde Harriman, interview; Joe Jensen, interview; Shirley Lally, interview; Phil Lestage, interview; and Howard Parkhurst, interview; Dan Parks, interview; Curtis Pease, interview; and Howard Reiche, interview. See also "S. D. Warren Union Okay Rejected Pact," *Portland Press Herald*, May 30, 1970; "S. D. Warren Company Strike Vote Monday," *Portland Press Herald*, June 16, 1973; "Warren Workers Vote Not to Strike," *Portland Press Herald*, June 19, 1973; "Warren Workers To Strike Tonight," *Portland Press Herald*, June 6, 1977; "S. D. Warren Workers Officially Begin Siege," *Portland Press Herald*, June 11, 1977; "4th Week of Strike Has Warren Employees End Strike, Start Returning to Work," *Portland Evening Express*, July 13, 1977; "Tentative Accord May Avert Strike at S. D. Warren, *Portland Press Herald*, June 15, 1979; "More Than 1000 of Union, UPIU, Struck at 12:00 PM Over Medical Benefits in New Contract Negotiations," *Portland Evening Express*, June 2, 1983; and "Union Ended 9 Day Old Strike, Voted to Accept Company's 2 Year Contract Offer," *Portland Evening Express*, June 11, 1983.

78. Arthur Gordon, interview.

79. The following two pargaraphs are derived from Marv Ewing, interview; and Arthur Gordon, interview.

80. Michael Gammon, "A GIS Analysis of Changing Democratic Voter Patterns in Westbrook and Madawaska, Maine after Significant Union Events, 1960–1976," unpublished GIS project, last modified, May 1, 2013, Microsoft Powerpoint file.

81. Marv Ewing, Bill Carver, and Howard Reiche, interviews.

82. Anonymous S. D. Warren manager, interview with author, Portland, Maine, September 21, 2000.

83. In addition to the many interviews with S. D. Warren Company workers, managers, and union officials, see Gary Cook, interview, and Peter Kellman, interview, February 13, 2003.

84. Karl Dornish, interview.

85. Anonymous S. D. Warren manager, interview.

86. Howard Reiche, interview.

4. MADAWASKA REBELLION

1. Net income dipped from $5.02 million in 1965 to 3.53 million in 1967, even though sales surged. Income dipped further in 1968 and 1969, averaging less than $1 million. Fraser's net income averaged $4.7 million annually from 1955–65. "Annual Minutes of Fraser Company Board of Directors' Executive Committee, 1955–1969," Fraser Company Archives (Edmundston: University of New Brunswick–Edmundston.

2. "New Fraser President Is Introduced at Annual General Meeting of the Company," *St. John Valley Times*, April 25, 1968.

3. Heuer was a towering, overweight, man. Peter Egan's father was an engineering manager in the mid-1960s and close associate of Heuer's at Great Northern Paper in the mid-1960s. Heuer joined the Egans weekly for dinner. Peter Egan recalls that Heuer would have many shots of whiskey, neat, while chain-smoking nonfilter cigarettes. Peter Egan, interview with author, Portland, Maine, October 4, 2014.

4. "Organization, Staff Changes at Fraser," *St. John Valley Times*, May 29, 1968.

5. "Strike Averted: About $100,000 Wage Boost Finally Break Jam, Drama at Acadia School Leaves Community Limp," *St. John Valley Times*, August 8, 1968.

6. This figure refers to the Canadian as well as U.S. side of the river. A contemporary estimate is about 14,000 residents on the U.S. side with a larger population of about 40,000 on the Canadian side. As this chapter further explains, it is historically one community. Aroostook County Tourism, accessed March 24, 2020, https://visitaroostook.com/story/st-john-valley.

7. *Acadian Culture in Maine*, accessed August 4, 2019, http://acim.umfk.maine.edu/. As discussed below in the section "The Acadians of the St. John Valley: French Identity and Conflict With the English," the original settlers of the St. John Valley were Acadians who were part of the 1750s diaspora from Nova Scotia, with an intermediary stop for a generation in southern New Brunswick. This diaspora also included the Cajun French of Louisiana. While technically hailing from New Brunswick, the relevance of the diaspora is deeply embedded in local lore and identity.

8. Mary Reinsmuth, *The Fraser Story* (Edmundston, New Brunswick: Fraser Paper Company, 1949).

9. Reinsmuth, *The Fraser Story*. The exchange rate between the United States and Canada has in fact fluctuated, and at times in 1940s and 1950s it was either at parity or the Canadian dollar was even a bit stronger. Since 1979, with the exception of a few years in the early 2010s, the U.S. dollar has been quite strong, ensuring Fraser the exchange rate advantage on pulp. "Foreign Currency Units Per 1 Canadian Dollar, 1950–2018," Pacific Exchange Rate Service, Sauder School of Business, University of British Columbia, Database Retrieval System, accessed March 24, 2020, http://fx.sauder.ubc.ca/etc/CADpages.pdf.

10. "Annual Minutes of Fraser Company Board of Directors' Executive Committee, 1932–1942," Fraser Company Archives (Edmundston: University of New Brunswick–Edmundston).

11. Nicole Lang, "La compagnie Fraser Limited, 1918–1974: Étude de l'évolution des stratégies économiques, des structures administratives et de l'organisation du travail à l'usine d'Edmundston au Nouveau-Brunswick," (PhD diss., University of Montreal, 1994); Nicole Lang, interview with author, Edmundston, New Brunswick, May 8, 2012; and Reinsmuth, *The Fraser Story*.

12. Fraser retained several other smaller pulp and lumber mill operations in New Brunswick and Quebec. Reinsmuth, *The Fraser Story*.

13. A commonplace management strategy in paper mill strikes from the 1950s into the early 1980s was to shift production to sister mills within a large company like Scott or St. Regis, and especially to temporarily transfer shop-floor supervisors who were experienced paper makers to staff a struck mill. Bruce Kaufman, "The Emergence and Growth

of A Non-Union Sector in the Southern Paper Industry," in *Southern Labor in Transition 1940–1995*, ed. Robert Zeiger (Knoxville, TN: University of Tennessee Press, 1997), 295–330, 321. The lack of other production sites in Fraser foreclosed use of this practice.

14. Reinsmuth, *The Fraser Story*.

15. See Lang, "La compagnie Fraser Limited, 1918–1974"; Nicole Lang, interview; "Annual Minutes of Fraser Company Board of Directors' Executive Committee, 1932–1974," Fraser Company Archives (Edmundston: University of New Brunswick-Edmundston); Reinsmuth, *The Fraser Story*.

16. These were K. S. MacLachlin in 1932 and then Aubrey Crabtree in 1941. After twenty-seven years, John Heuer succeeded Crabtree and brought in a new regime of management and investment that provoked the 1971 strike. Reinsmuth, *The Fraser Story*. Heuer died shortly after the strike and was replaced by C. P. Recor, who led the mill for three more years until 1974.

17. "Annual Minutes of Fraser Company Board of Directors' Executive Committee, 1938 and 1939," Fraser Company Archives (Edmundston: University of New Brunswick-Edmundston).

18. Paul Cyr, interview with author, St. David, Maine, July 8, 2008; Lang, "La compagnie Fraser Limited, 1918–1974"; Nicole Lang, interview; "Annual Minutes of Fraser Company Board of Directors' Executive Committee, 1932–1974," Fraser Company Archives (Edmundston: University of New Brunswick-Edmundston); and Reinsmuth, *The Fraser Story*.

19. Camille Bernier, interview with author, Frenchville, Maine, September 12, 2014; Paul Cyr, interview; Nicole Lang, interview; Richard Marston, interview with author, St. Agatha, Maine, September 10, 2014; Kim Ouellette, interview with author, South Portland, Maine, September 5, 2013; Judith Paradis, interview with author, Frenchville, Maine, September 11, 2014; and Lise Pelletier, interview with author, Fort Kent, Maine, May 8, 2012.

20. Camille Bernier, Kim Ouellette, interview; Richard Marston, interview; Judith Paradis, interview.

21. The literature on the family wage is enormous. Three foundational treatments are found in Ava Baron, ed., *Work Engendered Towards a New History of American Labor* (Ithaca, NY: Cornell University Press, 1991); Alice Kessler-Harris, *Out to Work: A History of Wage-Earning Women in the United States*, 20th anniversary ed. (Cambridge: Oxford University Press, 2003); and Kessler-Harris, *Gendering Labor History* (Urbana: University of Illinois Press, 2006).

22. Judy Paradis, interview with author, Frenchville, Maine, September 9, 2014.

23. "Wall of Silence up in Strikebound Madawaska," *Maine Sunday Telegram*, August 29, 1971.

24. Real Daigle, interview with author, Madawaska, Maine, July 6, 2008; and "Wall of Silence up in Strikebound Madawaska," *Maine Sunday Telegram*, August 29, 1971. As discussed at length below, the manning letters referred to agreements between the mill and the union locals that required certain staffing levels for various machines and work processes.

25. Nicole Lang, interview.

26. Lucien Mazzerolle, interview with the author, St. David, Maine, May 8, 2012.

27. Senior executives from Maine companies, including Howard Reiche, Richard Marston, Karl Dornish, and others, recall that it was in the 1970s that greater international and Southern production capacity in Maine's favored line of publication and specialty papers came online and began to reduce companies' pricing power.

28. Nicole Lang, interview; and "Fraser Launches Operation Big Thrust; To Increase Sales in Forest Projects," *St. John Valley Times*, September 25, 1969. Also from the

Edmundston French language edition of the *St. John Valley Times*—"Aux usines Fraser d'Edmundston et de Madawaska: Projet d'expansion de $60 millions," *Le Madawaska*, September 25, 1969; "Détails du programme d'expansion des Compagnies Fraser Limitées," *Le Madawaska*, October 2, 1969; and "L'Honorable Duffie souligne les avantages du projet d'expansion des 9ies Fraser," *Le Madawaska*, October 2, 1969, p. A-3 (Translation by Nancy Erickson, July 30, 2012).

29. On this, I queried Fraser historian Nicole Lang via email, June 1, 2012:

> *Michael Hillard*: Was the big thrust an effort, in part, to ward off takeover threats—besides being an effort to improve competitiveness, was it also a push to prevent another company from buying Fraser?
>
> *Lang*: I would say yes. . . . It was also a push to prevent another company buying it. In 1967, Price Company Limited tried to buy a majority of shares to take control of the company (wanted 51% of the shares). The Board of Directors sent a letter to the stockholders and recommended they say no to Price's offer—Price offered $1.40 per share and the value was then $1.94. So, the Directors of FCL maintained that Price's offer was less than the value of the company (*valeur comptable*). Price could not buy enough shares so it withdrew its offer. Then, a few months later Continental Co. of Canada tried to take-over the company. It did not succeed. After this, the Board of Directors and principal officers of Frasers wanted to reinforce the company's position.

30. Nicole Lang, interview.

31. "New Fraser President Is Introduced at Annual General Meeting of the Company," *St. John Valley Times*, April 25, 1968; and "Strike Averted: About $100,000 Wage Boost Finally Break Jam, Drama at Acadia School Leaves Community Limp," *St. John Valley Times*, August 8, 1968.

32. The literature on this topic is vast. The great labor historian David Montgomery documented how this issue shaped twentieth-century labor history, most notably in his *Workers' Control in America: Studies in the History of Work, Technology, and Labor Struggles* (New York: Cambridge University Press, 1980). A generation of feminist labor historians would criticize Montgomery not on the substance of his analysis but for his focus on male workers in telling the story. See Ardis Cameron, *Radicals of the Worst Sort* (Urbana: University of Illinois Press, 1993) for a corrective treatment in her history of the famous 1912 Bread and Roses strike, in which speed-up was a factor in Lawrence, Massachusetts textile strikes in 1882 and 1912. An early treatment, whose analysis rings true with the frustration of Fraser workers at a time, separated by nearly fifty years, is the classic of industrial sociology by Stanley Mathewson, *Restriction of Output among Unorganized Workers* (New York: Viking Press, 1931).

33. See Harry Braverman, *Labor and Monopoly Capital: The Degradation of Work in the Twentieth Century* (New York: Monthly Review Press, 1974). Since the 1970s, there has been a corollary literature on worker resistance to speed-up. It began with Harry Braverman's seminal but flawed analysis of scientific management in *Labor and Monopoly Capital*. Braverman posited that Frederick Winslow Taylor's pioneering scientific management centered on timing jobs and taking skill out of the hands of direct workers. It not only vastly increased workers' productivity but undermined the monopoly on skill workers once used to resist speed-up. The vast literature responding to Braverman's hypothesis focused on his useful (and Marxian) frame for raising questions about how work is managed in a profit-making capitalism in which intensifying work on assembly-like jobs is an obvious and central goal. Most studies departed from Braverman's biggest flaw—ignoring that workers often resist, and through resistance help to constitute the actual shop floor regimes to be found in cases studies. Two early responses in this vein were two books pub-

lished in 1979, and 1982, respectively: David Montgomery's *Workers' Control in America* and Michael Burowoy's *Manufacturing Consent: Changes in the Labor Process under Monopoly Capitalism* (Chicago: University of Chicago Press, 1982). For a thorough review of this literature, see Paul Thompson and Kirsty Newsome, "Labor Process Theory, Work, and the Employment Relation," in *Theoretical Perspectives on Work and the Employment Relationship*, ed. Bruce Kaufman (Urbana, IL: IRRA Series, 2004), 133–62.

Brody's view of workplace contractualism adds a compelling insight: job control contracts can be a vehicle for framing questions of shop-floor justice, and violations of contract promises and rules on a wide scale are a specific impetus to worker resistance. Fraser's locals sought first to resist through negotiation and grievances but later struck when these mechanisms were tried without success.

34. "Open Statement by UPIU Locals 347, Local 1251," *St. John Valley Times*, July 10, 1971; "Locals Give Views to Canadians and Public," *St. John Valley Times*, July 22, 1971; and Ron Albert, interview with author, Madawaska, Maine, May 6, 2012; Ron Chasse and Lucien Mazzerolle, joint interview conducted with author, St. David, Maine, May 8, 2012; Paul Cyr, interview; Jerry Cyr, interview with author, St. David, Maine, July 8, 2008; and Real Daigle, interview with author, Madawaska, Maine, July 6, 2008.

35. See note 28 above.

36. Camille Bernier, interview.

37. "The Fraser Situation: Talks between Local 365 and Management Stop, Workers Say Discharge of 12 Men 'Unsatisfactory,'" *St. John Valley Times*, October 1, 1970; "Local 365 Answers Fraser Statement," *St. John Valley Times*, October 15, 1970; "Open Statement by UPIU Locals 347, Local 1251," *St. John Valley Times*, July 10, 1971; and "Locals Give Views to Canadians and Public," *St. John Valley Times*, July 22, 1971. Also Ron Albert, interview; Camille Bernier, interview; Ron Chasse and Lucien Mazzerolle, joint interview; Paul Cyr, interview; Jerry Cyr, interview; Real Daigle, interview; Nicole Lang, interview; Judith Paradis, interview.

38. "Open Statement by UPIU Locals 347, Local 1251," *St. John Valley Times*, July 10, 1971; "Locals Give Views to Canadians and Public," *St. John Valley Times*, July 22, 1971.

39. This interpretation emanated from local historians, especially Nicole Lang and Lise Pelletier (see previously cited interviews). But it is also at the center of the memories of men who were young militants at the time of the strike, especially Ron Albert, interview; Paul Cyr, interview; Phil Dubois, interview; and Judy Paradis, interview.

40. *Acadian Culture in Maine* (website), accessed August 4, 2019, http://acim.umfk .maine.edu/.

41. "About Us," St. John Valley Chamber of Commerce, accessed August 4, 2019, https://www.stjohnvalleychamber.org/about-us.html.

42. Part of the Canadian diaspora located in southern New Brunswick; the second movement of Acadians from southern New Brunswick to the Saint John Valley was due to economic pressures from English settlers and American loyalists fleeing the Revolutionary War. It was part of this group that immigrated to the St. John Valley. Over the next seventy-five years, local French Canadians—Quebecois who also included New Brunswick French Canadians—heavily intermarried with St. John Valley Acadians. The primary source on this history is Beatrice Craig, *Backwoods Consumers and Homespun Capitalists: The Rise of a Market Culture in Eastern Canada* (Toronto: University of Toronto Press, 2009).

43. See *Acadian Culture in Maine*; "About Us," St. John Valley Chamber of Commerce; and Joseph E. Price, "The Status of French among Youth in a Bilingual American-Canadian Border Community: The Case of Madawaska, Maine." (PhD Diss., University of Indiana, 2007).

44. Some former Fraser workers interviewed for this essay were born in Canada, either because the Edmundston hospital was used (see, for example, Bob Gogan, interview with

author, St. David, Maine, July 8, 2008) or because the worker grew up somewhere in nearby New Brunswick before making their way to Madawaska on the U.S. side of the river to work for Fraser. See, for example, Lucien Mazzerolle, interview. An important caveat is that 9/11 tightened border security dramatically. This drastically reduced cross-border movement and thus has eroded the historic closeness of the cross-border community.

45. According to the website for the documentary *Réveil: Waking up French*, one factor that stoked xenophobia toward New England's Franco-Americans was their resistance to assimilation, especially embodied in the persistence well into the twentieth-century of the use of French as the Franco's daily language. *Réveil: Waking up French*, accessed August 4, 2019, http://www.wakingupfrench.com/about.shtm.

46. *Réveil: Waking up French*.

47. *Acadian Culture in Maine*.

48. Cecile Fontaine recalls the condescension of her Anglo teachers: "The teacher we had in my school would liken us to the Appalachians, you know, saying that they were 'missionaries,' and I always really resented that." Cecile Fontaine, interview with author, Portland, Maine, July 2004. Folklorist Lise Pelletier of *Acadian Culture in Maine* emphasized that "outside" "English" teachers and school principals organized students to "snitch" on other students as part of this process of enforcement. Anecdotes of punishment for speaking French in school (almost invariably getting caught on the playground) is a trope in most of the interviews the author did in the upper St. John Valley.

49. See *Acadian Culture in Maine*; *Réveil: Waking up French*; Price, *Status of French: "About Us,"* St. John Valley Chamber of Commerce. Also, Claire Bolduc, interview; Cecile Fontaine, interview; Nicole Lang, interview; and Lise Pelletier, interview.

50. David Brody, "The New Immigrants," in *Steelworkers in America: The Non-Union Years* (Cambridge, MA: Harvard University Press, 1960), 96–111. For Madawaska versus other Maine paper mill communities, see Peter Kellman, interview with author, Portland, Maine, December 5, 2012. Jefferson Cowie has demonstrated how the ethos of white ethnic working-class identity largely disappeared in the 1970s. See Jefferson Cowie, *Stayin' Alive: The 1970s and the Last Days of the Working Class* (New York: New Press, 2010).

51. Lise Pelletier, interview with author, Fort Kent, Maine, May 8, 2012. Former valley resident and lifelong political activist Claire Bolduc is quite eloquent on this point:

> People in northern Maine had a cohesion based on community, history—the French speakers had cohesion based on language, on culture, on food, and they were Catholics. . . . That gave them an edge about understanding organization, and being willing to be part of a group, and be dependent on each other. It gave them an edge that you don't have with the stalwart Yankee who is independent—to his death. . . . Whereas the Catholic—we have the communion of saints, we're all in this together, that's an old story.

Claire Bolduc, interview with author, Bangor, Maine, July 6, 2004.

52. *Acadian Culture in Maine*.

53. Paul Cyr, interview.

54. *Acadian Culture in Maine*.

55. Ron Albert, interview; Ron Chasse and Lucien Mazzerolle, joint interview; Paul Cyr, interview; Jerry Cyr, interview; Real Daigle, interview; Nicole Lang, interview; Judith Paradis, interview; and Lise Pelletier, interview.

56. Claire Bolduc, interview with the author, Bangor, Maine, July 6, 2004; William Butler interview with the author, Aurora, Maine, July 27, 2004; Jonathan Falk, digitally recorded interview with the author, Carmel, Maine, July 6, 2004; Donald Fontaine, digitally recorded interview with the author, Portland, Maine, July 14, 2004; Carroll Gerow, interview, Patton, Maine, August 11, 2004; Peter Hagerty, interview with the author, Portland,

Maine, August 15, 2004; and Larry Palmer, interview with the author, Patton, Maine, August 10, 2004. Also, *Acadian Culture in Maine*; and David Vail, "The internal conflict: contract logging, chainsaws, and clear-cuts in Maine forestry," in *Who Will Save the Forests? Knowledge, Power, and Environmental Destruction*, eds. T. Banuri and F. A. Marglin (London: Zed Books, 1993), 142–89.

57. Paul Cyr, interview. Cyr also pointed out that there was a very high degree of interest and participation in election campaigns for union posts.

58. Jerry Cyr, interview with author, St. Francis, Maine, July 8, 2008.

59. Paul Cyr, interview.

60. Michael Gammon, "A GIS Analysis of Changing Democratic Voter Patterns in Westbrook and Madawaska, Maine after Significant Union Events, 1960–1976" (Unpublished GIS project, last modified, May 1, 2013), Microsoft Powerpoint file.

61. This trenchant appeal is well illustrated by the experience of Franco-Americans in Westbrook. Westbrook workers of Quebecois descent recall the Ku Klux Klan marching through Franco neighborhoods in the 1920s. Phil LaViolette, the former long-time S. D. Warren worker and founder of Westbrook's Franco historical society, recalls that local Catholic priests led voter registration efforts to have Franco workers join the Democratic Party during FDR's presidency because of this appeal of the party to white ethnics. Phil LaViolette, interview with author, Westbrook, Maine, July 8, 2003.

62. The analysis in this paragraph comes from my interview with Nicole Lang, and also her "Fraser Company Limited: Family Firm to Modern Company, 1917–1974" (unpublished manuscript, May 14, 1999).

63. Nicole Lang, interview.

64. Ron Albert, interview with author, Madawaska, Maine, May 6, 2012.

65. Nicole Lang, interview.

66. Here I am using Portelli's framework for interpreting memory in oral history interviews. Alessandro Portelli, *The Death of Luigi Trastulli and Other Stories* (Albany: SUNY Press, 1991).

67. The vast majority of private-sector union contracts in the United States after 1950 contained no-strike clauses during the duration of the contract. Workers striking during the contract was unsanctioned by local union officials; it was therefore a wildcat strike. Typically, the international union's representatives, who are legally bound to uphold no-strike clauses and responsible for getting rank-and-file union workers to honor the contract, would often try to persuade—forcefully—that workers must end a wildcat and return to work. That happened in this case.

This legal situation grew out of the antiunion 1948 Taft-Hartley Act. This major antiunion legislation successfully restricted most forms of union militancy: "by undermining unions' ability and ultimate workers' right to strike . . . confine[d] unions into the straightjacket of collective bargaining structures. Collective bargaining pursued . . . orderly industrial relations by rendering most types of strikes illegal during the life of the contract. It transformed [union officials] into guardians of the rank and file insofar as they had to restrain workers' actions that violated the contract." Nicola Pizzolato, "Strikes in the United States since World War II," in *The Encyclopedia of Strikes in American History*, ed. Aaron Brenner, Benjamin Day, and Immanuel Ness (Armonk, NY: M. E. Sharpe, 2009), 226–38.

68. Local 365 of the International Brotherhood of Pulp, Sulfite, and Paper Mill Workers. "The Fraser Situation: Talks between Local 365 and Management Stop, Workers Say Discharge of 12 Men 'Unsatisfactory,'" *St. John Valley Times*, October 1, 1970; "Local 365 Answers Fraser Statement," *St. John Valley Times*, October 15, 1970.

69. "The Fraser Situation: Talks between Local 365 and Management Stop, Workers Say Discharge of 12 Men 'Unsatisfactory,'" *St. John Valley Times*, October 1, 1970; "Local 365

Answers Fraser Statement," *St. John Valley Times*, October 15, 1970; and Paul Cyr, interview.

70. "The Fraser Situation: Talks between Local 365 and Management Stop, Workers Say Discharge of 12 Men 'Unsatisfactory,'" *St. John Valley Times*, October 1, 1970.

71. Ron Chasse and Lucien Mazzerolle, joint interview.

72. Paul Cyr, interview.

73. Jerry Cyr recalls: "The mill didn't go completely down at the time. They were trying to make shiftwork and make the people staying to work longer, to achieve this goal of keeping the machines up." Jerry Cyr and Ron Albert, interviews.

74. "The Fraser Situation: Talks between Local 365 and Management Stop, Workers Say Discharge of 12 Men 'Unsatisfactory,'" *St. John Valley Times*, October 1, 1970; "Local 365 Answers Fraser Statement," *St. John Valley Times*, October 15, 1970. Also, Ron Chasse and Lucien Mazzerolle, joint interview; Jerry Cyr, interview; and Paul Cyr, interview.

75. "The Fraser Situation: Talks between Local 365 and Management Stop, Workers Say Discharge of 12 Men 'Unsatisfactory,'" *St. John Valley Times*, October 1, 1970; Paul Cyr, interview.

76. "Local 365 Answers Fraser Statement," *St. John Valley Times*, October 15, 1970.

77. Paul Cyr, interview.

78. Says Paul Cyr: "My father was one of a group of French-named managers who were purged. . . . There was a guy named Marty Roach who came up here. . . . He was a guy brought in by Fraser to sweep the house, and he essentially fired every manager in the mill who had a French name. Eventually a lot of them came back, or worked their way back. . . . But it was quite a contentious time." Paul Cyr, interview. Ouellette's 2001 study of Fraser's labor relations identified the same purge and captures community memory of the period as well. Ouellette writes: "In the mid to late 1960s, recalls a worker, there was a subtle shift in ownership. Fraser moved away from being a predominately family owned company toward one with outside stockholders. [The new ownership and management] created a rift [with] workers. The new investors made a clean sweep of management; the president was replaced and 20 foremen were let go as well. [Quoting the worker]: "A hatch [sic] man they call, came and said: 'you, you're out, you, you're out, we don't need you any more . . . that's when they [Fraser] weren't family owned any more. But it was still Fraser . . . and that's when they [management] started to turn." P. Kim Ouellette, "The History of Labor Relations at Fraser Papers" (unpublished paper, December 11, 2001).

79. In an open letter published a couple of days after the strike began, the striking locals stated:

> In 1968, the company asked for cooperation on the part of their employees, claiming a drop in profits and problems of survival. For three cents an hour more and promises of more job opportunities, the employees accepted a new contract. Management took it from there. Our new management immediately started their programs **of exploiting human resources**. Emphasis in original letter. "Open Statement by UPIU Locals 347, Local 1251," *St. John Valley Times*, July 10, 1971.

80. Ron Albert, interview.

81. Phil Dubois, interview with the author, Madawaska, Maine, May 5, 2012.

82. Boldface and capital letters as is in the original; I gave emphasis to "present management" because the union locals were all quite explicit in referring to Heuer and Roach. "Locals Give Views to Canadians and Public," *St. John Valley Times*, July 22, 1971.

83. "Locals Give Views to Canadians and Public," *St. John Valley Times*, July 22, 1971.

84. Paul Cyr, interview.

85. Paul Cyr, interview. In the paper industry, it was common practice in the postwar era, prior to 1980, for managers—often including managers from other mills under a company's ownership—to attempt to maintain production during strikes.

86. "What Does It Take to Move a Mountain?" *St. John Valley Times*, August 5, 1971. The advertisement makes clear that the company is anticipating, and willing to come down hard on, "illegal picketing," defined as threatening or using violence on picket lines to keep people out of the mill. The mill directly threatened criminal and civil prosecution and dismissal from the company on illegal picketers.

87. Paul Cyr, phone communication with author, March 26, 2020; and Ron Albert, interview; Paul Cyr, interview; and Bob Gogan, interview.

88. Reinsmuth, *Fraser Story*; Nicole Lang, interview.

89. Ron Albert remembers that the managers working in the mill during the strike "started loading cars with paper, and the word was getting around; there were some in management on the inside that were informing us what was going on." Ron Albert, interview.

90. Bob Gogan, interview.

91. The *Maine Sunday Telegram* reported that BAR had to enlist nonunion supervisors to run the train—avoiding the obvious problem of unionized rail workers refusing to cross a picket line. "Wall of Silence."

92. "State Police guard BAR Paper Train at Madawaska," *Portland Press Herald*, August 9, 1971.

93. "A call was made to get state troopers and regional sheriffs to the town, where they remained on the outskirts," quoted in "Wall of Silence up in Strikebound Madawaska," *Maine Sunday Telegram*, August 29, 1971.

94. This overview of the events of August 5–9, 1971 is derived from "State Police guard BAR Paper Train at Madawaska," *Portland Press Herald*, August 9, 1971; "Fraser Strike Cools; Boxcars Remain in the Yard," *Bangor Daily News*, August 10, 1971; and "Talks to Resume Thursday in Bitter Fraser Strike," *Portland Press Herald*, August 10, 1971. And Ron Albert, interview; Camille Bernier, interview; Ron Chasse and Lucien Mazzerolle, joint interview; Paul Cyr, interview; Jerry Cyr, interview; Real Daigle, interview; Bob Gogan, Nicole Lang, interview; and Judith Paradis, interview.

95. Taylor Branch, *Parting the Waters: America in the King Years* (New York: Simon and Schuster, 1988), 673–845.

96. Bob Gogan, interview.

97. In a statement released right after the confrontation, the committee of strike leaders of the four union locals fully distanced themselves from the events. "The union representative said the leadership did not question the company's right to deliver the paper and added: 'We're not behind the violence.'" "Talks to Resume Thursday in Bitter Fraser Strike," *Portland Press Herald*, August 10, 1971. Camille Bernier, who was president of Paper Makers Local 247 at the time of the strike, recalled having little knowledge of the activists' actions. Camille Bernier, interview.

98. Camille Bernier, interview.

99. Paul Cyr, interview.

100. Bob Gogan, interview.

101. "Fraser Strike Cools; Boxcars Remain in the Yard," *Bangor Daily News*, August 10, 1971.

102. According to newspaper accounts, the confrontation came as the BAR tried to move an engine into the mill to couple to the twenty-seven boxcars in the mill yard. "Fraser Strike Cools; Boxcars Remain in the Yard," *Bangor Daily News*, August 10, 1971.

103. "Talks to Resume Thursday in Bitter Fraser Strike," *Portland Press Herald*, August 10, 1971.

104. The following is drawn from interviews with Bob Gogan, Paul Cyr, Jerry Cyr, Phil Dubois, Ron Chasse, interviews; Real Daigle, interview with author, Madawaska, Maine, May 6, 2008; and Deborah Daigle, interview with author, Madawaska, Maine, September 9, 2014.

105. Here is a newspaper's account of this moment: "State Police captain ordered the crowd to disperse and when they refused, a tear gas shell was fired in front of them. The wind was blowing in a westerly direction and the gas fumes drifted back onto the officers. More tear gas was thrown. In all, witnesses said, eight canisters of gas were fired. While some of the crowd pelted the police with rocks, the men rushed forward and started pushing and pummeling the officers. The police beat a hasty retreat up the hill." "Wall of Silence up in Strikebound Madawaska," *Maine Sunday Telegram*, August 29, 1971; and Phil Dubois, interview.

106. "Fraser Strike Cools; Boxcars Remain in the Yard," *Bangor Daily News*, August 10, 1971.

107. Paul Cyr and Peter Kellman, interviews.

108. Paul Cyr, interview.

109. Bob Gogan, interview.

110. "Fraser Strike Cools; Boxcars Remain in the Yard," *Bangor Daily News*, August 10, 1971.

111. "Fraser Strike Cools; Boxcars Remain in the Yard," *Bangor Daily News*, August 10, 1971.

112. Neil Rolde, interview with author, Portland, Maine, September 28, 2011.

113. Governor Curtis met the parties on August 9 and 10. Negotiations resumed two days later on Thursday, August 12. "Mill, Union Talk Again, In Private," *Portland Press Herald*, August 13, 1971.

114. "Mill, Union Talk Again, In Private," *Portland Press Herald*, August 13, 1971; and "Unions Turn Down Fraser Paper Offer," *Portland Press Herald*, August 22, 1971.

115. Local union leaders thought it might be possible to have the wage increases applied to benefits, and they also thought that Nixon's move might also allow them to return to work under existing contract conditions, which would mean the manning letter would stay intact. According to a press report, these notions put workers in the "quandary" of thinking it might make sense to end the strike. "Wall of Silence up in Strikebound Madawaska," *Maine Sunday Telegram*, August 29, 1971.

116. "Five Striking Maine Unions Plan to Stay Out Despite Pleas," *Portland Press Herald*, August 18, 1971. The article quotes the Nixon administration's chief federal mediator as saying that 150,000 workers were out on a total of 363 strikes, including the entire West Coast dockworkers, with nearly 300,000 workers possibly going out on strike soon in bituminous coal and in aerospace and airlines in September.

117. See "Vote Set Today on Fraser Pact," *Portland Press Herald*, August 21, 1971; "Unions Turn Down Fraser Paper Offer," *Portland Press Herald*, August 22, 1971.

118. "Unions Turn Down Fraser Paper Offer, *Portland Press Herald*, August 22, 1971.

119. "Fraser Strike Over—Contract Signed, Workers Back, Machines Start Up," *St. John Valley Times*, September 16, 1971.

120. "Fraser Nine Week Strike Ends Sunday," *Kennebec Journal*, September 11, 1971; "Fraser Strike Over: Contract Signed, Workers Back, Machines Start Up," *St. John Valley Times*, September 16, 1971.

121. Paul Cyr, interview; Bob Gogan, interview.

122. Ron Albert, interview; Ron Chasse and Lucien Mazzerolle, joint interview; Paul Cyr, interview; Jerry Cyr, interview; Phil Dubois, interview; Bob Gogan, interview; and Real Daigle, interview.

123. Ron Chasse and Lucien Mazzerolle, joint interview; Paul Cyr, interview; Jerry Cyr, interview; and Ouellette, "The History of Labor Relations."

124. Jerry Cyr, interview.

125. Anonymous interviewee, interview with P. Kim Ouellette, November, 2001, cited in Ouellette, "The History of Labor Relations."

126. "Unions Vote Today," *St. John Valley Times*, July 3, 1974; "Mediation Next?" *St. John Valley Times*, July 10, 1974; and "Unions Accept Contract," *St. John Valley Times*, July 17, 1974.

127. For example, Westbrook, Maine's S. D. Warren mill hired a great number of union leaders. The mill manager at the time, Howard Reiche, saw union leaders as often the brightest and most motivated in the workforce and also knew he could improve relations with the mill's locals. See Howard Reiche, interview. Michael Hamel, a former union leader at Scott's Winslow, Maine mill painted similar picture of at his mill. Michael Hamel, interview with author, Waterville, Maine, April 8, 2003.

128. Paul Cyr, interview.

129. Ron Albert, Jerry Cyr, Paul Cyr, and Bob Gogan, interviews.

130. Deborah Daigle and Phil Dubois, interviews.

131. Paul Cyr, interview.

132. Ron Albert, interview; Ron Chasse and Lucien Mazzerolle, joint interview; Paul Cyr, interview; Jerry Cyr, interview; Bob Gogan, interview; and Real Daigle, interview.

133. Jerry Cyr, interview.

134. Judy Paradis and P. Kim Ouellette, interviews.

135. Phil Dubois, interview.

136. The community strike an early twentieth century phenomenom has its own of extensive literature in the field of U.S. labor history. See especially Elizabeth Faue, "Paths of Unionization: Community, Bureaucracy and Gender in the Minneapolis Labor Movement of the 1930s," in *We Are All Leaders*, ed. Staughton Lynd (Urbana: University of Illinois Press, 1996), 172–98; and Ardis Cameron's skillful use of oral history brings alive the community component in the 1912 Bread and Roses strike of Lawrence, Massachusetts. Cameron, *Radicals of the Worst Sort.*

137. See Barry Bluestone and Bennett Harrison, *The Deindustrializtion of America* (New York: Basic Books, 1982); Howell John Harris, *The Right to Manage: Industrial Relations Policies of American Business in the 1940s* (Madison: University of Wisconsin Press, 1982); and Kimberly Phillips-Fein, *Invisible Hands: The Making of the Conservative Movement from the New Deal to Reagan* (New York: W. W. Norton, 2009).

138. See David Roediger, *Working Towards Whiteness: How America's Immigrants Became White, the Strange Journey from Ellis Island to the Suburbs* (New York: Basic Books, 2005).

139. This phrase is Leon Fink's apt depiction of the term "political economy." My book's argument on strike activity in the 1960s follows Lichtenstein's critique of the capital-labor accord notion, with frequent strike activity, especially in the late 1960s through the mid-1970s, exemplifying that this period can be aptly characterized as the unquiet decades. In his words: "American unions proved remarkably combative. From the later 1940s through the early 1970s, strike levels in the United States stood higher than at any time, before or since. During the 1950s, organized labor averaged 352 big stoppages a year. That dropped to something like 285 a year throughout the next two decades, before plummeting to 83 in the 1980s and even less during the century's last decade." Nelson Lichtenstein, *State of the Union: A Century of American Labor* (Princeton, NJ: Princeton University Press, 2002), 136. See also Jefferson Cowie, *Stayin' Alive: The 1970s and the Last Days of the Working Class* (New York: New Press, 2010), 23–74.

5. CUTTING OFF THE CANADIANS

1. Some content in this article, including the chapter title, originally appeared in Michael Hillard and Jonathan Goldstein, "Cutting Off the Canadians: Nativism and the Fate of the Maine Woodsmen's Association, 1970–1981," *Labor: Studies in the Working Class History of the Americas* 5, no. 3 (2008): 67–89.

2. See Mel Ames, interview with author, Atkinson, Maine, August 12, 2004; William Butler, interview with author, Aurora, Maine, July 27, 2004; Claire Bolduc, interview with author, July 7, 2004; Jonathan Falk, interview with author, Carmel, Maine, July 24, 2004; Cecile Fontaine, interview with author, Portland, Maine, July 16, 2004; Donald Fontaine, interview with author, Portland, Maine, July 15, 2004; Peter Hagerty, interview with author, Portland, Maine, August 8, 2004; and Larry Palmer, interview with author, Patton, Maine, July 10, 2004. The author also consulted over twenty articles in the *Portland Press Herald* and *Bangor Daily News* from fall 1975.

3. Leon Fink, "Editor's Introduction," *Labor: Studies in the Working Class Histories of the Americas* 5, no. 3 (2008): 2.

4. The absence of unionization was specific to New England, especially Maine and New Hampshire. Loggers in the western South—especially Arkansas and Louisiana—and the Northwest have a long history of rebellion and radical unionism, dating to the early twentieth century when "wobbly" Industrial Workers of the World (IWW) organizers had great success in mobilizing discontent among the geographically male proletariat that formed these workforces. See James Green, *Grass Roots Socialism: Radical Movements in the Southwest* (Baton Rouge: Louisiana University Press, 1978); Jerry Lembcke and William Tattam, *One Union in Wood: A Political History of International Woodsworkers of America* (New York: International Publishers, 1984); Richard Rajala, "A Dandy Bunch of Wobblies: Pacific Northwest Loggers and the Industrial Workers of the World, 1900–1930," *Labor History* 37, no. 2 (1996): 205–34; and Robert Taylor, *Rebels in the Woods: The IWW in the Pacific Northwest* (Eugene: University of Oregon Press, 1967).

5. This chapter uses multiple terms to describe the fall 1975 woodcutters protest, primarily using action, protest and strike effort to depict this set of events. Protest participants refer to it as a strike at the time, as did Maine newspapers' accounts. I explore below why and how the event fits somewhere in between what is traditionally called a strike, versus a protest or attempted strike. The heart of the matter is that only a fraction of the woodcutter workforce were participants in various meetings and pickets at paper mills, and the protest led to only modest disruptions of paper production in mills. Company officials did not (then or now) consider it a strike, while at the same time successfully seeking court injunctions *against the MWA's strike* and attempt to collectively bargain with the companies. In a word, how to characterize the event is complicated.

6. Stewart Smith and Michele Marra, "Values and Community: The Promise of Sustainable Agriculture and the Role of Government," in *Towards a Sustainable Maine: The Politics, Economics and Ethics of Sustainability*, ed. Richard Barringer (Portland, ME: Muskie Institute of Public Affairs, 1993), 235–54.

7. Barbara Birmingham, interview with author, Cape Elizabeth, Maine, August 2, 2004.

8. Camille Bernier, interview with author, Frenchville, Maine, September 12, 2014; Barbara Birmingham, interview with author, Cape Elizabeth, Maine, August 2, 2004; Guy Dubay, interview with author, Madawaska, Maine, May 10, 2012; Carroll Gerow, interview with author, Patton, Maine, August 11, 2004; Kim Ouellette, interview with author, South Portland, Maine, September 14, 2012; Jonathan Falk, interview; and Larry Palmer, interview.

9. Claire Bolduc, interview.

10. Jonathan Falk, interview.

11. Larry Palmer, interview; Carroll Gerow, interview; and Barbara Birmingham, interview.

12. Jonathan Falk, "The Organization of Pulpwood Harvesting in Maine," (working paper, Yale University, School of Forestry and Environmental Studies, no. 4, 1977).

13. Claire Bolduc, interview; Jonathan Falk, interview; Cecile Fontaine, interview; Donald Fontaine, interview; and Peter Hagerty, interview with author.

14. Claire Bolduc, interview; Cecile Fontaine, interview; and Donald Fontaine, interview.

15. Mel Ames, interview with author, Atkinson, Maine, August 12, 2004.

16. Bill Butler, interview with author, Aurora, Maine, July 27, 2004.

17. On this passage on the history from the 1930s to 1960s, see William Parenteau, "The Rise of the Small Contractor: A Study of Technological and Structural Change in the Maine Pulpwood Industry, 1900–1975" (Master's thesis, University of Maine-Orono, 1986), 100; and David Vail, "The Internal Conflict: Contract Logging, Chainsaws, and Clear-Cuts in Maine Forestry," in *Who Will Save the Forests? Knowledge, Power, and Environmental Destruction*, ed. Tarique Banuri and Frederique A. Marglin (Atlantic Highlands, NJ: Zed Books, 1993), 149–50, 152.

18. Daniel Corcoran, interview with the author, Millinocket, Maine, June 22, 2006.

19. The latter is from the late 1940s to the 1970s. Falk, "The Organization," 8–9, 43–44.

20. See Falk, "The Organization"; Parenteau, "The Rise of the Small Contractor; David Vail, "The Internal Conflict."

21. See William Osborne, *The Paper Plantation: Ralph Nadar's Study Group Report on the Pulp and Paper Industry in Maine* (New York: Viking Press, 1974), 141–55. See Parenteau, "The Rise of the Small Contractor; Vail, "The Internal Conflict," 141–55.

22. See Falk, "The Organization"; Parenteau, "The Rise of the Small Contractor; Vail, "The Internal Conflict."

23. Falk, "The Organization," 10–11.

24. A government report of fatalities in logging for the years 1992–97, a period in which logging was already much safer due to mechanized harvesters' wide use, cited it the nation's second most dangerous occupation, with 126 mortalities per year, a rate twenty-seven times greater than the average for all occupations. Eric Sygnatur, "Logging is Perilous Work," *Compensation and Working Conditions* 3, no. 4 (1998): 3–4; Vail, "The Internal Conflict," 157; and Claire Bolduc, interview; Jonathan Falk, interview; Cecile Fontaine, interview; and Donald Fontaine, interview.

25. Vail, "The Internal Conflict," 156.

26. Vail, "The Internal Conflict," 153, 156; and Claire Bolduc, interview; Jonathan Falk, interview; Cecile Fontaine, interview; and Donald Fontaine, interview.

27. Falk, "The Organization," 21; and Vail, "The Internal Conflict," 156.

28. William Parenteau, "Bonded Labor: Canadian Woods Workers in the Maine Pulpwood Industry, 1940–1955," *Forest and Conservation History* 37, no 3, (1993): 108–19.

29. Cited in Parenteau, "The Rise of the Small Contractor," 97.

30. Parenteau, "Bonded Labor," 115.

31. Parenteau, "The Rise of the Small Contractor," 134.

32. John G. Peters, "An Economic Analysis of the Independent Pulpwood Production Industry in Maine" (Master's thesis, University of Maine-Orono, 1973).

33. Vail, "The Internal Conflict, "The Rise of the Small Contractor," 154; Falk, "The Organization"; and Parenteau, "The Rise of the Small Contractor."

34. As noted in chapter 2, companies also contracted with large contractors. These contractors were typically pass-through operations; their purpose was to relieve companies of finding jobbers and in some cases running larger logging camps; but these contracts

did not themselves directly employ woodcutting crews or truckers. Parenteau, "Bonded Labor," 113.

35. Carroll Gerow, interview.

36. Osborne, *Paper Plantation*, 137–54; David Vail, "The Internal Conflict," 164.

37. Bureau of Labor Statistics, "Historical Consumer Price Index for All Urban Consumers (CPI-U), Table 24," accessed April 16, 2020, https://www.bls.gov/cpi/tables/historical-cpi-u-201709.pdf.

38. Peters, "Economic Analysis," 25.

39. This is discussed extensively in Osborne, *Paper Plantation*, 133–55; also see Claire Bolduc, interview; Cecile Fontaine, interview; and Jonathan Falk, interview.

40. Contractors were hired on renewable, nonbinding six-month contracts but then also had to receive weekly tickets permitting wood deliveries. Companies could withhold issuing tickets when wood inventories were sufficient.

41. Osborne, *Paper Plantation*, 133.

42. Osborne, *Paper Plantation*, 137–54; David Vail, "The Internal Conflict," 154–59.

43. "Bank Prime Loan Rate Changes: Historical Dates of Changes and Rates," Federal Reserve Economic Data/Federal Reserve Bank of St. Louis, accessed July 28, 2018, https://fred.stlouisfed.org/series/PRIME.

44. As Maine forestry economist David Vail notes: "In 1970, the frequency of accidents in Maine remained 37 percent above the national rate for logging, and nearly three times the rate for all manufacturing. One worker in eight suffered a disabling injury each year, losing nearly a half-year of work. At least twenty loggers were killed yearly by falling trees, chainsaw kickback, and other hazards." David Vail, "The Internal Conflict," 157.

45. Claire Bolduc, interview.

46. Mel Ames, interview; and Bill Butler, interview. Also Osborne, *Paper Plantation*, 159–64; and Parenteau, "Bonded Labor," 112–16.

47. Falk, "The Organization"; "The Rise of the Small Contractor," and Vail, "The Internal Conflict."

48. For Canadians, a better alternative to bond status was to have a work visa. With a visa, woodcutters could jump to other employers. Small numbers—several hundred—of Canadians working in the woods in the postwar era gained visas.

49. Parenteau, "The Rise of the Small Contractor," 113.

50. Canadians achieved national universal hospital insurance in 1961, with complete public insurance coming 10 ten years later. See E. Vayda and R. B. Derber, "The Canadian Health Care System: An Overview," National Center for Biotechnology Information (website), accessed September 2, 2019, https://www.ncbi.nlm.nih.gov/pubmed/6422558.

51. Vail, "The Internal Conflict," 159.

52. Larry Palmer, interview.

53. Parenteau, "The Rise of the Small Contractor," 183–84.

54. Parenteau, "The Rise of the Small Contractor," 146.

55. Mel Ames, interview; Claire Bolduc, interview; Bill Butler, interview; Jonathan Falk, interview; Cecile Fontaine, interview; Carroll Gerow, interview; Peter Hagerty, interview; and Larry Palmer, interview. Vail, "The Internal Conflict," 163–65.

56. Claire Bolduc, interview.

57. Donald Fontaine, interview.

58. Parenteau, "The Rise of the Small Contractor," 183–84.

59. Parenteau, "The Rise of the Small Contractor," 181.

60. Claire Bolduc, interview; emphasis added.

61. Larry Palmer, interview.

62. The two prior studies of the protest drew this conclusion, which was self-evident in the many interviews of former MWA leaders. See "The Rise of the Small Contractor,"

and Vail, "The Internal Conflict"; and Mel Ames, interview; Claire Bolduc, interview; Bill Butler, interview; Jonathan Falk, interview; Cecile Fontaine, interview; Donald Fontaine, interview; and Peter Hagerty, interview.

63. Peter Hagerty, interview.

64. The following account of the strike effort is based on nearly two dozen articles in the *Bangor Daily News* and the *Portland Press Herald*, spanning October 4 through October 21, 1975; interviews with Mel Ames, Claire Bolduc, William Butler, Jonathan Falk, Cecile Fontaine, Donald Fontaine, Peter Hagerty, and Larry Palmer; Parenteau, "The Rise of the Small Contractor," and Vail, "The Internal Conflict."

65. The Sherman and Costigan plants were lumber mills.

66. "No Quick Woodsmen's Strike Accord Seen," *Portland Press Herald*, October 19, 1975.

67. Peter Hagerty, interview.

68. Peter Hagerty, interview.

69. Great Northern did face disruption but did not shutdown; contemporary newspaper reports cite a temporary layoff of about ninety workers due to the strike effort. "Great Northern, Woodsmen Confer," *Bangor Daily News*, October 14, 1975; and Parenteau, "The Rise of the Small Contractor," 185.

70. "Woods Activity Moves North," *Bangor Daily News*, October 14, 1975; "Loggers Appeal to Governor," *Bangor Daily News*, October 17, 1975; and "Contractors Ask Protection, *Bangor Daily News*, October 19, 1975.

71. See Willis Johnson, *The Year of The Longley* (Stonington, ME: Penobscot Bay Press, 1978).

72. William Butler, interview.

73. Donald Fontaine, interview.

74. Donald Fontaine, interview.

75. "Picketing Workers Go Back to Work," *Portland Press Herald*, October 20, 1975; "Woodmen's Rift Smoldered Before Coming to a Boil," *Bangor Daily News*, October 21, 1975; and "Pause in the Woodsmen's Strike," *Maine Times*, October 24, 1975.

76. At the beginning of the protest, the Bangor meeting reportedly had at least two hundred new MWA members in attendance. As noted, at the height of the strike effort, some five hundred to six hundred participated in a demonstration at the state house in Augusta on October 16, 1975. "Loggers Appeal to Governor," *Bangor Daily News*, October 17, 1975. An even larger group of an estimated 750 attended the Bangor meeting on October 19 when the MWA decided to end the strike. "Picketing Strikers Go Back to Work," *Portland Press Herald*, October 20, 1975. All of the former MWA leaders I interviewed described large meetings around the state during the uprising; for instance, one in southern Maine that Peter Hagerty said had between 150 and 200 participants. The last president of the MWA, Mel Ames, published the organization's newsletter in the late 1970s and recalled a mailing list of three thousand. Certainly, there were many contractors and jobbers, particularly larger ones with significant numbers of crews in their employ, who did not support striking and who were the targets in some instances of threats and sabotage, and of course between one and two thousand Canadian bonds employed at the time. Finally, Robert Bartlett, Great Northern Paper's chief woodlands manager, in testimony to the 1977 Senate Hearing in Bangor on Canadian labor in the Maine woods, contended that Wayne Birmingham's contention of MWA membership at 1,200 lacked credibility, commenting that no meeting ever held by the MWA had more than 150 participants. "Statement of Robert F. Bartlett, Manager of Woodlands, Great Northern Paper Co., Accompanied By Henry Deabay," *U.S. Senate Subcommittee on Employment, Poverty, and Migratory Labor, Canadian Labor in the Maine Woods,* 95th Cong. (1977), April 14, 1977, Bangor, Maine, 4–23; 5. (Washington D.C.: U.S. Government Printing Office, 1977), 5.

77. Parenteau, "The Rise of the Small Contractor," 188.

78. See Parenteau, "The Rise of the Small Contractor," and Vail, "The Internal Conflict"; and Mel Ames, interview; Claire Bolduc, interview; Bill Butler, interview; Jonathan Falk, interview; Cecile Fontaine, interview; Donald Fontaine, interview; Peter Hagerty, interview; and Larry Palmer, interview.

79. Jonathan Falk, interview; Falk, "The Organization," 34.

80. Klan antipathy, in Maine and across the United States at that time, was broadly anti-Catholic, but Maine Francos were especially a target because of their continued use of French language. See the website for the documentary *Réveil: Waking up French*; as previously noted, a key cause of xenophobia toward New England's Franco-Americans was their resistance to assimilation, especially embodied in the persistence well into the twentieth-century of the use of French as the Franco's daily language. *Réveil: Waking up French*, accessed August 4, 2019, http://www.wakingupfrench.com/about.shtm; Claire Bolduc, interview; Cecile Fontaine, interview; Peter Hagerty, interview; and Lise Pelletier, interview. Also see note 48 in Chapter 4.

81. Parenteau, "The Rise of the Small Contractor," 164.

82. See *U.S. Senate Subcommittee on Employment, Poverty, and Migratory Labor*; and Donald Fontaine, interview.

83. "Statement of Donald F. Fontaine, ESQ., Counsel, Melvin Ames, Sr., Vice President, and Wayne Birmingham, President, Maine Woodsmen's Association," *U.S. Senate Subcommittee on Employment, Poverty, and Migratory Labor, Canadian Labor in the Maine Woods*, 95th Cong. (1977), April 14, 1977, 129–42.

84. A 1968 Bowdoin study of the Maine woods workforce observed: "It is worth noting that the officials in the local offices, who know the most about the woods operations, tend to identify closely with the industry. It is not an exaggeration to suggest that they feel a closer identification with the industry and its problems than do with the individual job applicant." Cited in Parenteau, "Bonded Labor," 116. Following this, Parenteau concludes that "the commission acted as a service industry for the industry." Parenteau, "Bonded Labor," 116.

85. Donald Fontaine, interview.

86. William Butler, interview.

87. Claire Bolduc, interview.

88. Peter Hagerty, interview.

89. William Butler, interview.

90. Claire Bolduc, interview.

91. Cecile Fontaine, interview.

92. The author learned of this from a well-known veteran of Maine's labor movement. Anonymous union official, phone conversation with the author, July 23, 2005.

93. See Peter Kellman, interview with author, Portland, Maine, February 13, 2003. Kellman, lifelong Maine labor activist, published author on the history of Maine paper industry labor relations, and a leader of the IP Jay strike of 1987–88 first introduced this perspective to me in the 2003 interview, and it was borne out by the research presented in this chapter. While not a focus of Vail's study, his prior analysis of Maine woodcutter culture and history affirms this view, as do the interviews with principals in the strike, especially those with Claire Bolduc, Cecile Fontaine, Donald Fontaine, Jonathan Falk, and Peter Hagerty. See Vail, "Internal Conflict," 154–56.

94. Zeiger, *Rebuilding the Pulp and Paper Union*; and Kellman, *Divided We Fall*.

95. See Eldon Hebert's testimony to the U.S. Senate in 1977: "Statement of Eldon L. Hebert, Representative, United Paper Workers, International Union, AFL-CIO, CLC," *U.S. Senate Subcommittee on Employment, Poverty, and Migratory Labor*, 117–28.

96. See "Statement of Eldon Hebert," *U.S. Senate Subcommittee on Employment, Poverty, and Migratory Labor*, 123–28.

97. Especially Jonathan Falk, interview.

98. Donald Fontaine, Mel Ames, and Wayne Birmingham presented evidence of this in their 1977 Senate testimony. "Statement of Donald F. Fontaine, ESQ., Counsel, Melvin Ames, Sr., Vice President, and Wayne Birmingham, President, Maine Woodsmen's Association,"*U.S. Senate Subcommittee on Employment, Poverty, and Migratory Labor, Canadian Labor in the Maine Woods*, 95th Cong. (1977), April 14, 1977, 129–64.

99. Robert Bond, "Bonded Canadian Labor in New England's Logging Industry," in *U.S. Senate Subcommittee on Employment, Poverty, and Migratory Labor, Canadian Labor in the Maine Woods*, 95th Cong. (1977), April 14, 1977, 29–112.

100. See Falk, "The Organization"; Osborne, *Paper Plantation*; and Pan Atlantic Consultants, "Maine Logging Industry and Bonded Labor Program: An Economic Analysis," (Winthrop, ME: The Irland Group, 1999), figures 20, 61.

101. Jonathan Falk, interview.

102. Melvin Ames and Jonathan Falk, interviews.

103. Current and former paper company and independent foresters all downplayed and in some instances denigrated the MWA as a childish and ineffective organization, despite evidence to the contrary noted here. See Daniel Corcoran, interview with the author, Millinocket, Maine, June 22, 2006; David Edson, interview with the author, Old Town, Maine, June 23, 2006; James Pinkerton, interview with author, Madison, Maine, June 23, 2006; Carl Van Husen, interview with author, Madison, Maine, June 22, 2006; and anonymous interview with a former paper company woodlands manager, Portland, Maine, June, 28, 2006. See also Vail, "Internal Conflict," 164–5. Notably, Edson credited the MWA for bringing issues to the table that needed to be addressed.

104. See William Butler, Claire Bolduc, Peter Hagerty, and Jonathan Falk, interviews.

105. On scaling law, see Vail, "The Internal Conflict," 164; Claire Bolduc, interview; and Jonathan Falk, interview. On workers compensation, see Parenteau, "The Rise of the Small Contractor."

106. Also, Barbara Birmingham, interview; Claire Bolduc, interview; Jonathan Falk, interview; Carroll Gerow, interview; and Larry Palmer, interview.

107. "Statement of Eldon Hebert," *U.S. Senate Subcommittee on Employment, Poverty, and Migratory Labor*, 123–28.

108. At Scott, two attempts to unionize nearly succeeded, and company officials improved pay and benefits for woodcutters at this time, which helped the company to defeat the UPIU drive. James Pinkerton and Carl Van Husen, interviews.

109. "Statement of Eldon Hebert," *U.S. Senate Subcommittee on Employment, Poverty, and Migratory Labor*, 117–19; Falk, "The Organization," 27; and Vail, "The Internal Conflict," 167.

110. The research for this section with jointly conducted by the author and Jonathan Goldstein of Bowdoin College from 2004–06. The findings of this research are presented in Jonathan Goldstein and Michael Hillard, "Taking the High Road Only to Arrive at the Low Road: The Creation of a Reserve Army of Petty Capitalists in the North Maine Woods," *Review of Radical Political Economics* 40, no. 4 (2008): 479–509. We interviewed former forestry managers from companies that owned approximately six million acres in 1980, about 60 percent of the industrially owned forest land at that time. Daniel Corcoran, interview with the author, Millinocket, Maine, June 22, 2006; David Edsen, interview with the author, Old Town, Maine, June 23, 2006; James Pinkerton, interview with the author, Madison, Maine, June 15, 2006; Carl Van Husen, interview with the author, Madison, Maine, June 22, 2006; and anonymous former paper company woodlands manager,

interview with the author, Portland, Maine, June 28, 2006; anonymous former forester, digitally recorded interview with the author, Bingham, Maine, June 15, 2006; plus an additional interview with a woodlands manager, Brian Condon, interview with author, Ashland, Maine, July 7, 2008. Also see Falk, "The Organization," 42–56; and Irland, *Maine's Forest Industry: Essays in Economic History* (Wayne, ME: unpublished manuscript, 2007, 281 pages), 83–86. Vail, "The Internal Conflict," 166–68.

111. The number of bonded Canadian laborers fell from approximately 1500 to 500 between 1975 and 1980. Pan Atlantic Consultants, *Maine Logging*, figures 20 and 61.

112. Carl Van Husen, interview.

113. Anonymous forester, interview, June 28, 2006.

114. Pan Atlantic Consultants, *Maine Logging*, 38; Vail, "The Internal Conflict," 167–69. And Mel Ames, interview; Bill Butler, interview; Daniel Corcoran, interview; David Edsen, interview, 2006; Jonathan Falk, interview; James Pinkerton, interview; Carl Van Husen, interview; and anonymous former paper company woodlands manager, interview; anonymous former forester, interview.

115. Robert BaRoss, interview; Brian Condon, interview; James Pinkerton, interview; Carl Van Husen, interview; and anonymous former paper company woodlands manager, interview; anonymous former forester, interview.

116. David Edsen, interview; James Pinkerton, interview; Carl Van Husen, interview; and anonymous former paper company woodlands manager, interview; anonymous former forester, interview.

117. Anonymous forester, interview. Route 11 bisected the center and north of the North Maine Woods.

118. David Edsen, interview; Jonathan Falk, interview; James Pinkerton, interview; Carl Van Husen, interview; and anonymous former paper company woodlands manager, interview; anonymous former forester, interview.

119. Daniel Corcoran, interview; David Edsen, interview, 2006; Jonathan Falk, interview; James Pinkerton, interview; Carl Van Husen, interview; and anonymous former paper company woodlands manager, interview; anonymous former forester, interview.

120. This and related wage data came from the Maine Department of Labor, and is presented fully in Goldstein and Hillard, "Taking the High Road." Also, the author interviewed a mechanized crew in 2008 who described their earnings as $13–$14 per hour. With substantial overtime, one man said he had earned $37,000 the year before. Deflated to 1986, this was the equivalent of $18,500, roughly half of what unionized woodcutters on company crews earned that year. Author's field notes, Ashland, Maine, July 7, 2008.

121. See Jonathan Goldstein, Lloyd Irland, and J. Senick, E. Bassett, "The Intergenerational Supply of Loggers under Conditions of Declining Economic Well-Being," *Industrial Relations* 44, no. 2, (2006): 331–40.

122. Lloyd Irland, "Maine's Forest Industry: Essays in Economic History" (Unpublished manuscript, last modified in 2007), Microsoft Word file.

123. According to the Maine Department of Labor, wages declined sharply between 1986 and 1999:

PERCENT CHANGE IN REAL WAGES	1974–1986	1986–1999
Harvester/delimber operators	30	–61
Bulldozer operators	29	–27
Logging equipment mechanics	39	–52

Source: *Maine Department of Labor Annual Woods Wage Survey*

See Goldstein and Hillard, "Taking the High Road," 499.

124. Jason Newton, "Logging Bill Can Help Correct a Long History of Injustice in Maine Woods," *Bangor Daily News*, May 13, 2019; Beth Brogan, "Maine Loggers Poised to Unionize," *News Center Maine*, WCHS TV, September 4, 2019, accessed March 30, 2020,. https://www.newscentermaine.com/article/news/local/maine-loggers-poised-to-unionize/97-cc206261-9f39-450f-bd38-2b971fe05bcf.

125. In Great Britain, the triple alliance of miner, railroad workers, and longshoreman threatened a powerful general strike from 1911 through 1926, when it finally did start a strike that turned into a massive, if short, general strike joined by workers from a variety of industries. "1926: The General Strike," Libcom (website), accessed July 9, 2017, https://libcom.org/history/1926-british-general-strike.

6. FEAR AND LOATHING ON THE LOW AND HIGH ROADS

1. These developments are sketched in Michael Beer and Nitkin Nohria, *Breaking the Code of Change* (Boston: Harvard Business School Press, 2000); Barry Bluestone and Bennett Harrison *The Deindustrialization of America: Plant Closings, Community Abandonment, and the Dismantling of Basic Industry by economists* (New York: Basic Books, 1982); and Julius Getman, *The Betrayal of Local 14: Paperworkers, Politics, and Personal Replacements* (Ithaca, NY: Cornell University Press, 1998); Thomas Kochan, Harry Katz, and Robert McKersie, *The Transformation of Industrial Relations* (Ithaca, NY: Cornell University Press, 1994); Ira Magaziner and Robert Reich, *Minding America's Business: The Decline and Rise of the American Economy* (New York: Vintage Books, 1982); Ray Marshall and Marc Tucker, *Thinking for a Living: Education and the Wealth of Nations* (New York: Basic Books, 1992); and Lester Thurow, *Head to Head: the Coming Economic Battle Among Japan, Europe, and America* (New York: Morrow, 1992).

2. Getman, *Betrayal of Local 14*; and Timothy Minchin, "Permanent Replacements and the Rumford Strike of 1986," *New England Quarterly* 74, no. 1 (2001): 5–31.

3. I present evidence in support of this conclusion in the body of this chapter. A first look at these developments is found in Michael Hillard, "The Failure of Labor Management Cooperation at Two Maine Paper Mills: A Case Study," *Advances in Industrial and Labor Relations* 14 (2005): 127–71.

4. The concept of a choice between high and low roads emerged in the industrial relations (IR) literature of the mid 1980s. Arguments framing this as a choice, and evidence marshalled in support of the high road as a "win-win" model was fully developed by leading IR scholars including Eileen Applebaum, Rosemary Batt, Thomas Kochan, Ray Marshall, and Paul Osterman. See especially Eileen Applebaum and Rosemary Batt, *The New American Workplace: Transforming Work Systems in the United States.* (Ithaca, NY: Cornell University Press, 1994); Eileen Applebaum et al., *Manufacturing Advantage: Why High Performance Work Systems Pay Off* (Ithaca, NY: Cornell University Press, 2000). Thomas Kochan and Paul Osterman, *The Mutual Gains Enterprise: Forging a Winning Partnership among Labor, Management, and Government* (Boston: Harvard Business School Press, 1994); Marshall and Tucker, *Thinking for a Living*; and Paul Osterman, *Securing Prosperity: The American Labor Market: How It Has Changed and What to Do About It* (Princeton, NJ: Princeton University Press, 1999). Writers such as Marshall, Reich, and Lester Thurow popularized this thinking for a wider national audience. See Magaziner and Reich, *Minding America's Business*; Marshall and Tucker, *Thinking for a Living* and Lester Thurow, *Head to Head*.

5. Phyllis Austin, "Mill Town Blues," Alicia Patterson Foundation, accessed August 12, 2015, https://aliciapatterson.org/stories/mill-town-blues.

6. Adrienne Birecree, "Corporate Development, Structural Change, and Strategic Choice: Bargaining at International Paper Company in the 1980s," *Industrial Relations* 32,

no. 4 (1993): 343–66; Adrienne Eaton and Jill Kriesky, "Decentralization of Bargaining Structure: Four Cases from the U.S. Paper Industry," *Relations Industrielles* 53 no. 3 (1998): 486–516; and Bruce Kaufman, "The Emergence and Growth of a Non-Union Sector in the Southern Paper Industry," in *Southern Labor in Transition 1940–1995*, ed. Robert Zeiger (Knoxville: University of Tennessee Press, 1997), 295–330.

7. Eaton and Kriesky, "Decentralization of Bargaining Structure," 486–516; Getman, *Betrayal of Local 14*; Julius Getman and Ray Marshall, "Industrial Relations in Transition: The Paper Industry Example," *Yale Law Review* 102, no. 8 (1993):1804–95; Hillard, "Failure of Labor–Management Cooperation"; Bruce, Kaufman, "Emergence and Growth," 295–330.

8. Kochan, Katz, and McKersie, *Transformation of Industrial Relations*; and Richard Walton, Robert McKersie and Joel Cutcher-Gershenfield, *Strategic Negotiations: A Theory of Labor Management Relations* (Boston: Harvard Business School Press, 1994).

9. David Anderson, "Things Are Different Down Here: The 1955 Perfect Circle Strike, Conservative Civic Identity, and the Roots of the New Right in the Industrial Heartland," *International Labor and Working Class History* 74, no. 1 (2008): 101–23; Jefferson Cowie, *Capital Moves: RCA's Seventy-Year Quest for Cheap Labor* (Ithaca, NY: Cornell University Press, 1999); and Kim Phillips-Fein, *Invisible Hands: The Making of the Conservative Movement from the New Deal to Reagan* (New York: Norton 2009).

10. Eaton and Kriesky, "Decentralization of Bargaining Structure"; Kaufman, "Emergence and Growth"; Kochan, Katz, and McKersie, *The Transformation*; Timothy Minchin, *The Color of Work: The Struggle For Civil Rights in the Southern Paper Industry, 1945–1980* (Chapel Hill: University of North Carolina Press, 2001); Walton, McKersie and Cutcher-Gershenfield, *Strategic Negotiations*, 67–116.

11. Eaton and Kriesky, "Decentralization of Bargaining Structure"; Kaufman, "Emergence and Growth"; Minchin, *The Color of Work*; Walton, McKersie and Cutcher-Gershenfield, *Strategic Negotiations*. As Arthur Ross long ago noted, the political pressures on local leaders to be militant are far more intense than those faced by international leaders. Arthur Ross, *Trade Union Wage Policy* (Berkeley: University of California Press, 1948), 30–31.

12. As noted in chapter 3, the central and national union organization is known as the "International."

13. Eaton and Kriesky, "Decentralization of Bargaining Structure"; Kaufman, "Emergence and Growth"; Minchin, *The Color of Work*; Walton, McKersie and Cutcher-Gershenfield, *Strategic Negotiations*; and Shoshana Zuboff, *In the Age of the Smart Machine: The Future of Work and Power* (New York: Basic Books, 1988).

14. Kaufman, "Emergence and Growth," 319–20.

15. Walton, McKersie, and Cutcher-Gershenfield, *Strategic Negotiations*, 82.

16. The story of these developments and the new options I describe in the next section have been widely told; I summarize here for the convenience of the reader. Besides Nelson Lichtenstein, *State of the Union: A Century of American Labor* (Princeton, NJ: Princeton University Press, 2002). Accounts range from the timely and prescient 1982 work, *The Deindustrialization of America* by economists Barry Bluestone and Bennett Harrison to Joseph McCartin's gripping *Collision Course: Ronald Reagan, the Air Traffic Controllers, and the Strike that Changed America* (New York: Oxford University Press, 2011). See also Kochan, Katz, and McKersie, *The Transformation*, and Getman, *Betrayal of Local 14*.

17. McCartin, *Collision Course*.

18. Walton, McKersie, and Cutcher-Gershenfield, *Strategic Negotiations*, 80–81.

19. Kaufman, "Emergence and Growth," 309–18; and Walton, McKersie, and Cutcher-Gershenfield, *Strategic Negotiations*, 83–84. Note that the analysis here stresses the changing strategic choices made by national paper company leaders in the face of new pressures from Wall Street. One question a perceptive reader may raise: To what extent were auto-

mation and import penetration a factor in the sense of crisis that emerged in Maine in the 1980s and 1990s? I address this further in chapter 8. My main contention is that import penetration escalated after 1990 and was significant but modest before then. Obviously, competition from Southern mills was already a factor. New computer process controls were being introduced in the 1980s, and better command and better technology would make it a major factor in reducing labor requirements after 1990. With automation, labor productivity in the U.S. paper industry grew an epic 97 percent between 1990 and 2015. Lloyd Irland, "When the Mill Goes Quiet: Maine's Paper Industry, 1990–2015" (Wayne, ME: unpublished manuscript, 2017), 15.

20. Birecree, "Corporate Development."

21. Kaufman, "Emergence and Growth," 320.

22. Beer and Nohria, Breaking the Code of Change; Adrienne, M. Birecree, "Corporate Development, Structural Change, and Strategic Choice"; Getman, Betrayal of Local 14; Lazonick, Sustainable Prosperity; and Lazonick and O'Sullivan, "Maximizing Shareholder Value: A New Ideology for Corporate Governance," Economy and Society 29, no. 2 (2000): 13–35.

23. Walton, McKersie, and Cutcher-Gershenfield, Strategic Negotiations, 83.

24. Getman, Betrayal of Local 14, 32; Kaufman, "Emergence and Growth," 309–18; Minchin, "Permanent Replacements," 28.

25. Kaufman, "Emergence and Growth," 322–24.

26. Birecree, "Corporate Development"; Getman, Betrayal of Local 14, 16, 20, 23–24, 32–34; Kaufman, "Emergence and Growth," 319–22; Minchin, "Permanent Replacements," 9–10.

27. "Strategic" refers in general to all of the courses of action engaged by business, including engagement with consumers, relations with suppliers, sources of finance, and other methods beyond labor relations. In the 1980s, strategic change in labor relations was something of a common denominator, at least in U.S. manufacturing. See Beer and Nohria, Breaking the Code of Change.

28. Beer and Nohria, Breaking the Code of Change; Birecree, "Corporate Development"; Getman, Betrayal of Local 14; Lazonick, Sustainable Prosperity; and Lazonick and O'Sullivan, "Maximizing Shareholder Value."

29. There is a wide journalistic and academic literature on this. For a journalistic treatment, see Stephen Greenhouse, The Big Squeeze: Tough Times for the American Worker (New York: Anchor Books, 2008), 83–87. Michael Beer and Nitkin Nohria coined the term Theory E for this process, see Beer and Nohria, ed. Breaking the Code of Change, 3–12. William Lazonick aptly describes this process as "downsize and divest," see Lazonick, Sustainable Prosperity, 200–215. How this came to Maine's paper industry is a focus of Chapter 7.

30. "Lean" in its strictest sense was adopting Japanese style just-in-time inventory techniques—first in auto manufacturing and it later spread to other industries. Critical studies of these practices emphasized the stress and speed-up workers faced. See Egil Skorstad, "Lean Production, Conditions of Work and Worker Commitment," Economic and Industrial Democracy 15, no. 3 (1994): 429–55.

31. Stephen Greenhouse, The Big Squeeze: Tough Times for the American Worker (New York: Anchor Books, 2008), 83–87; former Scott executive, anonymous phone interview with author, June 17, 2003; Howard Reiche, interview with author, Harpswell, Maine, August 8, 2001; anonymous forestry manager, interview with author, Portland, Maine, June, 28, 2006.

32. As noted above, widely read popular authors, especially Robert Reich and Lester Thurow, argued for a "high road" strategy under the banner of the need for the U.S. to develop an industrial policy to match those of Japan and select western European nations. See Magaziner and Reich, Minding America's Business; Marshall and Tucker, Thinking for a Living; and Thurow, Head to Head.

33. See Magaziner and Reich, *Minding America's Business*; Marshall and Tucker, *Thinking for a Living*; and Thurow, *Head to Head*.

34. Michael Porter, *Competitive Advantage: Creating and Sustaining Superior Performance* (New York: Free Press, 1985); Peter Drucker, *Management Challenges for the 21st Century* (New York: Harper Collins, 2009); and Peter Senge, *The Fifth Discipline: The Art and Practice of Learning Organizations* (New York: Doubleday, 1990).

35. Michael Piore and Charles Sabel, *The Second Industrial Divide: Possibilities for Prosperity* (New York: Basic Books, 1984).

36. Applebaum et al., *Manufacturing Advantage*; Applebaum and Batt, *The New American Workplace*; Kochan and Osterman, *The Mutual Gains Enterprise*.

37. See Osterman, *Securing Prosperity*, 90–115.

38. Thomas Kochan and Saul Rubenstein, *Learning from Saturn: Possibilities for Corporate Governance and Employee Relations* (Ithaca, NY: Cornell University Press, 2001).

39. This argument was made most coherently and in depth by leading IR scholars. See Applebaum et al., *Manufacturing Advantage*; Applebaum and Batt, *The New American Workplace*; and Kochan and Osterman, *Mutual Gains Enterprise*.

40. The Gekko character was the fictional embodiment of Wall Street evil incarnate in Oliver Stone's popular 1987 film, *Wall Street*.

41. Michael Jensen and William Meckling, "Theory of the Firm: Managerial Behavior, Agency Costs, and Ownership Structure," *Journal of Financial Economics* 3 no. 4 (1976): 305–60.

42. Robert Hayes and William Abernathy, "Managing Our Way to Decline," *Harvard Business Review* 58, no. 4 (1980): 67–77.

43. Donald Mackenzie, *An Engine Not a Camera: How Financial Models Shape Markets* (Cambridge, MA: MIT Press, 2006), 1–88.

44. Local executives and Maine industry experts all described these developments in detail in interviews with the author. See especially anonymous former woodlands director executive, interview with author, June 28, 2006; Lloyd Irland, interview with author, Wayne, Maine, August 9, 2011; and Howard Reiche, interview with author, Harpswell, ME, August 8, 2001. Also see studies cited above, especially Eaton and Kriesky, "Decentralization of Bargaining Structure"; Birecree, "Corporate Development"; Getman, *Betrayal of Local 14*; Getman and Marshall, "Industrial Relations in Transition"; Hillard, "Failure of Labor–Management Cooperation"; Kaufman, "Emergence and Growth"; and Walton, McKersie and Cutcher-Gershenfield, *Strategic Negotiations*.

45. Eaton and Kriesky, "Decentralization of Bargaining Structure"; Getman, *Betrayal of Local 14*; Getman and Marshall, "Industrial Relations in Transition"; Hillard, "Failure of Labor–Management Cooperation"; Getman and Marshall, "Industrial Relations in Transition," 1804–95; Kaufman, "Emergence and Growth"; Minchin, "Permanent Replacements"; and Walton, McKersie and Cutcher-Gershenfield, *Strategic Negotiations*.

46. Julius Getman quotes CEO John Georges as estimating that the 1987–88 strike cost International Paper "over $1 billion" in lost earnings. Julius Getman, *Betrayal of Local 14*, 208.

47. Eileen Appelbaum and Rosemary Batt analyzed financialization's impact on workers, focusing on the rise of private equity. See Appelbaum and Batt, *Private Equity at Work: When Wall Street Manages Main Street* (New York: Russell Sage, 2014). Private equity funds indeed became the principal owners of Maine's mills and industrial forests after 2000, with mixed results. Interpreting the overall impact of financialization on manufacturing, as do Appelbaum and Batt and Sanford Jacoby, leaves us with averages showing that labor is less well off in employment and wages. Sanford Jacoby, "Finance and Labor: Perspectives on Risk, Inequality and Democracy," *Comparative Labor Law and Policy Journal* 30, no. 1 (2008): 17–66. Beneath the averages is the real story—for every turnaround story

where a hedge fund or private equity firm succeeds in turning around a failing factory, there are many others where enterprises are either run into the ground (after exorbitent fees and profits are ruthlessly extracted) or shutdown and sold off into parts to extract value while destroying the enterprises. A well-told exposé is Josh Kosman, *The Buyout of America: How Private Equity Is Destroying Jobs and Killing the American Economy* (New York: Penguin Books, 2010). I focus on the period of financialization that predates the rise of private equity, looking mostly at the 1980s and 1990s.

48. See Jonathan Rosenblum, *Copper Crucible: How the Arizona Miners' Strike of 1983 Recast Labor-Management Relations in America* (Ithaca, NY: Cornell University Press, 1998).

49. This proved completely successful at IP's Jay, Maine plant. See Getman, *Betrayal of Local 14*, 192–200.

50. Minchin, "Permanent Replacements," 10.

51. Minchin, "Permanent Replacements," 9–10.

52. Minchin, "Permanent Replacements," 16–21.

53. Minchin, "Permanent Replacements," 21.

54. Minchin, "Permanent Replacements," 20.

55. Minchin, "Permanent Replacements," 21–22.

56. On the Hormel strike, which presaged almost exactly what unfolded in the Jay strike, see Kim Moody, *An Injury to All: The Decline of American Unionism* (New York: Verso, 1998), 196–98.

57. Birecree, "Corporate Development," 353–54; Michael Hillard, "An Analysis and Perspective on the International Paper/Jay Strike," *Maine Business Indicators* 33, no. 3 (1988): 1–3; and Stuart Gilson and Jeremy Cott, "Scott Paper Company," *HBS No. 9-296-048.* (Boston, MA: Harvard Business School, 1997), 4.

58. Getman, *Betrayal of Local 14*, 32, 71–75; Kellman, *Divided We Fall*, 8, 117; and Minchin, "Permanent Replacements," 12.

59. Getman, *Betrayal of Local 14*, 31–40; Michael Hillard, "An Analysis and Perspective," 1.

60. Getman, *Betrayal of Local 14*, 32.

61. Bill Meserve, personal communication with author, June 15, 1987.

62. Getman, *Betrayal of Local 14*, 35–36; Getman and Marshall, "Industrial Relations in Transition, 1817–20.

63. As Getman, *Betrayal of Local 14* shows, another pivotal tactic was to expand the strike to a much larger group of IP mills as subsequent contracts ran out and other UPIU locals could legally join the strike. Getman goes on to describe how the UPIU international leaders and the company collaborated to prevent this.

64. Chapter 7 develops this point at length. Also, see Getman, *Betrayal of Local 14*, 89–96, 124–26.

65. Getman, *Betrayal of Local 14*, 105–12, 169–77, 201–9, 216–30.

66. Getman, *Betrayal of Local 14*, 212–13.

67. Getman, *Betrayal of Local 14*, 97–104, 138–44; and Kellman, *Divided We Fall*, 162–64; Peter Kellman, interview with author, Portland, Maine, February 13, 2003; and Ray Pineau, interview with author, Augusta, Maine, March 4, 2003.

68. Chapter 7 develops this point at length. Also, see Getman, *Betrayal of Local 14*, 77–96, 124–26; Gary Cook, interview with author, Augusta, Maine, March 4, 2003; Peter Kellman, interview, February 13, 2003; Ray Pineau, interview. Jane Slaughter, phone interview with the author, February 26, 2003.

69. Getman, *Betrayal of Local 14*, 89–90.

70. Peter Kellman, interview with author, Portland, Maine, December 14, 2011.

71. Ray Pineau, interview.

72. Peter Kellman, interview.

73. Getman, *Betrayal of Local 14*, 20–22, 35–36.

74. Ray Pineau, interview.

75. Chapter 7 develops this point at length. Also see Anonymous S. D. Warren Westbrook manager, interview with author, Portland, Maine, September 21, 2000; Ray Pineau, interview; Peter Kellman, interview, February 13, 2003; and Jane Slaughter, interview.

76. Labor historian Bruce Laurie describes Lawrence Goodwyn's concept of a "movement culture" as a way of accounting for "the ebb and flow of the labor movement": "To Goodwyn . . . cultures may therefore be either oppositional or accommodative; they may dare the status quo or confirm it. Oppositional cultures become movement cultures when they develop organizations and ideologies for mobilizing the dispossessed in the name of democracy or equality." Bruce Laurie, *Artisans into Workers: Labor in Nineteenth-Century America* (New York: Noonday Press, 1989), 74.

77. Chapter 7 develops this point at length. Also, see Getman, *Betrayal of Local 14*, 77–96, 124–26; Gary Cook, interview with author, Augusta, Maine, March 4, 2003; Peter Kellman, interview, February 13, 2003; Ray Pineau, interview. Jane Slaughter, phone interview with the author, February 26, 2003.

78. Richard Marston, interview with author, St. Agatha, Maine, September 10, 2014; Mike Walsh, interview with author, Waterville, Maine, January 24, 2013. Getman, *Betrayal of Local 14*, 23–24, 31–38, 99; and Getman and Marshall, "Industrial Relations in Transition."

79. Phyllis Austin, "Mill Town Blues," Alicia Patterson Foundation, accessed August 12, 2015, https://aliciapatterson.org/stories/mill-town-blues.

7. THE HIGH ROAD COMETH

1. Julius Getman and Ray Marshall, "Industrial Relations in Transition: The Paper Industry Example," *Yale Law Review* 102, no. 8 (1993): 1804–95.

2. Getman and Marshall, "Industrial Relations in Transition"; also, anonymous interview with former Scott executive, phone interview with author, June 17 2003; John Beck, phone interview with author, January 29, 2003.

3. Stuart Gilson and Jeremy Cott, "Scott Paper Company," *HBS No. 9-296-048.* (Boston, MA: Harvard Business School Publishing, 1997), 1–3; Getman and Marshall, "Industrial Relations in Transition." Also, anonymous former Scott executive, interview; and John Beck, interview.

4. Getman and Marshall, "Industrial Relations in Transition"; and anonymous former Scott executive, interview; and John Beck, interview.

5. Anonymous S. D. Warren Westbrook manager, interview with author, Portland, Maine, September 21, 2000; anonymous former Scott executive, interview; John Beck, interview; William Carver, interview; Gary Cook, interview with author, Augusta, Maine, March 4, 2003; Karl Dornish interview, Winslow, Maine, March 20, 2003; Michael Hamel, interview with author, Waterville, Maine, April 8, 2003; Tom Lestage, interview with author, Westbrook, Maine, July 24, 2000; Curtis Pease interview with author, Gorham, Maine, August 1, 2001; and Carl Turner, interview with author, Portland, Maine, April 7, 2003.

6. There is an important distinction here between two types of argumentation promoting high performance work systems during the 1980s and 1990s. The IR scholars previously discussed, especially Eileen Applebaum, Rosemary Batt, Thomas Kochan, and Paul Osterman, offered a nuanced advocacy for work reorganization. See Eileen Applebaum and Rosemary Batt, *The New American Workplace: Transforming Work Systems in the United States* (Ithaca, NY: Cornell University Press, 1994); Eileen Applebaum et al., *Man-*

ufacturing Advantage: Why High Performance Work Systems Pay Off (Ithaca, NY: Cornell University Press, 2000); Thomas Kochan and Paul Osterman, *The Mutual Gains Enterprise: Forging a Winning Partnership among Labor, Management, and Government* (Boston: Harvard Business School Press, 1994); and Paul Osterman, *Securing Prosperity: The American Labor Market: How It Has Changed and What to Do About It* (Princeton, NJ: Princeton University Press, 1999). Key nuances included recognizing and documenting that as a top down corporate strategy, success in pursuing work reorganization has both more efficacy and also equity if legitimate "mutual gains" are built in and if workers are effectively empowered over work practices over a long period of time. In turn, if neither of these prerequisites are present (a widespread fact increasingly evident in Osterman's field research at the time), worker resistance is likely and understandable. See Osterman, *Securing Prosperity*, 90–115. They also point to case studies showing these systems are better built in "greenfield" (i.e., new) workplaces. Kochan and Osterman further identified the barrier of financialized corporate governance to successful work reform, the main point made in this chapter, and Kochan was quick to recognize by the mid-1990s that a revival of a progressive political coalition was really a prerequisite to achieving policy change. In sum, the criticism raised here applies gently to this work, that is, that these scholars' argument that since work reorganization is the preferred mechanism for generating "win–win" employment outcomes, it is implied that everyone is better off "getting on board," but recognizing that without the right prerequisites, reform efforts are likely to fail and workers in particular won't reap a "win."

At the same time, consultants (such as those described in this chapter who were hired to assist Scott's Jointness campaign) and less nuanced policy writers did argue that it was imperative that "everyone gets on board." Two notable examples are Ray Marshall and Marc Tucker's, *Thinking for a Living: Education and the Wealth of Nations* (New York: Basic Books, 1992); and especially David I. Levine's, *Working in the Twenty-First Century: Policies for Economic Growth Through Training, Opportunity, and Education* (New York, NY: Routledge, 1998). Levine makes two concerning moves in the book, one stylistic, the other substantive. Stylistically, this work is typical of this movement in using "must" language: schools "must," employers "must," and workers "must" embrace change—that is, embracing this movement was something that required smart actors to get on board. The substantive problem is a labor supply side argument—to the effect, if we train enough workers in the right skills, employers would have an incentive to reorganize work and reward workers fairly. This view is a departure from a strength of institutional labor economics—recognizing that institutionally, it is the demand side of the labor market—employers—that sets the terms of worker opportunities and employment outcomes. See especially Richard Freeman, "Does the New Generation of Labor Economists Know More than the Old Generation?" in *How Labor Markets Work: Reflections on Theory and Practice by John Dunlop, Clark Kerr, Richard Lester, and Lloyd Reynolds*, ed. B. Kaufman (Lexington: MA: Lexington Books, 1988), 205–23; as well as Bruce Kaufman, *The Origins and Evolution of Industrial Relations in the United States in the United States* (Ithaca, NY: Cornell University Press, 1993).

7. Anonymous former Scott executive, interview.

8. Getman and Marshall, "Industrial Relations in Transition"; Gilson and Cott, "Scott Paper Company"; and anonymous former Scott executive, interview.

9. Anonymous former Scott executive, interview; and John Beck, interview.

10. Anonymous former Scott executive, interview.

11. John Beck, interview; William Carver, interview; Gary Cook, interview; Tom Lestage, interview; Jane Slaughter, interview, and Getman and Marshall, "Industrial Relations in Transition."

12. John Beck, interview. Livermore Falls is adjacent to the Jay IP mill; ten thousand IP strikers and supporters marched there at the peak of the Jay strike.

13. Anonymous former Scott executive, interview.

14. This chapter goes on to highlight four Scott mills, three of which were in Maine and the fourth in Mobile, Alabama. See anonymous S. D. Warren Westbrook manager, interview; anonymous former Scott executive, interview; John Beck, interview; William Carver, interview; Gary Cook, interview; Karl Dornish, interview; Michael Hamel, interview; Tom Lestage, interview; Curtis Pease interview; and Carl Turner, interview.

15. Also, see Applebaum, et al., *Manufacturing Advantage*, 8–9, 11–12; Kochan and Osterman, *Mutual Gains Enterprise*, 101–3; Osterman, *Securing Prosperity*, 113.

16. The quid here is the giving up of contract job rule and job allocation procedures.

17. Kochan and Osterman, *Mutual Gains Enterprise*, 111–40; Osterman, *Securing Prosperity*, 148–62; Lazonick, *Sustainable Prosperity*, 200–215; and William Lazonick and Mary O'Sullivan, "Maximizing Shareholder Value: A New Ideology for Corporate Governance," *Economy and Society* 29, no. 2 (2000): 13–35.

18. William Carver, interview; Karl Dornish interview; Arthur Gordon, interview; Michael Hamel, interview; Barry Kenney, interview; Tom Lestage, interview; Curtis Pease, interview; Howard Reiche, interview; and Carl Turner, interview.

19. William Carver, interview.

20. Patrick Peoples, interview with author, Westbrook, Maine, July 29, 2003.

21. Tom Lestage, interview. Lestage is referring here to the white safety helmets worn by supervisors.

22. As William Carver pointed out in this chapter's opening epigraph, this was an especially acute situation at S. D. Warren/Westbrook in the late 1980s and early 1990s. See also Karl Dornish interview; Arthur Gordon, interview; Michael Hamel, interview; Barry Kenney, interview; Tom Lestage, interview; Curtis Pease, interview; Howard Reiche, interview; and Carl Turner, interview. As prior chapters demonstrated, increasingly Maine mills were run by a mix of traditional managers who came up through these companies and new managers from outside.

23. William Carver, interview.

24. Curtis Pease, interview.

25. According to the former Scott executive, whose career spanned the pre- and post-Scott merger era: "And the other thing I'll fault Scott for, and I think one of the reasons, besides having a couple of guys that feathered their nest at the last of it, at the expense of the company, Scott never assimilated anybody that they bought. There was . . . very, very little Scott culture." Anonymous former Scott executive, interview; and Karl Dornish, interview.

26. Applebaum and Batt, *New American Workplace*; Kochan and Osterman, *Mutual Gains Enterprise*; Applebaum et al., *Manufacturing Advantage*.

27. William Carver, interview; Gary Cook, interview; Michael Hamel, interview; Peter Kellman, interview; Tom Lestage, interview; Curtis Pease, interview; Ray Pineau, interview; Carl Turner, interview; and Jane Slaughter, phone interview.

28. Michael Hamel, interview; anonymous former Scott executive, interview.

29. This account of Scott Mobile draws on the anonymous Scott paper executive interview, and on Connolly et al., "The Evolutionary Process of Establishing a High-Performance Work System," *Summary: The Seventh National Labor-Management Conference* (Washington, D.C.: Federal Mediation and Conciliation Service, 1994), 53–56.

30. Connolly et al., "The Evolutionary Process."

31. Connolly et al., "The Evolutionary Process"; and Michael Hamel, interview.

32. Michael Hamel, interview.

33. Michael Hamel, interview. Because of lower value to weight than coated publication papers, markets for tissues and paper towels are more regional than national or international.

34. Gary Cook, interview; Michael Hamel, interview; and Jane Slaughter, interview.

35. Michael Hamel, interview.

36. Michael Hamel, interview. If further workforce reductions were needed, they would be accomplished by voluntary early retirements and severance along the lines of the 1992 downsizing.

37. Michael Hamel, interview.

38. Anonymous former Scott executive, interview; Gary Cook, interview; Karl Dornish, interview; Peter Kellman, interview, February 13, 2003; Frank Poulin, interview; Ray Pineau, interview; and Howard Reiche, interview.

39. Karl Dornish, interview; Frank Poulin, interview; and Carl Turner, interview.

40. Karl Dornish, interview.

41. Frank Poulin, interview.

42. Frank Poulin, interview.

43. Karl Dornish, interview; Frank Poulin, interview; and Carl Turner, interview.

44. Karl Dornish, interview. Speaker's emphasis in the quote.

45. Mike Parker and Jane Slaughter, *Choosing Sides: Unions and the Team Concept* (Boston: South End Press, 1988); Mike Parker and Jane Slaughter, *Working Smart: A Union Guide to Participation Program and Reengineering* (Detroit, MI: Labor Notes, 1994). Also, Jane Slaughter, interview.

46. Jane Slaughter, interview.

47. Gary Cook, interview with author, Augusta, Maine, March 4, 2003; and Jane Slaughter, interview.

48. William Carver, interview; Tom Lestage, interview; Frank Poulin, interview; and Carl Turner, interview.

49. Carl Turner, interview. Turner pointed out that a notable exception to Local 9's refusal to participate in Jointness was the OSHA 200 program, an extensive and dramatically effective safety program developed at Hinckley in the early 1990s.

50. William Carver, interview; Gary Cook, interview; Peter Kellman, interview, February 13, 2003; Tom Lestage, interview; and Ray Pineau, interview.

51. William Carver, interview; Gary Cook, interview; Peter Kellman, interview, February 13, 2003; Tom Lestage, interview; Ray Pineau, interview; and Jane Slaughter, interview.

52. John Beck, telephone interview. Speaker's emphasis in the quote.

53. The quotation is from William Carver. John Beck, interview; William Carver, interview; Gary Cook, interview; Peter Kellman, interview, February 13, 2003; Tom Lestage, interview; Ray Pineau, interview; and Jane Slaughter, interview.

54. Anonymous S. D. Warren Westbrook manager, interview with author, Portland, Maine, September 21, 2000.

55. Tom Lestage, interview with author, Westbrook, Maine, July 24, 2000. Union locals representing skilled maintenance workers, who made up about a quarter of the mill's hourly workers, had accepted contract revisions, including cross-training in the trades, relaxation of work rules, and pay-for-knowledge.

56. Karl Dornish, interview.

57. Anonymous S. D. Warren Westbrook manager, interview.

58. Carver, interview; Lestage, interview; Pease, interview; and Reiche interview.

59. Anonymous S. D. Warren Westbrook manager, interview; Reiche, interview; Steven Page, interview with author, Portland, Maine, June 16, 2002.

60. William Carver, interview.

61. See Chapter 2.

62. William Carver, interview.

63. William Carver, interview.

64. William Carver, interview; and Tom Lestage, interview.

65. These mill managers included Robert MacAvoy, Charles Rose, and Richard Frost. See Tom Lestage, interview; Eric Blom, "Union: S. D. Warren Weakens Maine Mill," *Portland Press Herald*, November 10, 1992; "S. D. Warren Promotes Frost to Vice President and Mill Manager of its Somerset and Northeast Timberlands Operations," *Business Wire*, November 3, 1995; and Harry Foote, "Looking Back, 05/04," *American Journal*, May 3, 2005, accessed April 3, 2020, https://www.pressherald.com/2005/05/03/looking-back-0504/.

66. Tom Lestage, interview.

67. G. A. Akerlof, "Labor Contracts as Partial Gift Exchange," *Quarterly Journal of Economics* 97, no. 4 (1982): 543–69.

68. Dave Martin, interview with author, Westbrook, Maine, July 18, 2003.

69. Jeff Smith, "S. D. Warren Accused of 'Destructive' Action," *Portland Press Herald*, November 3, 1992; William Carver, interview; and Tom Lestage, interview.

70. William Carver, interview; and Tom Lestage, interview.

71. William Carver, interview; and Tom Lestage, interview.

72. Anonymous S. D. Warren Westbrook manager, interview.

73. William Carver, interview; and Frank Poulin, interview.

74. William Carver, interview; and Tom Lestage, interview.

75. William Carver, interview; and Tom Lestage, interview.

76. William Carver, interview.

77. Steve Keglovitz, phone interview with author, May 22, 2003.

78. Michael Beer and Nitkin Nohria, *Breaking the Code of Change* (Boston: Harvard Business School Press, 2000), 1–34; and Gilson and Cott, "Scott Paper Company," 2.

79. Beer and Nohria, *Breaking the Code*, 1–34; Gilson and Cott, "Scott Paper Company"; and Stephen Greenhouse, *The Big Squeeze: Tough Times for the American Worker* (New York: Anchor Books, 2008), 83–87. Dunlap's career pattern was to hopscotch across industries, bringing his brutal metrics and slashing techniques to wildly different companies. Dunlap next became head of Sunbeam Corporation. Besides shutting down a Maine plant in 1996, he later was barred from the business world altogether for fraudulent accounting practices at Sunbeam; after being forced to restate the financial condition of the firm in 1998, Sunbeam went bankrupt. In 2002, Dunlap paid a huge fine and accepted a lifetime ban from the corporate world. See Floyd Norris, "Former Sunbeam Chief Agrees To Ban and a Fine of $500,000," *New York Times*, September 5, 2002; and John Byrne, *Chainsaw Al: The Notorious Career of Al Dunlap in the Era of Profits at Any Price* (New York: Harperbusiness, 1999).

80. Wyatt Olson, "Mainers Struggle After Layoffs," *Bangor Daily News*, September 6, 1999; Maine Center for Economic Policy, *Life After Layoff in Central Maine*, (Augusta, ME, 1999); Ned McCann, ed., *Laid Off: Conversations With Maine Workers in Crisis, A Blue Print For Action* (Augusta, ME: 2003).

81. Dan Fastenberg, "Workplace Users and Abusers: Al Dunlap," *Time*, October 18, 2010, accessed April 3, 2020, http://content.time.com/time/specials/packages/article/0,28804,2025898_2025900_2026107,00.html; Norris, "Former Sunbeam Chief Agrees To Ban"; and Harrison Smith, "Albert J. Dunlap, Corporate Turnaround Artist Accused of Accounting Fraud, Dies at 81," *Washington Post*, January 28, 2019, accessed April 3, 2020, https://www.washingtonpost.com/local/obituaries/albert-j-dunlap-corporate-turnaround

-specialist-accused-of-accounting-fraud-dies-at-81/2019/01/28/652d3a34-230f-11e9
-90cd-dedb0c92dc17_story.html.

82. Appelbaum and Batt, *Private Equity at Work*; Beer and Nohria, *Breaking the Code of Change*; Justin Fox, *The Myth of the Rational Market: A History of Risk, Reward, and Delusion on Wall Street* (New York: Harper Business, 2011); Sanford Jacoby, "Finance and Labor: Perspectives on Risk, Inequality and Democracy," *Comparative Labor Law and Policy Journal* 30, no. 1 (2008): 17–66; Kosman, *The Buyout of America: How Private Equity Will Cause the Next Great Credit Crisis* (New York: Portfolio, 2010); Lazonick, *Sustainable Prosperity*, 200–215; and Lazonick and O'Sullivan, "Maximizing Shareholder Value."

83. Getman and Marshall, "Industrial Relations in Transition"; and anonymous former Scott executive, interview.

84. Peter Hall and David Soskice, eds., *Varieties of Capitalism: The Institutional Foundations of Comparative Advantage* (New York: Oxford University Press, 2001); Lazonick, *Business Organization and the Myth of the Market Economy* (New York: Cambridge University Press, 1992); Lazonick, *Sustainable Prosperity*; Lazonick and O'Sullivan, "Maximizing Shareholder Value"; and William Lazonick, "Varieties of Capitalism and Innovative Enterprise," *Comparative Social Research* 24 (2007): 21–69.

85. It is noteworthy that as a highly cyclical business, the strong economic growth of the late 1980s produced a burst of strong profitability, with profits for 1989 and 1990 averaging just under $400 million per year. With the subsequent recession and very weak recovery through 1994, profits averaged only $82 million the following three years, followed by a loss of $277 million in 1993, leading to Lippencott leaving as CEO. Gilson and Cott, "Scott Paper Company," 13, Exhibit 3.

86. Anonymous former Scott executive, interview.

87. Anonymous former Scott executive, interview.

88. Doug Harlow, "Sappi Celebrates $200 Million Investment in Skowhegan mill," *Portland Press Herald*, September 27, 2018.

89. Matt Wickensheiser, "Westbrook Mill to Cut 170 Employees: The Cost Cutting Move Will Take Place No Later Than Jan. 10, Officials of Sappi North America Say," *Portland Press Herald*, November 11, 2003. Employment followed this track: 1990 still at 2,300; in 1994 it drops to 1,053; in 1999 it drops to 550; in 2003, it falls to approximately 300.

90. Beer and Nohria, *Breaking the Code of Change*, 5; "Winslow Paper Mill to Close. 264 at Kimberly–Clark to Lose Their Jobs," *Bangor Daily News*, November 22, 1997; and "Bid to Sell Winslow Mill 'Exhausted' Kimberly Clark Announces Final Shutdown of Plant; Maine Officials Livid," *Bangor Daily News*, April 4, 1998.

91. Michael Hamel, interview.

92. Robert Langreth, "Kimberly-Clark's Sweeping Cutbacks Should Ease Overcapacity," *Wall Street Journal*, November 24, 1997.

93. Anonymous former Scott executive, interview.

8. MEMORY, ENTERPRISE CONSCIOUSNESS, AND HISTORICAL PERSPECTIVE AMONG MAINE'S PAPER WORKERS

1. Jackie Farwell, "Paper Money: Private Equity Firms Own Six of Maine's Major Paper Mills, For Better or Worse," Mainebiz, May 16, 2011; and "Map: Maine Paper Mills Operating or Closed Down," *Portland Press Herald*, July 19, 2017.

2. A balanced account of the overall decline of Maine's paper industry includes three causal factors—strategic decisions made by corporate leaders under the new lens of financialized capitalism, import competition, and automation. The case here is that the turn toward decline commenced with and was at the direction of financialized strategic decisions

that were set into motion in the 1980s and began as early as the 1960s. Moreover, Maine paper workers themselves keenly focused on strategic decision making by new corporate leaders in their explanations of their mills' deteriorating status. Import competition and automation accelerated only after 1990. Imports of publishing and printing grades to the United States were steady in the 1970s, began to grow in the 1990s, but exploded in the 1990s as the U.S. dollar appreciated (from 3.5 to 8 million tons), with the coup de grace coming as China gained entry in 2001 to the World Trade Organization and began plying new printing grades using advanced technologies supported by an ambitious government-supported research and development. Irland, *Maine's Forest Industry: Essays in Economic History* (Wayne, ME: unpublished manuscript, 2007), 28–48, 132–60. Also, see John Schmid, "Paper Cuts, Part One: An Industry Torn Up: Wisconsin's Place in Paper Industry Under Seige," *Milwaukee Journal Sentinel*, December 8, 2012, accessed April 7, 2020, http://archive.jsonline.com/business/paper-industry-digital-china -wisconsin-182612951.html/; and John Schmid, "Paper Cuts, Part Two: A Global Paper Trail; Bankrolled and Bioengineered, China Supplants Wisconsin's Paper Industry," *Milwaukee Journal Sentinel*, December 11, 2012, accessed April 7, 2020, http://archive .jsonline.com/business/bankrolled-and-bioengineered-china-supplants-wisconsins -paper-industry-183049221.html/.

In my epilogue, I ask the question—How might have decline been slower and more humane had a different form of corporate governance and the support of aggressive industrial policies here like those of China been in place?

3. See Mae Bachelor, interview with author, Westbrook, Maine, June 25, 2003; William Carver interview, Westbrook, Maine, December 9, 2001; Phil LaViolette, interview with author, Westbrook, Maine, July 8, 2003; Harley Lord, interview with author, Windham, Maine, June 6, 2003; Shirley Lally, interview with author, Westbrook, Maine, October 27, 2000; Phil Lestage, interview with author, Westbrook, Maine, August 29, 2001; Tom Lestage, interview with author, Westbrook, Maine, July 20, 2000; Dave Martin, interview with author, Westbrook, Maine, July 18, 2003; Jan Usher, interview with author, Westbrook, Maine, June 19, 2003; and; Chris Murray, interview with the author, Portland, Maine, September 7, 2000.

4. "Employee Buyout of Mill Makes Sense to Analysts," *Portland Press Herald*, December 13, 1991.

5. Alessandro Portelli, *The Death of Luigi Trastulli and Other Stories* (SUNY Press, 1991); also John Bodnar, "Power and Memory in Oral History: Workers and Managers at Studebaker," *Journal of American History* 75, no. 4 (1989): 1201–21; David Thelen, "Memory and American History," *Journal of American History* 75, no. 4 (1989): 1117–29; and Paul Thompson, *Voice of the Past: Oral History* (New York: Oxford University Press, 1980).

6. Tom Lestage, interview.

7. See Mae Bachelor, interview; Tom Lestage, interview; Harley Lord, interview with author, Windham, Maine, June 6, 2003; Dave Martin, interview; Jan Usher, interview; and Phil LaViolette, interview.

8. Frank Jewitt, interview with author, Buxton, Maine, July 20, 2001; Shirley Lally, interview with author, Westbrook, Maine, October 27, 2000; and John D. Glower and Ralph M. Hower, *The Administrator: Cases on Human Relations in Business*, 1st ed. (Homewood, IL: R. D. Irwin, 1949), 408.

9. Tom Lestage, interview with author, Westbrook, Maine, July 24, 2000.

10. Joe Jensen, interview with author, Westbrook, Maine, June 20, 2002.

11. For example, S. D. Warren Company, *A Hundred Years of S. D. Warren Company* (Westbrook, ME: S. D. Warren Company, 1954) and a compendium in the local library of 1888 funeral eulogies for founder Samuel Dennis Warren, *S. D. Warren: A Tribute from the People of Cumberland Mills* (Cambridge, MA: Riverside Press, 1888).

12. Chris Murray, interview with author, Portland, Maine, September 7, 2000.

13. Chris Murray, interview.

14. This justice notion is that the profits that the workers created for their employer was partially returned to them.

15. Shirley Lally, interview with author, Westbrook, Maine, September 9, 2000. Lally acknowledges that the Warrens were not truly or exclusively local; the company's headquarters from the start were in Boston. The last Warren to manage the entire mill was John E. Warren, who died in 1915. A small group of managers took control of the mill in the late 1910s and their sons and sons-in-law were still running the company and the mill when it was sold to Scott Paper in 1967. But the presence of John E. Warren's son Joseph in the mill into the 1950s, the company moniker Mother Warren, and the familiar names George Olmstead Senior and Junior—Warren chief executive officers from the 1920s until its sale in 1967—more than signaled the stability of the Warren era.

16. Shirley Lally, interview; emphasis added.

17. See Jacquelyn Dowd, Robert Korstad, and James Deloudis, "Cotton Mill People: Work, Community, and Protest in the Textile South, 1880–1940," *American Historical Review* 91, no. 2 (1986): 245–86.

18. Producerism is a particular view of the class structure of capitalism generated by the U.S. labor movement in the late nineteenth century. It distinguishes two classes: those who produced—including their small- to medium-sized industrial employers who helped to create the technology and organization of new factories—and nonproducers. The nonproducers were parasites—lawyers, financiers, and the like who leached or exploited off of producers. Labor historians, including Lawrence Glickman, Bruce Laurie, and David Montgomery, have noted how this differed from Marx's view of capitalism, in which any employer, large or small, always appropriated for free part of their workers' production— what Marx considered exploitation. In the United States, producerism, for some, took on a more Marxian bent as factory scale grew dramatically after 1880.

Here, paper workers' memory of a producerist class structure is counterposed to class parasites that ranged from takeovers by large paper companies (for example, Georgia Pacific's 1990 hostile takeover of Great Northern Paper) to the Wall Street financiers behind takeovers, and later hedge and private equity funds that became dominant owners of Maine mills after the late 1980s.

See Lawrence Glickman, *A Living Wage: American Workers and the Making of a Consumer Society* (Ithaca, NY: Cornell University Press, 1997), 5, 24–26, 93, 95–99; and Bruce Laurie, *Artisans into Workers: Labor in Nineteenth Century America* (New York: Noonday Press, 1989), 3–14, 149–55, 165–66, 213–15, 217; and David Montgomery, "Beyond Equality: Labor and the Radical Republicans" (Champagne: University of Illinois Press, 1981). On Marx's class theory, see Stephen Resnick and Richard Wolff, *Knowledge and Class: A Marxian Critique of Political Economy* (Chicago, IL: University of Chicago Press, 1987); and Bruce Roberts, "Class and Overdetermination: Value Theory and the Core of Resnick and Wolff's Marxism," in *Knowledge, Class, and Economics: Marxism Without Guarantees*, ed. Theodore Burczack et al. (New York: Routledge, 2018), 143–54.

19. Historian Philip Scranton shows that what makes paternalisms credible is the real technical or business acumen of mill owners. At Warren, this extended to the many inventions and hands-on production skills of middle and top management at the mill, made first by the poor Warrens into the early twentieth century and then by professional managers who ran the mill from the 1920s to the 1960s. Philip Scranton, "Varieties of Paternalism: Industrial Structures and the Social Relations of Production in American Textiles," *American Quarterly* 36, no. 2 (1984): 235–57.

20. Monica Wood, *When We Were the Kennedys: A Memoir from Mexico, Maine* (Boston: Mariner Press, 2012).

21. Wood, *When We Were the Kennedys*, 59.

22. Alfred Chandler, "Organizational Capabilities and the Economic History of the Industrial Enterprise," *Journal of Economic Perspectives* 6, no. 3 (1992): 79–100; William Lazonick and David Teece, eds., *Management Innovation: Essays in the Spirit of Alfred D. Chandler, Jr.* (New York: Oxford University Press, 2012), 3–24; C. K. Prahalad and Gary Hamel, "The Core Competencies of the Corporation," *Harvard Business Review* 68, no. 3 (1990): 79–91; and David Weil, *The Fissured Workplace: Why Work Became So Bad For So Many and What Can Be Done to Improve It* (Cambridge, MA: Harvard University Press, 2014), 49–52.

23. For instance, senior and middle mill and forestry managers including Howard Reiche and Karl Dornish, interviews; Steven Page, interview with the author, Portland, Maine, June 18, 2002; David Edson, interview with the author, Old Town, Maine, June 23, 2006; James Pinkerton, interview with author, Madison, Maine, June 23, 2006; Carl Van Husen, interview with author, Madison, Maine, June 22, 2006; and anonymous former paper company woodlands manager, interview with the author, Portland, Maine, June, 28, 2006.

24. See Howard Reiche, interview; Karl Dornish, interview; Steven Page, interview; and anonymous former paper company woodlands manager, interview.

25. David Edson, interview; James Pinkerton, interview; Carl Van Husen, interview; and anonymous former paper company woodlands manager, interview. As with the paper workers, the woodcutters who were active with the Maine Woodsmen's Association looked at the problems they were facing in terms of their relationships with their employer institutions.

26. See Howard Reiche, interview; Karl Dornish, interview; Steven Page, interview; and anonymous former paper company woodlands manager, interview.

27. Timothy Minchin, "'Just Like a Death': The Closing of the International Paper Company Mills in Mobile, Alabama, and the Deindustrialization of the South, 2000–2005," *Alabama Review* 59, no. 1 (2006): 52. Also, see Mae Bachelor, interview; William Carver interview; Phil LaViolette, interview; Shirley Lally, interview; Phil Lestage, interview; Tom Lestage, interview; Dave Martin, interview; Chris Murray, interview; and Dan Parks, interview.

28. Monica Wood's characterization of Hugh Chilsolm II echoes the memories of the Warrens:

> Hugh Chisholm the second was the big legend. He ran the mill for something like forty years, it was a long time. He was kind of a benevolent dictator; there was no unionizing earlier on. And so, there are photographs of people in that mill with bare feet and their shirttails hanging out, cooking vats of acid with no protection whatsoever, and yet Hugh Chisholm II is remembered as this benevolent guy, and in some ways he was really quite progressive when it came to . . . the well-being of the workers. He wanted them to have decent housing. . . . The way he puts it: the spiritual and physical health of the worker makes for a worker who will be a good worker, and *make beautiful paper*. . . . The workers whose rest of their lives are fulfilling would be good workers.

Monica Wood, interview with author, Portland, Maine, May 12, 2016.

29. Stuart Gilson and Jeremy Cott, "Scott Paper Company," *Case 9-296-048* (Cambridge, MA: Harvard Business School, 1997), 1–28; 2.

30. Tom Lestage, interview, July 20, 2000; Tom Lestage, interview with author, Westbrook, Maine, August 4, 2000.

31. These mill managers included Robert MacAvoy, Charles Rose, and Richard Frost. See Tom Lestage, interview; "Union: S.D. Warren Weakens Maine Mill," *Portland Press Herald*, November 10, 1992; "S. D. Warren Promotes Frost to Vice President and Mill

Manager of its Somerset and Northeast Timberlands Operations," *Business Wire*, November 3, 1995.

32. William Carver, interview; Tom Lestage, interview, August 4, 2000; Tom Lestage, interview with author, Westbrook, Maine, May 9, 2013.

33. "Workers Study Paper Mill Buyout," *Portland Press Herald*, December 12, 1991; "Employee Buyout of Mill Makes Sense to Analysts," *Portland Press Herald*, December 13, 1991; "S. D. Warren Deal Rejected," *Portland Press Herald*, October 24, 1992; and "S. D. Warren Accused of 'Destructive' Actions," *Portland Press Herald*, November 3, 1992. Also see William Carver, interview; Tom Lestage, interviews, August 4, 2000, and May 9, 2013.

34. Warren patented a variety of its Ultracast products; these products commanded $3,000–$4,000 per ton, compared to roughly $1,000 per ton at that time of its coated publication papers. Ultracast products are still produced in Westbrook and bring tidy profits to its current owners South African Pulp and Paper Industries (SAPPI). Tom Lestage, interview, May 9, 2013.

35. Karl Dornish, interview; Howard Reiche, interview.

36. "Workers Study Paper Mill Buyout," *Portland Press Herald*, December 12, 1991; "Employee Buyout of Mill Makes Sense to Analysts," *Portland Press Herald*, December 13, 1991. William Carver, interview; Tom Lestage, interview, August 4, 2000; Tom Lestage, interview with author, Westbrook, Maine, May 9, 2013.

37. Tom Lestage, interview, 2013.

38. Dave Martin, interview.

39. "Employee Buyout of Mill Makes Sense to Analysts," *Portland Press Herald*, December 13, 1991.

40. "S. D. Warren Deal Rejected," *Portland Press Herald*, October 24, 1991.

41. "Employee Buyout of Mill Makes Sense to Analysts," *Portland Press Herald*, December 13, 1991.

42. Dave Martin, interview.

43. Tom Lestage, interview, May 9, 2013.

44. "S. D. Warren Deal Rejected," *Portland Press Herald*, October 24, 1992.

45. Staughton Lynd, "The Genesis of the Idea of a Community Right to Industrial Property in Youngstown and Pittsburgh, 1977–1987," *Journal of American History* 7 no. 4 (1987): 926–58; Staughton Lynd, *The Fight Against Shutdowns: Youngstown's Steel Mill Closings* (San Pedro, CA: Singlejack Books, 1982); and John Russo and Sherry Linkon, *Steeltown U.S.A.: Work and Memory in Youngstown* (Lawrence: University of Kansas Press, 2002).

46. Jefferson Cowie and Joseph Heathcott, eds., *Beyond the Ruins: The Meanings of Deindustrialization* (Ithaca: NY: Cornell University Press, 2003). See their introduction, "The Meanings of Industrialization,"1–15; Steve May and Laura Morrison, "Making Sense of Restructuring: Narratives of Accommodation among Downsized Workers," 259–83; and Joy Hart and Tracy K'Meyer, "Worker Memory and Narrative: Personal Stories of Deindustrialization in Louisville, Kentucky," 284–304.

47. Cowie and Heathcott, *Beyond the Ruins*, 1.

48. Cowie and Heathcott, *Beyond the Ruins*, 13.

49. Cowie and Heathcott, *Beyond the Ruins*, 15.

EPILOGUE

1. David Harvey, *A Brief History of Neoliberalism* (New York: Oxford University Press, 2005).

2. Italian theorist Antonio Gramsci first made this point in describing what he called an organic intellectual. The extensive ethnography that is the foundation for *Shredding Paper* supports a claim that my observations here meet Gramsci's test. As Steve Jones puts it in his recent survey of Gramsci's writings:

> One danger with a progressive project is that it may appear intellectualized and abstract rather than concrete and grounded. . . . Furthermore, good sense has an affective or emotional aspect which is absent from abstract theorizing. The intellectual must combine the feelings that are prominent within good sense . . . with his or her philosophical understanding of the situation. Gramsci argues that any educational project that is not rooted in the concrete experience and popular conceptions is "like the contacts of English merchants and the negroes of Africa" since a fair exchange does not take place. The only way, he argues, in which the gap between leaders and led can properly be bridged is if intellectuals are themselves *organic* to those they educate and persuade. Steve Jones, *Gramsci* (New York: Routledge, 2006), 55.

Thus, conventional neoliberal orthodoxy, and especially its treatment of financialized capitalism as inevitable or immutable, puts orthodox advocates in the same position as Gramsci's English merchants.

3. Anonymous Portsmouth Naval Shipyard office, interview with John Bshara, Portsmouth, New Hampshire, April 26, 2013; Derek P. Langhauser, "The 2005 BRAC Process: The Case to Save Maine's Bases." *Maine Policy Review* 14, no.1 (2005): 38–48; United States Defense Base Closure and Realignment Commission, *BRAC Early Bird 6 July 2005.* UNT Digital Library, accessed April 8, 2020, http://digital.library.unt.edu /ark:/67531/metadc17650/; and William Yardley and Katie Zezima, "In New England, Sighs of Relief as Commission Votes to Save Submarine Base," *New York Times*, August 25, 2005, https://www.nytimes.com/2005/08/25/nyregion/in-new-england-sighs -of-relief-as-commission-votes-to-save.html. This research was conducted for the author by Christina Barnes and John Bshara.

4. Deborah McDermott, "Commander Says Kittery Shipyard Adding More Than 700 Workers," *Bangor Daily News*, April 13, 2015; Deborah McDermott, "Business is Booming at Maine Shipyard, with Hundreds More to be Hired, Captain Says," *Bangor Daily News*, August 25, 2018.

5. Ashley Conti, "Gov. Paul LePage Addresses Verso Paper Mill Closing," *Bangor Daily News*, October 3, 2014; Gabor Degre, "Verso Paper Co. Closing Bucksport Mill," *Bangor Daily News*, October 2, 2014; Robbie Feinberg, "Nearly 4 Years After Closing, Old Town Mill Reopens Under New Ownership," *Bangor Daily News*, August 14, 2019; Edward Murphy, "Buyers for Paper Mills Don't Grow on Trees," *Portland Press Herald*, October 13, 2014; Rachel Ohm, "Shutdown of Madison Mill is State's Fifth in Two Years," *Portland Press Herald*, March 14, 2016; Nick Sambides "Mill to Close September 2," *Bangor Daily News*, August 26 2008; Nick Sambides, "Baldacci Says Mills have Several Other Suitors," *Bangor Daily News*, February 4, 2011; Nick Sambides, "Timeline: The Often-dashed Hopes for Redevelopment of the Millinocket Paper Mill," *Bangor Daily News*, January 10, 2019; Matthew Stone, "Here's Where Redevelopment Stands at 6 Maine Paper Mills that Have Closed Since 2008," *Bangor Daily News*, December 18, 2019; and WSCH, "Governor Says Paper Mills Might Reopen," *News Center Maine*, November 10, 2014.

6. Mary Anne Lagasse, "Workers Expand Effort to Buy GNP > Millinocket Employees Seek All Maine Assets," *Bangor Daily News*, May 4, 1999; Mary Anne Lagasse, "GNP Mill Buyout Explored: Unions Fear Lost Jobs at Millinocket Plant," *Bangor Daily News*, January 19, 1999; Grady Trimble, "Old Town Mill Sold for $10.5 Million," *News Center Maine*, December 5, 2014; Jay Field, "Bankruptcy Judge Signs Off on Old Town Mill Sale to Wisconsin Firm," *Maine Public Radio*, December 5, 2014; and Grady Trimble "Lincoln Mill Sold to Liquidators for $5.95 Million," *Bangor Daily News*, December 5, 2014.

7. Darren Fishell and Nick Sambides Jr., "Great Northern Paper Files for Bankruptcy, Lists More than 1,000 Creditors," *Bangor Daily News*, September 23, 2014; "Buyout Plan

Altered to Save Hathaway," *Bangor Daily News*, September 19, 1996; "Hathaway Shirt Firm Plans Ad Campaign," *Bangor Daily News*, May 30, 1998; and Beryl Wolfe, "Brief History of Biddeford Textile Company," *Wolfenews*, April 9, 2001.

8. As previously noted, the seminal article for this perspective is: Michael Jensen and William Meckling, "Theory of the Firm: Managerial Behavior, Agency Costs, and Ownership Structure," *Journal of Financial Economics* 3, no. 4 (1976): 305–60. This conventional wisdom of mainstream economics (known within the professions as "neoclassical economics") is embodied in the best selling economics textbooks, particularly the theory of "perfect competition." See, for example, Gregory Mankiw, *Principles of Economics*, 6th edition (Mason, OH: South-Western Cengage Learning, 2012), 279–98. Nonneoclassical economists have long challenged neoclassical presumptions and methodology in ways analogous to but distinctive from the folk political economy analyzed here. See for example, James Crotty, "The Realism of Assumptions Does Matter: Why Keynes-Minsky Theory Must Replace Efficient Market Theory as the Guide to Financial Regulation Policy." In *The Oxford Handbook of the Political Economy of Financial Crises*, eds. Gerald Epstein and Martin Wolfson (New York: Oxford University Press, 2013), 133–58.

9. Lance Tapley, "Taxpayers Spending Millions on Mill that Keeps on Polluting," *Pine Tree Watchdog*, January 11, 2012.

10. The clearest example is of workers at GNP (see note 6 above). The more common practice has been union representatives and local workers meeting with statewide politicians to find a new corporate buyer, albeit with the hope that new buyers will restore the commitment to local enterprises that typified the Chandlerarian era before 1980 (see notes 6 and 7 above).

11. See Gar Alperovitz, *American beyond Capitalism: Reclaiming Our Wealth, Our Liberty, and Our Democracy* (Cambridge, MA: Democracy Collaborative Press/Dollars and Sense, 2011); J. K. Gibson-Graham, *A Postcapitalist Politics* (Minneapolis: University of Minnesota Press, 2006); J. K. Gibson-Graham, "Enabling Ethical Economies: Cooperativism and Class." *Critical Sociology* 29, no. 2 (2003): 123–61; and Richard Wolff, *Democracy at Work: A Cure For Capitalism* (Chicago: Haymarket Books, 2012).

12. See Peter A. Hall and David Soskice, *Varieties of Capitalism: The Institutional Foundations of Comparative Advantage* (New York: Oxford University Press, 2001).

13. See Jensen and Meckling, "Theory of the Firm"; and Mankiw, *Principles of Economics*.

14. Class justice here means that owners regularly shared a significant portion of company profits not just on good wages and benefits but on investment in community public works and other gratuities to mill workers and the community.

15. Judith Stein, *Pivotal Decade: How the US Traded Factories for Finance in the Seventies* (New Haven, CT: Yale University Press, 2010).

16. In particular, Germany, with a very different structure of corporate governance, offers a model that, at its peak between 1970 and 2000, supported continuing the kinds of organizational capacities that U.S. financialization helped destroy. From the 1950s through the 1990s, German industry thrived in part because of a continuation of patient financing by major banks that lasted into the 1990s. Worker voice was institutionalized through both unions and works councils, with councils in particular giving workers influence over technology and workplace issues in a way that goes beyond what most U.S. unions achieve. Most relevant is the legal requirement that worker representatives form 50 percent of the operational branch of each company's two boards of directors; this is a radical contrast to directors of U.S. corporations who recognize only shareholders (large institutional investors). This corporate governance model addresses the problem U.S. industrial workers have had with financialization, for instance that it cuts them and their communities out of being stakeholders in any meaningful sense (seen especially in Local

1069's desire to become the mill's economic principal.) Despite restrictive macroeconomic policies that kept German unemployment high after 1980, the combination of financial stability and worker power kept German manufacturing employment strong and wages very high. As scholar Peter Hall has observed, key elements of the German model still remain, despite a weakening of some of its pillars. Nonetheless, it provides an example of institutional arrangements that make workers sovereign stakeholders, giving them a significant voice in both the strategic and operational management of their companies. These arrangements have long boosted the capacity of German manufacturing firms to continue to maintain and enhance their organizational capacities, the very thing that financialization robbed U.S. industry of since 1980. Peter A. Hall, "The Fate of the German Model," in *The German Model as Seen by its Neighbors*, ed. Brigitte Unger (Brussels, Belgium: Social Europe, 2015), 43–62.

17. John Schmid, "Paper Cuts: Part One, An Industry Torn Up: Wisconsin's Place in Paper Industry Under Seige," *Milwaukee Journal Sentinel*, December 8, 2012; and John Schmid, "Paper Cuts, Part Two: A Global Paper Trail; Bankrolled and Bioengineered, China Supplants Wisconsin's Paper Industry," *Milwaukee Journal Sentinel*, December 11, 2012.

18. George Packer, "The Republican Class War," *New Yorker*, November 9, 2015.

19. Stephen Vogel, "Elizabeth Warren Wants to Stop Inequality Before It Starts," *New York Times*, January 3, 2019; and Stephen Silvia, *Holding the Shop Together: German Industrial Relations in the Postwar Era* (Ithaca, NY: Cornell University Press, 2011).

20. See Jennifer Klein, *For All These Rights: Business, Labor, and the Shaping of America's Public-Private Welfare State* (Princeton, NJ: Princeton University Press, 2004).

21. Jim Tankersley and Ben Casselman, "Wealth Tax and Free College Get Poll Support. Democrats Worry It Won't Last," *New York Times*, July 22, 2019.

Index

Page numbers in *italics* refer to figures and maps.

Acadians: communal solidarity of, 118, 125, 138, 139, 248n51; employment motivations of, 120; English oppression of, 124, 127, 139; exploitation of, 129–30; history of, 123–24, 244n7, 247n42; in management positions, 126–27, 136; political party identification, 125, 126, 142; union participation by, 125–26; xenophobia and, 124, 248n45. *See also* Fraser Paper Company
AFL-CIO, 97, 114, 176
Albert, Ron, 127, 129, 132–33, 251n89
American Federation of Labor. *See* AFL-CIO
American Wood Paper Company, 19–20
Ames, Mel, 143, 154
Applebaum, Eileen, 170–71
apprenticeship programs, 40, 59, 85
assembly line production, 49–50
automation, 96, 165, 188, 207, 263n19, 271–72n2

Babb, Dana, 72
Bachelor, Mae, 47–48, 54, 66, 81, 106, 109
Baldacci, John, 213
Bartlett, Robert F., 166, 257n76
Batt, Rosemary, 170–71
beaters, 17, 23, 55, 60, 77, 89
Beck, John, 183
Berle, Adolph, 33, 34
Bernier, Camille, 122, 133, 251n97
Big Thrust, 121–23, 246n29
Birmingham, Barbara, 141
Birmingham civil rights campaign (1963), 132
Birmingham, Wayne, 141–43, 151, 153–54, 159
Boise Cascade, 4, 100, 101, 165, 172–75
Bolduc, Claire, 141–43, 147, 149–50, 154, 156–57, 248n51
bonded labor program, 148–51, 155
bonus system, 47, 55, 66–67, 98, 105–6
Boyd, Fred, 187
Braverman, Harry, 246n33
Brennan, Joe, 114
Brody, David, 99, 247n33
Budd, John, 231–32nn23–24

Burton, Robert, 84, 107
business unionism, 97–98, 156
Butler, Bill, 143, 152, 154, 156, 157, 159

Canadian guest workers: activist efforts in regards to, 143, 162; bonded labor program for, 148–51, 155; citizen loggers replaced by, 140, 143, 144, 147, 155–56, 162; decline of, 158, 160–61, 260n111; exploitation of, 148–49; labor association for, 154; MWA perceptions of, x, 140, 151, 154–56; visas for, 158, 162, 256n48
capitalism: autopsies of, 2–3; characteristics of, 9; class structure of, 273n18; creative destruction and, 2, 214; critiques of, 4, 5; financialized, xi, 271n2; in folk political economy, 4, 203, 211; globalization and, 9–10, 216; inequalities within, 11; managerial, 34; Marx on, 2, 273n18; neoliberal, 212; reform proposals, 216–17; social Darwinian, 54; Taylorism and, 50, 246n33; welfare, 52, 71
Carver, Bill, 109, 180–85, 192–96, 200
chainsaws, ix, 144, *145*, 147, 160, 161
Chandler, Alfred, 31–33
Chandlerian companies, 31–42; corporate governance in, 32–36, 208; criticisms of, 36; evolution of informal firms into, 38–42; mass production by, 31–32; multidivisional, 32, 45; product innovation by, 32, 36–38, 41; profits as used by, 100–101; social democratic ethos of, 215
Chasse, Ron, 71, 128
Chisholm, Hugh: background of, 24, 206; characterizations of, 274n28; investment consortium of, 21, 22; mystique surrounding, 8, 24–25; paternalism of, 24, 33–34. *See also* International Paper Company; Oxford Paper Company
citizen loggers, 140, 143, 144, 147, 155–56, 162
civil disobedience, 117, 132, 138
civil rights movement, 132, 142, 176, 177
class justice, 205, 207, 215, 277n14
Clinton, Bill, 11

coated publication papers, 37–38, *38*, 40, 90
codetermination, 187, 199
collective bargaining, 111, 112, 120, 153, 168, 249n67
Collins, Susan, 213
community memory: Acadians and, 123, 127, 137–39; folk political economy constructed from, 5, 210–11; of Fraser Paper strike (1971), 137–39; functions of, 203; institutional, 184–85; of Scott Paper Company, 205–6; of S. D. Warren Company, 203–5, 207
company towns, 1, 53, 83
Congress of Industrial Unions. *See* AFL-CIO
Continental Bag Company, 25, 26
contract enforcement, 98–100
contractualism. *See* workplace contractualism
Cook, Gary, 190
corporate governance: in Chandlerian companies, 32–36, 208; defined, 10, 32; financialized, 10, 36, 207, 212, 214–15, 267n6; in folk political economy, 203, 206, 214–15; German model of, 215, 216, 277–78n16; managerial, 10, 33–36; reform proposals, 216; unions and, 199. *See also* management
corporate welfare movement, 51, 231n20
Cowie, Jefferson, 211
Crabtree, Aubrey, 126–27
creative destruction, 2, 200, 211, 214, 216
Curtis, Kenneth, 135
Cyr, Jerry, 57, 58, 126, 136–38, 250n73
Cyr, Paul, 125–34, 137, 138, 250n78

Day, Roger, 40
deindustrialization, 171, 203, 214, 216
Democratic Party, 83, 114, 125–26, 137, 142, 215
Denison, Adna C., 20
deskilling of workers, 50–52
digesters, 19, 52, 55, 65, 88, 186
discrimination, 95, 113
Dornish, Karl: in apprenticeship program, 59, 85; background of, 39–40, 189; on bonus system, 106; in contract negotiations, 113; on gross profit margins, 42; on Jointness initiative, 190; on management, 105, 107–9; paternalism and, 84; on product quality, 62; on sale of S. D. Warren Company, 44; on workforce composition, 103
Dorr, Bob, 70
Drucker, Peter, 170
Dubois, Phil, ix, 129–30, 134–35
Dunlap, Al, x, 10, 196–99, 222n25, 270n79

economies of scale, 32, 43, 90
economies of scope, 32, 36
employees. *See* workers
employment bargain, 48–54
employment security, 74, 79, 81, 86, 204
enterprise consciousness, 213–14
Ethyl Corporation, 34, 44, 173
Ewing, Marv, 112–14

Fair Labor Standards Act of 1938 (FLSA), 146
Falk, Jon, 142, 144, 154
familiar paternalism, 79
family wage, 86–87, 120, 132, 138
feller-bunchers, 160, *160*
females. *See* women
Fick, Oscar, Jr., 84
Fick, Oscar, Sr., 40, 229n101
filiopietism, 204
financial engineering, 169, 171, 196–97, 214
financialization: analysis of impact on workers and manufacturing, 264–65n47; of capitalism, xi, 271n2; Chandlerian companies and, 36, 216; of corporate governance, 10, 36, 207, 212, 214–15, 267n6; folk political economy and, 215–17; German strategies compared, 277–78n16; high road strategies and, 171–72, 204; Jensen/Meckling article and, 222n24; significance of, 12
finishing department: automation in, 188; bonus system in, 47, 55, 66–67, 98; duties of workers in, 62–67; shutdowns in, 194–95; supervision within, 55, 106; women in, 47, 55, *56*, 62–67, 108–9; work environment, 70
Fink, Leon, 12, 140
flexible specialization, 50
FLSA (Fair Labor Standards Act of 1938), 146
folk political economy: capitalism in, 4, 203, 211; community memory in construction of, 5, 210–11; corporate governance in, 203, 206, 214–15; as cultural artifact, 212; moral code underlying, 5, 12, 216
Fontaine, Cecile, 142, 143, 157, 248n48
Fontaine, Don, 142, 143, 149, 155
Ford, Henry, 1, 49–51, 57
foremen, 50–54, 104–9
fourdrinier machines: availability and use of, 18, 23, 26, 42; economies of scale and, 43, 90; invention and refinement of, 17, 18; in layout of production, *17*, 89; skilled labor for operation of, 75
Fraser Paper Company: Big Thrust at, 121–23, 246n29; contract negotiations at, 123, 135–37; downtime losses at, 57; family wage

at, 86–87, 120, 132, 138; homogeneity of workforce, 226n49; management of, 118–20, 126–27, 137; mobilization against closure of, 213; origins and growth of, 118–19; profitability of, 117, 244n1; strike against (1971), ix, 117, 129–39; takeover attempts at, 44–45, 117, 121; unionization at, 120; wildcat strike (1970), 123, 127–29. See also Acadians

Galbraith, John Kenneth, 34
gemeinschaft, 35, 231n23
Georges, John, 222n25
Germany, corporate governance in, 215, 216, 277–78n16
Gerow, Carroll, 142, 146
Getman, Julius, 176, 265n63
gift exchange, 71, 87, 194
globalization: capitalism and, 9–10, 216; flexible specialization and, 50; strategic change and, 170; in undermining of mature industries, 2; union decline and, 11
GNP. See Great Northern Paper Company
Gogan, Bob, ix, 129, 131, 133–34
Goodwyn, Lawrence, 179, 266n76
Gordon, Arthur, 70, 113–14
Gouldner, Alvin, 87
Gramsci, Antonio, 275–76n2
Great Depression: debt accumulation during, 74; employment security during, 81; labor supply during, 31; work-spreading scheme during, 66, 81, 230n2
Great Northern Paper Company (GNP): Canadian guest workers at, 149; immigrant labor at, 225n49; job cuts at, 166, 201; land plots distributed to workers, 86; mergers involving, 44; newsprint production by, 7, 22, 26–28, 38, 43; origins and growth of, 6, 22, 24, 26–28; paternalism in, 11; post-World War II peak of, 43; technology center at, 42; timberland purchases by, 24, 28; unionization at, 72, 159, 238n3; on workers' compensation, 146
greenfield facilities, 168, 195, 267n6
Green, Martin, 76, 228n96
Greep, Rudy, 59, 105
groundwood pulp production, 19–21
guest workers. See Canadian guest workers

Hagerty, Peter, 142, 143, 150–52, 154, 156–57
Hall, Peter, 278n16
Hammond, George Warren, 41, 228n96
harassment, sexual, 108–9

Harriman, Clyde, 102, 103–4, 108, 110–11
Heathcott, Joseph, 211
Hebert, Eldon, 158
Heuer, John "Pete," 117–23, 127, 129, 136, 244n3
high-performance work systems (HPWS): cost-cutting committees in, 195; decline of, 199; discipline of team members in, 189; implementation challenges, 171; investments required for, 184; opposition to, 172, 179, 183, 186, 193; radical analysis of, 192; shareholderism vs., 196, 197. See also Jointness initiative
high road strategies: advocacy for, 263n32; resistance to, 166, 172, 178–79, 190, 192, 204; strategic change through, 169; threats to implementation of, 171. See also high-performance work systems; Jointness initiative
Hollingsworth and Whitney Company, 23, 33, 38, 44–45, 99, 186
horizontal mergers, 25, 44
housing for workers, 24, 25, 78, 78–79, 237n155
HPWS. See high-performance work systems
human resource management, 51, 52, 87, 115
Hyde, John, 40, 64, 72–75, 84, 104, 229n101

immigrant labor, 28–29, 31, 49, 79, 225n49
import competition, 215, 271–72n2
income. See wages
indulgency pattern, 87, 103, 104
Industrial Workers of the World (IWW), 254n4
Ingalls, Everett, 105
innovation: by Chandlerian companies, 32, 36–38, 41; in large-scale enterprises, 16; in managerial practices, 49, 51; technology centers for, 42, 209; in undermining of mature industries, 2
International Brotherhood of Paper Makers Union, 96–98, 232n29, 239n13
International Brotherhood of Pulp, Sulfite, and Paper Mills Workers, 96–98, 102, 103, 110–12, 120, 239n13
International Paper Company (IP): bargaining pools at, 239n14; campaign to defeat unions, 96, 100; intentional provocation of strikes by, 4, 165; newsprint production by, 22, 26; origins and growth of, 6, 22–26; Project Productivity at, 174, 175; strike against (1987–88), 3, 5, 98, 174–79, 222n25; union busting by, 173–76
Irland, Lloyd, 237n155
IWW (Industrial Workers of the World), 254n4

Jackson, Jesse, 3, 177, 192, 204
Jacoby, Sanford, 51, 231n23
Jensen, Joseph, *102*, 110, 111, 204–5, 241n37
Jensen, Michael, 171, 208
Jewitt, Frank, 74
jobbers, 30, 31, 63, 107
job control unionism, 98, 116, 168, 171, 189, 199–200
job rotation, 195
Jointness initiative, 180–98; failure of, 188–91, 196; implementation challenges, 180–81; job rotation in, 195; proposal of, 182–85; shareholderism and, 197–98; skepticism regarding, 183–85; success of, 186–88; UPIU on, 183, 187, 191–94
Jones, Steve, 275–76n2

Kellman, Peter, 97, 176, 178
Kenney, Barry, 46, 66, 68
Kenyon, Ned, 62
Keyes Fiber, 43
Kimberly-Clark Corporation, 197, 199
Kochan, Thomas, 170–71, 184, 267n6
Ku Klux Klan (KKK), 124, 155, 249n61, 258n80

labor force. *See* workers
labor militancy. *See* militancy of unions
labor unions. *See* unions and unionization
LaFramboise, Bill, 136
Lally, Shirley, 66, 69–70, 74, 85, 108, 111, 205–6
Lang, Nicole, 121, 126–27, 246n29
L'Association des Forestiers de Sud-Est, 154
Laurie, Bruce, 224n13, 266n76
LaViolette, Phil, 77–78, 81, 82, 249n61
LePage, Paul, 213
Lestage, Phil, 66, 67, 107, 108, 242n61
Lestage, Tom, 65, 67–68, 72, 99, 191, 195, 209–10
Lichtenstein, Nelson, 223n29, 231n9, 253n139, 262n16
Lippencott, Phil, 181, 182, 197, 198
literacy rates, 15, 223n1
logging industry: citizen loggers in, 140, 143, 144, 147, 155–56, 162; hazards related to, 8, 29, 144, 147, 255n24, 256n44; immigrant labor in, 31; in make or buy decisions, 30; mechanization of, x, 88, 160–62, 207, 226n52; mud season in, 141; post-World War II peak of, 43; pulp peonage in, ix, 140, 143, 147; river drives in, 7, 27, 28, 88; unionization in, x, 140, 159, 162, 254n4; wage data for, 260n120, 260n123; wildcat strikes in, 149; workers' compensation in,

143, 146, 147, 151, 159. *See also* Canadian guest workers; Maine Woodsmen's Association
Longley, James, 140–41, 149, 151–54, 156
Lord, Harley, 81
low road strategies: costs of pursuing, 172; defined, 165–66; strategic change through, 169, 171; union busting, 165–67, 173–76, 222n25
lumber barons, 24, 27
Lutes, David, 148–49
Lynd, Staughton, 239n20

Maelot, Estelle, 66–67, 81
Magic City. *See* Great Northern Paper Company
Maine paper industry: decline of, x, 2, 9–12, 201, 206–7, 214, 271–72n2; deindustrialization and, 171, 203, 214, 216; feudal-like nature of, 3–4, 31; founding fathers and rise of, 21–29; geographic advantage of, 5, 20, 26–27, 43; layout of production in mills, 88–91; legacy of, xi, 203, 211; local character of, x, 44, 96; mergers within, 8–9, 24–26, 44; mill closings (1980–2016), 201, *202*; post-World War II peak of, 43–44; raw materials and, 5–7, 20, 24; work environment in, 68–71. *See also* Chandlerian companies; corporate governance; logging industry; paper production; unions and unionization; workers; *specific companies*
Maine Woodsmen's Association (MWA): on Canadian guest workers, x, 140, 151, 154–56; decline of, 159; formation and growth of, 149–50, 257n76; leadership of, 141–43, 154; militancy of, 156; nativism of, 154–55; relationship with UPIU, 141, 157–59; shortcomings of, 153–57; strike by (1975), ix–x, 140–41, 150–54, 160
maintenance workers, 35, 55, 65–66, 69, 90–91, 269n55
make or buy decisions, 29–30
management: Acadians in, 126–27, 136; apprenticeship programs, 40, 59, 85; of Chandlerian companies, 32–36; human resource, 51, 52, 87, 115; innovation in practices of, 49, 51; intramanagement conflict, 101; local character of, x, 44, 184; middle, 32, 54, 126, 198; mismanagement, 5, 40, 211; nepotism in, 39; open-door policies of, 74, 84, 87, 104, 108; paternalistic, 11, 33–34, 39, 74–75; of production, 58–64; professional, 33, 40, 119–20; scientific, 49,

246n33; strikes as viewed by, 168, 244n13; total quality, 42, 170, 192; in union negotiations, 115, 118; visible hand of, 32; in workplace hierarchy, 3, 86
management letters, 123, 129, 135, 136
manning letters, 123, 129, 135, 136, 245n24
Marshall, Ray, 170
Martin, David, 70–71, 81, 194, 209–10
Marx, Karl, 2, 192, 273n18
mass production: assembly lines in, 49–50; challenges of, 32; by Chandlerian companies, 31–32; employment bargain and, 49, 51; price wars and, 25; rise of, 16, 18, 30; work reorganization in, 170
Mayo, Elton, 51
Mazzerolle, Lucien, 71, 121, 128
Means, Gardiner, 33, 34
mechanization, x, 17–18, 88, 160–62, 207, 226n52
memory. See community memory
mergers, 8–9, 24–26, 44, 112, 117, 171
Meserve, Bill, 175, 176
middle management, 32, 54, 126, 198
militancy of unions: cultural influences on, 118; emergence of, 80, 95, 99–101; Fraser Paper strike (1971) and, 133–34; legal restrictions against, 249n67; in logging industry, 140, 156; paternalism in response to, 76; workplace contractualism and, 100–101, 118, 204. See also strikes; specific organizations
Mills, Janet, 162
Minchin, Timothy, 67, 174, 207
minimum wage, 82, 146, 237n138
monopolies, 22, 24–26
Morgan, J. P., 25–27
Mother Warren. See S. D. Warren Company
movement culture: anticorporate, 181, 203; class warfare and, 190, 204, 212; emergence of, 100, 179, 185, 204; oppositional nature of, 266n76
multidivisional companies, 32, 45
Murray, Chris, 5, 73, 205
MWA. See Maine Woodsmen's Association

National Labor Relations Board (NLRB), 103, 109, 112, 151, 175
nativism, 154–55
Nee, John, 112, 180, 182, 186, 243n74
neoliberalism, 11–12, 212–17, 223n29
nepotism, 39, 98, 104, 107–8, 203, 228n96
New Deal era, 10, 11, 71–72, 144, 221n22
newsprint production, 7, 22, 24–28, 38, 43
Newton, Jason, 30

Nixon, Richard M., 135–36
NLRB (National Labor Relations Board), 103, 109, 112, 151, 175

oligopolies, 21, 25–26, 35
Olmstead, George, Jr., 44, 59, 273n15
Olmstead, George, Sr., 40, 229n101, 273n15
open-door policies, 74, 84, 87, 104, 108
organic intellectuals, 275–76n2
Osterman, Paul, 170–71, 184, 267n6
Otis Falls Pulp and Paper Company, 25
Ouellette, P. Kim, xiii, 245n19, 245n20, 250n78, 254n8
Oxford Paper Company: Ethyl Corporation purchase of, 44; finishing department at, 56; origins and growth of, 6, 22, 23, 26; paternalism in, 11, 33–34; postcard contract received by, 26, 38, 56; post-World War II peak of, 43; technology center at, 42; union busting by, 173–74

Packer, George, 215–16
Palmer, Larry, 142, 148, 150
paper production: automation in, 96, 165, 188, 207, 263n19, 271–72n2; as capital-intensive industry, 7, 36, 69; challenges of, 56–58; coated papers, 37–38, 38, 40, 90; in consumer culture, 16; demand for, 5, 15–16, 18; handmade process of, 16–17; hazards related to, 7, 18, 48, 70–71, 233–34n80; industrial policy in, 215; layout of production in mills, 88–91; make or buy decisions in, 29–30; mechanization of, 17–18; nationalization of, 44; newsprint, 7, 22, 24–28, 38, 43; post-World War II peak of, 43–44; pulp-making for, 19–21, 26, 43, 88–89, 224n20, 232n45; raw materials for, 5–7, 18–20, 24; skilled labor for, 7, 8, 35; water utilization in, 6–7, 24. See also logging industry; Maine paper industry; mass production; workers
Paradis, Judy, 138–39
Parenteau, William, 148, 152, 153, 155
Parkhurst, Howard, 67, 108, 241n41
Parks, Dan, 101–2, 108–9, 111
PATCO (Professional Air Traffic Controllers Organizations), 168, 174
paternalism, 71–87; antiunion sentiments and, 72; credibility of, 75, 273n19; employment bargain and, 52; familiar, 79; gift exchange system and, 71, 87, 194; in industrial culture, 1, 11, 24, 46, 58; in management, 11, 33–34, 39, 74–75; in mass production operations, 51; motives for practice of, 76–77; political

paternalism (continued)
   influence and, 83, 113–14; principle features
   of, 77–79; social work elements of, 53, 83–86;
   welfare practices and, 51–52, 71, 79–81, 86;
   worker narratives of, 72–75, 204, 206, 207
Payne, Oliver, 27
Pease, Curtis, 185
PECs (private equity companies), 27, 201,
   225n41, 264–65n47
Pelletier, Lise, 125, 248n48
Penobscot Chemical Fiber Company, 21, 26
pensions, 77–79, 111, 236n121
Peoples, Patrick, 184
Pepper, Leslie, 145
Pineau, Ray, 177–78
Piore, Michael J., 50, 170
PNS (Portsmouth Naval Shipyard), 212–13
Portelli, Alessandro, 203
Porter, Michael, 170
Portsmouth Naval Shipyard (PNS), 212–13
postcards, 26, 38, 56
posttraumatic stress disorder, 85, 86, 103
Poulin, Frank, 99, 189
price wars, 25
private equity companies (PECs), 27, 201,
   225n41, 264–65n47
Procter and Gamble, 168, 182
producerism, 206, 273n18
production management, 40, 58–64
product life cycle, 32
Professional Air Traffic Controllers Organizations (PATCO), 168, 174
profit-sharing plans, 79–80
Project Productivity, 174, 175
pulp peonage, ix, 140, 143, 147
pulp production, 19–21, 26, 43, 88–89, 224n20,
   232n45

rank nepotism, 39, 228n96
Reagan, Ronald, 11, 168
Reiche, Howard, Jr.: in apprenticeship
   program, 40, 59, 85; background of, 39–40;
   on employment security during Great
   Depression, 81; giving fund maintained by,
   236n125; knowledge of S. D. Warren
   Company history, 234n91; on local mill
   buyout proposal, 210; on managerial coup,
   229n101; on paternalism, 84, 87; on political
   influence of mills, 83; retirement of, 194,
   208; on sale of S. D. Warren Company, 44;
   on shop-floor relations, 105; on supervisor
   behavior, 107–9; on unions, 95, 115, 116,
   253n127

Reich, Robert, 170, 263n32
Republican Party, 83, 113–14, 125, 215
Rittenhouse mill, 16–17
Roach, Martin, 118, 121–23, 129, 130, 136,
   250n78
Rolde, Neil, 135
Roosevelt, Franklin Delano, 10, 168
Rubinstein, Saul, 171
Rumford Falls Paper Company, 23, 23, 25, 26

Sabel, Charles F., 50, 170
St. John Valley Woodmen's Association, 143,
   149
salary. See wages
SAPPI (South African Pulp and Paper
   Industries), 197, 199, 275n34
satisficing strategies, 34–36, 100, 226n59
Saturn automobile company, 171, 199
Schenck, Garret, 21, 26–28
Schumpeter, Joseph, 2
scientific management, 49, 246n33
Scott Paper Company: community memory of,
   205–6; dismantling of, x, 197, 222n25;
   Hollingsworth and Whitney purchased by,
   44; S. D. Warren purchased by, x, 44, 71, 88,
   95, 102–3; Ultracast products from, 209, 210,
   275n34; UPIU strikes against, 5, 113, 114;
   worker buyout proposal, 208, 210. See also
   Jointness initiative
Scranton, Phillip, 77, 79, 273n19
S. D. Warren Company: accidents at, 48, 70,
   111; community memory of, 203–5, 207;
   corporate governance of, 32–33; departmental work within, 64–68; employment bargain
   in historical perspective, 48–54; evolution
   into Chandlerian company, 38–42; factory
   complexes, 6, 22, 28, 90; finishing department at, 47, 55, 62–67, 108–9; immigrant
   labor at, 28–29, 31, 79; managerial coup at,
   39, 74, 229n101; mismanagement of, 5, 40;
   nepotism within, 39, 104, 107–8, 203,
   228n96; origins and growth of, 4, 21, 224n26;
   paternalism in, 11, 24, 33–34, 39, 52, 71–87;
   post-World War II peak of, 43; production
   management at, 40, 58–64; sale to Scott
   Paper Company, x, 44, 71, 88, 95, 102–3;
   shop-floor relations at, 50, 51, 104–9; skill
   hierarchy at, 55; soda pulp production at, 19,
   224n20; strike against (1916), 39, 103,
   220n10, 235n103; supervision of workers at,
   54–58, 63, 104–9; testing lab and technology
   center at, 41–42; unionization at, 4–5, 95,
   109–12; wood procurement methods, 31

Senge, Peter, 170
sexual harassment, 108–9
Shaffer, Jim, 35
shareholderism, 182, 187, 196–98, 203–4, 211, 214
shareholder value movement, 10, 12, 34, 36, 171–73, 222n24
Sherman Antitrust Act of 1890, 25
shift work: in company towns, 53; daily schedule of, 229n2; in Great Depression, 230n2; night shifts, 69, 70, 190; rhythms of, 8; Southern swing shift, 69–70; on Sundays, 69, 70, 121–22, 169, 174–75; for women, 62
shop-floor relations, 50, 51, 104–9
Slaughter, Jane, 190–93, 204
Smith, Adam, 16
Smith, David, 19
Snowe, Olympia, 177
social Darwinian capitalism, 54
social work, 53, 83–86
soda pulp production, 19–21, 224n20
South African Pulp and Paper Industries (SAPPI), 197, 199, 275n34
Southern swing shift, 69–70
Stein, Judith, 215
strikes: average annual number of, 100, 253n139; family participation in, ix, 117, 132, 134, 137–39; Fraser Paper Company (1971), ix, 117, 129–39; intentional provocation of, 4, 165; International Paper Company (1987–88), 3, 5, 98, 174–79, 222n25; management view of, 168, 244n13; MWA (1975), ix–x, 140–41, 150–54, 160; S. D. Warren Company (1916), 39, 103, 220n10, 235n103; UPIU organization of, 5, 113, 114, 167, 173–76; wildcat, 123, 127–29, 149, 239–40n20, 249n67. See also unions and unionization
sulfite pulp production, 19–21, 26, 43
Sunbeam Corporation, 197, 270n79
Sunday shift work, 69, 70, 121–22, 169, 174–75
supercalendering, 59, 61, 90
supervision of workers, 51, 54–58, 63, 104–9

Taft-Hartley Act of 1948, 249n67
Taylor, Frederick Winslow, 49–52, 55, 57, 58, 246n33
Thurow, Lester, 170, 263n32
Tilghman, Benjamin, 20–21
total quality management (TQM), 42, 170, 192
trade unions. See unions and unionization
Trump, Donald, 215–16
Turner, Carl, 190, 191

UAW (United Autoworkers), 10, 11, 97
Ultracast products, 209, 210, 275n34
Umbagog Pulp Company, 25
union busting: as low road strategy, 165–67, 173–76, 222n25; neoliberalism and, 11; radical response to, 192; statewide movement against, x; in work reorganization schemes, 169, 173–76
unions and unionization: Acadian participation in, 125–26; anti-union legislation, 249n67; business unionism, 97–98, 156; collective bargaining by, 111, 112, 120, 153, 168, 249n67; contract enforcement by, 98–100; corporate governance and, 199; decline of, 3, 10–11, 72; grassroots activism by, 11, 177; job control unionism, 98, 116, 168, 171, 189, 199–200; in logging industry, x, 140, 159, 162, 254n4; national wave of, 96–97; in New Deal era, 10, 11, 71–72; spillover effects from, 72; women's role in, 110–11. See also militancy of unions; strikes; union busting; specific organizations
United Autoworkers (UAW), 10, 11, 97
United Papermakers and Paperworkers Union, 102, 103, 110–12, 239n13
United Paperworkers International Union (UPIU): contract enforcement by, 99, 204; emergence of, 112–13, 239n13, 243n76; in-plant resistance promoted by, 178–79; on Jointness initiative, 183, 187, 191–94; leadership of, 4–5, 113–15; mill buyout efforts led by, 208, 210; negotiation tactics of, 114–15, 137; relationship with MWA, 141, 157–59; strikes organized by, 5, 113, 114, 167, 173–76
United Steel Workers, 11, 213
UPIU. See United Paperworkers International Union
Usher, Ron, 103
U.S. Postal Service, 26, 38, 56

Vail, David, 145, 148, 256n44
Valente, A. J., 16
vanguard welfarism, 51

wages: family wage, 86–87, 120, 132, 138; in logging industry, 260n120, 260n123; minimum wage, 82, 146, 237n138; Nixon administration controls on, 135; for women, 77, 82
Warren, Elizabeth, 216
Warren, John E., 39–41, 73–77, 79, 228n96, 273n15

Warren, Joseph A., 39, 77, 83, 236n121, 273n15
Warren Merchants' Association (WMA), 41, 42
Warren, Samuel Dennis: antiunion sentiments of, 72; background of, 21, 39, 73, 75; community memory of, 204, 205; Congressional testimony by, 75, 76, 79; death of, 39, 73, 224n26; founder's culture established by, 75; home-building program of, *78*, 78–79; motives for business practices of, 76; mystique surrounding, 8, 75; procurement of rags by, 18, 75. *See also* S. D. Warren Company
Warren, Samuel Dennis, II, 39, 40, 228n96
welfare practices, 51–52, 71, 79–81, 86, 231n20
wildcat strikes, 123, 127–29, 149, 239–40n20, 249n67
WMA (Warren Merchants' Association), 41, 42
women: discrimination against, 95, 113; in finishing department, 47, 55, *56*, 62–67, 108–9; mill resting rooms for, 80; sexual harassment of, 108–9; strike participation by, ix, 132, 134, 137–39; as test girls, 60–61; in unionization efforts, 110–11; wages for, 77, 82; work-spreading scheme for, 81
woodcutting. *See* logging industry
Wood, Monica, 24, 206, 274n28
workers, 46–86; bonus system for, 47, 55, 66–67, 98, 105–6; departmental duties of, 64–68; deskilling of, 50–52; employment bargain and, 48–54; employment security for, 74, 79, 81, 86, 204; environment for, 68–71; in gift exchange system, 71, 87, 194;

housing for, 24, 25, *78*, 78–79, 237n155; immigrant, 28–29, 31, 49, 79, 225n49; in-plant resistance by, 178–79; longevity of, 47, 77–78, 230n2; maintenance, 35, 55, 65–66, 69, 90–91, 269n55; mill buyout efforts by, 208, 210; multigenerational, 7, 72, 81, 82, 86, 204; pensions for, 77–79, 111, 236n121; production, 58–64, 69; rules of conduct for, 79; skill hierarchy for, 55, 195; supervision of, 51, 54–58, 63, 104–9. *See also* Canadian guest workers; community memory; folk political economy; paternalism; shift work; unions and unionization; wages; women
workers' compensation, 143, 146, 147, 151, 159
workplace contractualism: Brody on, 99, 247n33; commitment to, 166–67, 183, 191; criticisms of, 239n20; exercise through grievances, 113; militancy of unions and, 100–101, 118, 204
work reorganization schemes: Big Thrust, 121–23, 246n29; corporate governance and, 36; failure of, 12, 188–91, 196; prerequisites for success of, 267n6; Project Productivity, 174, 175; team-based, 169, 170, 178–79; union busting in, 169, 173–76. *See also* Jointness initiative
work-spreading scheme, 66, 81, 230n2

xenophobia, 124, 147, 248n45, 258n80

Zeiger, Robert, 97, 238n12
Zuboff, Shoshana, 58